CAPTAIN COOK

Explorations and Reassessments

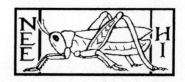

Regions and Regionalism in History

ISSN 1742–8254

Volume I: The Durham *Liber Vitae* and its Context, *edited by David Rollason, A.J. Piper, Margaret Harvey and Lynda Rollason*

This series, published in association with the AHRB Centre for North-East England History (NEEHI), aims to reflect and encourage the increasing academic and popular interest in regions and regionalism in historical perspective. It also seeks to explore the complex historical antecedents of regionalism as it appears in a wide range of international contexts.

Series Editor
Dr Peter Rushton, School of Health, Natural and Social Sciences, University of Sunderland

Editorial Board
Dr Richard C. Allen, University of Newcastle
Dr Barry Doyle, University of Teesside
Bill Lancaster, University of Northumbria
Bill Purdue, Open University
Professor David Rollason, University of Durham
Dr Peter Rushton, University of Sunderland

Proposals for future volumes may be sent to the following address:

AHRB CENTRE FOR NORTH-EAST ENGLAND HISTORY,
Department of History,
43 North Bailey,
Durham,
DH1 3EX
UK

CAPTAIN COOK

Explorations and Reassessments

EDITED BY
Glyndwr Williams

THE BOYDELL PRESS

First published 2004

Published by The Boydell Press
An imprint of Boydell & Brewer Ltd
PO Box 9, Woodbridge, Suffolk IP12 3DF, UK
and of Boydell & Brewer Inc.
PO Box 41026, Rochester, NY 14604–4126, USA
website: www.boydellandbrewer.com

ISBN 1 84383 100 7

A catalogue record for this book is available from the British Library

Library of Congress Cataloging-in-Publication Data
Captain Cook : explorations and reassessments / edited by Glyndwr Williams.
p. cm. – (Regions and regionalism in history ; 2)
Includes bibliographical references and index.
ISBN 1-84383-100-7 (hardback : alk. paper)
1. Cook, James, 1728-1779. 2. Explorers–Great Britain–Biography.
3. Oceania–Discovery and exploration–British. 4. Voyages around the world.
I. Williams, Glyndwr. II. Series.
G246.C7C29 2004
910'.92–dc22
2004008909

Typeset by Keystroke, Jacaranda Lodge, Wolverhampton
Printed in Great Britain by
Antony Rowe Ltd, Chippenham, Wiltshire

Contents

Illustrations

Contributors

Richard C. Allen is Lecturer in History at Newcastle University and Visiting Fellow at Northumbria University, Newcastle. He has published extensively on the history of the Society of Friends. Recent publications include '"Taking up her daily cross": Women and the Early Quaker Movement in Wales', in M. Roberts and S. Clark, eds, *Women and Gender in Early Modern Wales* (Cardiff, 2000); '"Mocked, scoffed, persecuted, and made a gazeing stock": the resistance of the Religious Society of Friends (Quakers) to the religious and civil authorities in post-toleration south-east Wales c.1689–1836', in G. Bonifas, ed., *Resistances, Cycnos* (Nice, 2002); 'An alternative community in North East England: Quakers, morals and popular culture in the long eighteenth century', in Helen Berry and Jeremy Gregory, eds, *Creating and Consuming Culture in North-East England* (Aldershot, 2004).

Rosalin Barker graduated from the University of Birmingham and has spent thirty years as tutor and counsellor in undergraduate and adult education, working variously for the Open University and Hull University. She is an Honorary Fellow of the Centre of Lifelong Learning at the University of Hull. She specialises in urban, regional, demographic and maritime history, and her publications include *Plague in Essex* (1982), *The Book of Whitby* (1990), *Prisoners of the Tsar: The Baltic Embargo of 1800–1801* (1992), and *The Whitby Sisters: A Chronicle of the Order of the Holy Paraclete* (2000).

Daniel Clayton is Lecturer in Human Geography at the University of St Andrews. He is the author of *Islands of Truth: The Imperial Fashioning of Vancouver Island* (2000), and of numerous articles on European-Native relations in the North Pacific and on the connections between geography and empire. His recent publications deal with the work of the French tropical geographer Pierre Gourou, and he is currently engaged on a book entitled *Colonialism's Geographies*.

Andrew S. Cook has been Map Archivist of the India Office Records, now in the British Library, since 1974. He is currently preparing for publication the catalogue of Alexander Dalrymple's charts and sailing directions, based on his doctoral thesis completed at the University of St Andrews. He is also developing a methodology for the historical bibliography of Admiralty charts and sailing directions. Arising out of his project to edit Dalrymple's hydro-graphic correspondence is his present investigation of the social connections of Dalrymple, Sir Joseph Banks, and their contemporaries, particularly through the Royal Society and its dining clubs. Andrew Cook has served as Honorary Secretary to the Hakluyt Society, and has contributed a number of papers to academic journals and conferences.

Robin Inglis is Director of the North Vancouver Museum and Archives in British Columbia, and is a Fellow of the Canadian Museums Association. As curator of major bicentennial exhibitions on the voyages of La Pérouse and Malaspina, he became involved in their stories. He has published and lectured widely on Northwest Coast exploration, and is a Contributing Editor to the Hakluyt Society's multi-volume edition of *The Malaspina Expedition 1789–1794: The Journal of the Voyage of Alejandro Malaspina* (2001–4).

Pauline Nawahineokala'i King studied history at Brown University and the University of Hawaii where she was awarded her doctorate. She is Professor of History at the University of Hawaii at Manoa in a position especially created to consider the rich indigenous society together with the growth of an American culture, and the dynamic between the two. She has published a biography of an American diplomat in Hawai'i in the 1850s, edited his journals and those of an American merchant, and also the journal of an Englishman who visited Hawai'i in 1825. Her present researches are concerned with early twentieth-century Hawai'i.

Andrew Lambert is Laughton Professor of Naval History in the Department of War Studies at King's College, London. His research interests are particularly concerned with nineteenth-century naval history, strategy and warfare. His most recent books include *The Foundations of Naval History: Sir John Laughton, the Royal Navy and the Historical Profession* (1998), *War at Sea in the Age of Sail* (2000), and *HMS Trincomalee: The Last of Nelson's Frigates* (2002). He took a break from teaching British strategic interests in the Mediterranean in the post-Napoleonic period to experience life as a topmast hand on an eighteenth-century ship when he joined the crew of the *Endeavour* replica off the Great Barrier Reef to advise the BBC on the television series, 'The Ship'.

Stuart Murray is Senior Lecturer in Commonwealth and Postcolonial Literature in the School of English, University of Leeds. He has published on the literature, film and cultural history of New Zealand, the South Pacific, Australia, Canada, and the Caribbean. He is author of *Never a Soul at Home: New Zealand Literary Nationalism and the 1930s* (1998); editor of *Not On Any Map: Essays on Postcoloniality and Cultural Nationalism* (1997); and co-editor of the forthcoming *Contemporary New Zealand Film* and *New Zealand Filmmakers*, both to be published by Wayne State University Press.

John Robson has travelled extensively in his career as a mining geologist and later as a librarian. He now works at the University of Waikato Library in Hamilton, New Zealand, and he is the New Zealand representative of the internationally-based Captain Cook Society. He is author of *Captain Cook's World: Maps of the Life and Voyages of James Cook R.N.* (2000), and is currently working on *The Captain Cook Encyclopedia.*

Anne Salmond is Professor of Social Anthropology and Maori Studies at the University of Auckland, where she has also been Pro-Vice-Chancellor since 1997. She received the CBE for services to literature and the Maori people in 1988, and in 1995 was made a Dame Commander of the British Empire for services to New Zealand history. She has worked extensively on Maori life and history, and among her many publications are *Two Worlds: First Meetings Between Maori and Europeans 1642–1772* (1991) and *Between Worlds: Early Exchanges Between Maori and Europeans 1773–1815* (1997). Her most recent book is *The Trial of the Cannibal Dog: Captain Cook in the South Seas* (2003).

Sujit Sivasundaram is Research Fellow in History at Gonville and Caius College, Cambridge. He has lectured at University College, London and the University of Cambridge. At present he is turning his doctorate, 'Nature speaks theology: colonialism, cultivation, conversion and the Pacific, 1795–1850', into a book, and is also working on a project on elephant hunting in colonial Ceylon. His most recent article is 'Natural History Spiritualized: Civilizing Islanders, Cultivating Breadfruit and Collecting Souls', *History of Science*, 39 (2001).

Simon Werrett trained in Slavonic Studies and the History of Science at the Universities of Leeds and Cambridge, where he completed his doctoral thesis in 2000 on the introduction of the sciences to eighteenth-century Russia. He is currently Assistant Professor at the University of Washington, Seattle. His research interests include the cultural history of science in eighteenth-century Russia, particularly the history of pyrotechnics, and relations between the sciences, art and the theatre.

Glyndwr Williams is Emeritus Professor of History at Queen Mary, University of London. Among his many books on the history of exploration is an edition of *Captain Cook's Voyages 1768–1779* (1997). His most recent book is *Voyages of Delusion: The Search for the Northwest Passage in the Age of Reason* (2002). In 2001 he was historical consultant to the BBC television series, 'The Ship', which was broadcast in August and September 2002.

Acknowledgements

Thanks are due to many who helped both with the conference and with the preparation of this volume: first and foremost to the Centre for North-East History, its Director Professor David Rollason, and its able administrator Margaret McAllister; and to the University of Teesside for its support and for hosting the meeting through local organisers Tony Pollard and Sophie Forgan. The British Academy and Redcar & Cleveland Borough Council gave their support, which was much appreciated. Through Cliff Thornton and Alwyn Peel, the Captain Cook Society gave helpful publicity and enthusiastic backing. Conference participants received hospitality and a warm welcome from the Captain Cook Birthplace Museum, Marton, the Whitby Museum, and the Captain Cook Memorial Museum, Whitby. Sophie Forgan helped immeasurably with the putting together of this volume, while Andrew David advised on specific issues. Finally, Peter Sowden and Sarah Pearsall did much to see the volume into print.

We are grateful to the following for permission to reproduce copyright material: Courtesy of the Public Record Office, Adm 55/21, fo. 150 (Plate I); Royal Naval Museum, Portsmouth (Plates II, V); Bibliothèque Centrale du Muséum Nationale d'Histoire Naturelle, Paris (Plate III); United Kingdom Hydrographic Office, Crown Copyright 2003. Published by permission of the Controller of Her Majesty's Stationery Office and the UK Hydrographic Office (www.ukho.gov.uk), (Plate IV); by permission of The British Library, BL Add. MS 21593 C (Plate VI); by permission of the British Library, BL Add. Ms 7085, fo. 17 (Plate VII); Bibliothèque Nationale de France (Plate VIII); University of Canterbury Library, New Zealand (Plates IX, XII); by permission of the British Library, BL Add. MS 15499, fo. 23 (Plate X); by permission of the British Library, Printed Books 455 a. 21–23 (Plate XI); by permission of the British Library, BL Add. MS 31360, fo. 44 (Plate XIII); Vancouver Maritime Museum (Plate XIV); Museo Naval, Madrid (Plate XV); Syndics of Cambridge University Library (Plates XVI, XVII, XVIII, XXI); The Rex Nan Kivell Collection, National Library of Australia (Plate XX); James Clerk and Co. (Plate XXII).

Abbreviations

Add. MSS	Additional Manuscripts, British Library
BCARS	British Columbia Archives and Records Service, Victoria, B.C., Canada
BL	British Library
CCMM	Captain Cook Memorial Museum, Whitby
HUA	Hull University Archives
NMM	National Maritime Museum, Greenwich
OA	Orkney Archives, Kirkwall
PRO	Public Record Office, Kew
RSA	Royal Society Archives
WLPS	Whitby Literary and Philosphical Society
	The Journals of Captain James Cook on His Voyages of Discovery, ed. J. C. B. Beaglehole
EV	I. *The Voyage of the Endeavour 1768–1771* (Cambridge, 1955)
RAV	II. *The Voyage of the Resolution and Adventure 1772–1775* (Cambridge, 1961)
RDV	III. *The Voyage of the Resolution and Discovery 1776–1780,* 2 parts (Cambridge, 1967)

Introduction

The conference on 'Captain Cook: Explorations and Reassessments' held at the University of Teesside, Middlesbrough, on 11–14 September 2002, was the sixth International Conference sponsored by the Arts and Humanities Research Board Centre for North-East England History. In one way it was an appropriate commemoration of local allegiances, for James Cook was born at Marton-in-Cleveland, only five miles from the conference hall, and his earliest experience of the sea and ships was at Whitby, less than thirty miles away. In another way the conference represented world history, for as with any meeting on Cook and his voyages the subject-matter of many of the papers concerned the Pacific. This association between the local and the global, between the Yorkshire background of the young Cook, and the ocean criss-crossed by the famous navigator, was a prominent feature of the conference. It was held at a time when Cook continued to attract both scholarly and popular attention. In those countries of the Pacific visited by Cook the current debate tends to concentrate on the larger implications of Cook's voyages, and the extent to which the individual explorer could be held responsible for the actions of his successors. In Britain there is perhaps less questioning of Cook's role and more celebration of his achievements. A six-part BBC 2 television series on Cook's first Pacific voyage was shown just before the conference began; in the weeks immediately after the conference Radio 4 broadcast a three-part series on Cook's voyages. The full-size replica of the *Endeavour* had reached Britain earlier in the year, while the summer months saw the publication of several books on Cook and his voyages. It was, then, a timely moment for a conference whose aim was to assess the present standing of Captain Cook as one of the leading figures in eighteenth-century history.

The chapters presented in this volume represent a range of disciplines and approaches. They have been grouped into four sections. Part I, 'The Years in England', opens with Rosalin Barker's chapter describing Whitby in the eighteenth century, and the environment that helped to provide the young James Cook with a good scientific and mathematical education as well as a practical training in seamanship. Richard Allen follows this by investigating the implications of Cook's apprenticeship with the Quaker shipowners, John and Henry Walker. Cook's nine-year stay in John Walker's household, and his

1

long-lasting relationship with his old master, have long attracted the interest of historians; but Allen argues that Cook's connection with Quakerism was a more tenuous and ambiguous affair than has often been assumed. Although Cook remained in contact with Walker when he joined the Royal Navy, after promotion from the Newfoundland survey to command the *Endeavour* and to observe the Transit of Venus, he began to move in very different circles from those of the North Yorkshire Society of Friends, as Andrew Cook shows in his chapter on the explorer and the Royal Society. His advancement, socially and professionally, was marked by his election as Fellow of the Royal Society in 1776, but the chapter argues that the Society's role in furthering Cook's career has been subject to misunderstanding and exaggeration.

Part II, 'The Pacific Voyages', takes a critical look at aspects of all three of Cook's voyages. Stuart Murray scrutinises the writings of the journal-keepers on the *Endeavour* during the ship's stay at the Endeavour River in order to explore the clash between the ship's crew and the Aborigines of the area. From there he considers other key moments of Pacific exchange in this period with a view to explaining how the writing of the Endeavour River episode wrestled with the demands placed upon it to function as both record and narrative. Anne Salmond traces the changes in Cook's behaviour and attitudes over the course of his three voyages as she argues that the contact experience was double-edged, and that in some respects both Cook and his crews were becoming more Polynesian. By the third voyage the humane and enlightened commander of the first two voyages had become altogether more capricious and unforgiving. It was not only islanders who experienced Cook's fits of temper and harsh punishments; his own crew also suffered, and their adoption of the Polynesian transliteration of his name, Toote or Tute, bore implications that were not altogether flattering to their captain. Some of the fiercest criticisms of Cook's behaviour have centred on his stay in Hawai'i and his apparent deification as *Lono* in the weeks before his death in February 1779. Pauline Nawahineokala'i King presents the research of two Native Hawaiian historians who throw new light on the relationship between Cook's visits to the Islands and the rise to power of Kamehameha I: Jerry Walker's examination of the significance of Cook's demonstration of the power of firearms, and Richard Paglinawam's evidence to show how Kamehameha used Makahiki, the four-month festival each year devoted to *Lono*, as well as the Cook legend, to strengthen his authority. Daniel Clayton shifts the locus of the debate from Oceania to the shores of Northwest America as he explores Cook's encounter with the Nuu-chah-nulth people of Nootka Sound in 1778. He contrasts the descriptive passages in the journals of Cook and his crew with the recollections of local oral evidence. Both sources raise issues of reliability and interpretation, and Clayton shows and questions how, in modern histories of the region, the European written records have invariably been given precedence.

Part III, 'Captain Cook and his Contemporaries', investigates the activities and attitudes of other Europeans in the Pacific in this period. John Robson compares the charts and maps produced by Cook on his first voyage with those of Louis-Antoine de Bougainville, and finds in favour of the former. Cook was a trained hydrographer, which Bougainville was not. In addition, Cook had specific instructions regarding surveying, whereas Bougainville's voyage had different objectives and priorities. Robin Inglis examines the Pacific voyages of both the French and the Spaniards, especially in the years after Cook's death. La Pérouse for France and Malaspina for Spain led expeditions to the Pacific that paid respectful attention to the Englishman's achievements but also hoped to rival them. In different ways both expeditions met with misfortune, and in the end neither challenged Cook's predominance. One country that appeared comparatively uninterested in Cook and his voyages was Russia, but Simon Werrett shows how an attitude of relative indifference changed after 1790 as a group of Russian navigators were able to fit Cook into their own traditions of maritime exploration, and looked to him for inspiration.

Part IV, 'The Legacy of Captain Cook', opens with Sujit Sivasundaram's comparison of the killing of the Revd John Williams on Eromanga in 1839 with the death of Cook sixty years earlier in Hawai'i. There are some similarities between these two men of humble birth who achieved fame in the Pacific, but Sivasundaram points to the important distinctions between the representations of their deaths. The missionary did not allow himself to be deified and in the end went to his death willingly. The editor's chapter seeks to set Cook in an historiographical framework, showing how his reputation has fluctuated from country to country and period to period, and that these variations have existed since the time of Cook's death. Andrew Lambert brings the representation of Cook and his men up to the present day, with his description of sailing in Australian waters in 2001 on the replica of the *Endeavour* during the filming of the BBC television series, 'The Ship'. As he says, a few weeks on shipboard, sharing the routines and hardships of an eighteenth-century mariner, gave him insights into Cook's voyages not possible for a study-bound scholar.

There was, however, unfinished business in the reassessment of Cook to which conference participants returned at the end of the proceedings. One issue which had surfaced several times during the sessions concerned the elusive matter of Cook's public reputation during his lifetime. On and after the first voyage, Cook shared the limelight with the more flamboyant Joseph Banks, and in Hawkesworth's *Voyages* the journals of the two men were merged in a way which made Cook's own contribution difficult to identify. Indeed since Cook was not an established officer or a gentlemen, if disaster had struck the voyage, his loss on what was a risky venture would not have been deemed a calamity. There were no rivals on the second voyage, and Cook's achievement was recognised on his return by such honours as an audience with the King, election to the Royal Society, and the award of its Copley Medal. Even so, his stay in England was relatively brief, and in terms of the London social calendar he returned from his second voyage too late for the 1775 'season', and left on his third voyage during the 1776 season. After his call at the Cape of Good Hope on the outward leg of that voyage there was no more news of Cook and his ships until the report of his death reached London in 1780, and this, it can be argued, caused the biggest stir of all. Cook dead was more famous than Cook alive, a thought which prompted some more general reflections on the nature of celebrity status in the eighteenth century.

Finally participants turned their attention to the records of the voyages – the jumble of logs and journals, personal diaries and letters, often cited as though they were of equal weight and value. Different officers, from Cook downwards, had their own way of keeping records; some were more conscious of possible scrutiny by the Lords of the Admiralty than others. Cook increasingly seems to have been writing for posterity as well as for his immediate superiors, while some of the frankest writing came from crew members who officially had no business recording events at all. As a postscript to this discussion the unexplained disappearance of Cook's journal that (presumably) he kept during his last days was pondered on. The wide-ranging speculation on what happened to the missing journal and what it might have contained was a fitting note on which to end a conference in which Cook enthusiasts from different countries and backgrounds learned much from each other's presentations, conversations and experiences.

Part I

The Years in England

1

Cook's nursery:
Whitby's eighteenth-century merchant fleet

ROSALIN BARKER

Whitby, in North Yorkshire, seems a very unlikely place to have owned the sixth largest outport fleet in England for most of the eighteenth century. It faces due north from its narrow estuary, at the mouth of a 24-mile-long river described, in 1720, as 'a little nameless river, scarce indeed worth a name' by Daniel Defoe.[1] There is no major river system such as that which backs the Humber or the Thames. Indeed, the tidal estuary is only one mile long, and at its maximum now 120 yards wide. There is no fertile hinterland and no great mineral deposit, and yet, as Defoe observed, 'they build very good ships for the coal trade, and many of them too, which makes the town rich'.

The port and its fleet

The size of the English merchant fleet in the middle of the eighteenth century is difficult to calculate, since the statistics submitted to London from the individual ports were very imperfect. The preamble to the principal source, BL Add. MS 11,255, states that it is:

> An account of the Tonnage of all Ships and Vessels belonging to each respective Port in England that have traded to or from foreign ports or coastwise or have been employed as Fishing vessels distinguishing each sort and each year and accounting each vessel once for the year.[2]

An accompanying letter dated 21 January 1782 from J. Dalley at the Customs House makes the point that during wartime, and especially during the War of American Independence, there was an apparent decrease in tonnage because of the number of vessels removed from trade as either privateers or

---

[1] Donald Woodward, ed., 'Descriptions of East Yorkshire, Leland to Defoe', *East Yorkshire Local History Series*, (No. 39 1985).
[2] It is clear from listings of Whitby vessels held within the port that vessel names were often repeated, so that there might be six or seven vessels of the same name, distinguishable only by the name of the master, and ranging from a 40-ton sloop to a 500-ton ship. This might well have led to much of the confusion.

transports. The latter counted as King's ships and did not report inwards or outwards.[3]

BL Add. MS 11,255 gives no figure at all for Whitby in 1747, when Cook first appeared on Whitby Muster Rolls, but the surrounding years' returns suggest a fleet during his time at Whitby of between 10,000 and 20,000 tons burthen. We know from later records held within Whitby that the totals given in BL Add. MS 11,255 are serious under-estimates, as Dalley suspected, and as they probably were for every other port. Suffice to say that Whitby's relative position in a league table of ship-ownership would have remained level for most of the century.[4]

The township of Whitby was small, a seigniorial borough, once of Whitby Abbey, and in Cook's day of the Cholmley family, one of the notable North Riding gentry and courtier families of the sixteenth and seventeenth centuries. It was squeezed into 48 acres of ancient burgage, of which half was and still is inter-tidal mud. Its population grew during the eighteenth century from about 3,000 in 1700 to some 7,500 at the first census in 1801, though by then there were a few of 'the better sort' in new developments in the suburb of Ruswarp. Yet that comparatively small population owned a very high proportion of the shares in the Whitby fleet.[5] From 1714 to 1718, there survives a series of lists of shareholders, naming the thirty-two individuals who variously held the sixty-four shares in *Hannah*, showing that 91 per cent of her shares were held by Whitby investors.[6] By 1782, when the fleet reached its maximum size of 315 vessels, with a total of 78,000 measured tons, local ownership seems to have stood at 83 per cent, compared to the 71 per cent of Liverpool-based shareholders in the Liverpool fleet at that time.[7] This tonnage figure was given in notes sent to the Board of Ordnance by the poet and dramatist Francis Gibson, in his capacity as officer commanding the Militia, but collated in his other capacity, as Collector of Customs.[8] It is higher than the figure shown in BL Add. MS 11,255 by a factor of six.

[3] BL Musgrave Papers, Add. MSS 11,255–6 consist of reports to the Customs authorities of clearances of vessels at the various headports and creek ports of England. They are discussed, together with their inherent problems, in R. Davis, *The Rise of the English Shipping Industry in the Seventeenth and Eighteenth Centuries* (first published, Macmillan, 1962, National Maritime Museum, Modern Maritime Classics Reprint No. 3, 1972), Appendix A, pp. 401–6.

[4] Rosalin Barker, work in progress

[5] Whitby Literary and Philosophical Society (hereafter WLPS), Chapman Papers; foliated volume containing, among other shipping and estate documents, the accounts of an unnamed shareholder in Whitby shipping, and the voyage accounts of *Judith*, 1677–82, and *Hannah*, 1714–17.

[6] At this time there were probably about 120 merchant vessels belonging to Whitby. *Hannah* is one of the only two for which a voyage book survives.

[7] S.K. Jones, 'A maritime history of the port of Whitby 1700–1914' (Ph.D. thesis, University College, London, 1982), pp. 75–6.

[8] PRO/T1/430, maps and notes sent by Francis Gibson, concerning the defence of Whitby, 1782.

Yet Whitby's fleet carried comparatively little trade to or from Whitby. It brought goods for the merchants who serviced the town, raw materials for sail and rope making, and timber to the thriving boat and ship building and repairing yards. The demand from the pastoral hinterland for goods was small. No raw materials were exported, save a little wool and dairy produce. The only mineral deposit exploited was alum, and that was processed before export, with a virtual cartel holding output down to under 4,000 tons lest the price fall below an economic level. During the latter half of the eighteenth century Whitby had virtually ceased to be a fishing station.[9]

Instead, the fleet carried goods to and from ports other than Whitby. It was a service fleet, carrying at different times in the eighteenth century up to 30 per cent of the coal exported from the northeast coal field,[10] 50 per cent of the timber imported from Norway,[11] and by the end of the century, 20 per cent of the enormous import trade from the Baltic to Great Britain.[12] It ventured into other trades, wherever money was to be made, for the shipowners of Whitby were opportunistic entrepreneurs. Apart from general cargo around the northern seas and across the Atlantic, there was Arctic whaling, from about 1753, and in time of war, the naval transport trade. Throughout the eighteenth and early nineteenth centuries, Whitby's large, heavy-duty vessels carried troops and stores to war, a lucrative and conservative trade for well-found ships, and for credit-worthy owners prepared to wait, sometimes for several years, for reimbursement of costs, and payment for the inevitable casualties.[13] When Cook, on his fatal return to the Hawaiian Islands from Alaska, struggling with inferior naval sails, praised the sails provided for merchant shipping, he would have been recalling the quality of sails in Whitby's well-maintained fleet.[14]

Indeed, Cook began his seafaring at a time when Whitby vessels were beginning to return from the War of the Austrian Succession, with considerable profit to their owners. The Whitby Muster Rolls for the Seamen's Sixpence, which begin, in great detail, in 1747, show Whitby's involvement in this war, as later in the Seven Years War, the War of American Independence, the French Revolutionary War and the Napoleonic Wars, as well as the American

---

[9] R. Robinson, A History of the Yorkshire Coast Fishing Industry 1780–1914 (Hull, 1987), p. 8.
[10] This calculation is based on current research on the Voyage Books of the Three Sisters and Four Brothers, in WLPS/Burnett Papers, and on M.W. Flinn (with D. Stoker), The History of the British Coal Industry, vol. 2, 1700–1830: The Industrial Revolution (Oxford, 1984).
[11] Ralph Davis, The Rise of the English Shipping Industry in the Seventeenth and Eighteenth Centuries (London, 1962), p. 64.
[12] N.E. Bang and K. Korst, Tabeller over Skibsfart og Varetransport gennem Øresund, 1497–1783 (Copenhagen/Leipzig, 1906–53), 7 vols.
[13] Jones, 'Maritime history of port of Whitby', pp. 96–8, table 14. There was the additional attraction that hired vessels were exempt from the attentions of the press-gang.
[14] EV, pp. 481–2.

War of 1812–14. When, during the Seven Years War, Cook served in Canada, he would have seen familiar Whitby ships, and men, serving in the transport service.

Not only did war involve Whitby shipping on hire to the Board of Transport, and to the Navy itself as armed vessels, but it also boosted the incomes of Whitby seamen in the trading fleet to an extraordinary degree, as the press-gang reduced the pool of available seamen, and as risk of capture or death reduced the number willing to take up such a career.[15] Table 1.1, which shows the annual wages of seamen on board *Three Sisters*, some of whom James Cook may well have known personally, makes clear the effect of war on the wages of men and officers. The war years are starred. The only crew member whose wages never varied was the Master. He appears to have earned his extra money on personal freight and from primage and other emoluments. There is also some shadowy evidence that ballast was a Master's perquisite.[16] Certainly, as the letters of James and Elizabeth Watt to Orkney show, masters managed to maintain a genteel, if not opulent, lifestyle.[17]

The period at which Cook first went to sea would have brought him into contact with men who had served either in the Navy or as the press-protected seamen of the Transport Service, so he would not have been ignorant of what the Navy might offer him. At the age of 18 he was an older servant who could talk to his shipmates, rather than a child. Although his career overlapped with the start of Whitby's whaling period by only two years, that was long enough for an intelligent mariner to listen to, and question, those of his friends who were engaged in this new trade, giving him an insight which would stand him in good stead on his second and third voyages, as he navigated through ice in both polar regions. His Baltic trips as a mate on John Walker's ships would also have given him experience of sea ice, since the Gulf of Riga froze for five months of the year.

The sources

Whitby has an enormously rich seam of documentary evidence for its shipping history, both within the community and in regional and national archives. Its role as a port involved a large geographical sphere of activity, and indeed influence, and its engagement in sea-borne trade introduced it to many different networks; these are reflected in the archives of the wider world. Those who work in the field of Whitby's shipping history become used to finding fragments of it on foreign shores. Indeed the earliest record of a particular ship being built

---

[15] WLPS: the voyage books of the *Four Brothers* and *Three Sisters* show that seamen's wages often doubled and occasionally tripled in wartime.

[16] Ongoing personal research.

[17] Orkney Archives (OA)/D3, Papers of Watt of Breckness; various letters.

Table 1.1 Annual wages of seamen on *Three Sisters*, 1761–87

Year	Annual earnings
* 1761	£27.22
* 1762	£30.67
* 1763	£21.66
1764	£14.13
1765	£12.75
1766	£12.10
1767	£14.00
1768	£17.00
1769	£20.00
1770	£22.16
1771	£24.00
1772	£17.50
1773	£17.50
1774	£17.50
1775	£20.00
* 1776	£19.50
* 1777	£37.60
* 1778	£36.55
* 1779	£42.00
* 1780	£37.85
* 1781	£42.16
* 1782	£35.26
* 1783	£26.50
1784	£20.00
1785	£22.25
1786	£15.25
1787	£21.00

Source: WLP/Swales Bequest/Voyage Books

in Whitby is of a ship commissioned by the Company of New England in 1625 – 500 tons burthen and 40 guns – making her the largest merchant ship in the English fleet at the time. Sadly the Company defaulted, and the *Great Neptune* was eventually bought by the Crown for the Navy.[18]

Many of the records, most notably the Port Books,[19] are in the Public Record Office, in the collections of the Exchequer, High Court of Admiralty, Board of Transport, Customs and Excise, Admiralty proper and even the Audit Office. Whitby was a creek of the headport of Newcastle upon Tyne, and spent a

[18] *Calendar of the Acts of the Privy Council, 1623–5*, pp. 439–40.
[19] Donald Woodward, 'The Port Books of England and Wales', *Maritime History*, III (1973), pp. 147–65, explains the system well.

great deal of time and effort trying to avoid both its dues to that port and the restrictive practices which the headport tried to impose upon its members. That this was not unusual is shown by the similar squabbles between Harwich and its headport Ipswich.[20] When the lesser port becomes successful, in the case of Harwich outstripping its ancient superior, pride and pocket both object to attempts at subjection.[21]

Whitby itself had subsidiary harbours at Staithes, Runswick and Robin Hood's Bay, at certain times only fishing stations, but at others small ports with merchant fleets of their own, though these, when registration was introduced in 1786, were registered at Whitby. Thus James Cook, apprenticed to grocer William Sanderson at Staithes, would have been in touch with merchant shipping, for William himself owned shares in shipping, and no doubt provided victualling and chandlery for local vessels.

While the sources held in the Public Record Office and other repositories match, in the main, those of other ports, it is the records held in Whitby Museum, in the archives of the Whitby Literary and Philosophical Society, that provide the most detailed account of the way in which Whitby conducted the business of its fleet. Three factors have contributed to the retention of this unique record of a merchant sailing fleet. First, the Society is itself of long standing, having been founded in 1823. Secondly, many of the principal shipowning families were Quakers, and the Quakers have always been known as diligent record keepers, and as people of great business integrity, with no need for secrecy over their business affairs. Thirdly, Whitby is a small town, where its inhabitants are greatly interested in their neighbours' affairs, and therefore disposed to keep any available evidence of its past. The town has long known of the length and continuity of its history, as might any community whose manorial government lasted from 1078 to 1894, with a continuing manorial presence into the new millennium, and which looks back to some 350 years before the previous millennium began.[22]

Part of the collection in Whitby Museum belongs to the Seamen's Hospital Charity founded in 1675 by Whitby shipowners for the relief of decayed and distressed seamen and their dependants.[23] Only an already confident shipowning port would have set up such an organisation, and in a way which gave it considerable economic and social control. It became the centre of Whitby's

[20] Leonard Weaver, *The Harwich Story*, 2nd edn (privately published, Harwich, 1976); Leonard Weaver was Hon. Archivist to the Borough of Harwich, and his book details much of the struggle and rivalry between Ipswich and Harwich.

[21] F.W. Dendy, *Records of the Newcastle upon Tyne Hostmen's Company*, Surtees Society 105 (1901), pp. 152–3, recounts the attempts to persuade the Collector of Customs at Whitby, Allan Wharton, to accept a moiety of the takings as collector of dues, in 1672. He declined after consulting Whitby merchants.

[22] The Abbey associated with St Hilda was founded in AD 657.

[23] There is a good account of the Charity in Richard Weatherill, *The Ancient Port of Whitby and its Shipping* (Whitby, 1908), pp. 393–9.

shipping life, its office used by Customs officers, the Ship-owners' Society, and any other body that wanted an official-looking address. In 1747 it came under the purview of the Seamen's Sixpence system, and from then until 1818 the original muster schedules for each vessel survive as well as the enrolled volumes made up from those schedules to remit that part of the Sixpence due to Greenwich Hospital.

There is a vast amount of information in the Muster Rolls, subject to continuing research – a probably endless task – and it is to these that we owe confirmation of James Cook's progress, from his indentures to John Walker, to his post as mate on Walker's ships, before he decided to join the Navy. Indeed, his career matches that of many promising men and boys who were indentured to the various shipowners of Whitby. As a well-grown youth at the start of his servitude, Cook served three years. Had he joined as a child, he would have been indentured until it seemed likely that he would be capable of a man's work, and there are cases of boys as young as 10 being indentured.[24] A man's work in the merchant fleet was, moreover, hard. The vessel might be propelled by wind in sails, and even occasionally encouraged along by the tide, but the real propellant was muscle power, and those muscles in the merchant fleet man-handled twenty tons per man as opposed to the three or four tons per man of the navy.[25]

An apprentice, described in the seventeenth century as an 'articulate', was usually mustered as a servant, so that it is not always easy to distinguish at first glance who was a ship's boy, likely to end up at most as a seaman; who was a carpenter's apprentice and might end his days as a master shipwright ashore; and who was expected to become a navigating officer. Few indentures survive, and it is from other evidence, or from tracing career patterns through the tens of thousands of musters, that distinctions can be made. The early rolls, which include those of James Cook's ships, are very detailed, and give the age and place of birth of all the crew. As always with a new system, the clerk was meticulous, and it has to be remembered that the document recorded not only the sea-career of each seaman or servant, but, by recording age and place of birth or residence, it paid at least lip-service to the Settlement Law of 1662, which determined entitlement to relief under the poor law. Inevitably, with custom and use, the information given became more sketchy. In any case, the Seamen's Hospital was a useful safety net between the parish Overseer of the Poor and the seafarer down on his luck.

Seafaring was a young man's life, and most would hope to come ashore before arthritis and chronic bronchitis set in. Servants' ages ranged from 10 to 27, so Cook was by no means the oldest servant of his day. Some men, of course, spent their whole working lives on one vessel or another, effectively homeless unless at sea, until they retired to the Hospital as almsmen. Others found employment

---

[24] A boy of 10 might well be indentured for nine years.
[25] Davis, *Rise of the English Shipping Industry*, pp. 58–61.

ashore, and even while still actively engaged with the sea would work ashore in the winter season when weather virtually closed down the North Sea trades. This was particularly true of ships' carpenters.

It often seems as if 'everyone' assumes that James Cook arose, in splendour to match the numerous depictions of his apotheosis after his death, as the only skilled and intellectual mariner to emerge from Whitby's fleet. The reality is far more prosaic; while James was a servant on board John Walker's ships, there were 1,276 servants altogether in the Whitby fleet, of an average age of 17, and median and mode ages of 16. They were all at various stages of their servitude, and not all would have been intended mariners (a distinction maintained, certainly in this region, to indicate a man who was capable of navigation and watch-keeping). However, many went on to become masters, and owners themselves. Some even achieved fame and recognition for their outstanding capabilities. Whitby had been home to the Arctic explorer Luke Foxe, who died there in 1637. It also nurtured the careers of the Scoresbys, father and son, whaling captains, both of whom, like Cook, were elected Fellows of the Royal Society. Captain John Beecroft, esteemed as one of the heroes of the struggles against slavery on the coast of West Africa, was born and trained in Whitby.[26]

The few surviving indentures, the notebooks of the costs of training kept by shipowners, and the day-books of schools, give us some small idea of how the system worked.[27] Those who hoped to become mates and masters would learn navigation, from skilled teachers in the town, as well as seamanship while on shipboard, but they would also have learnt 'mercantile accompts' from one of Whitby's schools or tutors. Jonathan Hornby's school at Danby in the Esk Valley, at the end of the eighteenth century, records the distance from which his pupils came, and the subjects they studied, including a classical or 'polite' education. This is later than Cook's time, but Cook was trained during the working life of the surveyor, cartographer, mathematician and classicist Lionel Charlton, who taught, wrote and surveyed in Whitby for many years.

A premium would have been paid for the servant's indenture, by a parent or friend, or by the Hospital for a son of a dead seaman, and from that, and from the wages which the owner took from the ship for his labour while on board, would have been paid his keep, as well as the cost of new clothes and washing and mending. Whitby's large number of vessels' Voyage Books, or accounts, show a complex financial structure, in which the ship is clearly an entity. Goods were bought by the ship; wages paid by it. The owner drew his share of the profit, but only after all dues had been met. The ship had a sum

---

[26] There is a fine portrait of Beecroft, who is buried in Africa, in Whitby Museum, together with mementoes of his work, and a collection of African ethnography.

[27] WLPS, Crispin Bean's Apprentices Notebook (see Table 1.2); Scottish Record Office, GD217/676, Apprenticeship indenture, Alexander Sibbald to John Calvert of Whitby, 1732; WLPS, Jonathan Hornby's School Accounts.

Table 1.2 Crispin Bean's Account Book for Apprentices, 1789–99 (Whitby Literary and Philosophical Society)

This is a small notebook. Each apprentice has at least one page, and sometimes the facing blotting-paper, to himself, although in three cases a page is shared, once by two brothers, one of whom was taken by the press-gang at Hull, once where a page has been used upside down for an incomplete account, and once where a boy was entered, indentured, conveyed to Hull, and ran away. This transcribed excerpt gives a brief account of the dealings with William Masterman from 1789.

	[£.	s.	d.]
W[illia]m Masterman			
at Diff[eren]t times on acc[oun]t of Wages	13	3	10
[17]89 [12]90 [17]91			
Aprill at Hull, Jackett Trows[ers] shirts			
& Stock[ing]s	1	3	6
Elsinure from Stolpl 4 Sugar		3	0
Cash D[itt]o		1	0
Hull cash of me		1	0
24 June of me		7	0
Petersburgh Voyage of the Master	1	3	0
Memell Voyage	1	8	4
2nd Jan 1792 his Mother (*paid for his winter lodging*)	1	1	0
Mr Tong a Jackett 15 June 1792		12	6
of Mr Atkinson the Memel Voyage	1	3	4
Petersburgh Voyage		17	0
2nd Memell Voyage		9	2
	5	4	1
Hull 19 Nov[embe]r	1	1	0
	22	13	8
	16	0	0
his Board [17]92 a[nd] [179]3 if all[owe]d	6	13	8
	2	12	0
B D f[ro]m him	4	1	8
Paid Mr Nicholson for Shirts		8	0

of money called 'the stock', a fixed sum, adjusted from time to time for inflation, which had to be made up at the end of each voyage year before any profit could be taken. All non-officer seamen were paid at the same rate, whether they were 'able' or merely servants, so that the apprentice-master collected a full man's wage for each servant, even if he was only a child. That went towards his keep and his equipment, and even some pocket-money. Trousers for work on board would be bought, but also knee-breeches and stockings for respectable company. Boots were provided if boys went to the Arctic whale fishery, and shoes for normal wear. Boys grew, and garments and footwear had to be replaced – or perhaps they were just boys, and out at knees, elbows and toes, as boys often are. Handkerchiefs were also provided, for these were the officers, masters and even shipowners of the future and must be decent in their manners.

The notes are *aides-mémoire*, rather than strict accounts, but enlighten us as to why James Watt found it a very harassing and difficult task to take on apprentices, especially those who were not of the 'better sort'.[28]

A strong element of gentility seems to have featured among the sea officers of Whitby. It is perhaps significant that the long run of accounts kept by successive 'Coal-meters' in Ipswich, a town notably conscious of the hierarchy of its burgesses, routinely referred to the masters of Whitby colliers by the honorific 'Mr', unlike those from other ports.[29]

The quality of the education available in Whitby is seen in the bound volume of mathematical exercises done by Henry Simpson between 1711 and 1718, while he was a servant. It represents a thorough grounding in mathematics and navigation, neatly illustrated, with six-figure logarithms accurately calculated, if with somewhat erratic spelling. However, it was accurate calculation rather than impeccable spelling that would keep Henry and his crew safe at sea. He went on to found a shipping and banking dynasty. Whitby's seafaring community was a sophisticated and well-educated one.

That this continued is made clear in a letter to his parents in Orkney, written on 5 September 1763, by William Manson, servant to Jonas Brown: 'Going over Navigation again [here in Whitby] as for that I learned at home did not seem a Great Deal of Good.'[30] That William's training served him well is clear from his early promotion at 20 as a master, having married Brown's step-daughter, but more significantly in his successful voyages in his brig *Flora*, 240 tons, to America and north of the Arctic Circle to Archangel. His log survives in Whitby Museum, and his Voyage Book in the Orkney Archives. Like Cook, Manson was interested in navigation, and though he did not join the Navy, he wrote his own 'rutters' and detailed 'remarks' for the testing parts of his voyages around the coast by Savannah and later to Archangel, and in much later life he surveyed a hitherto impossible navigation of the James River in Jamaica.[31]

What is clear from the musters is that the fleet was a very stable one. The smallness of the elite group of owners, and their interaction as members of the

[28] OA/D3/201, Papers of Watt of Breckness, letter, James Watt to brothers, 16 January 1791.

[29] Rosalin Barker, 'Ipswich Coalmeters' Accounts', *Suffolk Review*, n.s., 19 (1992); Michael Reed, 'Economic structure and social change in seventeenth century Ipswich', in Peter Clark, ed., *Country Towns in Pre-Industrial England* (Leicester, 1981), pp. 88–141.

[30] OA/D2/9/14, Balfour Papers, Letter, William Manson to parents, 5 September 1763, explaining that he will spend the winter in Whitby at school.

[31] Rutters were pilotage instructions, noted by conscientious masters for the future, or because the given instructions were inaccurate.

Society of Friends, or of kinship groups, and through the Seamen's Hospital, led to a great measure of social control. Unlike Rediker's samples in the Atlantic trade,[32] these crews had little need of brutal boatswains, and few deserted from their vessels.[33] Masters stayed in post for many years, and servants sometimes rose to command the vessels on which they had served their time. An example of how the Muster Rolls can be used to trace a specific career can be seen from the progress of William Barker as a servant on the *Three Sisters* to his appointment as her master over a ten-year period, a similar length of time to that of Cook on John Walker's ships.

One must not paint too rosy a picture of life at sea in eighteenth-century Whitby. Conditions were hard, dependent on life in a wooden box exposed to wind and weather in some of the most dangerous seas in the world. Records from the Seamen's Hospital make clear the high risk of injury from falls and back-lashing ropes, as well as the chest ills to which young men were particularly vulnerable in the northern seas, yet also show a care for their treatment. Medical expenses incurred by Whitby masters in other ports for the care of sick or injured crew were reimbursed, *provided* that the Trustees were satisfied as to the cause of the injury. There were no refunds for the treating of the results of any suspected abuse of servants or crew.

Perhaps the saddest word in Whitby's maritime archive is 'lost'; lost when driven on to a lee shore; lost after last seen crossing the bar at the mouth of the Tyne in a gale; lost, as so many vessels were, on the treacherous shifting sands of the East Anglian coast, like the *Alliance*, an Usherwoods ship, with

Table 1.3 William Barker's career on the *Three Sisters*, owner George Galilee

Year	Post on board	Period
1772	Servant	8 months, 2 days
1773	Servant	7 months, 5 days
1774	Servant	8 months, 5 days
1775	Servant	8 months, 3 days
1776	Seaman	7 months, 3 days
1776	Mate	1 month, 14 days
1777	Mate	8 months, 18 days
1778	Mate	8 months, 14 days
1779	Mate	8 months, 26 days
1780	Mate	8 months, 22 days
1781	Master	9 months, 21 days
1782	Master	7 months, 6 days

[32] Marcus Rediker, *Between the Devil and the Deep Blue Sea* (Cambridge, 1987), pp. 205–53.
[33] WLPS Muster Rolls. A 5 per cent database analysis of some 1,700 voyage years between 1747 and 1787 shows a low rate of desertion, and only three vessels carrying bosuns.

all hands, including her young master, William Usherwood junior; lost in a Baltic storm, desperately trying to reach the safety of Danzig harbour, like the *General Carleton*, currently being excavated by Polish archaeologists. And yet, despite the dangers of the Baltic, the proportion of Whitby ships which went through the Sound eastwards and failed to return is very small. In the five decades between 1740 and 1790, the recorded loss is less than 1 per cent.[34]

But these same archives also reveal something which throws light on Cook's success in tackling scurvy. In all the ills recorded in the Hospital archives, there is no single case of fatal scurvy. Despite the fact that Whitby vessels had long been used to 'blue-water sailing' – across the Atlantic; into the Davis Straits for whales; round to Archangel and Murmansk for trade – there is no mention of scurvy save on the circumnavigation voyages of the two Whitby ships[35] which went with the First Fleet to Botany Bay, 1787–8. And even they went hunting, in the Falkland Islands, among other places, for the cures which Cook knew, and which he himself sought when necessary. The scurvy grass, wild cabbage and wild celery (or lovage), all grow on Whitby cliffs, and even in Whitby churchyard.

It is to another great collection of documents in Whitby Museum that we owe our knowledge of how the fleet was run, to a miscellaneous group of varying documents accumulated by the great shipping families, the Swales, the Barrys, the Chapmans, the Usherwoods and others. They left for posterity their logs, Voyage Books, insurance schedules and letters, many of which are contemporary with John Walker. It is from these, often made up ashore from notes made on board, from dockets and bills, sometimes by masters' wives, like Elizabeth Watt, or by a grandfather, retired but still involved, like Robert Usherwood senior, that we learn most of the minutiae of life on board a Whitby merchantman.

Above all it is from these that we discover the source of much of Cook's humanity, and his technical and practical skill. As a young servant he would have learnt to make the fothering mat that years later saved *Endeavour* after she struck the Great Barrier Reef. It is a striking fact that the first things the master of a brand-new vessel bought were old rope and old sailcloth. Cook may have turned his midshipman, who had sailed in a fothered ship before, to the laborious task of placing the huge mat, but the method of construction with sailcloth, wool, oakum and fat, was Cook's, and probably Whitby's.[36]

The cleanliness of Whitby vessels is shown by the expenditure on brooms and brushes; the care for health and adequate diet is seen from the detailed

[34] WLPS Policies at Lloyds (Barry Bequest); in the nineteenth century the insurance average at Lloyds for a trip to the Baltic was 3 per cent, far higher than the losses experienced at Whitby in the eighteenth century.
[35] *Fishburn* and *Golden Grove*, both of which eventually rejoined the merchant fleet of the northeast.
[36] *EV*, p. 347 and n. 4.

lists of food bought – cabbages, carrots and potatoes, as well as oatmeal and biscuits, to supplement the meat, fresh and salted. To drink there was beer, a certain amount of spirits, and on coastal trips, milk for the boys. Fresh fish was bought at sea, soft bread whenever a port was visited. The cook was paid extra, as a petty officer, in the wages bills. The cabin was provided with tea – for the officers. As a mate Cook would have reached the 'tea' grade, and the right to sit and drink it in the cabin. As a servant he would have worked during the winter lay-off learning the rigging and repairing of his ship. He would have run errands ashore, shopping for a wide range of smaller items, and building up the network of tradespeople with whom he could have dealt on a larger scale as a master.

The extent of these micro-networks can be seen from the Voyage Books of the *Three Sisters*, 1761–88. No fewer than 250 different named chandlers and tradespeople appear in these, and there are many transactions with others not named. As masters changed, infrequently, a slightly altered cohort of suppliers appears. It must have been well worth the while of a dockside victualler to make a favourite of a bright youngster sent ashore for small shopping. Extra buns here and there, or a warm drink on a cold day, might yield dividends in regular orders when the inevitable promotion occurred.

Cook's ships probably over-wintered, as most larger Whitby vessels did, in either the Tyne or the Thames, depending on whether they were engaged as colliers or as Baltickers, so Cook would have learnt the workings of these great port areas, and met men from all over the world, and, on the Thames, from the Navy as well. Ralph Jackson's diary of his days as an apprentice to a leading Newcastle hostman reveals the social interchange between ship and shore in the mid-eighteenth century.[37]

There is much debate as to why Cook left the merchant fleet to join the Navy. However, one thing *is* certain; he did not turn down the command of a Whitby ship to avoid the press-gang in the forthcoming war. As a mate of a collier he had been exempt, as every Whitby sea-officer would know, and as a master he was extremely unlikely to be taken. In fact, masters of small vessels were exempt altogether. Whitby had, and still has, a carefully preserved eighteenth-century manuscript copy of the rules for the Officers of the Impress.[38] The port's long history of involvement with the Transport Service, and with other 'protected' seafaring such as whaling, would have ingrained the awareness of how the Impress Service worked, and how to manipulate it.

One wonders what Cook felt, secretly, when in 1768, after his long years in the Navy, he was given his first command as a commissioned officer, and was told that she was a Whitby collier, a command he had turned down fifteen years before in favour of the Navy. What resulted from Cook's career, however,

[37] Clifford Thornhill, ed., *Bound for the Tyne; Extracts from the Diary of Ralph Jackson, Apprentice Hostman of Newcastle upon Tyne* (Newcastle, 2000).
[38] WLPS Chapman Papers.

was the fact that he served far longer at sea than he would have done as a master in Whitby's merchant fleet. Herein may lie the clue to his apparent psychological changes in the exhausting processes of the last voyage, when he was in his late forties. Figure 1.1 shows that most masters were aged between 21 and 40, and epistolatory evidence shows that they felt themselves hard done by when their aching limbs were still at sea at the age of 40.[39]

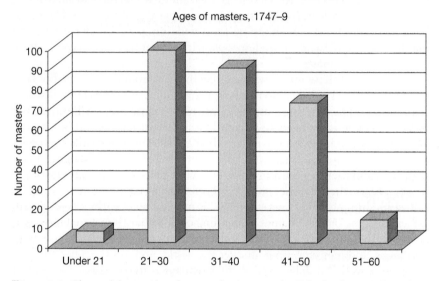

Figure 1.1 Chart of the age distribution of masters in the Whitby fleet, 1747–9, from the Muster Rolls

For all the hardships of the work, and the dangers of the North Sea and the Baltic, Cook's nursery was a relatively humane place, with well-trained servants, steady crews and long-serving masters, who were encouraged to think for themselves, and to work scientifically. It is not difficult to recognise in it the potential for a clever, diligent youth to become one of the world's greatest navigators.

[39] OA/D3/263, Papers of Watt of Breckness, letter, James Watt to his father and brothers, 17 September 1776, laments the fact that James was still active at sea at the age of 35.

2

'Remember me to my good friend Captain Walker': James Cook and the North Yorkshire Quakers

RICHARD C. ALLEN

James Cook's formative years in and around the port town of Whitby have been well documented. In his early childhood, he moved with his family from Marton-in-Cleveland to Great Ayton, near the Cleveland Hills, where he received a basic education at the village school. In 1745, he gained employment at William Sanderson's haberdashery and grocery shop at Staithes, a small fishing village near Whitby.[1] The lure of the sea, however, had a stronger calling, and in July 1746 Cook, aged 17, entered into an apprenticeship with John Walker (1706–85),[2] a prominent Quaker shipowner and coal merchant at Whitby. From the time that Cook became an apprentice, and throughout his career, Walker remained a close friend.

A great deal has been made of Cook's connection with the Quaker community both at Cleveland, North Yorkshire, and in London, and yet much of this has been written by historians and biographers who have only the most tenuous appreciation of the Quaker way of life. In her recent study, Julia Rae has attempted to throw more light on Cook's association with the Quaker community, but even this biography fails to establish why Cook did not embrace its religious ethos. This new analysis aims to address the lacunae in the literature and consider the deeper ambiguities of his relationship with Quakerism. It will draw upon the hitherto unexplored Quaker records of the Scarborough and Whitby Quaker meetings, trace the connection between the North Yorkshire Quakers, particularly the Walker family, and Cook, and provide a more textured reading of the North Yorkshire Society of Friends and their alternative way of life. In doing so it will question whether Quaker

---

[1] Details of his early life and education, and local Quakerism, are provided in George Young, *A History of Whitby and Streoneshalh Abbey* (2 vols, Whitby, 1817), II, pp. 850–2; George Young, *The Life and Voyages of Captain James Cook* (London, 1836), ch. 1; Robert Tate Gaskin, *The Old Seaport of Whitby* (Whitby, 1909, reprinted 1985), p. 382; J.C. Beaglehole, *The Life of Captain James Cook* (London, 1974), ch. 1; Julia Rae, *Captain James Cook: Endeavours* (London, 1997), chs 2, 3, 12; Vanessa Collingridge, *Captain Cook. Obsession and Betrayal in the New World* (London, 2002), chs 1, 3.

[2] See Young, *History*, II, p. 851; idem, *Life and Voyages*, pp. 6–8.

beliefs held any real currency for Cook as a young man and in his later life. Particular attention will be paid to the benefits of a solid and disciplined education, apprenticeship and training for life, the Quakers' work ethic and their value system.

Tom and Cordelia Stamp note that 'apart from the possibility of early Quaker influence at Ayton, there can be no doubt that Cook's coming to the Walker household at Whitby helped to shape his character along Quaker lines'.[3] Certainly, Cook's relationship with the Walker family lasted throughout his lifetime, and it may have left a marked impression on his later career. His apprenticeship with John Walker was a standard three-year contract to become a merchant sailor, whereby Cook agreed 'Not to play at dice, cards, bowls or any other unlawful games . . . [nor] haunt taverns or play houses . . . commit fornication nor contract matrimony.'[4] For his part, Walker agreed to provide instruction and training in the 'trade, mystery and occupation of a mariner' as well as offering 'meat and drink, washing and lodging'.[5] Living in the Walker household at Grape Lane, Whitby,[6] also meant that Cook was able to observe at first hand the Quaker value system: simplicity, honesty, moderation, and discipline.

Cook thrived in this rather austere environment and developed a long-term friendship with the Walkers. The five letters he is known to have written to John Walker between August 1771 and September 1775,[7] as well as his visit to the Walker household between December 1771 and January 1772,[8] illustrate the close and lasting friendship between the former apprentice and his employer. In 1771, he promised Walker, 'should I come into the North I shall certainly call upon you',[9] while in 1772 he wrote to Captain William Hammond, a Hull shipowner, 'if you should happen to go to Whitby remember me to my good friend Captain Walker'.[10] In 1775, Cook acknowledged receipt of Walker's 'obliging letter' and 'kind enquiryes after me during my absence'. He signed himself as Walker's 'Most affectionate friend and Humble Serv[t]', and offered his and his wife's 'respects to you and all your family'.[11]

---

[3] Thomas and Cordelia Stamp, *James Cook. Maritime Scientist* (Whitby, 1976), p. xi.

[4] J. Geoffrey Graham, *Captain James Cook, 'Servant and friend' of Captain John Walker* (Whitby, 1986), unpaginated.

[5] Ibid.

[6] For details, see Collingridge, *Captain Cook*, p. 28. The house is now the home of the Captain Cook Memorial Museum (hereafter CCMM).

[7] Printed in *EV*, pp. 505–9, *RAV*, pp. 689, 696–9, 960.

[8] For details see Graham, *Captain James Cook*.

[9] Whitby Literary and Philosophical Society (hereafter WLPS). MS.C126. Cook to Walker, 17 August 1771. Printed in *EV*, pp. 505–6.

[10] CCMM. MS C185.1. Cook to Captain William Hammond, 1 August 1772.

[11] Peabody Museum, Salem, Mass. Phillips Collection MS.C107.1. Cook to Walker, 19 August 1775; printed *RAV*, p. 960.

To make sense of Cook's association with Quakerism and its influence upon his life and career, some attention needs to be paid to the environment in which he spent his formative years. In the mid-eighteenth century Whitby was an expanding town[12] and the sixth shipowning port in England outside of London whose shipbuilding expanding dramatically during the century. The alum- and coal-carrying trade dominated the busy shipping lanes, and Whitby played an important role in ferrying coal from North Shields to London.[13] The Walker brothers, John and Henry, along with other Quaker shipowners, mariners, shipbuilders and suppliers such as the Chapmans, Taylors and Sanders, assumed a significant role in this lucrative but dangerous trade.

The Friends, far removed from their radical seventeenth-century roots,[14] were by the eighteenth century a religious community maintaining a healthy reputation as amiable neighbours, and distinguished by their desire for equality and pacifism.[15] But their detestation of ungodly places of public diversion led them to oppose some traditional social activities. Indeed, the remarkably buoyant consumer culture of eighteenth-century English society and the Quaker response to the rise of consumerism offer a new perspective upon the nature of popular traditions and the existence and workings of a counter-culture. For Quakers and Methodists in particular 'culture was a serious culture, with no time for the frivolity and self-indulgence of drama, painting, sculpture, music and dance, or even less serious forms of popular leisure'.[16] The Quaker code of conduct, founded upon strict moral principles, developed throughout the seventeenth century, and was enforced by the local preparative, monthly or quarterly meetings. The Walker family, as members of the Society of Friends, would have been expected to uphold such values, and in turn these may also have been impressed upon the young James Cook.

The divergence between popular culture and reformed behaviour, and the problems associated with calls for plainness and a simple, godly life nevertheless led many members to challenge the beliefs of their meetings. Consequently, this austerity, which ran counter to eighteenth-century social mores, led to a relentless decline in membership, as many Friends were unable to uphold this moral code. The Whitby Preparative Meeting and Scarborough Monthly Meeting minutes throughout the eighteenth century clearly reflect this tendency, most notably the disownment of Friends for 'marrying out' of the Society. In 1734, the Quarterly Meeting for North Yorkshire Friends expressed the hope

---

[12] Statistical information in Young, *History*, II, pp. 514–18.

[13] Ibid., ch. 3; Peter Clark, ed., *The Cambridge Urban History of Britain* (Cambridge, 2000), vol. II, pp. 128–9, 711ff.

[14] Nicholas Morgan, *Lancashire Quakers and the Establishment 1660–1730* (Halifax, 1993); David Scott, *Quakerism in York, 1650–1720* (York, 1991); Adrian Davies, *The Quakers in English Society, 1655–1725* (Oxford, 2000); Rosemary Moore, *The Light in their Consciences: Early Quakers in Britain, 1646–1666* (Philadelphia, 2000).

[15] In 1746, the North Yorkshire Quaker population was approximately 250–300 members.

[16] B. Reay, *The Quakers in the English Revolution* (London, 1985), p. 118.

that members would avoid 'superfluity of all kind',[17] and later called on them to reject 'unnecessary fashions which is Inconsistent with the Principles we profess'.[18] The refusal to condemn or at least to acknowledge their failings would lead to the expulsion of the 'unworthy' member. In such cases a paper of disownment was presented, and the Friend barred from membership unless he or she repented to the meeting's satisfaction. Disownment was not a measure that Friends took lightly; rather it was only invoked if the recalcitrant member failed to repent. But by rejecting many of the traditional customs associated with rites of passage they set themselves apart from the wider community.

For the Friends, a solid and disciplined education, coupled with an exacting but practical apprenticeship, meant that a young adult was provided with training for life. Quaker parents were required to ensure that their children were brought up in a temperate manner, while the monthly meetings were also encouraged to support the instruction of fellow members and to increase their levels of literacy. For example, the North Yorkshire Quarterly Meeting enquired whether Friends were 'carefull to put into practice former advises touching the education of children and keeping them as may be to Friends schools, and bringing them up in the fear of God'.[19] They were anxious to ensure that children behaved themselves, and called on members to provide clear advice on 'morality and in plainness of habit, speech and things agreeable to our profession'.[20] Thus in August 1764, the London Yearly Meeting 'being sorrowfully affected' called on members to forsake:

> the hurtful tendency of reading Plays, romances, Novels, & other pernicious Books [and] do earnestly recommend to every member of the Society to discourage & suppress the same and particularly to acquaint all Booksellers under our name with the painful anxiety occasioned to this Meeting by the reports of some Instances of selling or lending such Books, entreating they would avoid a Practice so inconsistent with the purity of the Christian Religion.
>
> And we further request that Frds everywhere woud be very careful of the choice of all Books wch their children read, seeing there are many under the specious Titles of the Promotion of Religion & Morality, containing sentiments repugnant to the Truth, as it is in Christ.[21]

At the heart of the Quaker way of life and its absolute rejection of worldly self-indulgence was a belief that work was an end in itself, which should satisfy

---

[17] Hull University Archives (hereafter HUA). DQR.12/9, Whitby Women's Preparative Meeting minutes 1719–56 (unpaginated), minutes 6.3.1734.

[18] HUA. DQR.12/9, minutes 6.5.1742.

[19] HUA. DQR.11/3, Scarborough Monthly Meeting minutes 1719–48 (unpaginated), Quarterly Meeting enquiries appended.

[20] HUA. DQR.11/4, Scarborough Monthly Meeting minutes 1748–67 (unpaginated). Quarterly Meeting enquiries appended.

[21] HUA. DQR.11/4, minutes 7.8.1764 citing the 1764 Yearly Meeting epistle.

individual creative needs and exploit God-given talents. Members thereby sought to provide appropriate education and training. Apprenticeships, whether for Quaker children or others, were regarded as the optimum means of equipping members for a life of hard work and financial stability. Friends who were apprenticed to other members of the Society were strictly supervised in order to ensure that they did not associate too freely with the wider community. For example, the Quarterly Meeting stressed that members should show great care in the placement of apprentices and servants with other Friends, and where 'any difficulty occurs in yt case to either m[a]st[e]rs or serv[an]ts that they apply to the particular monthly or Quarterly Meeting for assistance'.[22] In addition, as shown earlier, apprentices were denied the opportunity to attend musical festivals, dances and playhouses, or to socialise with women. There were occasions, however, when Quaker apprentices did not comply with the wishes of the Society. For example, in 1755 Scarborough Friends testified against John Adamson after it was proven that he was 'guilty of divers evil & unjust practices & disorder'.[23] Unfortunately, the minutes do not give details of these activities.

As an 'uncommonly serious, focused and studious' apprentice,[24] Cook was actively encouraged by his beneficent employer and the Walker family in general. They responded to his 'sober deportment and studious turn of mind',[25] and the housekeeper, Mary Prowd, provided him with additional candles and a table to continue his studies.[26] He spent nine years living in Walker's Grape Lane house: three during his time as an apprentice, and another six years while he was employed by the Walkers on their 'Cats' or coal colliers, the *Freelove*, *The Three Brothers*, *Mary* and *Friendship*. In accordance with their Quaker values, the Walker household was furnished in a plain style, which privileged function over the ostentatious display that increasingly became associated with the middling sorts in the eighteenth century. The accommodation was commodious but not extravagant, and Cook would have shared meals and spent many hours in the company of the family.[27]

Cook made good use of his time as an apprentice and quickly became proficient in navigation and the day-to-day running of a merchant ship – skills which would later be invaluable to him as an eighteenth-century explorer. The apprenticeship and his experiences on these 'Cats' meant that Cook 'matured

---

[22] HUA. DQR.11/3, Quarterly Meeting enquiries appended.

[23] HUA. DQR.11/4, minutes 7.10.1755, 4.11.1755.

[24] Collingridge, *Captain Cook*, p. 29.

[25] Young, *Life and Voyages*, p. 7.

[26] See Beaglehole, *Life*, pp. 8–14; Julia Hunt, *From Whitby to Wapping* (London, 1991), pp. 3–14.

[27] A discussion of the Quaker lifestyle in the eighteenth century can be found in Richard C. Allen, 'Establishing an alternative community in the north-east: Quakers, morals and popular culture in the long-eighteenth century', in Helen Berry and Jeremy Gregory, eds, *Creating and Consuming Culture in North-East England, 1660–1832* (Aldershot, 2004).

into a confident and driven young man with good skills, a good reputation and a good boss'.[28] Like Walker and a slightly later mariner, Henry Taylor of North Shields, Cook certainly would have recognised the importance of decent accommodation for his crew, fresh victuals for a healthy constitution, and firm discipline. Walker housed his crew, including his apprentices, at *The Bell* near Wapping High Street, a reputable establishment close to the Quaker meeting house. On board his merchant ships he ensured that fresh provisions were always provided, and Cook adopted this wholesome attitude when he embarked on his voyages. In 1792, Taylor published *Instructions for Mariners*, a text which stressed the demands on an apprentice. He wrote that:

> their minds should be strongly impressed with a sense of piety and virtue; quali-
> fications absolutely necessary in those that must be exposed to great temptations,
> and continual danger. . . . If it has been the misfortune of some young sailors to have
> had parents who either neglected, or had it not in their power to give them a suitable
> education, they will have frequent opportunities of improving themselves at sea,
> and while their ships lay in port.[29]

Masters were also to use good judgement and appeal to their apprentices' sense of pride in their work. Taylor recommended that masters should display a 'cheerful, calm, and dispassionate manner', which would set a good example for the crew.[30]

As an astute entrepreneur, John Walker was well equipped to teach Cook about business practices, particularly shrewd long-term financial or personal planning. For example, Walker never recklessly speculated or entered into dubious deals, unlike some contemporary merchants.[31] Rather he invested his wealth in land and securities, owning property at Haggersgate and farms at Danby, Hawkster and 'Lowly Lights' at North Shields. He also inherited a share in the family home at Grape Lane, and became the owner of Bagdale Hall in Whitby.[32] Friends in North Yorkshire, like Walker, believed in honesty and fairness in all of their business dealings. In September 1726 the Yearly Meeting at London exhorted Yorkshire members to discipline those who were engaged in smuggling and other nefarious activities.[33] Not all Friends complied. In 1772, the Whitby Preparative Meeting testified against Robert Pearson for smuggling, obstructing the law, and assaulting a customs officer.[34] While

[28] Collingridge, *Captain Cook*, p. 30.
[29] Henry Taylor, *Instructions for Mariners* (London, 1792), pp. 4, 6.
[30] Ibid., pp. 5–6.
[31] For details of Quaker partnerships and financial calamities, see Rae, *Endeavours*, pp. 9–10, 17, 21.
[32] Graham, *Captain James Cook*.
[33] HUA. DQR.11/3, minutes 3.8.1723; HUA. DQR.12/1, Whitby Preparative Meeting minutes 1726–1777 (unpaginated). Quarterly Meeting enquiries (*c*.1755) appended.
[34] HUA. DQR. 12/1, minutes 5.7.1772; Rae, *Endeavours*, pp. 7–9.

Quakers in business were also cautioned against the dangers of excess, they helped members who fell victim to bankruptcy provided that they had paid due attention to Friends' warnings. The temptations of the business world were all too real, and inevitably some members found themselves in difficulties. Thomas Clarkson of Scarborough was a prime example. In 1722, Friends testified against Clarkson and his wife for 'running into debt beyond wt he was able to pay'.[35] In spite of some notable cases, very few Friends in North Yorkshire were testified against for their business dealings.

Cook spent his formative years in this competitive environment. After passing his examinations in 1752, Walker promoted him to the position of mate aboard the *Friendship*, a position he held until 1755, when Walker offered him the post of master on one of his vessels. Cook, however, had decided to enlist in the Royal Navy.[36] The reasons why he chose to do this have been the subject of considerable speculation, and a number of plausible explanations suggest themselves. He may have been expressing patriotic loyalties by enlisting during a period of tension between Britain and France, or he could have been influenced by his experiences in London, where he had often voyaged on one of Walker's vessels. The sedate nature of Whitby was possibly too quiet for him. Either way, Cook's passion for exploration would not have been satisfied by a career as a merchant seaman. Clearly, he was a restless spirit, and Whitby could not appeal to him in the long term, as it was 'the kind of place that's for the homely rather than the progressive; the kind of place that cannot hold on to those with dreams'.[37] Cook seized the chance to demonstrate his abilities and carve out a career based on his belief that the English society was providing greater opportunities to men of talent.[38] By doing so, he distinguished himself from his Quaker benefactor and acquaintances. The inner peace that many Whitby Quakers exemplified had not permeated his soul, nor did he embrace the quiet life in his later years. A letter to John Walker in August 1775 would indicate that 'a fine retreat and a pretty income' did not appeal to his 'active mind'. He confided to Walker that he doubted whether he could bring himself to like 'ease and retirement'.[39]

In other respects Cook's personal life and career suggest that he did adopt some elements of Quakerism. His fair dealing with the native peoples he encountered is characteristic of Quaker egalitarianism. For example, the agreement he negotiated with the inhabitants of Tahiti in April 1769 stated that 'every fair means' was to be used to 'cultivate a friendship with the Natives and to treat them with all imaginable humanity', while any crewman found illicitly trading would be severely punished.[40]

---

[35] HUA. DQR. 11/3, minutes 4.10.1722.
[36] Beaglehole, *Life*, p. 15.
[37] Collingridge, *Captain Cook*, p. 36.
[38] Beaglehole, *Life*, p. 17.
[39] Peabody Museum. MS.C107.1. Cook to Walker, 19 August 1775.
[40] EV, pp. 75–6.

Quaker marriages were based on sobriety, compatibility and financial security. Courtships and marriage proposals had to satisfy the requirements of the local meeting. Any ill-conceived alliance was referred to the overseers for judgement, and they would assess the prospects of a successful relationship and the reputations of those involved. Occasionally marriages were delayed due to earlier engagements, or prohibited if one or both of the contracting partners was considered to be acting contrary to the Society's wishes. In March 1720, George Wilson of Whitby was obliged by his Monthly Meeting to acknowledge his unseemly behaviour in proposing marriage so soon after the death of his wife, and he repented his 'too hasty going from one woman to another'.[41] By the early eighteenth century the rules governing marriage, especially to non-members, were resolutely applied; for mixed marriages were believed to have a deleterious effect on Quaker unity. Friends who infringed the rules risked disownment. In 1729, Whitby Friends admonished George Hill for his 'outrunnings and marrying by a priest',[42] but the difficulties faced by Quakers seeking marriage partners were significant and many of them fell foul of the regulations. In April 1750, eight Whitby Friends were reported to have 'run out and transgressed as to marriage',[43] and this was replicated throughout the eighteenth century. The Walker family were not immune from such transgressions. Between 1726 and 1727, Whitby Friends counselled Henry Walker about his marriage with Ann Hudson, particularly his reluctance to acknowledge his 'outrunnings'. His stubborn failure to comply would normally have been met with a swift disownment, but as the affair had caused 'great uneasiness among friends of that meeting' it was decided to suspend deliberations.[44] Other members of the Walker family were also testified against for marrying outside the Society in 1734 and 1740.[45] The practice of disownment for 'walking disorderly' or 'marriage before a priest' served to undermine the Quaker community. It was this reason, rather than any other transgressions, which led to the severe reduction in membership in the eighteenth and nineteenth centuries.[46]

Cook, who lived in a Quaker household but was not a Friend, would have been accepted among the community, but not have been welcome as a potential marriage partner. Nevertheless, some aspects of his courtship with Elizabeth Batts, the daughter of the landlord of *The Bell*, and his subsequent marriage in December 1762, show an attachment to Quaker values. Cook was thirteen years older than Elizabeth (1741–1835), and had known her since

[41] HUA. DQR.11/3, minutes 1.1.1719–20.
[42] HUA. DQR.12/1, minutes 3.9.1729.
[43] HUA, DQR.12/1, minutes 29.2.1750, 3.4.1750.
[44] HUA. DQR.11/3, minutes 6.7.1726, 3.11.1726, 7.1.1726, 4.2.1727, 5.7.1727.
[45] HUA. DQR.11/3, minutes 3.10.1734 (John Walker Senior), 2.7.1740, 7.8.1740 (John Walker Junior).
[46] T.H. Woodwark, *The Quakers of Whitby* (Whitby, 1926), pp. 7–8.

she was 10 years old.[47] Although it may have been an unusual courtship, Cook was attracted by the family's sobriety, their financial solvency despite the sudden death of Elizabeth's father in 1743, and possibly by her quiet nature which promised to offer the long-term stability and compatibility he sought. Cook was not a man 'to indulge in a whirlwind courtship when on leave, and nothing would be more in character than for him to marry a girl that he had known for a long time'.[48] Friends would have approved of his choice, and his decision to have a quiet wedding.[49]

Cook was an able negotiator and appears to have disliked being involved in any unnecessary disputes. His knowledge of arbitration can possibly be traced back to his Whitby years. Disagreements between Quakers, although infrequent, were dealt with internally by the Society, as Friends were required to voice their grievances to the Meeting for Business and not to the law courts. For example, in January 1727 Whitby Friends arbitrated in a dispute between Benjamin Lazenby and Sarah Foster.[50] Arbitration proceedings were formalised in 1761 when the Quarterly Meeting offered advice on how to conduct meetings, particularly when differences between members were raised. They should be

> orderly & solemnly conducted to the Edification of our youth & one another that Each Friend, who hath any thing to offer to the meeting, do stand up & speak deliberately & audibly without Interruption, that all may understand & judge of what is offered & Two not to speak at once, & all whispering & going into parties to be avoided, & Friends are desired as much as possible to keep their seats & solidly attend to the Business of the meeting.[51]

Cook assumed a conciliatory stance when dealing with his crew and with the peoples of different countries. In his journal, he notes that while buying provisions at Rio de Janeiro in November 1768:

> the Viceroy . . . obliged me to employ a person to buy them for me, under a pretence that it was the custom of the place, and he likewise insisted . . . on putting a Soldier into the Boats that brought any thing to and from the Ship, aledging that it was the Orders of his Court . . . this indignity I was obliged to submit . . . being willing as much as in me lay to avoide all manner of disputes.[52]

Later, in May 1770, Cook recorded that he had 'always been ready to hear and redress every complaint that have been made against any Person in the Ship'.[53]

[47] Rae, *Endeavours*, pp. 22–3, 25–9, 67–9; Beaglehole, *Life*, pp. 61–2.
[48] Rae, *Endeavours*, p. 28.
[49] Collingridge, *Captain Cook*, p. 63.
[50] HUA. DQR.12/1, minutes 1.11.1727.
[51] HUA. DQR. 11/4, minutes 7.7.1761.
[52] EV, p. 23.
[53] EV, p. 324.

Cook would have been very familiar with the Quaker preference for simplicity of living and the reasons for their 'plain' lifestyle. The Quakers advocated a well-ordered life, though members who attained great wealth must have been tempted by the conspicuous consumption of fashionable eighteenth-century society. As elsewhere, Yorkshire Friends opposed many pastimes, notably theatrical performances, musical festivals, dances, and sporting events, which they regarded as vain, gratuitous, and encouraging immoral behaviour. Friends called on members to be 'careful to avoid all vain Sports, Places of Diversion, [and] gaming'.[54] In July 1737 the Whitby monthly meeting warned those who visited Seaborough Spa to be aware of the 'snares of the place'.[55] Two years later Scarborough Friends accepted Richard Park's testimony against his 'weakness and offence in meddling with a parcel of French playing cards lately seizd in his custody',[56] while in March 1765 they censured Jacob Blackbeard, John Linskill and Hannah Swales for various 'irregularities': Blackbeard was accused of 'frequenting Billiard Tables & play houses', Linskill and Swales of 'frequenting the play house'.[57] This was not a precept that Cook took seriously. He certainly did not regard dancing as in any way immoral activity, and took great delight in the performances of the native peoples he visited. At Lifuka in May 1777, he commented that such a display would have been met with 'universal applause on a European Theatre'. He also recorded his observations about the music and dances performed by the islanders, noting that their voices were

> extreemly musical and their actions gracefull and decent, if we except some few which in a English assemb[l]y would be thought otherwise. But these indecent actions few as they are, do not arrise from any wanton ideas, but merely to increase the variety, for it is as[t]onishing to see the numbers of actions they observe in their dances and songs.[58]

Quakers sought to keep their clothes plain and admonished members who dressed inappropriately. For example, women Friends in North Yorkshire were told to avoid

> imitating the Fashions of the World in their head-cloaths; some having four pinner Ends hanging down & handkerchiefs being too thin; some having them Hollow'd out, & put on far of their necks; and their Gown sleeves & short Lappetts; wth A great deal to pin up in the Skirts; also their Quilted petticoats set out in Imitacon of hoops; some wearing two together; also Cloath-shoes of light colours bound wth

---

[54] HUA. DQR.12/1, Quarterly Meeting enquiries (c.1755).
[55] HUA. DQR.11/3, minutes 5.5.1737.
[56] HUA. DQR.11/3, minutes 4.7.1739.
[57] HUA. DQR.11/4, minutes 5.3.1765, 7.5.1765.
[58] *RDV*, p. 110.

different colours, and heels white or Red, wth white Rands & white colour'd Cloggs and strings; also scarlet or purple stockings, and Petticoats made short to Expose them.[59]

Men were expected to wear traditional Quaker clothing, particularly knee breeches, white bibs and unmistakable wide-brimmed hats, and this clearly distinguished them from the rest of North Yorkshire society. For example, Ambrose Rigge, a Yorkshire Quaker, wrote to Friends imploring them to avoid wearing wigs and 'all superfluities or haughtiness whatsoever'. He wrote that God had 'bestowed on many a Plentifull quantity of Hair to keep them warm of one colour Some of another'. It was, however, natural if one's hair was thinning that 'a suitable modest supply may then be very reasonable and no offence to God or good men', but he concluded that, for some, wearing a wig was a sign of immodesty and 'without any Just occasion any yt have sufficient Hair do cutt It of, Esteeming it not ffashionable or modish, or yt it Dont Curle Enough'.[60]

Cook's correspondence and journals reflect his own preference for plainness and modesty. He hoped that the public would remember him as a plain man, 'Zealously employed in the Service of his Country'.[61] Indeed, the journals were designed to provide an accurate record of events rather than an embellished text for the gratification and amusement of the public. He justified his plain-speaking in the following terms:

> It is a work for information and not for amusement, written by a man, who has not the advantage of Education . . . nor Natural abilities for writing, but by one who has been constantly at sea from his youth, and who, with the Assistance of a few good friends gone through all Stations belonging to a Seaman, from apprentice boy in the Coal Trade to a Commander in the Navy.[62]

Cook was, however, not immune from uttering a few profanities, notably his weakness for the phrase 'God dam', which clearly was very unquakerly. He was, however, normally a reserved individual who would arrive at important decisions after quiet contemplation. In August 1770, Cook praised the simple life of the inhabitants of New Holland, who he suggests were 'far more happier than we Europeans'. They were

> wholy unacquainted not only with the superfluous but the necessary Conveniencies so much sought after in Europe, they are happy in not knowing the use of them. They live in a Tranquillity which is not disturb'd by the Inequality of Condition:

---

[59] HUA. DQR.18/8. Miscellaneous records. A Testimony of Women's Meeting against fashionable clothes (c. eighteenth century) addressed to Scarborough Friends.
[60] HUA. DQR.18/8. Ambrose Rigge against wigs (c. eighteenth century).
[61] *RAV*, p. 2
[62] *RAV*.

The Earth and sea of their own accord furnishes them with all things necessary for life, they covet not Magnificent Houses, Houshold-stuff &c . . . they think themselves provided with all the necessarys of Life and that they have no superfluities.[63]

The following year he described life on some of the South Sea Islands to John Walker in glowing terms:

These people may be said to be exempted from the curse of our fore fathers, scarce can it be said that they earn thier bread with the sweat of thier brows, benevolent nature hath not only provided them with necessarys but many of the luxuries of life.[64]

His correspondence too showed evidence of a remarkable modesty. In a letter to Walker in August 1771, Cook recalled a meeting with George III who commended him on his achievements, but he maintained that he had 'made no very great Discoveries'.[65] To some extent this accorded well with Quaker egalitarian attitudes, but although Friends refused to remove their hats or 'hat-honour' their social superiors or address them according to their titles,[66] Cook was always formal in his letters to Walker and other associates, addressing them as 'Sir'.

Along with other nonconformists, Friends sought to curtail immoderate behaviour, especially the baneful influence of alcohol, and consistently advised members to be more temperate, avoiding 'all unnecessary frequenting of Ale Houses or Taverns, Excess in Drinking, & Intemperance of every kind'.[67] In 1766, Whitby Friends were concerned about Solomon Chapman's intemperance and they encouraged him to amend his behaviour.[68] It would be wrong to assume that Friends were simply concerned about alcohol abuse or keen to preserve their reputation in the local community. By attacking excess, the Society was also trying to limit the consequences of such behaviour, namely the dangers posed to family relationships and business probity. For example, in 1722 Friends remonstrated with Robert Robinson of Whitby and his 'many years addicted to Excess in Drinking, and neglect of paymt of his Just Debts'. He was cautioned, therefore, to resist these indulgences or risk disownment. In spite of his warning, Robinson persisted and in March 1723 he was eventually disowned.[69]

---

[63] *EV*, p. 399.
[64] Cook to Walker, 13 September 1771. *EV*, p. 507.
[65] WLPS. MS.C126; *EV*, p. 505.
[66] A.M. Gummere, *The Quaker: A Study in Costume* (Philadelphia, 1901), pp. 67–71, 75–86; C. Horle, *The Quakers and the English Legal System, 1660–1688* (Philadelphia, 1988), pp. 15–16.
[67] HUA. DQR.12/1, Quarterly Meeting enquiries (c.1755).
[68] HUA. DQR.12/1, minutes 5.1.1766.
[69] HUA. DQR.11/3, minutes 7.1.1721/2, 5.1.1722/3.

Cook took an equally strong line on immoderate behaviour, particularly the excesses of drunkenness on board ship. In August 1764, while he was acting as the 'King's Surveyor' at Newfoundland and Master of the schooner *Grenville*, some of his crew took advantage of his indisposition after an accident, and in their drunken state planned a mutiny. It came to nothing. As punishment two of the seamen were confined to the deck, while the ringleader was forced to run the gauntlet.[70] Another case of drunkenness was recorded on the *Endeavour* in April 1770. Cook's clerk, Richard Orton, who had drunk himself into a stupor, was the victim of two attacks by his fellow crewmen. Initially they cut off all his clothes, but later they returned and mutilated his ears while he slept. Cook assumed that this was the 'drunken frolicks' of a midshipman, James Magra, who Cook described as a 'good for nothing'; but, without supporting evidence, Cook could only confine him to quarters.[71] Again, in February 1771, Cook had to punish another member of his crew, Thomas Rossiter, for his drunken behaviour and assault upon a fellow crewman.[72] In general, Cook tolerated the hard-drinking lifestyle of his crew, but only within certain limits.

The Quaker code of conduct expressly condemned sexual misconduct or inappropriate relationships. Among various examples in the North Yorkshire meetings, in March 1765 William Hill was accused of fornication, but Friends were unable to admonish him because he was away at sea. On his return, he expressed his regret and was allowed to remain a member of the Society.[73] Those members who were expelled for their immoderate behaviour effectively became social outcasts, unwelcome among those who had provided kinship and security and with no claim upon the wider community. Cook attempted to instil into his crew a disciplined approach to their work and sexual behaviour, particularly in their dealings with the native peoples. Moderation, friendship and humanity were the watchwords of any encounters, and he sought to ensure that the natives were not maltreated nor exploited, physically or sexually. His humane attitude towards the peoples of the Pacific also reflected the Admiralty's official policy and particularly the 'Hints' offered by the Earl of Morton, the President of the Royal Society.[74]

In a letter to Walker written in September 1771, Cook described the Aborigines of New South Wales as a 'timorous inoffensive race' who 'go wholly naked'. He compared them to Adam and Eve as they were 'naked and are not ashame'd',[75] but he was equally aware of their vulnerability. Several of Cook's

---

[70] Beaglehole, *Life*, pp. 80–1; Rae, *Endeavours*, pp. 73–4.
[71] It was later discovered that Magra was innocent; the culprit, Saunders, later deserted. See *EV*, pp. 323–4, 347 n. 5; Beaglehole, *Life*, pp. 232–3.
[72] *EV*, p. 451.
[73] HUA. DQR.11/4, minutes 5.3.1765, 1.4.1766.
[74] *EV*, pp. cclxxxiii, 514–19; Beaglehole, *Life*, pp. 150–1.
[75] *EV*, p. 508.

modern biographers have noted that Cook was disinclined to prohibit some of the relationships his men had with the Tahitian women.[76] Indeed, his journal entry for May 1769 notes that astronomical instruments were stolen while his men were 'diverting themselves with the natives'. Disease was an inevitable outcome and, as Cook noted, the 'women were so very liberal with their favours . . . that this distemper very soon spread it self over the greatest part of the Ships Compney'.[77] Although Cook exercised tolerance in such matters he nevertheless was quick to reprimand and punish those whose behaviour threatened the safety of the ship and crew or infringed the boundaries of common decency. For instance, when Cook was Master of the *Pembroke* in May 1758 he punished one of the crew, William Murray, for attempted sodomy.[78] Later, in July 1769, a dangerous situation arose at Tahiti when two of his men deserted the ship because 'they had got each of them a Wife', and were being protected by the native population. The unwillingness of the Tahitians to give up the men forced Cook to abduct several chiefs until his crewmen were returned. When the chiefs were released the two crewmen were given two dozen lashes each.[79]

Cook's use of force represented a major departure from Quaker principles. On many occasions, most notably during his encounters with the Hawaiians on the third voyage, force was used. This is not nearly so remarkable given that John Walker and other Whitby Quaker shipowners allowed armaments on their ships, ostensibly to defend their goods from marauding pirates. Such activity drew severe criticism from Yorkshire Friends who remained extremely concerned about such practices.[80] In April 1756, Scarborough Friends reported that the Quarterly Meeting was extremely dissatisfied with the attitudes of some Quaker shipowners and masters in arming themselves for 'their defence contrary to our professed principles & that Christian frame of mind, that the followers of Christ have walked in'. They therefore called on the overseers of the local meetings to labour with a 'Spirit of love' in order to persuade members to

> desist from such practice, & put their trust in that arm of power, that is able to preserve beyond any contrivance of man: And we desire they would weightily consider the distress of mind they bring upon their Brethren, on acco[un]t of the inconsistency that appears among us, as many cannot for conscience sake take up arms.[81]

---

[76] Peter Aughton, *Endeavour* (Moreton-in-Marsh, Glos., 1999), pp. 63, 93–7; Collingridge, *Captain Cook*, pp. 137–8, 363.

[77] EV, pp. 88, 99.

[78] Rae, *Endeavours*, p. 44.

[79] EV, pp. 114–16; Beaglehole, *Life*, pp. 191–2.

[80] In 1706, Friends considered the issue of carrying guns on ships, while in 1714 Joseph Linskill offered a 'sorrowful confession' for arming his ships. See Woodwark, *The Quakers of Whitby*, p. 10; Isaac Sharp, 'Friends in current literature', *Journal of the Friends' Historical Society*, 7 (1910), p. 37.

[81] HUA. DQR.11/4, minutes 6.4.1756.

In 1760, Quarterly Meeting representatives reported that there was 'some uneasiness' concerning the carrying of guns on ships and other unquakerly activities, and required members to be careful 'in walking more agreeable to the Truth in these Respects'.[82] The issue continued to cause distress among Friends, and in 1781 a Quarterly Meeting committee informed members that they had compiled a list of Friends who owned ships in which guns were carried. Among those listed were the Whitby Quakers: Abel Chapman, Thomas Linksill and John Walker. The committee concluded that they had 'insufficient grounds of hope that an alteration of conduct . . . is likely at present to take place with any of them'. Shortly afterwards the Quarterly Meeting at York disowned Thomas Scarth, and refused to accept the subscriptions of Abel Chapman until he sold his ship. In 1783, the Quarterly Meeting recommended that fifteen Friends from Scarborough and Whitby should not be allowed to decide on matters of discipline in meetings and that their subscriptions should be refused. Later testimonies were given against fourteen Friends for arming their vessels, but the clerk of the Whitby meeting refused to publicly admonish them.[83] It is notable that upon his death on 5 October 1785, the Quarterly Meeting classified Walker as a non-member, presumably because of his refusal to disarm his ships.[84]

Walker's dilemma in trying to protect his business interests and conform to Quaker principles was not one which Cook had to wrestle with. Once he enlisted in the service of the Royal Navy, he accepted that physical force might be necessary when diplomatic efforts had been exhausted. In September 1771 he described to Walker how on the east coast of New Zealand he had encountered

a strong well made active people, rather above the common size . . . they are also a brave warlike people with sentiments voide of treachery, thier Arms are spears, Clubs, Halbarts, Battle Axes, darts and Stones. . . . We had frequent skirmishes with them . . . our fire arms gave us the Superiority; at first some of them were kill'd.

Here as elsewhere Cook endeavoured to limit the violence whenever possible, commenting that 'we at last learnt how to manage them without takeing away their lives, and when once Peace was settled they ever after were our very good friends'.[85] It can be suggested that Cook was 'humane, tolerant, patient, anxious for peaceful relations, deeply interested in their customs and manner of life. But there was a strict and firm boundary to his tolerance and patience.'[86]

---

[82] HUA. DQR.11/4, minutes 1.4.1760.
[83] Woodwark, *The Quakers of Whitby*, pp. 10–11.
[84] Library of the Society of Friends, London. Unpublished 'Dictionary of Quaker Biography' (entry John Walker).
[85] *EV*, p. 507.
[86] Philip Edwards, ed., *The Journals of Captain Cook* (London, 1999), p. 612.

Once that patience was tested he resorted to punitive measures: confiscation and the destruction of property, the detention of tribal leaders, and ultimately physical force.

On balance, then, Cook's attachment to Quakerism is not nearly as certain as his biographers would have us believe. They have mostly assumed that his lifelong friendship with Walker could only have been possible if Cook had conformed to the Quaker value system. In assuming that Walker was a devout and committed Quaker, all too keen to instil that value system among his apprentices, they have read too much into Cook's Quakerly characteristics. It could be argued that Cook's life does not demonstrate anything other than a commitment to his job, except that he was perhaps a more enlightened or at least a less brutal leader of his men than some of his contemporaries.

In the eighteenth century, the Quakers constituted a separate and distinct community. Quakerism was not just a one-day-a-week, take-it-or-leave-it religion, but rather it had become a defensive and inflexible code which dominated an individual's life, forcing members to retreat from the world, and especially from materialism. It is clear that even for the average Quaker it was difficult to accept such restrictions, particularly for one such as John Walker whose livelihood depended upon safeguarding his vessels, but in the process he contravened the Quaker code. Walker was a realist, a man of the world, who had to live both in the bellicose and turbulent society of eighteenth-century commercial shipping and in the largely inflexible Quaker community. Ultimately it was impossible for him to remain in both camps. For Cook there were no such restrictions. Although he had witnessed and been a key member of a Quaker household, he was nevertheless not a member of this strict, restrictive and clannish community, and never likely to be one. He may have appreciated the disciplined order of the Walker household, with its calmness and stability, but his free spirit forced him to make the decision to leave the security of Whitby and the alternative community of Friends for the unrestricted world of exploration.

Finally, despite the abundance of information concerning Cook, little is known about the private man, and, as such, he remains an enigma. He was a man of iron reticence, having both a tendency for engagement with new 'worlds' and a detachment from the old one that he had previously rejected. Many aspects of his life epitomise the Quaker virtues: discipline, sobriety, fastidiousness, hard work, moderation, modesty, faithfulness and tolerance; but he also displayed an ambitious, ruthless, determined and imperialist/militaristic nature which does not accord well with the claims made by several of his modern biographers that the Quaker influence was uniquely formative.

3

James Cook and the Royal Society

ANDREW S. COOK

The standard view of James Cook's three voyages of exploration embraces the idea that the Royal Society was a thoroughly involved participant in their preparation, execution and results. Because, perhaps, of his early death, the status and fame which James Cook achieved by the time of his third voyage and posthumously, have been casually transferred by many writers back to the time of his selection in 1768 for naval promotion from master to lieutenant and command of the converted *Earl of Pembroke*.[1] Cook had no later life for historians to plot the rise and rise of his career into old age. Joseph Banks has been more tenderly treated: certainly there have been writers who have similarly attached the eminence of the older Sir Joseph to the opportunist venture of the young naturalist in applying in 1768,[2] through the Royal Society of which he was a new Fellow, to government for permission to accompany the Transit of Venus expedition. But biographers of Banks, more perhaps than those of Cook, have managed to put their central character's early activities into perspective.[3]

Cook's first voyage was properly the Royal Society's expedition: the initiative and the planning for observing the Transit of Venus in the southern hemisphere came from the Royal Society.[4] It was the government agenda for exploration which took charge of the expedition once the Transit of Venus observations at Tahiti were completed in 1769, even though many of the subsequent discoveries later came to be interpreted to the public through Banks's position

---

[1] It is invidious to particularise, but Alan Villiers, *Captain Cook the Seamen's Seaman* (London, 1967), and Hugh Carrington, *Life of Captain Cook* (London, 1939), come most readily to mind, and more recently, Michael E. Hoare, 'Captain James Cook: man, myth and reality', *Pacific Studies*, I, (1978), pp. 71–6, though this was given as a conference introduction. J.C. Beaglehole, *The Life of Captain James Cook* (London, 1974) is regarded as *parti pris*. R.T. Gould, *Captain Cook* (London, 1935) is a useful corrective. R.A. Skelton, *Captain James Cook after Two Hundred Years* (London, 1969) summarises the positions of earlier biographers.
[2] For example, H.C. Cameron, *Sir Joseph Banks: The Autocrat of the Philosophers 1744–1820* (London, 1952).
[3] Particularly Harold B. Carter, *Sir Joseph Banks 1743–1820* (London, 1988).
[4] Harry Woolf, *The Transits of Venus: A Study of Eighteenth-Century Science* (Princeton, 1959), especially pp. 161–70.

in the Royal Society. Chroniclers of the Royal Society have suggested (or assumed) that the Society, as an institution, was similarly central to the planning and results of Cook's second and third voyages.[5] But this is by no means certain. The interests of the Royal Society and the mechanisms by which it operated in the later mid-eighteenth century have yet to be put properly under the microscope of Cook studies.

Four lines of enquiry suggest themselves. What was James Cook's involvement in the Royal Society's preparations in 1767 and 1768 for the Transit of Venus expedition? What was the Royal Society's involvement in the planning of Cook's second and third voyages? What reception did the Royal Society give to James Cook on his return from his first and second voyages? And how did the Royal Society receive the news of Cook's death in 1780?

It is easy for the present-day observer of the Royal Society, persuaded by the Society's traditional image of its historical self, to import to his understanding of the eighteenth-century Society a sense of its twentieth-century presence, conferring lustre on the careers and achievements of its elected Fellows. But the Royal Society of the 1760s was barely a century from its creation, and, though it had enjoyed the presidency of Sir Hans Sloane, it had not yet submitted to the formative influence of the forty-three years' presidency of Sir Joseph Banks. The Royal Society of the 1760s was hardly more than a forum for gentlemen of scientific interests, its corporate means meagre in comparison with the private wealth of its officers and active Fellows.[6] The Society had certain responsibilities, though the most notable of these, that of providing Visitors to the Royal Observatory, had fallen into abeyance after the failure to apply for the renewal of the Royal Warrant after 1714. Particular scientific matters, such as advising on the form of lightning conductors for St Paul's Cathedral and for gunpowder stores,[7] were from time to time referred by government, but a considerable part of *Philosophical Transactions* records papers read on physical abnormalities or on antiquarian subjects. The Society was in essence a useful vehicle for government to utilise the scientific interests of individual Fellows, and for Fellows to turn their scientific interests into formal applications for government assistance.

Even so, the Royal Society was in a quiescent period in the mid-eighteenth century. Historians of the Society have no great events to report for the decades

---

[5] Sir Henry Lyons, *The Royal Society 1660–1940: A History of its Administration under its Charters* (Cambridge, 1944), e.g. p. 189: 'West's presidency only lasted from 1769 to 1772 during which the Council were very fully occupied with the preparation of detailed instructions for Captain Cook's voyage to the Antarctic, on which he sailed in 1772.' I. Kaye, 'Captain James Cook and the Royal Society', *Notes and Records of the Royal Society of London*, 24 (1969), pp. 7–18, makes the most (pp. 8–9) of some tenuous connections.

[6] E.N. da C. Andrade, *A Brief History of the Royal Society* (London, 1960), p. 7: 'His [Sloane's] presidency saw the beginning of a period of decline in the scientific activities and reputation of the Society, during which, however, the Fellowship steadily increased in numbers.' On finances, see Lyons, *Royal Society*, pp. 166–70.

[7] Lyons, *Royal Society*, pp. 192–3.

after the early 1740s, the end of the consecutive presidencies of Newton and Sloane in 1741, and the death of Edmond Halley in March 1742.[8] Andrade, in his *Brief History*, reports: 'Hardly a remembered name was elected as Fellow from the end of Newton's reign until 1760.'[9] Henry Cavendish's election in the year of George III's accession marked the start of a new scientific constituency among Fellows, and a new royal patronage of the Society.

It was in acting in 1760 on the long-range call in Halley's paper in *Philosophical Transactions* of 1716 for proper observation of the Transit of Venus in 1761 that the Royal Society established the precedent of a Treasury grant for specific astronomical observations. A grant of £1,600 enabled the Council of the Society to dispatch observers to Bencoolen and to St Helena on East India Company ships.[10] The observations were less than satisfactory, the Bencoolen observers being delayed at the Cape of Good Hope, and Nevil Maskelyne at St Helena suffering adverse observing weather. (Complete transit observations require the sun to be visible throughout the period of transit, and, because transits occur close to the solstices, while observable widely in the summer hemisphere, can be seen only in narrow 'cones of visibility' of the short daily sunlight in the winter hemisphere.) Thomas Hornsby, Savilian Professor of Astronomy at Oxford, who had carried out the 1761 observations at the private observatory of the Earl of Macclesfield, President of the Royal Society, at Shirburn Castle, Oxfordshire, and who subsequently published the unsatisfactory observations from the various stations, alerted the Royal Society in 1766 to the need to make proper provision for the 1769 Transit of Venus.[11]

In his 1766 paper in *Philosophical Transactions* Hornsby drew attention to the 'cone of visibility' for the 3 June 1769 transit which, though visible widely in the northern hemisphere summer, would be seen in the southern hemisphere only in a small area of the Pacific Ocean. From his own study of the voyages of Mendaña, Torres and Tasman, he drew up a table of seventeen 'suitable' island groups between 4° and 21° south and between 130° and 190° west of Greenwich. He gave the source of his table of the geographical positions of the Pacific islands as 'Mr de Lisle's map of the southern hemisphere', that is, Guillaume Delisle's 'Hemisphere Meridionale' of 1714.[12] All Hornsby's

---

[8] Lyons, ibid., headed his 1741–78 chapter (pp. 159–96) 'A growing administration', and highlighted the Society's activities in respect of the standard yard measure as an indicator of its activity.

[9] Andrade, *Brief History*, p. 8.

[10] E. Halley , 'A particular method by which the parallax of the Sun, or its distance from the Earth, may be ascertained by the assistance of the Transit of Venus over the Sun', *Philosophical Transactions of the Royal Society*, 29 (1716), pp. 454–64; Woolf, *The Transits of Venus*, pp. 71–96.

[11] Thomas Hornsby, 'On the Transit of Venus in 1769', *Philosophical Transactions*, 55 (1765), pp. 326–44. Hornsby's paper was read on 13 February 1766.

[12] Guillaume Delisle, 'Hemisphere meridionale pour voir plus distinctement les Terres Australes' (Paris, 1714).

island names and positions were those of the 1714 Delisle map, except that he overrode Delisle's longitude for the Marquesas with a calculation based on Mendaña's estimate of 1595. Hornsby's 'Terra Australis' was simply Delisle's 'Terra Australis de Espiritu Sancto', and all his supposed longitudes had long since been revised by Bellin, Green and Robert de Vaugondy.[13] Yet it was this paper which was to form the basis of the work of the Royal Society committee which met on 17 November 1767 'to consider of the places proper to observe the ensuing transit of Venus; and the methods, the persons fit, and the particulars relative to the same'.

Such a committee derived its authority from the Council, the effective executive body of the Royal Society, and not from the fellowship at large. An examination of its surviving records shows how the Society operated in the eighteenth century. The formal weekly meetings of Fellows to hear prepared papers are recorded in the Journal Books: these meetings took place each Thursday from January to June (except the Thursdays before and after Easter, and after Whitsunday), after which the Society went into recess until the Anniversary meeting on 30 November, before resuming the annual cycle of Thursday meetings in the January following. The minutes do not record the names of all Fellows attending, only those introducing guests (and their guests' names). Some sense of Fellows attending can be gained from the certificates of election of Fellows, which were 'suspended' as proposals to receive supporting signatures for a number of meetings before election. The Register Books record the texts of papers delivered, often by one of the Secretaries on behalf of a Fellow, while the original papers and correspondence concerning them reside in the Early Letters and Classified Papers series, combined after 1741 as the Letters and Papers series.[14]

The Anniversary meeting elected the president, officers and Council members for the ensuing year, and the Council met routinely on Thursdays, though not every Thursday, throughout the session. The Council met on other days during the session, and at times in the July-to-November recess, as business

---

[13] J.N. Bellin, 'Carte reduite des mers comprises entre l'Asie et l'Amerique . . .' (Paris, 1742), and 'Observations sur la construction de la carte des mers comprises entre l'Asie et l'Amerique', *Mémoires pour l'histoire des sciences et des beaux arts* (Paris, 1742), pp. 866–94 and 942–71. Some of Bellin's improvements were incorporated in John Green [Bradock Mead], *A Chart of North America and South America, including the Atlantic and Pacific Oceans* . . . (London, 1753), and discussed by him in his *Remarks, in support of the New Chart of North and South America* (London, 1753), pp. 43–4. Didier Robert de Vaugondy, *Carte générale qui répresente les Mers des Indes, Pacifique, et Atlantique, et principalement le Monde Austral* . . . (Paris, 1756), appears to have used Green as one of his sources.

[14] For the arrangement of the Royal Society Archives generally, see Keith Moore and Mary Sampson, *A Guide to the Archives and Manuscripts of the Royal Society* (London, 1995). The archive series mentioned here are: Journal Book, Original and Copy; Register Book, Original and Copy; Early Letters; Classified Papers; Letters and Papers; Certificates of Election and Candidature. The manuscripts of papers read at meetings are found in *Philosophical Transactions* if published, and in Archived Papers if they remained unpublished.

dictated, and routinely each year for a 'salaries-and-bills' meeting a week or two before the Anniversary meeting. The President answered to the Anniversary meeting for the Council's business during the year, but not to the January-to-July Thursday meetings of the Society, where the only normal business, other than the reading of scientific papers, was the election of new Fellows. The various archive series of Council Minutes, Domestic Manuscripts, Royal Society Letters, and Account Books represent the main record of the executive actions of the Council and its committees.[15]

The only body connected to the Royal Society which met throughout the year was the Royal Society Club, or the Club of the Royal Philosophers as it was called until 1795.[16] As a dining club, composed of a number of Fellows wishing to dine and talk together before Thursday meetings, the Royal Society Club had its own constitution and rules. The President of the Royal Society for the time being was normally elected to the Club, if not already a member, and generally presided at the dinners at the Mitre Tavern each Thursday. Otherwise Fellows were proposed for election to the Club at its annual meeting on the last Thursday in July, to a maximum of forty members. Members of the Club dined together each Thursday throughout the year, often as many as twenty-five, sometimes as few as two, the only exception being when 30 November fell on a Thursday. In those years the Society's annual dinner following the Anniversary meeting took precedence. Many Fellows, and some officers of the Society, did not choose to join such a dining club, but the Club constituted, year-round, a forum where gregarious Fellows at the centre of the Society's activities could meet to discuss matters of common interest. Increasingly the Royal Society Club dinners became a meeting-place into which Fellows, particularly Council members and officers, could introduce visitors to the Royal Society milieu, certainly on meeting days in session, and especially when visitors arrived in London during the annual recess. The Dining Books, recording Fellows and guests present each Thursday (as well as menus), and the Minute Books of the annual meetings, are preserved in the Society's archives.[17]

The Council delegated particular scientific questions to committees, who met and reported their recommendations to the Council, whose approval gave them the weight they then carried as the Society's considered opinion. Often the only official activity of the Royal Society during the period of recess

[15] Royal Society Archives [hereafter RSA]: Council Minutes, Original and Copy; Domestic Manuscripts; Royal Society Letters; Account Books.
[16] On the Club generally, see Sir Archibald Geikie, *Annals of the Royal Society Club: The record of a London dining-club in the eighteenth & nineteenth centuries* (London, 1917), and T.E. Allibone, *The Royal Society and its Dining Clubs* (Oxford, 1976). Older works still of use are W.H. Smyth, *Sketch of the Rise and Progress of the Royal Society Club* (London, 1860, re-issued with 'An additional word', 1861), and Sir John Barrow, *Sketches of the Royal Society and the Royal Society Club* (London, 1849).
[17] RSA: Royal Society Club Archive.

and on Tuesday 29 March the Navy Board reported to Stephens that it was buying *Earl of Pembroke* and asking in what name she was to be registered.[29]

The Royal Society as 'customer' appears at first not to have been involved in the week's activity at Deptford, except for one curious circumstance. Dalrymple later recorded, in an autobiographical account eventually published in *The European Magazine* in 1802:

> Afterwards, when the Royal Society proposed to send persons to observe the Transit of Venus, in 1769, Alexander Dalrymple was thought of as a proper person; and the Admiralty approving of his being employed for this service, as well as for prosecuting discoveries in that quarter, Alexander Dalrymple accompanied the Surveyor of the Navy to examine two vessels that were thought fit for the purpose. The one he approved was accordingly purchased.[30]

And as part of the controversy which surrounded Hawkesworth's publication in 1773 of the account of the voyage, Dalrymple wrote:

> When I gave as a reason for preferring the Endeavour to the other ship which was smaller, that being able to carry another anchor and cable might be of the utmost consequence, a navy Oracle told me 'I was much mistaken if I thought I should have just what stores I pleased, that there was an Establishment, altho' I might be allowed an anchor and cable extraordinary on such a voyage'.[31]

Dalrymple, the Royal Society's chosen observer for the South Seas, and therefore 'a proper person' in the Society's eyes, appears to have been sufficiently understood by the Admiralty as the Society's representative to have been accepted as one of the party inspecting ships in the Thames in the last week of March 1768. He was not necessarily trying to show that *Earl of Pembroke* was purchased *because* he approved it: he was concerned later to show that, before his subsequent withdrawal from the expedition the following Easter Sunday, he had been present at the centre of the events of the selection of the vessel. Dalrymple's writing in the autobiographical account has generally been found both accurate and sophisticated.[32]

[29] *EV*, p. 606.

[30] 'Memoirs of Alexander Dalrymple, Esq.', *The European Magazine and London Review*, 42 (1802), pp. 323–8, *321–*7, 421–4, particularly *325.

[31] Alexander Dalrymple, *Mr. Dalrymple's Observations on Dr. Hawkesworth's Preface to the Second Edition* [of *Account of the Voyages . . . undertaken for making Discoveries in the Southern Hemisphere*] ([London], 1773), p. 19. For the significance of Dalrymple's reference to 'the other ship', see note 28 above.

[32] For a discussion of the autobiographical sources for, and probable veracity of, 'Memoirs of Alexander Dalrymple, Esq.', see Andrew S. Cook, '"An author voluminous and vast": Alexander Dalrymple (1737–1808), Hydrographer to the East India Company and to the Admiralty, as Publisher', Ph.D., St Andrews, 1992, p. 7 n. 12, and p. 17 n. 2.

Philip Stephens's letter of Good Friday 1 April to the Royal Society announced the purchase of the vessel, and asked to know the 'number and quality' of the persons the Royal Society wished to send. The Admiralty further desired the Royal Society 'to consider and propose to them what instructions they conceive it may be necessary for their Lordships to give to the Commander of the said vessel, towards his proceeding to the places where the observations of the Transit are to be made'.[33] This brought the Earl of Morton to his meeting with Admiral Hawke on Easter Saturday 2 April, at which he 'recommended Mr Dalrymple to the Lords of the Admiralty, for the command of a vessel, according to his letter read to the Council Decr. 18th 1767'.[34] Hawke's reaction is now well known to historians, that he would not tolerate a man other than a naval officer in command.[35] The events of the previous week, and Morton's straightforward manner of approach to Hawke, suggest that, in the rapid developments after the Royal Society received the Admiralty's notice on 24 March, the two parties were unwittingly proceeding on different assumptions. The Royal Society assumed that they had the responsibility to propose a commander and observer, and continued with their choice of Dalrymple on his own expectation of being placed in command; the Admiralty assumed that the Royal Society were advancing the names of observers to travel under the command of a naval officer of the Admiralty's choice.

A Council meeting was convened for the Easter weekend, unusual for a Royal Society meeting in any event.[36] Dalrymple was present,[37] to hear Morton

---

[33] EV, p. 606 where Beaglehole remarks that 'The Royal Society's reply to this has not been found.' Any possibility of a formal reply would seem to have been overtaken by the face-to-face meeting the following day (see note 34 below).

[34] RSA: Council Minute Book V, pp. 293–4.

[35] Different authors convey this differently, but Gould, *Captain Cook*, p. 36, expresses it succinctly: 'He [Hawke] swore roundly that, sooner than sign a Captain's commission for a man who was not a King's officer, he would cut his hand off.'

[36] RSA: Council Minute Book V, pp. 292–4. The Original [CMO] and Copy [CMC] Council Minute Book both head the minutes for this meeting 'Thursday 3rd April', which is a calendar impossibility, 3 April 1768 falling on a Sunday. The Secretary's rough minute book (see note 37 below) gives 'Saturday 3rd April', also a calendar impossibility. An Easter weekend day is clearly indicated for the meeting, but we cannot be certain, without corroborative details of the private movements on Saturday 2 April and Sunday 3 April of individual Council members, on which weekend day the meeting took place. The Society did not hold general Thursday meetings in the week following Easter Sunday and Whitsunday, and though a Council meeting might exceptionally be called in such a week, a weekend meeting, particularly an Easter weekend meeting, was highly unusual, and should be taken as indicative of the urgency of the business to be transacted.

[37] The minutes of the meeting, which are more comprehensible in the rough minute book (RSA: Manuscripts (General), MS. 633), indicate that Dalrymple ('who now attended the Council') was questioned during the meeting. Errors in transcribing from a much-corrected rough book to the fair minute book have resulted in a nonsense at one point in the formal minutes.

report the misunderstanding and Hawke's refusal to consider other than a naval officer in command. Despite considerable pressure, Dalrymple held to his stated position and declined to travel as a Royal Society observer under naval command. The rough notes taken by the Secretary, as a basis for the formal minutes of the Council meeting, exhibit an abnormal amount of correction, word-choosing and interlineation at this point, seemingly so as not to rule out, for Dalrymple, other opportunities which might arise for overseas voyages of observation or exploration.[38] But he falls from the formal record of the Royal Society at this point, at least two days before the first inkling that the Admiralty had James Cook in mind for the command of the Transit of Venus expedition vessel. Although the precise date when the name of James Cook, master, came into the minds of the Lords of the Admiralty as a candidate for command of the expedition vessel has been the subject of some speculation, the Admiralty's decision has been dated no more precisely than 'some time between 5 and 12 April',[39] the latter date being that of a minute by Sir Hugh Palliser first noting the consequences for the Newfoundland survey of Cook being employed 'elsewhere'.[40] Though assigned to survey in Newfoundland since 1763, Cook was present, as usual, in London in April: the persistence of ice in the Strait of Belle Isle and in Newfoundland waters did not usually allow survey work to commence until May or June, and the annual departure of Cook's ship *Grenville* from the Thames usually took place in mid- or late April.[41] Even if the Admiralty had brought Cook to mind for command of the Whitby collier sooner than it did after the purchase of *Earl of Pembroke* on 29 March had been notified by the Navy Board, it would not have been as a point of contention with the Royal Society's nomination of Dalrymple as one of the two observers. The Admiralty assumed it had the responsibility, as was customary with naval vessels, to appoint the commander of *Earl of Pembroke*. Whether Hawke had private information, before the 2 April meeting with

[38] RSA: Manuscripts (General), MS. 633. 'The President reported to the Council, that he had recommended Mr Dalrymple to the Lords of the Admiralty, for the command of a vessel, according to his letter read [to the Council *added above the line*] Decr. 18, 1767. But had been informed by their Lordships, that such ap appointment would be entirely [utterly *added above the line in replacement and deleted*] contrary [repugnant *added above the line*] to the usage- [regulations *added above the line*] of the Navy, and Mr Dalrymple, who [now *added above the line*] attended the Council, having persisted in declining the employment of observer for the Society [*altered crudely to* on this occasion] [unless he could be vested with the sole command *added above the line*] it was resolved to consider of a proper person at a future council.'
[39] Glyndwr Williams, 'The *Endeavour* voyage: a coincidence of motives', in Margarette Lincoln (ed.), *Science and Exploration in the Pacific: European Voyages to the Southern Oceans in the Eighteenth Century* (Woodbridge, 1998), pp. 3–18, particularly p. 17.
[40] *EV*, p. 607.
[41] Victor Suthren, *To go upon Discovery: James Cook and Canada, from 1758 to 1779* (Toronto, 2000), ch. 7: Cook's earliest spring departure for Newfoundland was 10 April 1767, his latest 15 May 1763.

the Earl of Morton, that the Royal Society was intending to propose Dalrymple also as commander, is not likely now to be discovered, but the hasty convening of the Easter weekend meeting of the Royal Society Council, and the manner of the minuting of Morton's report of his meeting with Hawke, suggest that the Royal Society was not prepared for Hawke's plain statement of the Admiralty's duty and responsibility.

The Royal Society was plainly embarrassed by the events of 2 and 3 April: having petitioned the King for a vessel to carry its observers to the South Pacific, it found itself suddenly short of one (and possibly both) of its chosen representatives. Dalrymple had withdrawn; Green's terms, previously considered excessive, had not yet been agreed; and the Society's other observers were already committed to their northern observing stations. The Royal Society Council, on 3 April, had 'resolvd to consider of a proper person in his [Dalrymple's] place', and quickly agreed terms with Green, now their chief observer of the Transit in the South Pacific.[42] It was with mingled relief and alacrity that the Council minutes of 5 May showed also the proposal and appointment of Cook as the Society's second observer: he was immediately called in and accepted the office in return for 'such gratuity as the Society shall think proper'.[43] Green accepted the office of observer on 5 May for 200 guineas, plus 100 guineas a year after two years; Cook was offered, on 19 May, a single payment of 100 guineas as second observer.[44] Each was allowed £120 a year on the Society's account for victualling. There was little else the Society could do at such short notice.

The question still remained as to where the Royal Society wished *Endeavour* to go. A suitable, but unspecified, island in Maskelyne's area of observation was the best the Admiralty had to work with, until Wallis returned on 20 May with news of the discovery of King George III's Island or Tahiti.[45] Dr Morton's letter of 9 June to the Admiralty specified for the first time that 'the Council desire to have their observers, who are destined for the Southern latitudes, conveyed to Port Royal in George-land, lately discovered by Capt. Wallis in His Majesty's ship Dolphin', and that 'The Council have appointed Mr. Charles Green, and Capt. Cook, who is commander of the Vessel, to be their Observers'. In the same letter Morton continued:

[42] RSA: Council Minute Book V, p. 299.
[43] RSA: Council Minute Book V, p. 299. Skelton, *Captain James Cook*, p. 11, mistakenly suggests, perhaps through ellipsis, that Cook was appointed by the Admiralty because he was observer for the Royal Society, rather than the other way round.
[44] RSA: Council Minute Book V, pp. 304–5. Cook's gratuity was supplementary to his Navy pay.
[45] Hugh Carrington, ed., *The Discovery of Tahiti: A Journal of the second voyage of H.M.S. Dolphin round the world, under the command of Captain Wallis, R.N. in the years 1766, 1767 and 1768 written by her master George Robertson* (London, 1948), pp. xxiv–xxv.

besides whom, Joseph Banks Esqr. Fellow of this Society, a Gentleman of large fortune, who is well versed in natural history, being desirous of undertaking the same voyage, the Council very earnestly request their Lordships, that in regard to Mr. Banks's great personal merit, and for the advancement of useful knowledge, He also, together with his suite being seven persons more (that is eight persons in all) together with their baggage, be received on board the Ship under the command of Capt. Cook.[46]

Quite apart from extending the courtesy title of 'Captain' to Cook even before he was commissioned Lieutenant on 25 May, the Society had subtly changed its relationship with the voyage, at least in public perception, by Morton's intercession with the Admiralty on behalf of Joseph Banks. Given the unusually public character of the Transit of Venus voyage to Tahiti, it is conceivable that the Admiralty acquiesced in the presence of Banks and his retinue as 'cover' for the movements envisaged in the secret post-Tahiti instructions prepared for Cook. What becomes clear later is that the Royal Society, having interceded for Banks, had no formal locus in his activities on the voyage nor subsequent claim on his observations or collections. Nor, it seems, in the further preparations for the voyage in the summer of 1768: only the Earl of Morton's 'Hints', a comprehensive code of conduct for Cook, Banks, Solander 'and the other Gentlemen', compiled on 10 August,[47] keep the Society in the historians' picture.

It has already been explained that the executive business of the Royal Society was not brought to its regular weekly meetings of Fellows, but retained in the meetings of the Council which, for convenience, were held on some of the same days. The informal connections of Society officers with the preparing expedition could have been maintained rather through the Dining Club, particularly after the regular session ended in July, but no clear pattern of attendance at dinners emerges. The Earl of Morton, as President, abruptly ceased to dine after 31 March for four months; Maskelyne had no regular pattern of attendance, dining only five times between April and August, and introducing no guests. Dalrymple dined as a guest three times in April, July and August, but these occasions did not coincide with Banks's sole appearance as guest on 14 April.[48] The Royal Society Council, having provided observers in December 1767 in response to the recommendations of Maskelyne's committee, concerned itself with other, internal matters.[49]

---

[46] Draft letter from Morton to Philip Stephens, Admiralty (RSA: Council Minute Book V, pp. 313–15). In case Tahiti was not found, Maskelyne provided a reserve 'Table of the limits of Latitude and Longitude, within which it is proper to observe the next transit of Venus', which was incorporated in the expedition instructions.

[47] Manuscript in the National Library of Australia, printed in *EV*, pp. 514–19.

[48] 28 April, 14 July and 4 August 1768 (RSA: Royal Society Club Archives, Dinner Book 5). Dalrymple had dined on 10 March as the guest of the President while still the Society's nominated observer.

[49] In particular with the fraud committed on the Society by its clerk E.M. da Costa, who

Inevitably there was no communication from the expedition after *Endeavour* left Rio de Janeiro in early December. Cook and Green had written to the Royal Society from Funchal and Rio, reporting on the voyage and recording having drawn on the victualling allowance. Banks and Daniel Solander addressed letters to the Earl of Morton on 1 December, unaware that the President had died some weeks before.[50] The first news to reach London of the safe arrival of *Endeavour* at Batavia on 10 October 1770 is recorded in Admiralty minutes for 7 May 1771,[51] the news arriving from the East Indiaman *Harcourt*, coincidentally in Batavia Roads when *Endeavour* arrived.[52] A newspaper report had been circulating since January,[53] but, without confirmation, there was official scepticism until May: 'it was feared the said Vessel was lost'.[54] Cook's first letter to the Admiralty, of 14 October 1770, apparently miscarried, and his letters of 23 October, to the Admiralty and to the Royal Society, were the first reports in his own hand of the voyage since 2 December 1769.[55] The Royal Society Council met on Monday 20 May 1771 (the Monday after Whitsunday) to read the letter sent from Batavia, a letter which is remarkable for its meticulous omission of everything which did not concern the Royal Society. To Philip Stephens, Secretary to the Admiralty, the same day Cook gave a full account of the voyage he had made from Rio de Janeiro to Batavia, including the observations of the Transit of Venus at Tahiti on 3 June 1769, and enclosing a copy of his journal with such charts as he had been able to copy.[56] To the President and Council of the Royal Society he gave the same account of the Transit of Venus observations, but prefacing it only with the single sentence, 'I did myself the Honour to write to you from Rio de Janeiro which place I left on the 8th of Decem[be]r 1768 and arrived at Georges Island in the South Seas on the 13th of Ap[ri]l following', and following it only with: 'We left Georges Island the 13th of July [17]69 and Arrived at this place the 10th inst [i.e. 10 October 1770].'[57] Green enclosed with Cook's letter the results of the Transit observations, but the Royal Society was given then

---

had been appropriating to his own use the arrears of subscriptions paid by Fellows. He made the mistake of thus siphoning off Joseph Banks's fellowship payments. See Lyons, *The Royal Society*, p. 169, and Marie Boas Hall, *The Library and Archives of the Royal Society 1660–1990* (London, 1992), p. 12 and n. 21.

[50] *EV*, pp. 624–6.

[51] *EV*, p. 631.

[52] *Harcourt* is recorded arriving at Batavia on 5 September 1770 *en route* from London to Benkulen (India Office Records: L/MAR/B/558G), returning to the Thames on 20 September 1771. The intelligence is likely to have been transferred to a homeward bound East Indiaman at Benkulen.

[53] *EV*, p. 627, n. 3.

[54] *EV*, p. 631.

[55] *EV*, pp. 627–8.

[56] *EV*, pp. 499–501.

[57] *EV*, p. 502.

no other information about the rest of the voyage, despite the presence of Banks and his retinue on board. The Royal Society Council met again routinely on Thursday 30 May, there being no meeting of the Society on the Thursday of Whitsunday week, and the Society was then in recess from 20 June to 7 November.[58]

Cook and *Endeavour* spent a month at the Cape, from 14 March to 14 April 1771, and joined *Portland* at St Helena on 1 May ready to sail with a homeward convoy on 4 May. *Endeavour* lagging behind the convoy because of her poor condition, Cook sent journals and letters to the Admiralty and the Royal Society on board *Portland* on 10 May off Ascension.[59] His 9 May letter thus transmitted to Maskelyne, which he brought to the specially convened meeting of the Royal Society Council on 11 July,[60] announced the death of Green on 29 January shortly after leaving Batavia. *Endeavour* was only three days behind *Portland* coming home, and Cook sent a letter to the Royal Society ashore on a cutter off Start Point on 11 July,[61] before anchoring in the Downs on 13 July. Cook, Banks and Solander went ashore there, leaving the pilot to take *Endeavour* to Gallion's Reach in the Thames on 18 July. After 11 July the Royal Society Council next met on 25 July, when Cook's letter of 11 July was read. Cook himself attended the Royal Society that day, and was called into the Council meeting as the sole survivor of the Society's two observers. The minutes of the Council meeting and the interview with Cook, two years and more after his appointment, were succinct. Cook was asked for, and delivered at the table, the instruments entrusted to Green and himself as observers for the Society. Maskelyne was due the return of his watch which he had lent to Green, and Cook delivered that too at the table. The Council then granted Cook £150 as his gratuity (rather then the 100 guineas originally proposed), thanked him for his services, and he left.[62] Subsequently the Council ordered the results of the Transit of Venus observations to be published in *Philosophical Transactions* under the names of Cook and Green.[63] There was no further meeting of the Council until 7 November.

This is not to say that individual officers and Fellows of the Royal Society did not engage with Cook on his return, but the Royal Society as a body showed only a formal connection with its observer. The Lords of the Admiralty thoroughly approved of Cook's conduct of the voyage, and Stephens communicated this to him on 2 August 'at his house at Mile End'.[64] The news of his unsolicited

---

[58] RSA: Council Minute Book VI, pp. 101–2; Journal Book XXVII.

[59] *EV*, p. 631.

[60] RSA: Council Minute Book VI, pp. 101–2.

[61] RSA: Council Minute Book VI, pp. 107–9.

[62] RSA: Council Minute Book VI, pp. 110–12.

[63] 'Observations made, by appointment of the Royal Society, at King George's Island in the South Sea, by Mr. Charles Green and Lieut. James Cook', *Philosophical Transactions*, 61 (1771), pp. 397–421.

[64] *EV*, p. 635.

promotion to a Captain's (i.e. Commander's) commission apparently came to him first in a letter from Banks early in August, for he replied to Banks, in a letter from Will's Coffee House at Charing Cross dated tentatively 11 August, that he had in consequence that morning waited on the Earl of Sandwich at the Admiralty.[65] Banks had been elected to the Royal Society Dining Club at its election meeting on 25 July, and, immediately a frequent diner, brought fellow-botanist and shipboard companion Daniel Solander as his guest on 7 November. Cook was invited to dine on 21 November, as Maskelyne's guest, on a night when twenty were present. He dined again with the Club the following week, this time with Commander Tobias Furneaux as Banks's guest and with Solander also present.[66]

Furneaux's presence with Cook at the Royal Society Club on 28 November 1771 may have had more to do with planning for the next voyage of exploration than with the past Transit of Venus expedition. The President, James West, brought to the Council meeting of Friday 29 November a report of the meeting of the Board of Longitude the day before, at which the plan of the voyage was considered.[67] His purpose, and Maskelyne's as Astronomer Royal, was to gain from the Royal Society Council its suggestions to improve or elaborate the Board's plan, and at its 12 December meeting the Council transmitted, through Maskelyne, suggestions for incorporation in the Board of Longitude proposal to the Government for the expedition.[68] It is noteworthy that the initiative for Cook's second voyage did not come from the Royal Society, and that, if Maskelyne had not chosen himself to bring the Board of Longitude's deliberations before the Society's Council in December 1771, the Society would not have been consulted at all. In the Board's proposal the chief function of the Royal Society was to be asked to lend instruments from its collection to the expedition, to supply wants at the Board of Longitude. Cook's departure from London on 21 June 1772, and his sailing from Plymouth on 13 July on board *Resolution*, in company with Furneaux in *Adventure*,[69] passed without formal notice by the Royal Society.

In 1775, on his return from the South Pacific, Cook arrived at Spithead on 30 July, having spent a month (21 March to 27 April) at the Cape and some days in May at St Helena.[70] Immediately on his return to London he was Daniel Solander's guest dining at the Royal Society Club on 3 August.[71] (Solander had been elected to the Club in 1773, and became its Treasurer the following

[65] *EV*, p. 637–8.
[66] RSA: Royal Society Club Archives, Dinner Book 5.
[67] RSA: Council Minute Book VI, pp. 118–19.
[68] RSA: Council Minute Book VI, pp. 122–8. On Maskelyne, see Derek Howse, *Nevil Maskelyne: The Seaman's Astronomer* (Cambridge, 1989).
[69] *RAV*, pp. 9 and 16–17.
[70] *RAV*, pp. 654–65.
[71] RSA: Royal Society Club Archives, Dinner Book 6.

year on the death of Josiah Colebrooke.)[72] There is no sign of formal letters from Cook to the Royal Society from the Cape or from St Helena *en route*. Solander, in his correspondence with Banks in 1775, was much taken up with Furneaux's earlier return with Omai, and relayed information to Banks from Cook's letters, particularly that of 24 May to the Admiralty.[73] Though the Royal Society Council met a number of times during the 1775 recess, chiefly concerned with repairing damage to instruments at the Royal Observatory after the routine visitation of 21 June, no part of its formal business concerned Cook's voyage.[74]

Cook was proposed for fellowship of the Royal Society at the meeting which he attended on 23 November 1775: 'a gentleman skilfull in astronomy, & the succesful conductor of two important voyages for the discovery of unknown countries, by which geography and natural history have been greatly advantaged and improved'. Banks, Solander and Constantine John Phipps (later Lord Mulgrave) headed the list of those nominating Cook, and among other names were those of Henry Cavendish, Philip Stephens and Nevil Maskelyne.[75] Cook was Banks's guest at the Royal Society Club that day, and dined again on 14 December, 25 January and 8 and 22 February as guest of Solander or of Sir John Pringle, the President, when attending Society meetings, while his nomination 'hung' to receive signatures.[76] On 29 February his nomination was balloted and he was elected Fellow, and followed the convention of not attending his ballot.[77] On 7 March he was admitted Fellow, and dined as the President's guest.[78] As a Fellow his attendance at particular meetings is not recorded thereafter, but he became a regular guest at the Club, guest of Solander on five further occasions between March and June 1776.[79] It was at the 18 April dinner that the diarist Boswell was also present, making the pun 'I have had a good dinner, for I have had a good Cook.'[80]

While Cook was away on his second voyage, the Royal Society Council in 1773 and 1774 proposed to the Admiralty further discovery voyages, though at no time was Cook's name mentioned as a possible commander. In 1773 Daines Barrington, proceeding on the basis of the conviction of others of the existence of an ice-free north polar sea, advanced a case, taken up by the Royal Society, for a naval expedition to make a polar voyage to the East Indies.[81]

[72] RSA: Royal Society Club Archives, Minute Book 1 (entries for 1773 and 1774 meetings).
[73] *RAV*, pp. 952–3 and 957.
[74] RSA: Council Minute Book VI, pp. 268–78.
[75] RSA: Certificates of Election and Candidature, III, p. 237 (EC/1775/27).
[76] RSA: Journal Book XXVIII, p. 653.
[77] RSA: Journal Book XXIX, p. 48.
[78] RSA: Journal Book XXIX, p. 52; Royal Society Club Archives, Dinner Book 6.
[79] RSA: Royal Society Club Archives, Dinner Book 6.
[80] RSA: Royal Society Club Archives, Dinner Book 6. Beaglehole, *Life of Cook*, p. 452.
[81] Glyndwr Williams, *The British Search for the Northwest Passage in the Eighteenth Century* (London, 1962), pp. 164–6.

Constantine John Phipps, a Fellow and Council member, led the expedition, and narrowly extricated the sloop *Racehorse* from the polar ice north of Spitzbergen to retreat southwards.[82]

Barrington pressed on the Royal Society Council a second idea, in 1774, this time to send an expedition *via* the East Indies, revictualling at Canton, to the Pacific coast of North America in search of a Northwest Passage.[83] Dr Maty's letter, as Secretary, to Lord Sandwich at the Admiralty, was met with the regret that the year's estimates would not allow for it, but Sandwich subsequently convinced Barrington that on Cook's return from his second voyage such an expedition would be fitted out, and there the matter rested.[84] The Society's role in what became Cook's third voyage was indirect, inadvertent and unfortunate: its Secretary, Dr Maty, was involved in the translation and publication of Jacob von Stählin's *An Account of the New Northern Archipelago*, which so misled and infuriated Cook on his final voyage.[85] During 1776 the Royal Society Council was preoccupied with the revision of the Society's statutes and with the inadequacy of Sir William Chambers's plans for the Society's new premises, and those of the Society of Antiquaries, at Somerset House.[86] No part of its deliberations concerned preparations for Cook's third voyage, for which he departed from London on 25 June, and set sail from Plymouth on 12 July 1776.[87] There was time before his departure from Plymouth for Cook to hear of the award to him of the Copley Medal, resolved by the Royal Society Council at its recess meeting on 1 July.[88] The award was made for Cook's paper on methods of preserving the health of seamen, composed as a letter to Sir John Pringle and read at the Royal Society on 7 March 1776.[89]

The news of Cook's death at Kealakekua Bay on 14 February 1779 came to London in a letter of 8 June 1779 from Clerke in Kamchatka.[90] Clerke was to die before it was delivered early in January 1780. Sandwich wrote to Banks on 10 January 1780: 'What is uppermost in our mind allways must come out first, poor captain Cooke is no more.'[91] Banks, who had become President of

---

[82] Ibid., pp. 164–6.

[83] Ibid., pp. 165–7.

[84] Ibid.

[85] J. von Stählin, *An Account of the New Northern Archipelago, Lately Discovered by the Russians in the Seas of Kamtschatka and Anadir* (London, 1774). For Cook's outrage at the deficiencies of Stählin's work see *RDV*, p. 456.

[86] RSA: Council Minute Book VI, pp. 285–98.

[87] *RDV*, p. 8.

[88] RSA: Council Minute Book VI, p. 299.

[89] RSA: Journal Book XXIX, pp. 53–6. 'The Method taken for preserving the Health of the Crew of His Majesty's Ship the Resolution . . . by Captain James Cook F.R.S.', *Philosophical Transactions*, 66 (1776), pp. 402–6.

[90] *RDV*, pp. 1535–40.

[91] *RDV*, pp. 1552–3.

the Royal Society in 1777 in succession to Pringle, brought to the 20 January Council meeting the desirability of recognising Cook's very singular services as 'meriting some public act'.[92] On 27 January the Council, thus prompted, ordered a medal to be struck 'expressive of his deserts', though with the rider 'as the expence of striking a proper medal would fall too heavy on the fund of the corporation . . . a voluntary subscription be opened to the members thereof and them only'.[93] The medallist Pingo was selected, and on 17 February the decision taken to invite subscriptions for the commemorative medal at 20 guineas for gold, one guinea for silver, and a free bronze issue.[94] Thus the wheel turned full circle: the lack of funds in the Royal Society of 1767 which provoked the petition to the King for a vessel to take observers to the Transit of Venus in the South Pacific was the same lack of funds which prohibited even Joseph Banks, participant in that expedition, from doing more thirteen years later than opening a subscription for a medal to honour James Cook, commander of three expeditions.

The truth is that the Royal Society's formal role in Cook's voyages, however much the exploits of the circumnavigator are claimed as an integral part of the Society's history, was limited to the astronomical observations of 1769. Once he had delivered for publication the results of the Transit of Venus observations, Cook, as fall-back observer for the Society, had no further official dealings with the Society in the Admiralty planning of the second and third voyages. As an explorer of renown, and the associate of Joseph Banks from their shared experience of the *Endeavour* voyage, but particularly for the medical, scientific and chronometer results of his second voyage, Cook was welcomed into the milieu of the Royal Society, a Fellow among Fellows whose reputation outshone that of the Society which served as their meeting place.

The Royal Society was accustomed to having its Fellows gracing the Society's scene, the meetings, the Council (if elected), and the Dining Club (if so inclined and welcomed), long into old age. The antiquary Daniel Wray wrote to the Earl of Hardwicke in 1775 that Cook had resumed his customary place at the Mitre tavern, not a public-house 'regular' as Beaglehole seems to infer, but a frequent guest at the Royal Society Dining Club.[95] Cook enjoyed only a short period of active association with the Royal Society in the interval between his second and third voyages, and partook of the benefits of fellowship in London for less than six months overall in 1776. In Royal Society terms he had established his position by his two voyages, particularly by the science of the second voyage of 1772–5. In 1775 he held the retirement appointment of Fourth Captain of Greenwich Hospital (though with the express right of

92 RSA: Council Minute Book VII, p. 36.
93 RSA: Council Minute Book VII, p. 37.
94 RSA: Council Minute Book VII, p. 38.
95 Beaglehole, *Life of Cook*, p. 450.

reversion to more active duty).[96] He was elected Fellow of the Royal Society, attended meetings, and was deemed good company at the Club. The citation in his nomination for the Society speaks of the sufficiency of his past achievements. Sir John Pringle's advancement of Cook's communication on scurvy into a paper meriting the award of the Copley Medal within six months of election suggests the Society's wish to claim Cook for themselves. In this context the third voyage was unnecessary; a Fellow going on expedition to the Pacific (*pace* Banks, and Phipps, of course) was almost unheard of; and the death, the violent death, of a Fellow on the far side of the world, something the Royal Society was unaccustomed to cope with. Banks, who never had the opportunity to enjoy Cook's company in London while President of the Society whose fellowship they shared, was the first to have to suggest a form of untimely commemoration of his late colleague. The Society, not being able to enjoy Cook's fellowship into old age as they did with Colebrooke, Cavendish, Marsden, even Dalrymple, and Banks himself, strained (and still strains) to connect with Cook posthumously in all his works. In truth, Cook came to the Royal Society's employ as a Royal Navy master through an opportunity created by a minor incompetence of the Society's officers in progressing an application from astronomer Fellows to have a series of observations made, and at the end of that employ they paid him and bade him farewell. The Society welcomed him again four years later as a gentleman of science who had continued to establish a considerable reputation, but as a Society they had no part in his advancement to the position of celebrated circumnavigator.

---

[96] *RAV*, p. 958.

Part II

The Pacific Voyages

4

'Notwithstanding our signs to the contrary': textuality and authority at the Endeavour River, June to August 1771

STUART MURRAY

Gananath Obeyesekere's 1992 study *The Apotheosis of Captain Cook* marked the high point of a critical postcolonial approach to the dynamics of Pacific exploration. Obeyesekere's ferocious attack on the methodology of those non-Pacific/non-indigenous scholars, here with special reference to Marshall Sahlins, who seek to read the processes of culture contact and exchange in the region, ultimately offered not so much another way of reading events, as a completely different idea of rationality at the heart of the construction of history.[1] In a similar vein, Dennis Foley's insistence that only Aboriginal commentators can interpret the full meaning of Cook's contacts in Australia in 1770 promotes a forceful sense of Cook as the instigator of the colonial period that would follow the arrival of the First Fleet.[2] Such readings invoke the language of cultural primacy, of the rights of interpretation associated with this position.

We make a mistake if we try to see through the prose of the ships' journals to the events of Cook's *Endeavour* voyage as if the writing were some form of clear glass. This is not a point about language so much as a consequence of textual exchange, the problems that writing carries as it tries to express both the modernity of its own approach and the nature of the contact involved. It is clear that the scholarship focused upon the investigation of the journal writing of the period needs to improve. To understand the complexities of such production we need to know what writing a journal meant in the late eighteenth century, why it was so popular, the forms it could take, the generic codes such writing had already established by the 1760s, and the demands these contexts and codes placed upon anyone who sought to write down experiences.

The two points above are intertwined. Obeyesekere and Foley, while making crucial and valid points about the frequently blinkered nature of European

---

[1] Gananath Obeyesekere, *The Apotheosis of Captain Cook: European Mythmaking in the Pacific* (Princeton, NJ, 1992).
[2] Dennis Foley, *Repossession of Our Spirit: Traditional Owners of Northern Sydney* (Canberra, 2001).

scholarship regarding culture contact, are nevertheless themselves over-deterministic in their categorisation of Cook as simply an exemplar of empire. There is disingenuousness in such thinking. Equally, the method of reading Cook's prose that allows for an idea of an unmediated originality, a clear route from the events of the *Endeavour* voyage to the character of the figure commanding the ship, makes a great error. It excludes any real comprehension of the systems at work in exploration and culture contact, the forms of authority and culture involved, even the nature of philosophy, in favour of a reading of history as theatre, where characters dominate and psychology and biography become the tools of subsequent comprehension.[3] The analysis that follows here seeks to locate the writing of the *Endeavour* voyage as a fluid and complex space where expressions of power are mixed with moments of clear vulnerability, and where the task of representing events was itself a challenge that was fraught with difficulties.

Of all the Pacific voyages originating in the 1760s, Cook's first on the *Endeavour* between 1768 and 1771 is the fullest in terms of the range of manifestations of the modern it contained. It has been described as 'the first organized and thoroughly equipped voyage of biological exploration', and in addition to its botanical practice, the scientific activity surrounding the observation of the Transit of Venus and the cartography and meteorology mark it as deeply important in the history of exploration as a process of empirical enquiry.[4] Harold B. Carter, the biographer of Joseph Banks, summed it up well when he noted that the intersection of national maritime exploration with Enlightenment concepts of science was 'a collaboration of civilian science under royal patronage with royal finance, joined with private enterprise funded from a country rent roll and executed under Admiralty management', and Glyndwr Williams, in a neat phrase, has talked of 'a coincidence of motives' for the voyage.[5] The *Endeavour* voyage was also a voyage of record. As well as Sydney Parkinson and Alexander Buchan (the artists who accompanied Banks), and the naturalists Daniel Solander and Herman Spöring, Cook himself was ordered in the 'Secret Instructions' to make a number of specific observations. In line with a tradition dating back to the Royal Society's 'Directions' of 1665, he was told to note both the 'Genius, Temper, Disposition and Number of the Natives', and 'the Nature of the Soil, and the products

---

[3] Paul Carter, *The Road to Botany Bay: An Essay in Spatial History* (London, 1987), pp. 1–33.

[4] W.T. Stearn, quoted in Richard Hough, *Captain James Cook* (London, 1994), p. 2.

[5] H.B. Carter, *Sir Joseph Banks* (London, 1988), p. 75. The Royal Society had secured both a Navy ship and some £4,000 following an appeal to George III. The *Endeavour* voyage was originally planned as one of astronomical observation. For its origins, see H.B. Carter, 'The Royal Society and the voyage of HMS *Endeavour* 1768–1771', *Notes and Records of the Royal Society of London*, 49 (1995), pp. 145–60, and Glyndwr Williams, 'The *Endeavour* voyage: a coincidence of motives', in Margarette Lincoln, ed., *Science and Exploration in the Pacific: European Voyages to the Southern Oceans in the Eighteenth Century* (Woodbridge, 1998), pp. 3–18.

thereof; the Beasts and Fowls that inhabit or frequent it, the fishes that are to be found in the Rivers or upon the coast and in what Plenty', as well as to bring back to Britain minerals and plant specimens found on the voyage.[6] Instead of the range of responsibilities suggested here, I want to focus on the pressure this places upon the writing of the documents that might contain such information, not just in the journal of Cook but in those of others aboard the *Endeavour*.

What needs to be considered is that the issues of the apprehension of other spaces and cultures in the journals, and its *writing* in particular, are as much a part of the expansion of the concerns of modernity as the more tangible practice of botany or the observation of the Transit of Venus that took place aboard the *Endeavour*. It is an orthodox enough observation to note how the *practices* of natural history, physical science, cartography and representation (among others) constitute markers in the development of the modern age. But, this acknowledgement made, the development of critical analyses of modernity from this point can, and does, differ widely. In the specific context of the expansion of a modern Europe that was to lead, in the nineteenth century, to the organisation of a regulated and systematised colonialism, the modern practices of late eighteenth-century exploration are sometimes read as a will-to-power that codifies and begins the processes of control over non-European space. In another context, the Pacific quest for *Terra Australis*, the Great South Land of imaginative geography, is read as a modern secularisation of a Christian desire for knowledge capable of rendering the world in its entirety, in which a modern notion of 'progress' displaces earlier religious categories. From those standpoints not especially concerned with the development of colonial practice, or resistant to the idea of modernity's false consciousness, however, the organisational aspects of late eighteenth-century Pacific exploration exemplify dynamic examples of new accretions of rationality, record and technology.[7] These various positions tend to misrepresent the effect of writing, seeing either only slippages of meaning that reveal a hidden agenda of control, or a flat and featureless prose that is an easily read form through which to observe the significant actions of the modern. The writers of the journals, as they wrestled to document and explain the situations in which they found themselves, produced texts that inhabit spaces more complex than this.

The ships of exploration in the Pacific were, literally, vessels of modernity. Possibly the most graphic example of this was the French expedition to the

---

[6] Quoted in Bernard Smith, *European Vision and the South Pacific: A Study in the History of Art and Ideas* (London and New York, 1969), p. 14.
[7] The first of these positions is a standard post-Edward Said postcolonial position, but also one of certain postmodernists and other critics of the perceived totalising project of modernity. The second is a social theorist position adopted by figures such as Weber and, later, Lowith. The last is more Habermasian, and also typical of the kind of maritime history exemplified by Beaglehole.

Pacific which left Brest in September 1791. Two ships, the *Recherche* and the *Espérance*, under the initial overall command of Antoine-Raymond-Joseph de Bruni d'Entrecasteaux (who died at sea in July 1793), rehearsed the events of the French Revolution in miniature, with the expedition collapsing in early 1794 when at port in the Dutch East Indies.[8] Regardless of the specific politics at work in this instance, however, d'Entrecasteaux's expedition was typical of the majority of post-Cook voyages in the inclusion of hydrographers and botanists among the ship's complement, now seen, along with artists and draughtsmen, as essential members of any voyage of exploration. The writing of the voyages conveys the limits of the expressible modernity surrounding the ships themselves. Like the scientific practices it complements, such writing emerges not as an arbitrary modern commitment, but as the evolution of previous questions and methods now functioning in different contexts. As with the instances of natural history or cartography concerning Tahiti, New Zealand or Australia, it appears involved in a process of attempted clarification. Seen in these terms, the journals allow for a consideration of the natural sense of self-assertion that marks the voyages, where voyagers sought to both intuit and record their circumstances with the only tools they had available. Such a view, that the processes of record must be seen as legitimate in a projected sincerity, is as vital to a reading of the processes of exploration as an understanding of the often fatal consequences of culture contact. It also allows for a refutation of the too simple idea that the voyages only constitute an example of the 'inevitable progress' thesis of modernity as pathology. But, equally, seen thus the journals can also be understood as a marker of those moments when writing slipped away from the objects it attempted to name, when the processes of the modern can be seen to find one of their limits.[9]

The writing itself emerges as often fractured and deeply ambiguous about the possibility of conveying any representative truths, and the desire on the part of the journal keepers to be descriptive reveals time and time again the limits of language at the moment of culture contact. This is not, I would want to stress, a point about the limits of language *per se*. A figure such as Cook or George Robertson (Master of the *Dolphin* during Samuel Wallis's voyage, and the author of one of the most important journals of eighteenth-century Pacific encounter), or indeed any of the knowledgeable journal writers of the period, would have been able to write accounts of, say, continental European travel, and may have produced more stable texts given the greater wealth of

[8] John Dunmore, *French Explorers in the Pacific*: vol. I, *The Eighteenth Century* (Oxford, 1965), pp. 283–341. D'Auribeau, the expedition's commander following d'Entrecasteaux's death, hearing partial accounts of the development of the Terror in Paris, arrested all suspected Republicans aboard the two ships and declared himself for the *émigré* cause. He died later while revolutionary delegates were on their way to arrest him.
[9] The concept of self-assertion is a vital part of Hans Blumenberg's thesis on modernity. See his *The Legitimacy of the Modern Age*, trans. Robert M. Wallace (Cambridge, MA, 1983).

previous documentation on such travels. But for all the empiricism surrounding the 1760s voyages in the Pacific, from sounding and charting to the detailed copies of flora and fauna made by artists such as Parkinson and Buchan, the writing of these voyages remains unsure and deeply problematic. The journals expose what Jonathan Lamb has referred to as 'the two sides to the absence or hollow formed by European ignorance of the Pacific: the empowerment of fantastic desires when based on nothing more restrictive than "a wide-extended and opprobrious *blank*" and the bringing home of such fantasies as barefaced lies, sheer fictions, or domestic nightmares'.[10] With all of this juxtaposed with the desired precision of the scientist's or the sailor's prose, the journals enshrine a complexity that is characteristically modern.

An extended example to begin with. Having left New Zealand the *Endeavour* sighted the coast of Australia on 19 April 1770 (Cook wrote that the land looked 'very agreeable and promising'), and the first sight of Aboriginal inhabitants came on 22 April. The *Endeavour* proceeded north, sighting Aborigines but failing to establish any sustained contact with them. Cook notes with some frustration in an entry for 6 May, concluding the visit to Botany Bay: 'we could know very little of their customs as we were never able to form any connection with them, they had not so much as touch'd the things we had left in their hutts on purpose for them to take away'.[11] Other journals record a similar lack of exchange. The gunner, Stephen Forwood, writes on the same day: 'During our stay here we saw Parteys of the Indians several times but not come near enough to make any kind of friendship with them but they always made signals with us to be gone.'[12] On 11 June the *Endeavour* struck the Great Barrier Reef and was severely damaged. Cook was forced to bring the ship into what was subsequently named the Endeavour River for repairs, and these were not completed until 4 August, a period of great vulnerability for both vessel and crew. The interim period saw the first real occasion of violence between the crew and the Aborigines. Following a week of sporadic contact, Thursday 19 July saw a conflict on board the *Endeavour* that led to Aborigines setting fire to the immediate shoreline, threatening a considerable amount of the crew's provisions which were ashore, including a tent erected by Banks. Cook fired at one of the Aborigines involved, wounding him, and a later meeting some two hours later restored the peace.

The incident was the most dramatic to date during the time spent on the Australian coast. It came at the end of a month made fraught by the necessary

---

[10] Jonathan Lamb, 'Introduction', *The South Pacific in the Eighteenth Century: Narratives and Myths*, special issue of *Eighteenth-Century Life*, 18, 3 (1994), pp. 1–2. Lamb continues: 'Underneath all explorations of the Pacific . . . there is a principle of uncertainty at work that transforms intentions, actions and reports into the opposite of what they were meant to be.'

[11] *EV*, p. 312.

[12] Forwood, Sunday 6 May, *Endeavour* journal, PRO ADM 51/4545.

repairs to the *Endeavour*, and concluded a series of non-communications with the Aboriginal inhabitants who singularly refused to match either the civility of the Tahitians or the aggression of the Maori, both encountered earlier on the voyage and possibly explicable in the minds of the crew because they fitted into existing European discourses on, and perceptions of, Polynesian behaviour.[13] The differing log and journal entries for 19 July display a marked feature that prompts a series of questions about the *writing* of the encounter. The entry for the log kept by Master's mate Richard Pickersgill reads:

> Some Indians on board who went ashore at 9 o'clock and fired all the country around us. Mr. Banks' markee was with difficulty saved. The Indians continuing to increase the no of fires notwithstanding our signs to the contrary were fired at by the captain and one of them wounded with small shot. They now dispers'd and in about 2 hours time return'd without arms and seemingly good friends.[14]

In his own journal, Pickersgill gives slightly more detail to the event ('we with difficulty preserv'd Mr. Banks' markee which was up and obliged to be pulled down', 'we was obliged to fire and wound one of them') but maintains the basic structure of the log entry. Stephen Forwood's entry for the same date is:

> Several Indians about the ship and aboard at 9 they went on shore and fir'd all the country round us. Mr. Banks' markee was with much difficulty saved from the flames by being very hastley pulled down. They still continued to increase the fire not withstanding our signs to the contrary the Captain wonded one of them with small shott which effectively dispursd them, In about 2 hours after they returnd with out Arms semingly very good friends.[15]

Midshipman John Bootie has the following in his journal:

> Sev'l Indians on bd ship about 9 they went in shore and fired the country round about us. Mr. Banks' markee was with difficulty saved from the flames by being

---

[13] As Samuel Wallis and Abel Tasman had visited Tahiti and New Zealand respectively prior to Cook, discourses concerning 'soft' and 'hard' primitivism with regard to Polynesian societies were already in existence. In addition, the *Endeavour*'s arrival off Poverty Bay in New Zealand on 7 October 1769 led to a confrontation and the killing of four Maori two days after landfall. This certainly would have affected the nature of the contact with the Aborigines in the Endeavour River. See *EV*, pp. 168–70; also Anne Salmond, *Two Worlds: First Meetings between Maori and Europeans* (Auckland and London, 1991); Stephen Turner, 'Captain Cook finds himself in a state of nature', in Alex Calder, Jonathan Lamb and Bridget Orr, eds, *Voyages and Beaches: Pacific Encounters, 1769–1840* (Honolulu, 1999), pp. 89–99; and Jonathan Lamb, 'A Sublime Moment off Poverty Bay, 9 October 1769', in Graham McGregor and Mark Williams, eds, *Dirty Silence: Aspects of Language and Literature in New Zealand* (Auckland, 1991), pp. 97–115.
[14] Pickersgill, Thursday 19 July, *Endeavour* journal, PRO ADM 51/4547.
[15] Forwood, Thursday 19 July. PRO ADM 51/4545.

hastily pulled down . . . they continuing to Increase the fire notwithstanding our signs to the Contrary therefore the Captain wounded one of them with small shott which effectively dispersed them . . . in about 2 hours they returned without their arms and seemingly very good friends.[16]

Charles Green, the *Endeavour*'s astronomer, has an entry almost word-for-word identical to those of both Bootie and Forwood, as does Master's mate Frank Wilkinson and an unnamed, untitled journal. In addition the log of the *Endeavour*'s Master, Robert Molyneux, repeats the paragraph. Others have slight differences, as in the entry for 19 July in the journal of Lieut. Zachary Hicks:

AM several Indians sett fire to the grass near the ship and continued spreading it notwithstanding our signs to the contrary, till the Captain fired on them by which some of them was wounded. They then retired and about two hours after returned unarmed seemingly good friends.[17]

The similarity is striking, especially the use of the central phrase 'notwithstanding our signs to the contrary', the key point that validates the use of technical force, and the excuse given for opening fire. Given the difficulties already encountered with Aborigines during the voyage, it seems explicable that the crew's 'signs' should have failed in their attempted communication. No form of meaningful dialogue had, after all, been established up to this point. But the point to be stressed is that it is the idea of communication at the heart of these signs that is of most interest here.

On one level there is no mystery about the identical nature of so many of the entries. None of the *Endeavour* journals, as opposed to the logs, were written entirely as 'daily diaries'. Days were missed, and missing sections filled later, especially in the time leading up to the arrival in Batavia in October 1770, at which point Hicks collected all the journals in accordance with Admiralty policy. In such circumstances it is natural that details should have been based on log entries made at the time, and other dates display similar textual congruencies.[18] Such copying was a routine shipboard activity. Discussing Cook's own journal, J.C. Beaglehole notes that Cook returned to the entry for 12 June, the day following the *Endeavour*'s striking the reef, to add a sentence that both personalises and dramatises the event: 'This was an alarming and I may say terrible Circumstance and threatend immediate destruction to us as soon as our Ship was afloat.' Similarly, the entry for 10 June, the day before the collision, notes Cook's decision to name a prominent landmark Cape Tribulation

---

[16] John Bootie, Thursday 19 July, *Endeavour* journal, PRO ADM 51/4546.

[17] Zachary Hicks, Thursday 19 July, *Endeavour* journal, PRO ADM 51/4546. The other journals are in ADM 51/4545, ADM 51/4547 and ADM 51/4548.

[18] For example, following a confrontation Cook fired at two Aborigines on 29 April. All the journals discussed here have near identical descriptions of the event.

'because here begun all our troubles', a clear piece of retrospective naming.[19] In his account of what he terms the 'Subordinate MS Sources' for the voyage, Beaglehole remarks that very few of the other *Endeavour* journals are worth even a footnote to that of Cook, and that on the whole they only record technical details. He continues: 'there is a great deal of dog-eat-dog among them; who copies whom is impossible to determine, apart from the common basis in the ship's log. . . . Most of our men were no doubt better at yarning over their grog than at reducing experience to the written word.'[20]

Beaglehole's observations reflect part of the world aboard the *Endeavour*, yet his account of the function of journal-keeping cannot explain a nagging desire to understand further the nature of encounter. The clash in the Endeavour River was a key moment of activity and tension, and as such we might expect writing that reflects this even in subtle forms. The simple fact that so many of the writers had felt the need to return to an original source (probably the ship's log) to find expression for this act of non-communication merits more investigation than the casual outlining of the practices of journal-keeping aboard ship. The writing of encounter is not to be apprehended in purely functional terms.

Exempt from Admiralty demands because of his non-naval status (and, we might add, free from Beaglehole's criticisms), Banks's journal describes the events with a surer sense of narrative fluidity. He also explains the origins of the 'markee', which is such a common factor to the other *Endeavour* journals:

> they seized their arms in an instant, and taking fire from under a pitch kettle which was boiling they began to set fire to the grass to windward of the few things we had left ashore with surprising dexterity and quickness; the grass which was 4 or 5 feet high and as dry as stubble burnt with vast fury. A Tent of mine which had been put up for Tupia [the Society Islander taken on board the *Endeavour* at Tahiti in August 1769] when he was sick was the only thing of any consequence in the way of it so I leapd into a boat to fetch some people from the ship in order to save it, and quickly returning hauld it down to the beach Just time enough. The Captn in the meantime followed the Indians to prevent their burning our Linnen and the Seine which lay on the grass just where they were gone. He had no musquet with him so returnd to fetch one for no threats or signs would make them desist. Mine was ashore and another loaded with shot, so we ran as fast as possible towards them and came just time enough to save the Seine by firing at an Indian who had already fird the grass in two places just to windward of it; on the shot striking him, tho he

---

[19] *EV*, pp. 345, 343. It is worth noting that the textual nature of the *Endeavour* journal as a whole is far from stable. As Beaglehole notes in his textual introduction to his edition of the journal, it is compiled from four different copies, each of which was amended and re-drafted. The edition preserved by Beaglehole's editing then is a composite text. Ibid., pp. cxcii–cclxiv.

[20] *EV*, pp. ccxxvii–ccxxviii. Beaglehole's discussion of the other *Endeavour* journals is to be found in his introduction to the textual production of Cook's journal, pp. ccxxvi–cclxiv.

was full 40 yards from the Captn who fird, he dropd his fire and ran nimbly to his comrades who all ran off pretty fast.[21]

Though he does not use the same phrase as the other journals, Banks's words 'for no threats or signs would make them desist' convey the same meaning, an attempted communication that was not, or cannot be, read.

As we might expect, Cook's journal entry for 19 July is the most detailed. It is worth quoting in full:

In the AM we were viseted by 10 or 11 of the natives, the most of them came from the other side of the River where we saw six or seven more the most of them women and like the men quite naked; those that came on board were very desirous of having some of our turtle and took the liberty to haul two to the gang way to put over the side, being disapointed in this they grew a little troublesome and were for throwing every thing over board they could lay their hands upon; as we had no victuals dress'd at this time I offer'd them some bread to eat, which they rejected with scorn as I believe they would have done any thing else excepting turtle. Soon after this they all went a shore, Mr Banks my self and five or six of our people being a shore at the same time; emmidiatly upon their landing one of them took a handfull of dry grass and lighted it at a fire we had a shore, and before we well know'd what he was going about he made a large circuit round about us and set fire to the grass in his way and in an Instant the whole place was in flames, luckily at this time we had hardly any thing ashore besides the forge and a sow with a Litter of young pigs one of which was scorched to death in the fire. As soon as they had done this they all went to a place where some of our people were washing and where all our nets and a good deal of linnen were laid out to dry, here with the greatest obstinacy they again set fire to the grass which I and some others who were present could not prevent, until I was obliged to fire a musquet load[ed] with small shott at one of the ri[n]g leaders which sent them off. As we were apprised of this last attempt of theirs we got the fire out before it got head, but the first spread like wild fire in the woods and grass. Notwithstanding my fireing, in which one must have been a little hurt because we saw a few drops of blood on some of the linnen he had gone over, they did not go far from us for we soon after heard their Voices in the woods; upon which Mr Banks and I and 3 or 4 More went to look for them and very soon met them comeing towards us. As they had each 4 or 5 darts a piece and not knowing their intention we seized upon six or seven of the first darts we met with, this alarmed them so much that they all made off and we followd them for near half a Mile and than set down and call'd to them and they stoped also; after some little unintelligible conversation had pass'd they lay down their darts and came to us in a very friendly manner; we now returned the darts we had taken from them which reconciled every thing. There were 4 strangers among them that we had not seen before and these were interduced to us by name by the others; the man which we suppos'd to have been struck with

[21] J.C. Beaglehole, ed., *The Endeavour Journal of Joseph Banks 1768–1771*, 2 vols (Sydney, 1962), II, p. 96.

small shott was gone off but he could not be much hurt as he was at a great distance when I fired. They all came along with us abreast of the ship where they stay'd a short time and then went away, and soon after set the woods on fire about a Mile and a half and two miles from us.[22]

The details here give the clear narrative of events. The scene seems a typical one of much eighteenth-century Pacific exploration, the escalation of an instance of theft into a conflict between the two communities involved. Interestingly, Cook talks of being 'obliged to fire' but makes no mention of any 'signs to the contrary'. His 'notwithstanding' is partly a narrative device, a return to the action, and partly a simple 'despite', as in the other journals.

But if Cook's version is clearly the fullest available and thus to be taken as the closest to a record of events, problems remain. No other writer (Banks included) mentions the subsequent firing of the woods that Cook remarks upon at the close of his entry, despite it surely being an obvious action that might call for comment. More intriguingly, Cook makes no mention of Banks's tent or marquee, which in nearly all the other journal entries is the focal point for the rescue of the *Endeavour*'s materials that were on shore. Indeed, Cook notes that 'luckily at this time we had hardly any thing ashore', and his journal has absolutely no record of the setting up of any tent following the *Endeavour*'s arrival in the river on 18 June subsequent to its striking the reef.

It is impossible and pointless to seek a primary narrative that resolves these inconsistencies. No pure version can be worked towards. In part this is clearly consistent with Beaglehole's reading of the conditions of the journals' production, and the lack of literacy of the writers involved especially. Nevertheless, it is clearly not inappropriate to note that at one of the moments of greatest tension and drama during the Australian section of the voyage, and at a moment when the technical (in terms of armaments) superiority of Cook and his crew is displayed, the writing of the event collapses into a near total uniformity. In particular the phrase 'notwithstanding our signs to the contrary' seems to offer a sense of a profound lack of articulation, a complete inability to say what is meant, that is then immediately turned to legitimise a violent act. Given the Admiralty directions for the keeping of journals, and the widely known popularity of voyage narratives, and given what we might call the heightened circumstances that culture contact must have brought, and the genuine drama of this particular moment, might we not expect something more from the *Endeavour*'s journal writers, even if it might be something we could clearly recognise as fiction?[23]

A possible answer to these questions lies with the writing of earlier voyages. Just five years before Cook sailed the *Endeavour* towards the coast of

---

[22] *EV*, pp. 361–2.

[23] It is worth noting that both Hawkesworth in 1773 and Wharton in 1894 rewrote Cook's journal to emphasise the dramatic nature of events.

New Holland, Byron, in the midst of his circumnavigation, sent a letter via the storeship *Florida* to the Earl of Egmont, the First Lord of the Admiralty. The February 1765 letter was an account of Byron's trip up to that point, but was especially noteworthy because of his descriptions of the inhabitants of Patagonia, rumoured since the visit of Magellan's expedition of June 1520 to be giants. Byron knew the previous accounts of voyages to the region. John Wood, of John Narborough's 1670 expedition which visited Patagonia, commented that none of the seven Patagonians he met were much above six feet, and certainly not of 'such Exterordenary Stature as is reported by Magellanes & other Spaniards'. Harrington and Carmen returned in 1704, however, with stories which appeared to corroborate the Spanish version. In 1741 John Bulkeley and John Cummins, shipwrecked survivors in Patagonia from one of Commodore Anson's vessels, agreed with Wood that the inhabitants were 'of a middle Stature', and Byron had a copy of Bulkeley's account when the *Dolphin* arrived off the coast of Patagonia in December 1764.[24] He wrote to Egmont that:

> I never was more astonish'd than to see such a set of People, the stoutest of Our Grenadiers would appear nothing to them. . . . Nothing in Nature could appear more terribly frightful than these People did both Men & Women. Our People before We landed swore they were all mounted on Guanicoes, their Horses appear'd so small in Comparison to their Riders, tho' when I was near them I observ'd that their Horses were of the Common Size, and Our People on Board, who were looking at Us thro' their Glasses, said We look'd like meer Dwarfs to the people We were gone amongst . . . these People who in Size come the nearest to Giants of any People I believe in the World.[25]

The letter is a more or less faithful reproduction of Byron's journal entry for 21 December 1764, although it is impossible to know the exact order of writing. The Admiralty kept the contents of the document secret until Byron's return in 1766, when it became reported among the French intelligence services that he had encountered men 'nine feet high'. Charles Clerke, later of the *Endeavour*, but at this time a midshipman with Byron aboard the *Dolphin*, wrote an account of the Patagonians which was subsequently read to the Royal Society on 12 February 1767, and published in the *Philosophical Transactions* of that year, in which he asserted that 'there was hardly a man there less than eight feet, most of them considerably more'.[26] Byron's voyage across the Pacific was spectacular in its failure to find anything worth documenting (ignoring orders to search for the Northwest Passage, he sailed across the ocean missing

---

[24] Helen Wallis, 'The Patagonian Giants', in Robert E. Gallagher, ed., *Byron's Journal of his Circumnavigation, 1764–1766* (Cambridge, 1962), pp. 185–6.
[25] Ibid., pp. 153–9. See pp. 45–8 for the relevant journal entry.
[26] Ibid., p. 188.

all the major island groups), but his accounts of the Patagonian giants made his expedition a talking point of the late 1760s.

Bernard Smith has noted that, unlike Cook, Byron lacked a professional artist on his expedition. An illustration of the encounter was added both to the 1767 publication of A Voyage round the World, in His Majesty's Ship the Dolphin, Commanded by the Honourable Commodore Byron, and to John Hawkesworth's Voyages, published in 1773, in which the Captain is suitably dwarfed by a Patagonian chief, but this was 'simply an illustration based on a written statement'.[27] Without the empirical recording ability of the trained artist, all that remains in Byron's version of his contact is *writing*. The written word here seems far more prone to the seductions of previous narratives. It seems as if the slippage of fact into fiction cannot be avoided, and indeed that writing is not expected to reproduce the actuality of the experience. In this sense, Byron's account is not exceptional but typical of many eighteenth-century voyage narratives, where as Philip Edwards has noted:

> The vagueness about the aims and purposes of an official publication, and in particular about the balance between the entertainment and edification of the general reader on the one hand, and the provision of scientific and technical information on the other, was a part of the extraordinary lack of clarity in all major voyage-accounts.[28]

Byron's writing renders his journal an extremely unstable text. Set in the context of the recording nature of the journal – the accounts of navigation, wind speed and direction, the distance from the coast, the status of the crew and ship's stores – such writing belongs to the authoritative domain of the factual and the measurable. It seems a clear part of the rational empiricism of modern exploration. Yet it is clear that other roots for Byron's writing belong to the far-fetched, the gestural and dramatic world of an encounter with other peoples. These roots of course pre-date the scientific precision of late eighteenth-century travel considerably, and in part are subsumed by what might be described as Byron's lacklustre style, but they clearly surface in the descriptions of the Patagonian giants.

In the voyage that followed Byron's, both Captain Samuel Wallis on the Dolphin and Captain Philip Carteret on the Swallow reported on the Patagonians. Indeed Carteret was expressly commissioned by Dr Matthew Maty, Secretary of the Royal Society, to do so as soon as possible.[29] Both captains reported that, though 'stout', the Patagonians were not gigantic. Carteret, in a January 1767 letter to Maty, noted that they 'were in general all from six feet, to six

---

[27] Smith, *European Vision and the South Pacific*, p. 20.
[28] Philip Edwards, *The Story of the Voyage: Sea Narratives in Eighteenth-century England* (Cambridge, 1994), p. 7.
[29] Gallagher, *Byron's Journal of his Circumnavigation*, p. 190.

feet five inches, although there were some who came to six feet seven inches, but none above that'. Wallis, who had brought special measuring rods to obtain empirical observations, wrote in the *Dolphin's* log that 'the major part of them were from 5 feet 10 inches to six feet', seeming to set the record straight, though other anonymous letters from the voyage again talked of figures between seven and eight feet tall.[30]

Wallis's voyage in the *Dolphin* is, however, more important for the fact that it was the first with official instructions to search in the Pacific for the Southern Continent, and for its account of the first encounter between Europeans and Tahitians. That contact occurred some six months after the visit to Patagonia, and followed the ship's arrival at Tahiti on 19 June 1767 and the subsequent landing in Matavai Bay on 26 June. The journal of George Robertson, the *Dolphin's* Master, records the unease of contact, where it is clear that Tahiti held for the arriving Europeans both the exotic potential of untold riches and the terrifying nature of savage otherness.[31] What is of particular interest in relation to the *Endeavour* journals, however, is the descent into violence in the seven-day stand-off following the *Dolphin's* arrival, the initial recording of native 'insolence' and lack of trust, and then the confrontation following a sounding expedition that took place on 21 June:

> The instant that we tackd and stood off all the people ashoar set up a load cry and those in the canoes began to hoot us – and several of them attempted to board us, and seemed greatly inraged at us when they found we would not land, When we got within a mile and half of the ship – one of the Large Canoes run aboard of the Cutter, and caried away her bumphen and tore the mizen – but they soon got clear of her by using the picks and Bayonets, at same time another attempted to board us but we soon got clear of him, a few minutes after three of the largest Attempted to board us all at once – I then ordered the Marins to point the musquets at them, but they Laughd at us and one struck his prow right into our Boat stern, and four of the stoutest fellows immediately Jumpt on the prow of the canoe, as if they meant to board us, with their paddles and clubs in their hands, when I found them so very resolute, I orderd one of the marins to fire his musquet right across their canoe, in hopes of frightening them, without dowing them any more hurt, but this hade not the desired Effect it only startled them a little and when they found non of them was hurt, they all gave a shout and run directly for our boats starn again, and the oyther two came right for the middle of our Boat, fully resolved to board us, which

[30] See Helen Wallis, ed., *Carteret's Voyage Around the World, 1766–1769*, 2 vols (Cambridge, 1963), II, pp. 315–22. The original letter was actually never received in London, but was read to the Royal Society later in January 1770. See also Helen Wallis's note on the Patagonian giants on pp. 322–6; Samuel Wallis, Log of the *Dolphin*, 17 December 1766, PRO Adm 55/35.

[31] Peter Hulme describes Columbus's first voyage to the Caribbean in such terms. See his *Colonial Encounters: Europe and the Native Caribbean, 1492–1797* (London and New York, 1986).

if they hade their prows would have sertainly sunk our boat, and all of us must have inevitably perishd – at same time they were attempting to board the cutter, I then found it was too leat to treat them with tenderness espetially as the ship took no manner of notice of us, altho they saw the whole transaction very plain, hade their been a nine-pound shot fired over their heads, perhaps it may have frightened them from hurting us – But that not being done I thought myself under a necessity of using violent means, I therefor orderd the serjent and one of the Marins, to wound the two most resolute like fellows, that was in the boat which first Boarded us, this orders was Complyed with and the one was killd which the serjent fired at, and the oyther was wounded in the thigh, and both fell overboard, when the oyther fellows in the canoe saw this they all Jumpt overboard, and the other two Canoes immediately steerd of, when we pointed the musquets to them they hield up their paddles before their faces and dropt astern clear of us.[32]

As Cook would feel likewise some three years later at the Endeavour River, Robertson here 'thought myself under the necessity of using violent means'. Robertson's entry writes an escalation of the conflict to violence through a narrative hierarchy. The development of the scene, though not fictional, is a clear example of narrative tension (in a later entry describing the *Dolphin*'s bombardment of the shore in response to a stone-throwing attack, Robertson notes 'it would require the pen of Milton to describe').[33] The narrative tension here, however, is used to reinforce the legitimacy of the violent act, Robertson presenting himself as having no other choice (these are, in effect, his 'signs to the contrary'). His writing clings both to the authority of the sailor, the necessity of the sounding mission and the safety of the ship, and to the authority of the author, forced to account for his actions with regard to the treatment of a different culture and aware of a potential audience. No other journal of the late eighteenth century comes close to Robertson's for the interpenetration of these issues of text, authority and representation. His characterisation of the sick Wallis, the over-assertive First Lieutenant William Clarke (referred to as 'Growl' or 'Lieut. Knowall'), and his own hurt when his advice is ignored, at times presents the clear shape of imaginative fiction.[34] Yet,

---

[32] George Robertson, *The Discovery of Tahiti: A Journal of the Second Voyage of HMS Dolphin around the World under the Command of Captain Wallis, RN, in the Years 1767, 67, 68*, ed. Hugh Carrington (London, 1940), p. 144. There are a total of seventeen journals relating to the voyage, in differing states of completion. Robertson's differs widely from that of Wallis, and is by far the fullest.

[33] Ibid., p. 154.

[34] On 23 June, Robertson writes: 'The Capt. now being very bade and not able to keep the Deck, he consulted with his Officers what was best to be done, our first Lieut. was likesway bade and not able to do any duty upon Deck, but though himself very Able to Advise, what Advice he gave the Capt. at this time I know not, but I afterwards found it was opposite to mine, at a time when it hurt me greatly.' Ibid., p. 148. A few days later, Lieut. Clarke publicly rebuked Robertson on the quarterdeck for his actions during a sounding expedition, and as Robertson notes, 'this speech made my heart ake' (p. 150).

conscious of his role as a representative of the nation and a man of enlightenment with a responsibility for the understanding of the new culture he was meeting, Robertson finds his prose torn between the demands of record and those of narrative description. The result is an often fraught locutionary position that nevertheless exemplifies the nature of the modernity it enacts and seeks to capture.

In their differing ways, the writings of Byron and Robertson help to bring us back to the Endeavour River. When we seek a view of the journals that asks more of them than simply to be the straightforward site of record and observation, the uniformity and the mistakes can be seen to belong to a specific moment where writing fails to carry the responsibilities and sensibilities that are asked of it. The closed world of the ship was a place of discipline, authority and, as Greg Dening has noted, a kind of theatre.[35] It was a vessel of modernity. But the nature of the reality experienced on the voyage did not allow the open sensibility of modern thought to find its formulation. As it was written in the journals of contact, it found its limits, unable to negotiate the range of material it encountered. As Jonathan Lamb puts it:

> The difficulties of producing probable narratives of Pacific discovery arose from both the assumptions with which the eyewitness began his account and the material he had to include. Lying behind a buccaneer's tale and a scientist's treatise was a common dependence upon a system of differences that rendered the wonderful and the marvellous intelligible and believable. The differences between human and animal, adult and child, mine and yours, sexual relations and kinship structures, food and human flesh, wealth and privation, and so on defined the perspective of civil society and its emissaries upon the new world opened up by this 'door of the seas.' However, these were the very differences destined to be blurred by entering through it.[36]

This analysis is far from earlier ideas of Cook's writing. Commenting upon the *Endeavour* journal, Beaglehole notes that Cook's writing is in fact properly viewed as an extension of his maritime skills:

> He regards words unromantically, as concrete things with a precise use, much in the way he regards a block and tackle or a tiller-brace; and as he merely wished those articles to work efficiently in the ship's economy with no splendid, if difficult, aura of their own, so he is never tempted to give his words any extrinsic value.[37]

Thus Cook is a functional writer, but, as in navigation, the function is the virtue (Beaglehole notes that Cook's prose is the 'sort that might be expected'

---

[35] Greg Dening, *Mr. Bligh's Bad Language: Passion, Power and Theatre on the Bounty* (Cambridge, 1992).
[36] Lamb, 'Introduction', *The South Pacific in the Eighteenth Century*, p. 4.
[37] *EV*, p. cxciii.

and that he has 'a magnificent lack of imagination').[38] It is noticeable that, for Beaglehole, the one point of the *Endeavour* journal where Cook's writing fails is the Australian section. What Beaglehole has in mind here is the kind of philosophical and ethnographic speculations, rare in Cook's prose, such as those he offers when recalling and recording the Aborigines as the voyage nears its end:

> From what I have said of the Natives of New-Holland they may appear to some to be the most wretched people upon Earth, but in reality they are far more happier than we Europeans; being wholy unacquainted not only with the superfluous but the necessary Conveniencies so much sought after in Europe, they are happy in not knowing the use of them. They live in a Tranquillity which is not disturb'd by the Inequality of Condition. . . . In short they seem'd to set no Value upon any thing we gave them, nor would they ever part with any thing of their own for any one article we could offer them; this in my opinion argues that they think themselves provided with all the necessarys of Life and that they have no superfluities.[39]

Beaglehole places this kind of prose in the company of Commerson's commentary on Tahiti, and Hawkesworth's rewriting of the post-1763 journals in his 1773 publication. He comments: 'And as Commerson wrote nonsense about Tahiti, and Hawkesworth about New Zealand, so Cook, the genius of the matter-of-fact, writes nonsense about Australian society.'[40] Cook's writing is 'nonsense' because it departs from the unimaginative clarity of record that Beaglehole sees as the prime requisite for a journal of exploration. In fact, the tension of the writing of the Australian section of the *Endeavour* journal is founded precisely upon, first, Cook's problematic lack of exchange with the Aborigines, which meant he had little choice other than to speculate, and secondly the variety of purposes the writing carried, which meant the *inscription* of this lack of exchange was continually threatened with the possibility of empty words (a peculiar form of cultural entanglement). As we have seen, this is true not just of Cook, but of the other writers of the *Endeavour* experience. With the possibility of both technical and imaginative models to use, the prose falls flat, almost self-aware of its inability to do justice to the

---

[38] *EV*, p. cxciii.

[39] *EV*, p. 399.

[40] *EV*, pp. cxciii–cclxiv. It is noticeable that Cook's ethnological observations on the Aborigines often seek to work against previous texts, here those of Shelvocke and Jeffreys, and especially that of Dampier's 1697 *New Voyage*. See Smith, *European Vision and the South Pacific*, pp. 125–7; also Glyndwr Williams, '"Far more happier than we Europeans": reactions to the Australian Aborigines on Cook's voyage', *Historical Studies*, XIX (1981), pp. 499–512. It is worth noting that Hawkesworth left out Cook's comments on the Aborigines in his later compilation, which is of course in itself a different example of the journals being edited to find an audience.

scene. That the words employed might be empty, even given the dramatic events that unfolded, is striking, but the truth about the 'signs to the contrary' is that they were often, in all senses of the word, gestural.[41]

In keeping with the provisional nature of the material under analysis here, it is perhaps fitting to conclude with some appropriate moments of conjecture. By his third voyage, after a decade of travel, Cook was increasingly drawn into a world of ever-increasing cross-cultural complexity. Quite possibly it was the demands created by this position that led to his actions both on board and on shore after that voyage left Queen Charlotte's Sound and headed across the Pacific to the Hawaiian Islands. In terms of the textuality of Cook's journals, though, it is possible to invert this model and see the problems of writing coming sooner, and not later, on the first voyage and not the third. By the third voyage Cook had acquired such knowledge of the Pacific that writing of its events had a history for him – he had himself extended the genre. And, given that writing is always potentially a mask, maybe even Cook, the plain man with his Quaker heritage of moderation, saw that words could be something he could use or even hide behind. But on the *Endeavour* voyage, when his journal writing (and that of many of his crew) was new to culture contact, possibly it was more difficult to write, to find the words that would describe the scene.

Secondly, might it not be that the kind of vulnerability seen here in the writing of the Endeavour River episode might be explained by the vulnerability of the *Endeavour* itself? With the ship seriously holed and in need of significant repairs, could it be that all the issues the voyage contained – the ideas of authority, of King and country, of science and exploration – were under threat and that this was a situation felt by all of the crew? Following on from this, and attempting to reposition the positive nature of Obeyesekere and Foley's work in a less deterministic fashion, might it not be somehow appropriate to see the writing of the Endeavour River as a fitting language for the development of an Australian society that was to follow? In the gaps and pauses and disjunctures of the journal-keepers, might we not see the anticipation of a country founded upon the wilful blindness of the *terra nullius* principle, where there was no real effort on the part of the settler community to have a vision of a colony that included its indigenous peoples, where the machinations of cultural nationalism became the dominant fiction that sought

---

[41] Discussing the writing of exploration and voyage narratives, Stephen Greenblatt notes: 'Textual authority is fraught with particular difficulties, not only because of perennial tensions in overburdened command structures, but because of the immense distance from Europe of the newly discovered lands and, consequently, the immense problem of verification, a problem exacerbated by the strangeness of the stories that had to be told. At the moment that Europeans embarked on one of the greatest enterprises of appetite, acquisition and control in the history of the world, their own discourses became haunted by all that they could not control.' Greenblatt, 'Introduction: New World encounters', in Stephen Greenblatt, ed., *New World Encounters* (Berkeley and Los Angeles, 1993), p. xvii.

to justify settlement, where dialogue across the racial divide did not exist (some might say still does not), and ultimately where the late twentieth century saw a collapse in the values that had encompassed the Australian mind for so long? In that idea of difficulty that hampered the journal writers, in the problems of exchange, possibly the Endeavour River is strangely foundational, in its own lack of communication a sign itself of a difficult future.

5

Tute: the impact of Polynesia on Captain Cook

ANNE SALMOND

Without doubt, Captain James Cook was one of the world's great explorers. During his three Pacific journeys his wooden ships circled the world, navigating the ice-bound fringes of the Antarctic and Arctic circles, where sails froze solid and the rigging hung with icicles; sailed into tropical seas, where they survived hurricanes, lightning strikes and volcanic eruptions; edged around uncharted lands and islands, always in danger of shipwreck; and in one harbour after another, found unknown peoples. For any time and in any culture, these were remarkable voyages, like the journeys of Odysseus, or the Polynesian star navigators.

At the same time, Captain Cook has become an icon of imperial history. His voyages epitomise the European conquest of nature, fixing the location of coastlines by the use of instruments and mathematical calculation, classifying and collecting plants, animals, insects and people. As the edges of the known world were pushed out, wild nature – including the 'savages' and 'barbarians' at the margins of humanity – was brought under the calm, controlling gaze of Enlightenment science, long before colonial domination was attempted. Cook's Pacific voyages, and his life and death, thus provoke reflection about the nature of history, and the impartiality of its explanations. Tales of the European discovery of the world are still shaped by imperial attitudes; and accounts of the great voyages of exploration are often written as epics in which only the Europeans are real. They travel in seas which had been traversed for centuries, 'discovering' places long inhabited by others. Yet *terra nullius*, the 'empty lands', were only empty because their people had been reduced to ciphers, 'savages' without the power to shape the future, to influence the Europeans and to change them.

In reflecting upon these great voyages, one must avoid the trap of Cyclops, with his one-eyed vision. Rather, we can draw on the perception, shared by James Cook himself, that in his journeys of Pacific exploration, Europeans and 'natives' alike were only human. On each side, there was savagery and kindness, generosity and greed, intelligent curiosity and stupidity. Maori, Tahitians and other Pacific Islanders engaged with Cook's men in ways that were defined by their cosmology and culture, just as Cook's men were shaped by the cosmology and culture of Georgian England. During their successive

77

encounters with Polynesians, European voyagers and Polynesians alike were transformed. In those meetings, perceptions and practices were *mutually* altered. Both sides were caught up in contradictory influences, and in this 'space of wondering' people were vulnerable to confusion. By the third voyage, Cook's ships were not pure exemplars of Europe – far from it; and Cook's behaviour had shifted significantly. He became increasingly volatile and violent, and his men called him 'Tute', his Tahitian name, and spoke of him as a Polynesian despot.

The trial of the cannibal dog

During this last voyage to the Pacific, Alexander Home was a master's mate on board Cook's consort ship, *Discovery*. In his old age there was a yarn he used to spin about an incident that happened while they were anchored at New Zealand in 1777, in Totaranui (Queen Charlotte's Sound):

> When we were in New Zealand, Neddy Rhio, one of my messmates had got hold of a New Zealand dog, as savage a devil as the savages from whom he got it, and this same dog he intended to bring home to present to the Marchioness of Townsend, his patroness. But one day, when Neddy was on shore on duty, a court-martial was held on the dog, and it was agreed *nem.con.* that, as the dog was of cannibal origin, and was completely a cannibal itself, having bit every one of us, and shewn every inclination to eat us alive if he could, that he should be doomed to death, and eat in his turn, we being short of fresh provisions at the time. The sentence was immediately executed, the dog cooked, dressed, and eat, for we could have eat a horse behind the saddle, we were all so confoundedly hungry; but, considering that Neddy had a best right to a share, we put past his portion in a wooden bowl, and by way of having some sport, we cut a hole in the dog's skin, and as Neddy came up the side, I popped his own dog's skin over his head with the tail hanging down behind, and the paws before. He looked the grin horrid, told us we were all a set of d—d cannibals, as bad as the New Zealanders we were amongst, and dived down below quite in the sulks.[1]

Cannibalism was a sore subject with Cook's men during their visit to Totaranui in 1777. Just three years earlier, during Cook's second Pacific voyage, local Maori had attacked a boat-load of the *Adventure*'s crew in the Sound, and killed them all. This had been the fifth visit by Cook's ships, and during those visits there had been affrays with local people, including several shootings. Revenge, when it came, though, was shocking. A launch commanded by the ship's second lieutenant, James Burney, sent out to search for the missing cutter, found rowlock ports and a shoe, and then human flesh bundled up in

---

[1] *RDV*, pp. xcviii–xix.

flax food baskets in a small bay. When the boat's crew rounded the point to the next bay they found Grass Cove 'throng'd like a Fair', attacked the crowd with muskets and wall-guns, landed, and found dogs chewing on the discarded roasted hearts, lungs, heads, hands and feet of their comrades.

This 'shocking scene of Carnage and Barbarity' was described in detail in Burney's report and imprinted on shipboard memory. Cook's men had known about Maori cannibalism since their circumnavigation of New Zealand in 1769–70, but did not expect to encounter it so closely. This was the stuff of sailors' nightmares, a tale of man-eating 'savages' come true. Now, early in Cook's third voyage to the Pacific, Lieutenant Burney, several of his shipmates and their Polynesian companion Mai from the *Adventure*, were returning to the Sound for the first time since that experience. Many others, including Cook and Charles Clerke, their captains, were making their second visit since the killings. They had been on board the *Resolution* when she came back to the Sound in October 1774, hoping for news of her consort. Rumours of a fight between the crew of a shipwrecked European vessel and local people had reached them during the visit, but they had been persuaded that although the *Adventure* had been in the Sound, nothing untoward had happened.

When he finally learned about the fate of the *Adventure*'s boat crew at the Cape of Good Hope in March 1775, Cook thought that the sailors might have been responsible. In his journal at the time, he commented: 'I shall make no reflections on this Melancholy affair untill I hear more about it. I must however observe in favour of the New Zealanders that I have allways found them of a Brave, Noble, Open and benevolent disposition, but they are a people that will never put up with an insult if they have an oppertunity to resent it.'[2] He was still keeping an open mind about the cause of the affray. Until he knew what had provoked it, Cook was determined to take no action. For local Maori, though, this was difficult to grasp. As Cook had noted, they would 'never put up with an insult if they have an opportunity to resent it'. To kill and ritually eat members of another group was the epitome of insult, 'biting the head' of their ancestors, an act which annulled their mana, their capacity to act effectively in the world of light (the everyday world of human affairs). A true rangatira (leader) was bound to retaliate with all the force at his command to such an insult, or his gods would withdraw their presence (or tapu), leaving both rangatira and people bereft. Mai, the young Raiatean who had been on the *Adventure* and since spent two years in England, knew this very well, and reacted to Cook's discretion during this final visit with incredulity. Many of the sailors, too, were thirsty for revenge. They were fundamentally offended that people who had cooked and eaten their comrades should walk about unscathed.

Towards the end of their visit, then, when Cook let Kahura sit in his cabin on board the *Resolution* and questioned him about the killings, then had

---

[2] *RDV*, p. 653.

Webber paint his portrait, this was too much for many of Cook's men. Certainly Mai, when he was asked to bring Kahura to the great cabin, was furious. As Kahura entered he exclaimed, 'There is Kahura, kill him!' When Cook ignored him Mai walked out in disgust, only to return soon afterwards, vehemently protesting: 'Why do you not kill him, you tell me if a man kills an other in England he is hanged for it, this Man has killed ten and yet you will not kill him, tho a great many of his countrymen desire it and it would be very good.'[3]

Cook, though, had promised Kahura that he would do him no harm. He wrote, 'as to what was past, I should think no more of it as it was sometime sence and done when I was not there, but if ever they made a Second attempt of that kind, they might rest assured of feeling the weight of my resentment'.[4] Many of the sailors, though, were of a mind with Mai. Burney spoke for them when he wrote: 'It seemed evident that many of them held us in great contempt and I believe chiefly on account of our not revenging the affair of Grass Cove, so contrary to the principals by which they would have been actuated in the like case.'[5]

During the last days in Queen Charlotte's Sound, then, the scene was set for the trial on board the *Discovery*. James Burney, the living witness of what had happened at Meretoto and the ship's first lieutenant, was chafing at Cook's inaction. The *Discovery* was Cook's consort ship, so the burlesque trial was staged at a safe distance from the crew's commander. It was a marvellous way of letting Cook and Clerke know what the sailors (and some of their officers) thought of Maori cannibals, and how they ought to be handled.

Such exemplary trials of animals were not unprecedented in Europe. In *The Great Cat Massacre*, Robert Darnton tells a tale of an eighteenth-century printer's apprentices in Paris, who lived a hard life with their master, sleeping in a filthy, freezing room, working long hours and being beaten and abused. The master's wife in this workshop adored her cats, especially *la grise* (the gray), a favourite, and fed them well, while the cook gave the apprentices cat's food – old, rotting scraps of meat. Finally the apprentices rebelled. For several nights one of their number, who had a gift for mimicry, yowled and meowed above the master's bedroom until he and his wife thought they were bewitched. In desperation they ordered the apprentices to get rid of the cats, except of course *la grise*, who must on no account be frightened. The apprentices, armed with weapons, went after every cat they could find, beginning with *la grise*, and beat them until they were half-dead, then dumped their bodies in the courtyard where the entire workshop staged a trial. The cats were charged with witchcraft, tried, convicted and hung. When their mistress came out and saw a bloody cat dangling from a noose, she let out a great shriek, to the joy of all the workers.

---

[3] RDV, p. 68.
[4] RDV, p. 69.
[5] Burney in Robert McNab, ed., *Historical Records of New Zealand*, II (Wellington, 1914), p. 199.

For weeks afterwards the apprentices re-enacted their trial and killing of the cats with roars of laughter and 'rough music', running their composing sticks across the type cases, pounding the cupboards and meowing horribly.[6] They had managed to let their master and mistress know just what they thought of them, without exposing themselves to punishment, and the memory was both hilarious and intensely satisfying.

Such trials, not always burlesque, also happened in England. Tom Paine once wrote a satire on the true story of a Sussex farmer whose dog was sentenced to be hanged by local judges, who disliked the way his master had voted in a Parliamentary election.[7] On board English ships, too, as Joseph Banks recounted for the *Endeavour* voyage, animals were involved in similar rough rituals. Dogs and cats as well as men who had not yet 'crossed the Line' were ceremonially ducked on crossing the Equator, unless someone paid in rum to redeem them.

The trial of the cannibal dog, then, was not aberrant behaviour for Europeans at that time. It was rough humour, and, like all such trials, not quite a joke. As Claude Lévi-Strauss has pointed out,[8] domestic animals such as dogs and cats were part of human society in Europe, serving as metonymns (partial representations) of their masters. In the trial of the kurii (Polynesian dog), the sailors were treating it as part of Maori society. By trying and convicting the kurii of cannibalism, they were saying what they thought of Kahura and his compatriots. The trial was on board ship, though, where their captains were the masters. The *Discovery*'s men were telling Cook and Clerke what they thought of their failure to take revenge, sending a message to their commanders at least as much as to anyone on shore.

If the shipboard trial was not weird behaviour, though, eating the dog certainly was, in European terms. As Lévi-Strauss has also noted, cats and dogs in Europe, as metonymns of people, were under a dietary taboo.[9] The thought of eating their flesh was abhorrent, akin to cannibalism. How, then, could Neddy Rhio's mess-mates eat his pet kurii? It may have been that Cook and his sailors (or some of them) were no longer purely European. This was not the first time that Cook's men had eaten dogs in Polynesia. During the *Endeavour*'s first three-month visit to Tahiti in 1769, they had learned to eat dog flesh as feast food, served by hospitable chiefs. As Cook noted at the time, 'Dogs . . . we learned to eat from them and few were there of us but what allowe'd that a South Sea Dog was next to an English lamb.'[10] They

[6] Robert Darnton, *The Great Cat Massacre and Other Episodes in French Cultural History* (New York, 1985), pp. 75–104.

[7] In 'The Trial of Farmer Short's Dog Porter'; see J. Keane, *Tom Paine: A Political Life* (London, 1995), pp. 70–1. Such trials of animals also had antecedents in the classics; see for example *The Wasps* by Aristophanes, trans. David Barnett (London, 1964).

[8] Claude Lévi-Strauss, *The Savage Mind* (Chicago, 1962), pp. 204–8.

[9] Ibid., p. 205.

[10] *EV*, pp. ccvi, 103.

learned, too, that Polynesians kept dogs in their houses, fed them with vege-tables, tied them with strings around the belly and even buried them in special burial grounds.[11] During the *Endeavour*'s voyage, just before they rounded the far southern end of New Zealand, the crew had celebrated the birthday of one of the officers with a feast of dog meat – the hindquarters roasted, the forequarters in a pie, and the guts made into a haggis.[12] On the second voyage, after their first visit to Queen Charlotte Sound, a black dog from the Cape was cooked and eaten in the gun-room, leading Johann Reinhold Forster to muse upon the European prejudice that treated cats and dogs as unclean animals, unfit to eat. And when Cook fell desperately ill off Easter Island and they despaired of his life, Forster sacrificed another dog to feed him. As Cook commented later: 'a favourite dog belonging to Mr Forster fell a Sacrifice to my tender Stomack; we had no other fresh meat whatever on board and I could eat of this flesh as well as broth made of it, when I could taste nothing else, thus I received nourishment and strength from food which would have made most people in Europe sick'.[13]

By the third voyage, far from feeling sick at the thought of eating dog meat (whether European or Polynesian), the sailors' mouths had begun to water. They had come under Polynesian influence – not surprisingly, since some of them had spent more time in the Pacific than anywhere else in recent years. They had learned something of the power of mana, how to resent an insult to it, and how to express that resentment. After almost a decade of visits to Polynesia, if Cook's sailors could eat a kurii after convicting it of cannibalism, that is no great cause for amazement. For the rest of this chapter, I will sketch these processes of transformation, offering some notes on the first two voyages before discussing Cook's last expedition in more detail.

Cook's first two Pacific voyages

During Cook's Pacific voyages, contacts with Polynesians were close and of some long standing. During the first voyage, the *Endeavour* spent three months at Tahiti, where the men seemed generous, and the women were bare-breasted and compliant. Many of the men had love affairs; others had tattoos, or learned to speak Tahitian; and most acquired their own taio (ceremonial friends). They acquired a lasting liking for Polynesians, and when the *Endeavour* sailed from this glorious island, the Raiatean high-priest navigator Tupaia sailed with them. As he piloted the ship through the Society Islands, Tupaia tried to teach Cook and Banks about Tahitian cosmology and navigation, producing a remarkable chart of the Polynesian islands. A six-month circumnavigation of New Zealand

[11] *RAV*, pp. 419–20.
[12] *EV*, p. 262 n. 3.
[13] *RAV*, pp. 333–4.

followed, when the ship anchored in one harbour after another; and Cook worked out ways of dealing with Maori challenges, which were usually vigorous and assertive. In New Zealand the *Endeavour* was often remembered as Tupaia's ship – he took the lead in encounters with Maori, and they thought this was his expedition. During the second voyage, the *Resolution* and *Adventure* returned on a number of occasions to Queen Charlotte's Sound and the Society Islands, and visited Eua and Tongatapu, where they received tumultuous welcomes. Two young Polynesians, Mai and Hitihiti, joined the ships in the Society Islands, intent upon visiting 'Peretane'. The ships were separated in a storm off the coast of New Zealand, and the *Adventure* put into Queen Charlotte's Sound on her own, where Mai and his *Adventure* shipmates discovered the mangled, cooked remains of their comrades at Grass Cove. They fled back to England, while Hitihiti sailed with the *Resolution* down to the Antarctic ice edge, remarking with astonishment on the 'white stones' (or hail) in these 'white, evil useless lands' before returning home to the Society Islands. Over this time Cook's men came to take pride in their Pacific adventures, tattooing their chests with stars and calling themselves the 'Knights of Tahiti', sprinkling their conversation with Polynesian words and eating dog as a mark of their initiation into island customs.

At the same time, during the first two voyages Cook tried to act as an 'enlightened' leader – cool, rational and humane, but maintaining strict 'superiority'. At first he was inspired by the Earl of Morton's instructions, his experiences with the Quakers and Joseph Banks's youthful idealism – but by the second voyage, he came to epitomise these values, leading by example. As midshipman John Elliott commented:

> No man could be better calculated to gain the confidence of Savages than Capn Cook. He was brave, uncommonly Cool, Humane – and Patient. He would land alone unarm'd, or lay aside his Arms, and sit down, when they threaten'd with theirs, throwing them Beads, Knives, and other little presents, then by degrees advancing nearer, till by Patience, and forbearance, he gain'd their friendship, and an intercourse with them; which to people in our situation, was of the utmost consequence.[14]

Cook also tried to stop his men from spreading venereal diseases, to their intense frustration; and punished them for offences against local people, musing in his journal:

> It has ever been a maxim with me to punish the least crimes any of my people have commited against these uncivilized Nations, their robing us with impunity is by no means a sufficient reason why we should treat them in the same manner. . . . The best method in my opinion to preserve a good understanding with such people is first to shew them the use of fire arms and to convince them of the Superiority they

---

[14] *RAV*, p. 124 n. 3.

give you over them and to be always upon your guard; when once they are sencible of these things, a regard for their own safety will deter them from disturbing you or being unanimous in forming any plan to atack you, and Strict honisty and gentle treatment on your part will make it their intrest not to do it.[15]

Such punishments did not endear him to his men, however. In the New Hebrides, for example, towards the end of the second voyage, when some boys were shot for throwing stones, Cook ordered the marines to observe greater discretion. Before his eyes, a sentry shot a man who had lifted his bow, and shattered his arm with a musket ball, so Cook ordered the sentry to be seized, and taken back to the ship and flogged. When the officers disputed this order, there was a heated argument between them and their captain. The sailors sided with the officers, arguing that it was unfair that a shipmate should be flogged for defending himself. As Elliott noted, 'Tho I have several times said that Captn Cook was a Most Brave, Just, Humane, and good Man, and the fittest of all others for such a Voyage; yet I must think, that here . . . He lost sight, of both justice, and Humanity.'[16]

Despite these tensions, Cook upheld his authority, keeping Polynesians and his men alike in line by the use of limited violence. During the first voyage, when he had just the *Endeavour* to manage, twenty-one men out of the crew of eighty-five were punished, five of them twice, with a maximum of twenty-four lashes – a total of 342 lashes. During the second voyage, when the ships were often separated, just nineteen of the *Resolution*'s men were punished, with one sentence of twenty-four lashes, two sentences of eighteen lashes, sixteen of twelve lashes, and six of six lashes (a total of 288 lashes over three years at sea), a more moderate tally; and the *Resolution* was reckoned to be a happy ship. At the end of the voyage, Elliott commented, 'I will here do them the justice to say that *No Men* could behave better, under every circumstance than they did, the same must be said of the officers; and I will add that I believe their never was a Ship, where for so long a period, under such circumstances, more happiness, order, and obedience was enjoy'd.'[17] During the third voyage, though, when the *Resolution* and *Discovery* were constantly together, their arrival in any Polynesian port was formidable. It was a drain on local supplies, and as the sailors amused themselves on shore they created major disciplinary problems, both for Cook and for his Polynesian counterparts. These tensions eventually spiralled out of control, fuelled by the long-standing debate between Cook and his men about how natives should be handled.

[15] *RAV*, p. 292.
[16] *RAV*, p. 500.
[17] *RAV*, pp. xxxiii–iv.

Cook's third Pacific voyage

As I have noted, during Cook's last Pacific expedition, the *Resolution*'s contingent included many first- and second-voyage men. Charles Clerke, the *Resolution*'s favourite humorist, was given command of her consort ship *Discovery*, although he had been in prison for his brother's debts, where he contracted the tuberculosis that would kill him. This time, too, there were no civilian scientists to act as independent witnesses. After Banks's earlier antics and Forster's grumblings, Cook had exclaimed 'Curse the scientists, and all science into the Bargain!', and ensured that the scientists for this voyage were naval men. In addition there was Mai, the young refugee from Raiatea. He had had a wonderful time in England, meeting the King and the professors at Cambridge (whom he regarded with great admiration), learning to ice-skate and ride, dining with nobility, flirting with women and acquiring a taste for opera and wine, before being sent home on board the *Resolution*.

The voyage began uneventfully enough. Some of the sailors were punished for fighting, neglect of duty or absenting themselves from the ship without permission, but this was routine, and not unusual. And then came the visit to Queen Charlotte's Sound, where Cook failed to avenge the killing and eating of the *Adventure*'s men. The local people seemed at first puzzled, and then contemptuous. Gore commented that they now seemed 'Confident of their own Power', expecting gifts as 'Tribute for their friendship'.[18] Kahura's provocative behaviour sparked Mai's outburst, which Cook ignored, and the trial of the cannibal dog on board the *Discovery* soon followed. Relationships between Cook and his men became strained. When the *Resolution* and *Discovery* sailed from Totaranui in late February 1777, Clerke wrote:

> Whilst you keep the command in your own hands you are at leisure to act with whatever lenity you please, but if you relax so far as to lay yourself open to their machinations, you may be deceiv'd in your expectations. There are few Indians in whom I wou'd wish to put a perfect confidence, but of all I ever met with these shou'd be the last, for I firmly believe them very capable of the most perfidious & most cruel treachery, tho' no People can carry it fairer when the proper superiority is maintaind.[19]

Here, and in pointed comments by Burney and some of the sailors, Cook's handling of local people was being questioned. There was also a new note in Cook's own journal, however. He, who had so often described Maori as 'brave, noble, and open' people, now spoke with disgust about their treachery in warfare, when they 'kill every soul that falls in their way . . . and then either feast and gorge themselves on the spot or carry off as many of the

---

[18] *RDV*, p. 66 n. 1.
[19] *RDV*, p. 69 n. 2.

dead as they can and do it at home with acts of brutality horrible to relate'.[20] These comments were uncharacteristic of Cook, and mark the beginning of a transformation.

Bernard Smith has said that changes in Cook's behaviour during the third voyage might be described as '"the loss of hope", "an increased cynicism", "familiarity breeds contempt", "power tends to corrupt and absolute power corrupts absolutely"'.[21] I think that this transformation began at Totaranui. Cook realised how far he had been hoodwinked during his previous visit, and felt the sting of disrespect not only from local people, but from his own sailors. As an 'enlightened' leader, he had tried to act with calm detachment, even in the face of cannibalism. Many of his men had no such scruples, however. They wanted to revenge their shipmates, and kill the cannibals. When Cook took no action against local Maori, their faith in their commander was shaken, and discipline was threatened.

Almost as soon as the *Resolution* sailed from the Sound, there were rumblings on board the ship. According to Lieutenant King, there was an 'appearance of general disobedience among the people' and a rash of minor thieving. Cook cut the men's meat rations until the offenders were identified, but the crew refused to co-operate, which he considered 'a very mutinous proceeding'. From this time on, the voyage was plagued with outbreaks of violence. At Nomuka in Tonga, a chief was flogged, and when commoners were sent instead to take things from the ships, flogging became routine, and people's heads were shaved as a further deterrent. When the ships carried on to Lifuka, accompanied by one of the chiefs, his son was clapped in irons on the *Discovery* for stealing a cat. Although Mai recommended that this man be given a hundred lashes, on the grounds that the higher the rank, the worse the crime, Clerke let him off with just one lash, but this was still a deadly insult. A great night feast was put on, which Mai attended wearing a captain's uniform. According to William Mariner, a plan was made to seize Cook and his officers and marines at this feast and kill them all. Only a dispute over the timing of the attack saved them.

The ships carried on to Tongatapu, where the violence intensified further. Cook and the Tui Tonga exchanged gifts and became 'friends', and Cook was showered with gifts and entertainments. At the same time, Tongans (including old people) were punished with twenty-four, thirty-six, forty-eight, sixty and seventy-two lashes, while according to midshipman George Gilbert:

> Capt. Cook punished [theft] in a manner rather unbecoming of a European viz: by cutting off their ears; fireing at them with small shot, or ball, as they were swimming or paddling to the shore and suffering the people (as he rowed after them) to beat them with the oars; and stick the boat hook into them, where ever they could hit

---

[20] *RDV*, p. 71.

[21] Bernard Smith, *Imagining the Pacific: In the Wake of the Cook Voyages* (New Haven and London, 1992), p. 207.

them; one in particular he punished by ordering one of our people to make two cuts upon his arm to the bone one accross the other close below his shoulder; which was an act I cannot account for any otherways than to have proceeded from a momentary fit of anger as it certainly was not in the least premeditated.[22]

For Cook, this was unprecedented behaviour. During the first two voyages, the worst sentence meted out to anyone had been twenty-four lashes, and then only for serious offences. As ship's corporal William Griffin explained, 'The rules of the Navy dont admit of more than a Dozen lashes at one time for one Crime, although more is often given by severe Commanders.'[23] Strictly speaking, sentences of twenty-four lashes were illegal, although commanders on long voyages sometimes administered such punishments. Nicholas Rodger notes in his study of the Georgian Navy that anything above that was uncommon.[24] Sentences of thirty-six, forty-eight, sixty or seventy-two lashes were beyond captains' legal powers, as well as agonising. During the third voyage, then, Cook was breaching naval rules (although some of the worst punishments happened on board the *Discovery*, which suggests that Clerke was at least as much to blame), and worse still, acting in anger. In taking the high chiefs hostage, moreover, Cook was asking for trouble. Corporal of marines John Ledyard wrote:

> Perhaps no considerations will excuse the severity which he sometimes used toward the natives. . . . He would perhaps have done better to have considered that the full exertion of extreme power is an argument of extreme weakness, and nature seemed to inform the insulted natives of the truth of this maxim by the manifestation of their subsequent resentments; for before we quit Tongataboo we could not go any where into the country upon danger or pleasure without danger.[25]

At the same time, Cook was being tough on the *Resolution*'s crew. During this voyage, he punished twice as many men as on the previous two voyages, with a total of 736 lashes. Nor was this Cook's only uncharacteristic behaviour. Before they left Tongatapu he forced his way into a ritual staged by the Tui Tonga for his son, letting down his hair and baring his chest to comply with the tapu of the proceedings. His men thought that this was playing the Polynesian too far. Williamson commented, 'I do not pretend to dispute the propriety of Captn Cook's conduct, but I cannot help thinking he rather

---

[22] Christine Holmes, ed., *Captain Cook's Final Voyage: The Journal of Midshipman George Gilbert* (Horsham, 1982), pp. 33–4.
[23] *RDV*, p. 244.
[24] Nicholas Rodger, *The Wooden World: An Anatomy of the Georgian Navy* (London, 1986), p. 220.
[25] J.K. Munford, ed., *John Ledyard's Journal of Captain Cook's Last Voyage* (Corvalis, Oreg., 1963), p. 38.

let himself down.'[26] In the visit to Eua that followed, Cook reasserted his authority by flogging the sailors. Five men were flogged, one each day during their short stay on that island.

When the ships carried on to Tahiti, Cook met his ceremonial friend Tuu, who asked him to assist him in an attack on the neighbouring island of Mo'orea. Cook refused, but upon visiting Mo'orea shortly afterwards, he and Mai led a punitive expedition for the theft of a goat, burning down houses and twenty-five large war canoes belonging to the people of that island. According to Gilbert, neither tears nor entreaties moved Cook on this occasion; he seemed 'very rigid in the performance of His orders, which every one executed with the greatest reluctance except Omai; who was very officious in this business; and wanted to fire upon the natives . . . I can't well account for Capt Cook's proceeding on this occasion as they were so very different from his conduct in like cases in his former voyages'.[27] Williamson added, 'I cannot thinking the man totally destitute of humanity . . . I must confess this once I obey'd my Orders with reluctance . . . I doubt not but Captn Cook had good reasons for carrying His punishment of these people to so great a length, but what his reasons were are yet a secret.'[28] Gilbert offered the most likely explanation: 'If anything may be offered in favour of [the captain's proceedings] 'twas his great friendship for Otoo (king of Otaheite) to whom these people were pro-fessed enemies.'[29] Cook was still reluctant to shoot local people with ball, however; floggings, ear cropping and the destruction of property were used to punish pilfering in preference to outright killing.

From Mo'orea, Cook went on to Huahine, where Mai decided to stay on with his two young Maori companions. There, Mai and the local chiefs pleaded with Cook to attack Raiatea and free that island from Porapora invaders. Again Cook refused, but when the ship's sextant was taken several days later, Mai identified a Porapora man as the thief, and Cook had him put in irons and flogged 'until particles of his skin came away in shreds'.[30] Several days later when the Porapora man raided Mai's garden, and threatened to burn down Mai's house that the ship's carpenters were building, Cook had his ears cut off and clapped him back in irons on the ship, intending to carry him away from the island. Some of the crew evidently thought this was too harsh, and the next night unbolted the prisoner's irons and let him escape. Cook was furious that his authority had been flouted, and had the marines on duty punished with twelve and thirty-six lashes.

[26] RDV, p. 151 n. 1.

[27] Holmes, Cook's Final Voyage, pp. 46–7.

[28] RDV, p. 231.

[29] Holmes, Cook's Final Voyage, p. 47.

[30] F.W. Howay, ed., Zimmerman's Captain Cook: An Account of the Third Voyage of Captain Cook Around the World, 1776–1779 (Toronto, 1930), p. 58.

At Raiatea, some men deserted the ships, and Cook held the daughter, son-in-law and son of a local high chief hostage on the *Discovery* until the local people delivered up the deserters. This time, the local men planned to capture Cook and Clerke when they went to bathe on shore, in revenge for their insulting behaviour. Only a warning from a Huahine woman, who had travelled on the ship with her officer lover, saved them on that occasion.

Several weeks later the ships arrived at Kaua'i, perhaps the first European arrival at the Hawaiian islands. Venereal disease was rife on board, and Cook unsuccessfully tried to prohibit all intercourse with the local women. The people were astonished at the Europeans, and gave them an awe-struck welcome. When one of the locals took the butcher's cleaver and escaped in his canoe, the pinnace was sent off to chase him. Muskets were fired, to the terror of the local people, but no one was hit. When the pinnace came to land, it was surrounded by men who began to carry it ashore, to the sailors' consternation. When a man grabbed a boat-hook, Lieutenant Williamson shot him dead with ball, which infuriated Cook when he heard of it later. In his account of this incident, Williamson made it clear that there was still a deep division of opinion between Cook and Clerke, and many of his officers, about how 'Indians' ought to be handled:

> Cn Cook & I entertain'd very different opinions upon ye manner of treating indians, He asserts that he always found upon his first going among them, that ye firing wth small shot answers ye purpose, but Cn Clerke & many of ye Officers that have sail'd with him declare, that ye firing with small shot always had bad effects.[31]

When Cook landed at Waimea soon afterwards, the people prostrated themselves and presented him with cloth and pigs, then took him to a local heiau, or 'temple', where they clustered around the Europeans, opening their shirts to look at their bodies, and asking them if they could eat. As they left the island, the 'king' and his 'queen' came out to the *Discovery* with ceremonial gifts, which Clerke reciprocated. The pattern of prostration before Cook, which he understood 'is done to their great chiefs',[32] was also followed at Ni'ihau Island. Here, an old 'priestess' 'whom we supposed to be mad' stayed with the shore party, conducting daily ceremonies and arranging for offerings of food to be brought.

It is interesting that during the following months, as the ships headed for the northwest coast of America, punishments on board returned to routine levels, and there were few violent disputes with local people. As soon as they returned to Polynesia at the end of 1778, however, trouble flared up again between Cook and his men. He cruised around the Hawaiian islands of Maui and Hawai'i for seven weeks without landing, to the sailors' intense

---

[31] *RDV*, pp. 1348–9.
[32] *RDV*, p. 269.

frustration. He prohibited sexual contacts with the local women, but gave up when he realised that venereal disease had already been established among them, probably during their earlier visits to Kaua'i and Nihau. And when he had a beer brewed from sugar cane juice, and issued this instead of the crew's daily ration of grog, none of his men would drink it. They wrote and delivered a letter of protest about this and the 'scanty Allowance of Provisions serv'd them', which Cook, as the ship's purser, greatly resented. Several days later, he had a sailor flogged for tampering with the cask of sugar cane beer, and 'address'd ye Ships Company, telling them He look'd upon their Letter as a very mutinous Proceeding & that in future they might not expect the least indulgence from him'.[33]

By this stage in the voyage, Cook often seemed harsh and capricious. The men called him 'Toote' (the Polynesian transliteration of Cook), as in this snatch of shipboard doggerel by Trevenen:

> Oh Day of hard labour, O day of good living!
> When TOOTE was seized with the humour of giving –
> When he clothed in good nature his looks of authority,
> And shook from his eye brows their stern superiority.[34]

'Toote' was prone to violent rages, which the crew also linked with his experiences in Polynesia. Trevenen wrote of the Tahitian term heiva, for example:

> *Heiva*: the name of a dance of the southern islanders which bore so great a resemblance to the violent motions and stampings upon deck of Captain Cook in the paroxysms of passion into which he frequently threw himself upon the slightest occasion that they were universally known by the same name, and it was a common saying, both among officers and men, 'The old boy has been tipping a heiva to such and such a one.'[35]

From being 'cool' and rational', Cook had become 'hot-tempered' and 'passionate' (in anger, at least). Unrestrained passion, however, was the way that 'savages' were thought to behave. In a perceptive analysis of his captain, Zimmermann said that Cook was strict and hot-tempered, and hated being crossed by his men, but added that he

---

[33] Midshipman John Watts, quoted in ibid., pp. 479–80n.

[34] C. Lloyd and R.C. Anderson, eds, *A Memoir of James Trevenen, 1760–1790* (London, 1959), pp. 27–8.

[35] Ibid., p. 21. Banks was similarly treated when he arrived back in England. As tales of his amorous exploits in Tahiti began to circulate, he was satirised in doggerel poems as 'Opano', lover of the 'Queen of Tahiti'. He was described as 'very dark'; and even years later, he was still sometimes referred to as that 'old Otaheitean'.

was born to deal with savages and he was never happier than in association with them. He loved them and understood the languages of the different islanders and had the art of captivating them with his engaging manner. This was probably the reason that they honored and at times even worshipped him, and also further reason that when they ceased to honor him, or sometimes even ridicule him, he burned with rage. . . . He did everything he could to give them pleasure; and, by means of gifts, by imparting information, by entertaining them and by the representation of our European customs . . . Etc., endeavored to win their friendship.[36]

If Cook had become 'Toote' during his Pacific voyages, however, this was scarcely surprising. Over the past ten years he had exchanged gifts, including his own clothing, and sometimes his name, with a series of Polynesian leaders. During the course of these exchanges, according to Polynesian understandings, something of the life force of those people entered his wairua, or spirit. Such relationships, especially between leaders, were often turbulent and dangerous. When high chiefs came together, their ancestor gods also met. Ariki were the 'living face' of their gods, and imbued with their power. A man caught between two sets of gods was 'two-sided', and could be torn in contradictory directions.

During his first two Pacific voyages, as Bernard Smith has noted, Cook had tried to act as an exemplar of enlightened reason. These were scientific expeditions, equipped for systematic observation and enquiry. The man of reason was 'objective', 'detached' and 'dispassionate', free from emotion and weakness. And the epitome of such men was the great discoverer – 'I whose ambition leads me . . . farther than any man has been before me', bringing the edges of the unknown into the light of rational understanding.

For the last decade of his life, though, James Cook, as a discoverer, had spent much of his time in Polynesia, where reality and the self were understood quite differently. Mind and heart were not split, nor mind and matter – they had a generative relation. The world was patterned by spiralling lines of relationship, named in a genealogical language. The exemplary Polynesian leader was the man of mana, who had mastered the art of successful exchange (or utu) in the relational networks. Successful exchange meant revenge for insults, however, as well as generous gifting. As Cook said of Totaranui Maori in 1775: 'I have allways found them of a Brave, Noble, Open and benevolent disposition, but they are a people that will never put up with an insult if they have an oppertunity to resent it.'[37] During his first two voyages to the Pacific, Cook had often spoken of Tahitians or Maori as his 'friends', and advocated 'Strict honisty and gentle treatment'. After his experiences at Totaranui, however, he began to lose his faith in power of reason. Maori had killed and eaten his men, and then deceived him about what had happened. Cook became

[36] Howay, *Zimmerman's Captain Cook*, pp. 100–1.
[37] *RAV*, p. 653.

increasingly cynical, and prone to violent outbursts of anger. He was now also known as 'Toote' on board his ships, a passionate, unpredictable character.

There is a story to be told about the killing of Cook – but not on this occasion. He died as he lived throughout his last voyage, caught in intractable contradictions. As the trial of the cannibal dog in Queen Charlotte's Sound showed, when Cook acted with calm restraint, he invited humiliation. When he acted in anger and sought revenge, he invited retaliation. At Lifuka and on Raiatea during this voyage, plots were made to destroy him. At Hawai'i it happened, but there was no one cause. It was a cross-cultural combination of forces which killed him. Nor was Cook the only one caught in these paradoxical entanglements. During his fatal visit to Kealakekua Bay Cook gave his Hawaiian name 'Kuki' and his naval sword to the high chief Kalaniopu'u; and in return, Cook was given Kalaniopu'u's name. Exchanges of names, and life force, between great leaders in Polynesia had all kinds of consequences. According to the official record of the voyage, after Cook's death, Kalaniopu'u 'retired to a cave in the steep part of the mountain, that hangs over the bay, which was accessible only by the help of ropes, and where he remained for many days, having his victuals let down to him by ropes'.[38] The intensity of the kapu is not surprising. The man who sat in the cave was not only Kalaniopu'u, but, in a sense, also Captain Cook. For it was not only 'Kuki' and 'Lono' who had been killed and sacrificed at Kealakekua Bay, but also 'Kalaniopu'u'. It was fitting, then, that Cook's bones were honoured by Kalaniopu'u and his people, and that by 1793, or so Lieutenant Puget was told, the two men were buried together: 'They told us Capt Cooks Remains were in the Morai [temple] along with those of Terreobo [Kalaniopu'u], which faces the place [Ka'awaloa shore] where the above skirmish happened.'[39]

Polynesian as well as European practice and thought – the World of Light as well as the Enlightenment – played their part in Cook's death, just as Kuki's and Kalaniopu'u's bones were mingled. Polynesian as well as European thinking is needed again, to illuminate those cross-cultural exchanges. In the words of the favourite chant of my long-time mentor, the Maori tribal scholar Eruera Stirling:

Whakarongo! Whakarongo! Whakarongo!	Listen! Listen! Listen!
Ki te tangi a te manu e karanga nei	To the cry of the bird calling
Tui, tui, tuituiaa!	Bind, join, be one!
Tuia i runga, tuia i raro,	Bind above, bind below
Tuia i roto, tuia i waho,	Bind within, bind without
Tuia i te here tangata	Tie the knot of humankind

---

[38] Marshall Sahlins, *How 'Natives' Think: About Captain Cook, For Example* (Chicago, 1995), p. 147.
[39] Ibid., p. 96.

Ka rongo te poo, ka rongo te poo   The night hears, the night hears
Tuia i te kaawai tangata i heke mai   Bind the lines of people coming down
I Hawaiki nui, I Hawaiki roa,   From great Hawaiki, from long Hawaiki
I Hawaiki paamamao   From Hawaiki far away
I hono ki te wairua, ki te whai ao   Bind to the spirit, to the day light
Ki te Ao Maarama!   To the World of Light!

6

Some thoughts on Native Hawaiian attitudes towards Captain Cook

PAULINE NAWAHINEOKALA'I KING

Captain James Cook on his third voyage of exploration created the circumstances that resulted in the beginning of modern Hawaiian history,[1] for a major consequence of the voyage was the opening of the northeastern quadrant of the Pacific Ocean, including the Hawaiian Islands, to world commerce and international politics. The effects on the eight populated Polynesian islands were revolutionary. The four domains ruled by high chiefs of Kaua'i, O'ahu, Maui, and Hawai'i were united into one kingdom. The subsistence economy was transformed by its role in trans-Pacific commerce. Its cultural life gradually blended with Christian-British-American values to create a new Hawaiian society that was neither ancient Hawaiian nor typically western. Change has occurred so swiftly over the last 225 years that Hawaiians today identify the changes that they feel have been most detrimental to them as a people and see them in a negative light.

Towards Cook, Native Hawaiians[2] have mixed feelings. A number consider him to be a brilliant navigator, geographer, scientist – a remarkable and admired man. A larger number, if they think of him at all, are more or less indifferent about forming an opinion on the subject. The largest number, or perhaps it is better to characterise them as the most vocal, regard him with hostility and bitterness.

Today, Hawai'i is experiencing the force of the contemporary indigenous movements that seek to assert the dignity and richness of native cultures unhampered by misrepresentations of their past by western interpreters. In this context, it has not been difficult to identify Captain Cook with western imperialism, colonialism, dependency, capitalism, greed – whatever the popular epithet might be. And many do. A more serious group use the current interest

---

[1] Whether the Spaniards visited the Islands, traded with Hawaiians, and left before Cook's arrival, does not change this statement. Spanish visits have yet to be proven and there is no hard evidence that they had any significant influence on the Islands, although there are indications that castaways, probably Spanish, were washed ashore.

[2] In recent years the term 'Native Hawaiian' has become one used in legislation and in social programmes to distinguish this particular group. The term is best identified by capitalising it.

in non-western cultures to conduct research into the ancient past for under-standing themselves and their forebears. Even among these investigators Cook is not admired. Their first criticism points to the introduction of disease – venereal – through the Cook expedition. They cannot consider the massive depopulation of the Hawaiian people in the eighteenth and nineteenth centuries without pointing to this introduction on Kaua'i or Ni'ihau in January or February 1778, and again on the ships' return in November. Secondly, they question Cook's allowing himself to be worshipped by the *Lono* priests as an incarnation of the god, *Lono*. How could this man from a western culture accept a pagan religious ceremony unless he was mocking it? Other minor comments are made to the detriment of the reputation of Captain Cook.

Native Hawaiian historians and researchers[3] are delving into their past through traditional research methods including oral histories. They also ana-lyse by performing or recreating an event or ceremony, incorporating art, poetry and music. Their purpose is to take the culture as a whole including both physical and metaphysical aspects in the context of place and time. For example, it is obvious to them that the Hawai'i of modern times is directly the creation of a *wohi*[4] chief from Hawai'i Island named Kamehameha. Modern Hawaiian history began with the revolutionary changes that he instituted over the Islands from 1795, sixteen years after Cook's ships departed.

Perhaps, then, the consideration of the ancient past has eluded the writers of many contemporary studies, particularly those in the academic professions. It is the purpose of Native Hawaiian historians to explore the past in their own terms. They realise that it is a difficult process as they are faced with an ancient society superimposed with Christian and materialistic precepts. Moreover, their work, while central to their personal and group interest, has had little influence on academic historians and anthropologists.

It is the purpose of this chapter to consider the issue of indigenous history and its importance by taking the comments and work of two Native Hawaiian historians, examining these comments in their historical context, and iden-tifying how their work has added a significant dimension to an understand-ing of Hawai'i's past. Although their interest in Captain Cook on Hawai'i is of secondary importance to them, no history of these Islands can ignore the experiences of Cook and his crews in 1778 and 1779. Finally, an attempt will be made to indicate how indigenous history informs the work of the professional historian.

Dr Jerry A. Walker, Jr. and Richard K. Paglinawan have multiple interests in Hawaiian themes. Walker is working on such aspects of the past as genealogy,

---

[3] Native Hawaiian historians, as distinct from historians of the Hawaiian Islands, concern themselves primarily with their ancient culture, and how the precepts and customs from the past continue and/or change in modern times. Historians of Hawai'i encompass the totality of the past including the present.

[4] This rank is considered to be more or less a third rank. The *ni'aupi'o* and *naha* are higher in rank than the *wohi*.

Hawaiian martial arts, and training for war. Paglinawan has studied for many years with Hawaiian experts and is an important source of knowledge about the past. He is now concentrating on Hawaiian martial arts and a detailed examination of the Makahiki Festival. Both have opinions on the importance of Captain Cook in Hawai'i.

Introduction to firearms

'Discovery?' asks Dr Jerry Walker.[5] 'If Cook had not landed here, someone else would have. And in about the same era. To me, the visits of Captain George Vancouver in 1792, '93, and '94 are much more significant. Kamehameha agreed to place his Island under the protection of the British monarch. It is the beginning of diplomatic relations that led to the Kingdom of Hawai'i.' 'The major influence of Captain Cook', he continued, 'was the demonstration he and his men gave us of western weapons. We experienced the effect of muskets and cannon both when they were used to kill and when they were shot as a warning. By the time the British left the archipelago we had learned the range of their cannon and knew how to move out of harm's way.'[6]

Firearms for Cook were a form of defence against the alien peoples he met on his expeditions. He himself did not believe in using muskets and cannon as a hostile expedient. And Cook had had many experiences in meeting such peoples. His crew numbers were small in comparison to the crowds who gathered to see the strangers. He knew Polynesians saw his ships as luxurious islands of 'power' with quantities of iron everywhere. Hawaiians were eager to know more about the *haole*.[7] Islanders crushed around the British, touching them, as well as taking whatever iron object they could lift. Firearms were then used to control the situation, preferably shot over the heads of the Hawaiians. Shooting to kill was held to be a last resort by Cook. Unfortunately, sometimes his men were unable to follow his orders as they became frightened by the swirling mobs around them.

The first sound of gunfire occurred at Waimea, Kaua'i, on 20 January 1778, the second day of contact between the British and the Islanders. Cook wrote in his journal that when Lieutenant John Williamson was sent on shore to check out potentials for supplies and fresh water,

> the Indians coming down to the boat in great numbers . . . and pressed so thick upon
> him that he was obliged to fire, by which one man was killed. But this unhappy

---

[5] Dr Jerry Walker received his Ph.D. in public health from the University of Hawaii. He has worked for thirty years for the State of Hawaii on public health issues, education and Hawaiian affairs. He has published two collaborative works: one on the Kamehameha genealogy and a second on Hawaiian martial arts.
[6] Author's discussion with Dr Jerry Walker, 4 August 2002.
[7] *Haole* refers to the 'stranger'. Through usage it now refers to 'westerners'.

circumstance I did not know till after we left the islands. . . . It did not appear to M'r Williamson that they had any design to kill or even hurt any of the people in the boat but were excited by mere curiosity to get what they had from them, and were at the same time, ready to give in return any thing they had.[8]

William Griffin described the incident saying that 'the natives flocking around the boat though with no hostile intent, he [Williamson] shot one of them a Cowardly, dastardly action for which Cap't Cook was very angry'.[9] David Samwell reported that the Islanders 'were astonished at the report of the Gun'.[10] In Williamson's explanation, he gave an indication of the response of the Islanders to the incident:

the man that was shot was a tall handsome man about 40 years of age & seemed to be a Chief, the ball entering his right pap, he instantly dropt down dead in y'e water, y'e natives seeing the surface of the water cover'd with blood immediately quitted y'e boat & fled to y'e shore [and later returned] took up y'e dead body & carried it along the beach, upon the shoulders of six men stretched full length, & were followed by hundreds of the natives.[11]

The news of this extraordinary event, these remarkable men, incredible possessions, and quantities of iron was passed down the chain of islands immediately after the two ships left Kaua'i. The stick that breathed fire and killed was also noted.

When the ships returned to the Islands about ten months later in November 1778, they hovered off the northern coast of Maui. There they met the ali'i nui of Hawai'i Island, Kalaniopu'u. He was on Maui with his army preparing for battle with the ali'i nui of that island, Kahekili. The British also met Kalaniopu'u's nephew, Kamehameha, a young chief who had already established his reputation as a great warrior. Looking for a safe harbour, Cook led the two ships from Maui around the Island of Hawai'i, sailing from the north down the east coast of the Island , around the southern point, and about halfway up the western coast. At Kealakekua, Cook decided the two ships could find safe berths in the Bay. To Hawai'i Islanders this journey replicated the circuit of the god, Lono. In his manifestation as the great chief, Lono travelled north from his resident area of Kealakekua, down the east coast of Hawai'i, around South Point, and halfway up the western coast until he reached his starting point at Kealakekua. He then left, promising to return again, bringing with him great riches. The Islanders elevated him to a place as one of the four major gods in their pantheon,[12] and celebrated his story with an annual festival, the Makahiki Festival.

---

[8] *RDV*, p. 267.
[9] *RDV*, p. 267 n. 1.
[10] *RDV*, p. 1083.
[11] *RDV*, p. 1348.
[12] *RDV* The four major gods were *Kane, Ku, Kanaloa, Lono.*

As the two ships approached the Bay, about a thousand canoes surrounded them. Cook noted that 'not a man had with him a weapon of any sort'. He thought that trade and curiosity were their only motivation. There were so many Hawaiians crowding on board and surrounding his ship that he considered 'this is a good opportunity to shew them the use of firearms. . . . As it was not intended that any of the Shot should take effect, the Indians seemed rather more surprised than frightened.'[13] Samwell also described the scene: 'We have had more Canoes about us to day than in any place this Voyage. . . . Capt'n Cook ordered 2 or 3 of the great guns to be fired with ball in order to shew the Chiefs the effect of them & to what distance they would carry, at which they were much astonished.'[14]

By 14 February 1779, the Islanders knew the difference between 'small shot' and 'shot with a ball'. They knew the second killed, and they knew the range of the cannon balls. In circumstances where friendly relations between the two groups no longer existed, the Islanders did not fear the guns and cannon. Those circumstances came to pass on 14 February 1779. On that day the British did not realise that the Hawai'i Islanders had become accustomed to their fire power, and even Cook assumed that his superiority in firearms would protect him from the Hawaiians. John Law reported that Cook believed that 'the blast of a musket would disperse the whole island',[15] while James Burney wrote that Cook 'was very positive the Indians would not stand the fire of a single musket. Indeed, so many instances occurred which have all helped to confirm this opinion that it is not to be wondered at if everybody thought the same.'[16]

Instead, on the fatal day when Cook went ashore at Ka'awaloa to invite Kalaniopu'u aboard the *Resolution* to hold him captive until the ship's stolen property was returned, the Hawai'i Islanders appeared hostile even when faced with the threat of firearms. As a result of trying to protect their Chief, the Islanders turned to violence. A riot broke out and Cook and four marines were killed. After Cook's death there was a period of bitter fighting between the British and the Islanders. The ships bombarded the villages with cannon and destroyed property. But the Islanders retreated beyond the range of the cannon and fought back with surprising resolution.

Captain Charles Clerke, now in charge of the expedition, established peace with the assistance of the *Lono* priest. Once the remains of Cook were returned to the British and a solemn burial performed at Kealakekua Bay, Captain Clerke insisted that the ship had to be repaired. When this work was completed, the British left the Islands.

---

[13] *RDV*, p. 490.

[14] *RDV*, p. 1158.

[15] John Law, 'Journal of Cook's Third Voyage': microfilm 1205 (old series), University of Hawaii Hamilton Library, typescript, p. 17. Original in British Library.

[16] James Burney, 'Journal of the Proceedings of the Discovery': microfilm 697 (old series), University of Hawaii Hamilton Library. Original in Mitchell Library, Sydney.

The use of firearms was immediately recognised by the *ali'i nui* as the means to advance their ambitions. The eighteenth century was one of periodic warfare, as Ralph Kuykendall notes: 'Until the year 1796, war was the characteristic note in the islands, with various chieftains engaged in a fierce struggle for supremacy. The actual fighting was intermittent, but until supremacy was settled, the warring chiefs grasped every chance to strengthen their positions.'[17] The subsistence economy could not support long periods of warfare. The limitations of native weapons prevented chiefs from achieving their ambitions. Sometimes a chief was able to unite all districts of an island only to have it split into warring districts again. As soon as a chief achieved some control over his island, he would launch an attack against the chief of a neighbouring island.

The British arrival opened a major trade route between China and the Pacific Northwest. The Hawaiian Islands became a way-stop on that route. As soon as trading vessels began to make regular calls at the Islands, chiefs turned to the possibility of obtaining cannon, muskets and ammunition. They employed foreigners as interpreters, assistants in trading arrangements, and trainers of their warriors in the use of firearms. By 1795 there had been about forty-one visits by trading vessels, both British and American.

Weapons were not immediately a trade item. At first western traders would not sell firearms. The chiefs' relationships with the ship captains were often hostile and arbitrary. As an alternative, Islanders resorted to stealing cables and anchors from western ships and trading them back to the merchant. Market demands were met. Traders began to sell weapons to ambitious chiefs beginning about 1790. By 1793 all *ali'i nui* had stockpiles of western weapons as well as western advisers and employees.

A direct result of Cook's expedition, then, was the ultimate conquest of all Hawai'i Island, all Maui, Lana'i, and Moloka'i, and all O'ahu by Kamehameha of Hawai'i Island by the late summer of 1795. Immediately Kamehameha began to reorganise the conquered territory and at the same time he prepared for the invasion of the last holdout: Kaua'i. By 1804 Kamehameha

> had a reported arsenal of 600 muskets, 14 cannon, 40 swivels, and 6 small mortars. . . . The fleet carrying Kamehameha's army to O'ahu included twenty to thirty vessels of European model, some copper-bottomed, averaging perhaps twenty or twenty-tons burthen . . . also the famous peleleu fleet: a great number of European rigged, Hawaiian-hulled double canoes . . . with some seven to eight thousand warriors.[18]

---

[17] Ralph Kuykendall, *The Hawaiian Kingdom, 1778–1854* (Honolulu, 1953), I, p. 22.
[18] Patrick Kirch and Marshall Sahlins, *Anahulu: The Anthropology of History in the Kingdom of Hawaii* (Chicago, 1992), I, p. 43.

Native Hawaiian historians find Kamehameha a source of continuing study as a great hero, a remarkable warrior, an astute politician and diplomat, and a canny trader. He is admired as a man who adjusted to the modern world while still remaining true to his Hawaiian heritage. His use of western firearms, his continuing battles, and his massive preparations for war from 1782 to 1804 are viewed in a positive light as part of his wisdom in using all at his command to unite the Islands. A single kingdom was then prepared to cope with modern realities. These historians acknowledge that the introduction of the use of firearms by Cook is one legacy of the British expedition that they consider a benefit to Hawaiians.

Cook and Kamehameha

What was Kamehameha's relationship with Cook? The two men are in themselves symbolic of two fundamental themes in Island culture. Cook represented the god *Lono*, symbolising peace in the four months of the Makahiki season. Kamehameha represented the tradition of the warrior watched over by the god *Ku*, symbolising war in the eight months following Makahiki.

As noted above, the British arrived at a point in Island history when a great warrior chief was attempting to achieve his ambition to become the unifier of the Islands into a kingdom. Once Kamehameha had won by warfare all Islands except Kaua'i by the summer of 1795, he was able to bring Kaua'i under his control by agreement in 1810. He entered into trade with merchant sea captains and began to negotiate with European naval officers. He was described in their logs and journals, and his reputation spread beyond the Islands. Often he was referred to as 'The Great Kamehameha' and 'The Napoleon of the Pacific'.[19]

The timing of the British visits was such that Cook was identified as the living manifestation of a Hawaiian god. When Cook stepped on shore on Hawai'i Island on 17 January 1779, he was accompanied by a man the British learned was a priest. On shore, at the priest's direction, Islanders greeted the Captain with the name 'Erono' and the crowds recognised the Captain with the prostration *kapu*. Thereafter he was always referred to as *Lono I ka Makahiki*, Lono of the Makahiki. The recognition accorded Cook led to his veneration by Hawai'i Islanders but eventually resulted in his death.

How did this come about? A repetition of the chronology of the two visits by the British will help identify the issue from the Native Hawaiian point of view. The British first stopped at Kaua'i and Ni'ihau between 18 January and 2 February 1778. The two ships returned off Maui Island in November of 1778 and finally anchored in Kealakekua Bay on Hawai'i Island on 17 January 1779.

---

[19] See Stephen L. Desha, *Kamehameha and His Warrior Kekuhaupi'o*, trans. Frances N. Frazier (Honolulu, 2000), p. 22 and throughout.

Cook was killed on 14 February 1779. Both visits occurred during the Makahiki season, and for the Native Hawaiian historian, the issue becomes one of how to understand the meaning of that season as it was known in ancient days.

Richard Paglinawan[20] is a Native Hawaiian scholar who has spent many years studying ancient Hawaiian culture with such experts as Mary Kawena Pukui. His admiration for Kamehameha has led him to study Makahiki among many other subjects related to the great Chief. This concentration has resulted in his reaching interesting conclusions about Kamehameha and his role in the interpretation of the Festival.[21] Paglinawan has formed a group called 'Pa Kuʻi a Kua' which studies all aspects of Makahiki. Members make the tools and fabrics used at the time, recreate the religious ceremonies and games conducted then, and check the research materials. Each fall they hold an annual ceremony mirroring the Makahiki Festival, and on one day they conduct a Makahiki procession open to the public.

Paglinawan uses the most detailed description of the events of Makahiki, written by the Hawaiian scholar, David Malo.[22] Malo was born about 1793, was educated by American Protestant missionaries, and died in October 1858. He was a devoted supporter of Kamehameha and his successors. Paglinawan also refers to the work of the first Hawaiian historian, Samuel Kamakau,[23] who was born in October 1815, educated by American Protestant missionaries at Lahainaluna Seminary, and died in 1876. He wrote articles in the Hawaiian language newspapers, many of which have been translated into English and published. He also was an admirer of Kamehameha. Paglinawan took his group to Hawaiʻi Island and used Malo's essay to duplicate the record on the ground. By this means and with the totality of the work of his group, he has concluded that Malo's description is of the Festival as it was re-created after Kamehameha united all the Islands except Kauaʻi. One of the Chief's techniques for control and the unification of his recent conquests was to extend the cultural practices of Hawaiʻi Island uniformly over the conquered islands. But now, Paglinawan discovered, the Chief-become-King changed much of the ceremony and its emphases to suit his objectives.

Among the innovations Paglinawan identifies is the name of the Festival image. Where once the image was called *Lono Makua*, now it was called *Lono I ka Makahiki*, the very name given to Cook when he landed on the Island of Hawaiʻi. Kamehameha also added many aspects to the ceremonies that were

---

[20] Richard Paglinawan has worked extensively as an executive in Hawaiian organisations in the Hawaiian Homes Lands and the Office of Hawaiian Affairs, and in social services for the State of Hawaii. He is now project manager for the Queen Emma Foundation.

[21] Author's discussions with Paglinawan during spring and summer 2002 up to final interview on 9 August 2002; hereafter cited as Paglinawan discussions.

[22] David Malo, *Hawaiian Antiquities*, trans. Nathaniel B. Emerson (Honolulu, 1951), pp. 141–59.

[23] Samuel Kamakau, *Ka Poʻe Kahiko*, trans. Mary Kawena Pukui (Honolulu, 1964/1991), pp. 19–21.

part of the traditions from all the conquered islands. For example, Paglinawan
has collected photographs of the many images that Kamehameha added to
his depiction of the Festival. These images had been used in the celebration
on Maui, Moloka'i and O'ahu. 'He added them to his repertoire, so to speak',
notes Paglinawan. Another innovation was the ka'ai or casket woven of sennit
that was strapped to a pole and added to the ceremonial processions. It was
reported to contain the bones and possessions of Captain Cook. Paglinawan
has noted that these innovations introduced by Kamehameha were all part of
his programme to bring peace and unity to his Kingdom. He often expressed
sorrow at Cook's death. It was an unfortunate incident which should be kept
in the past; Cook should be admired as a great navigator, and his memory held
in esteem.[24]

How does Paglinawan's work conflict with or modify the present interpretations of the period and the man by professional historians and anthropologists?
It appears that here is an example of how western interpreters have mis-
construed the Hawaiian past. The story of Cook worshipped as a Hawaiian
god has captured the imagination of Americans and Europeans ever since the
knowledge of the events surrounding Cook's death reached the western world.
The Hawai'i-Cook story shows that history and mythology are one. Makahiki,
then, has become one of the most studied aspects of ancient Hawaiian culture.
The competition between two religious groups is a familiar theme in western
history. The famous event has led to many interpretations, often simplistic,
explaining its inner meaning. The bibliography is extremely large as scholars
mull over the events of January and February 1779.

Marshall Sahlins has been the leading scholar in recent years in the
published accounts and interpretations of Cook in Hawai'i. His *Historical
Metaphors and Mythical Realities* set out his interpretation of Hawai'i's past
including the acceptance of Cook as a manifestation of the god *Lono*.[25] His
work has been challenged on many counts. One criticism has been to question
whether Hawaiians venerated Cook as a manifestation of the god, or if there
was even a Makahiki Festival in the ancient society before the Islands were
influenced by western material goods and capitalistic imperialism. Sahlins
has responded to this criticism from those he calls the 'Copenhagen group'.[26]
He analysed their sources and arguments and found them lacking in knowledge of fundamental factors of the period under question. He believes that
their commitment to historical materialism in their interpretation of history
caused their misunderstanding of Hawai'i's past.

---

[24] Information in this and preceding paragraph from Paglinawan discussions.
[25] Marshall Sahlins, *Historical Metaphors and Mythical Realities: Structure in the Early History
of the Sandwich Island Kingdom* (Ann Arbor, 1981).
[26] See Steen Bergendorff, Uta Hasager and Peter Henriques, 'Mythopraxis and history: on
the interpretation of the Makahiki', *Journal of the Polynesian Society*, 97 (1988), pp. 391–408;
Sahlins's answer, 'Captain Cook in Hawaii', appeared in the *Journal*, 98 (1989), pp. 371–425.

A later challenge came in 1992 when Gananath Obeyesekere debunked Sahlins's claim that Hawaiians accepted Cook as one of their gods. In his work, *The Apotheosis of Captain Cook: European Mythmaking in the Pacific*, he identified the theory with the myth of imperialism, civilisation and conquest, and claimed that Sahlins was perpetuating the myth of the western civiliser of savages. His work caused an explosion of articles, panels of discussion at history and anthropology conferences, and lectures on the subject in university classes. At first Sahlins 'thought to let it pass'. He wrote that he felt Obeyesekere had such a 'flimsy case' that the scholarly professions would 'perceive the humbug he put out about my work'. Instead, he learned that the American Society for Eighteenth Century Studies had awarded Obeyesekere's book the Louis Gottschalk prize for 1992. As a result Sahlins published his own work, *How 'Natives' Think: About Captain Cook For Example*, in which he challenged the idea that, as a native Sri Lankan, Obeyesekere had a 'privileged insight into how Hawaiians thought'.[27]

To Richard Paglinawan it is immaterial whether history can best be understood by historical materialism, by structuralism, by world systems analysis, or by any other historical model. He believes that much of the academic concern about the Islands' past misrepresents what the ancients thought by placing their history in a foreign context. Instead, through study and doing, he believes that Native Hawaiian historians have a more sensitive understanding of the thinking of the ancients. He has emphasised for many years the concept of duality in Hawaiian thinking where all principles combine with their opposite to form a perfect and harmonious whole. In his study of the Hawaiian martial art, *Lua*, he emphasises this principle. In western thinking, there often tends to be the opposition of forces, and an either/or conceptual form. Thus, in the instance of Cook in Hawai'i, writers tend to posit Cook against Kamehameha, or peace against its alternative, war.[28]

How does his work inform our understanding of the period? First, it is useful to describe Makahiki as we know it from the work of scholars who have depended primarily on Malo's essay. E. S. Craighill Handy and Elizabeth Green Handy in collaboration with Mary Kawena Pukui have noted this Hawai'i Island connection. They state that Malo's

> reference . . . to the names of the months preceding and during the festival accord with the nomenclature of the island of Hawaii, but not with the month names used on the other islands. . . . The celebration differed on other islands, undoubtedly. . . . The Makahiki festival in honor of Lono commenced with the first rising of the

---

[27] Marshall Sahlins, *How 'Natives' Think: About Captain Cook For Example* (Chicago, 1995), p. 1.

[28] Information in this paragraph from Paglinawan discussions; see also his 'The art of Lua: Hawaiian martial arts', Hawaiian Cultural Lecture Series, Kamehameha Schools Press, 9 May 1991.

constellation of the Pleiades over the horizon at sunset (as seen in Kona, presumably from Lono's temple Hiki'au at Kealakekua).[29]

Most writers agree that the Festival lasted for about four months from the end of October until early in February. It was also the rainy season when storms over land and rough seas made it necessary for the farmer and the fisherman to refrain from their usual duties. Instead, the period was devoted to *Lono* in his specific form that appeared only at Makahiki time. The period opened with a formal procession of the carrying of an image of the god used only at Makahiki. The image was named *Lono Makua* or *Lono* the Father, as noted above. The image was a long pole with a face carved at its top. For the season a crosspiece was lashed about a third of the way down from the face. Strips of tapa cloth were hung from the crosspiece and ferns adorned the image. Throughout the four months, a grand procession of the image accompanied by other images, sennit caskets, and important artefacts was conducted from district to district on an island. After taxes were paid and solemn religious ceremonies performed, the district was free to begin a period devoted to poetry, music and dance, and boxing matches. At the end of Makahiki the image was undressed and that personification of the god was placed in a specific *heiau* or temple until the following year. During Makahiki war was forbidden in general and absolutely for at least one month during the season. Besides the religious ceremonies, the tax collecting, the boxing matches and games, the dance and poetry, the season ended with the reaffirmation of the authority of the ruling chief.

Along with the worship of the god *Ku*, and intimately intertwined with the war mode, was the power of the highest *ali'i*. His primary activity and responsibility in the eighteenth century was the conduct of war. This included his role as overlord of the *Ku Heiau*, or temples. When Makahiki was over, it was his power alone that could open the *laukini heiau* of *Ku*. Malo states that at the time of Kalaniopu'u's reign, the *Ku* cult, its priests and its adherents dominated society.[30] During the Makahiki season, all Hawaiians acknowledged the ascendancy of *Lono* and participated in the ceremonies and events of the season. But beginning in early February, eager warriors were pressuring and importuning the *ali'i nui* to begin the religious and civil activities in preparation for war. It is apparent that the beginning and end of Makahiki were closely monitored by the *Ku* priesthood, the chiefs, and their warriors.

On the first contact between Islanders and Cook on Kaua'i the Captain was not called *Lono*. But he and Captain Clerke were given the prostration *kapu*, a mass kneeling before the two men, in recognition of their status as leaders or chiefs of the two remarkable ships.[31] On Hawai'i Island, Cook was

---

[29] E.S. Craighill Handy and Elizabeth Green Handy, with Mary Kawena Pukui, *Native Planters of Hawaii: Their Life, Lore, and Environment* (revised edn, Honolulu, 1991), p. 329.
[30] Malo, *Hawaiian Antiquities*, pp. 159–62.
[31] *RDV*, p. 509.

met by a priest, was given the prostration *kapu*, and was led with some of his officers to Hiki'au *heiau*. There, Cook was invested in what was obviously a solemn ceremony. To Islanders the posture and the ceremony were reminiscent of the god in his Makahiki role. The priest held one of Cook's arms extended from his shoulder. The priest directed Lieutenant King to hold Cook's other arm in a similar manner.[32] It was then that Cook was given the name *Lono I ka Makahiki*, *Lono* of the Makahiki . Wherever he went, Hawai'i Islanders called him by that name.

The British realised that their Captain held some religious position for the Islanders, but they appear not to have recognised the superior place of the warrior in the culture. Their ignorance is demonstrated by the attitudes toward, and description of, Kamehameha when they met him on Maui and saw him on Hawai'i. Kamehameha does not appear to have been close to Captain Cook. He was instead friendly with Captain Clerke, who referred to the Hawaiian as 'an old friend of mine'.[33] Others among the visitors expressed a negative opinion of the warrior chief. At his first appearance off Maui, Law noted that 'This young man whose name is Ka Mea Mea is nephew to Kirri Oboo who seems to take great Notice of him and as I suppose a Favourite – tho' for what reason I cant tell as he is one of the Most Savage looking Men I've ever seen here . . .'[34] King recognised the primacy of his place among the men surrounding Kalaniopu'u:

> Maiha-Maiha, whose hair was now paisted over with a brown dirty sort of Paste or Powder, & which added to as savage a looking face as I ever saw, it however by no means seemed an emblem of his disposition which was good natured & humorous; . . . his manners shew'd somewhat of an overbearing spirit & he seem'd to be the Principal director of this interview.[35]

Finally, Samwell referred to him as a chief 'of great consequence . . . but of a clownish & blackguard appearance'.[36]

What the visitors did not understand fully was that Kamehameha was one of the most noted warriors of the Island at that time. His posture, his demeanour, his stride, his hair were all part of his war mode which would come into full play once Makahiki was over.[37] His 'disposition' would also change. During battle he would adopt harsh and fierce expressions and make intimidating gestures. In ancient society one season melds into another when there is a time for war and a time for peace. On 14 February Kamehameha was probably not at Ka'awaloa when Cook was killed. Kekuhaupi'o, his closest friend and

---

[32] *RDV*, pp. 504–6.
[33] *RDV*, p. 545.
[34] *RDV*, pp. 512–13 n. 5.
[35] *RDV*, p. 512.
[36] *RDV*, p. 1190.
[37] See Malo, *Hawaiian Antiquities*, pp. 53–4, 68, 77, 163, 179, 189, 194, 196, 203.

instructor in the arts of war, was there, and was one of the warriors who persuaded Kalaniopuʻu not to board the *Resolution* with Cook.[38] Kamehameha did participate in the days of hostility that followed Cook's death, and was wounded then.[39] He was also one of the great chiefs along with Kalaniopuʻu who wished to establish peace again with the ships' crews.[40] What has happened here between the Hawaiian warrior and the British is the demonstration of the role of the warrior in relation to the priest. To the people of the Islands the periods of war and peace were essential parts of the natural, seasonal, political rhythm.

Paglinawan's interest in Kamehameha has led him to study how the Chief/King deliberately used the Cook legend to add respect to his position as the conqueror of all the Islands except Kauaʻi. He believes that Kamehameha used the legend as part of his pacification process of a united kingdom. As noted above, he changed the name of the Makahiki image and added the sennit casket, both of which were said to refer to the Captain.[41]

Kamehameha had been either preparing for war or in the midst of battle for over twenty years. After his conquests and his agreement with King Kaumualiʻi of Kauaʻi to accept his control over foreign agreements and defence, Kamehameha had achieved a sense of security. He was known now to be affable, outgoing, jolly. The transformation had taken some time. In 1793, when he met Captain George Vancouver, he told the Englishman about his difficulties with his enemies, who were active and restive under his rule.[42] Stories and chants exist that indicate a growing tradition to support his superior standing among all Islanders. One story concerns the *naha* stone. The stone, situated in Kohala on the Island of Hawaiʻi where Kamehameha was born, could only be moved by a chief of the highest rank. Kamehameha moved the stone with great ease. A chant exists that indicates that Kahekili of Maui was his father. While it is impossible to date when the story or chant were first repeated, their importance is clear. Both story and chant have the effect of raising his rank from that of third place to that of second place, from that of *wohi* to *naha*. The *naha* rank is accorded the burning *kapu*, an important privilege in Hawaiian thought.[43]

Besides lauding the memory of Captain Cook, Kamehameha also emphasised the connection between Hawaiʻi and Great Britain. During his lifetime both the man and his country were held in high esteem. After his death in

---

[38] Samuel Kamakau, *The Ruling Chiefs of Hawaii* (revised edn, Honolulu, 1992), p. 102; see also Desha, *Kamehameha and Kekuhaupiʻo*, p. 29 and throughout.

[39] *RDV*, pp. 545, 562.

[40] *RDV*, pp. 566–7.

[41] See Kamakau, *Ruling Chiefs*, ch. XVI, for the changes that Kamehameha instituted over the conquered islands.

[42] W. Kaye Lamb, ed., *The Voyage of George Vancouver, 1791–1795* (London, 1984), III, p. 816.

[43] See Desha, *Kamehameha and Kekuhaupiʻo*, pp. 76–82; Kamakau, *Ka Poʻe Kahiko*, pp. 4–5.

1819 and according to his wishes expressed many years before that date, the Kingdom succeeded to his son Liholiho, a chief who held the rank of *ni'aupi'o/ naha* from his mother and from his Maui and Hawai'i connections. His security as King was supported by a group of chiefs and chiefesses most easily identified as the Maui Ma. During this period and to about 1839, Cook's reputation began to decline. His memory became part of the competition between American and British political and commercial interests of the day. Liholiho and the Maui Ma were in agreement on their control of their own people but divided in their preference for either the United States or Great Britain. Liholiho (Kamehameha II) admired Great Britain, whereas the Maui Ma became more and more connected to American political, cultural and commercial interests.

When the British Government sent HMS *Blonde* under the command of Captain Lord (George Anson) Byron to the Islands in 1825 to return the bodies of Kamehameha II and his queen who had died in London, ugly stories were current about the treatment of Cook's body by Hawaiians.[44] By this date American Protestant missionaries of the American Board of Commissions for Foreign Missions had begun to establish their dominant influence with the Maui Ma. To the missionaries, Cook represented a British influence as well as the cold logic of the scientific spirit. American influence and Christian faith were to be the emphases of the nineteenth century in Hawai'i, during which time the Hawaiians became identified as an ignorant, barbaric, child-like people who believed that a human being could appear on earth as one of their pagan gods.[45] Now there would be a constant denigration of the Hawaiian people and their ancient culture.

Stewart Firth, in an essay, described the colonisers' point of view toward native peoples. Their ethnocentrism can as easily be attached to the western historian and anthropologist He wrote that their 'most significant ideological achievement was the innovation of the Native. . . . The Native lacked European virtues such as application and foresight. His mind – the Native Mind – worked in mysterious ways.'[46] Paglinawan states, 'Today we like to blame the haole for the loss of our culture. Kamehameha contributed his own influence to the process. He did away – emasculated – much of the old ways and set in motion a whole new set of things preparing us for the modern world.'[47] Paglinawan appeared as much saddened by this necessary process as elated by the conqueror's wisdom.

---

[44] See Robert Dampier, ed. Pauline King Joerger, *To the Sandwich Islands on HMS Blonde* (Honolulu, 1971), pp. 35, 119.

[45] Hiram Bingham, *A Residence of Twenty-One Years in the Sandwich Islands* (Rutland, Vt. and Tokyo, 1981, reprint of revised third edn, Hartford, 1849), pp. 30–5.

[46] Stewart Firth, 'Colonial administration and the invention of the Native', in *Cambridge History of the Pacific Islanders* (Cambridge, 1977), p. 262.

[47] Paglinawan discussions.

Dr Dennis Foley of Australia notes that Aboriginal history is often a painful process for the Aboriginal scholar. But he maintains that Aboriginal history can only be understood fully by the Aboriginal scholar. He finds the vocabulary of academia about that history to be a form of colonialism. In colonial thinking indigenous issues are dissected without any recognition of indigenous thinking.[48] His description mirrors the approach of Native Hawaiian historians. They are adamant that their studies must include the thinking of their ancient forebears. They continue to study and assume that they are achieving an understanding of their ancient society that is closest to reality. To these historians, the third voyage of exploration of Captain Cook is peripheral to the central themes of their work. Yet they realise that the records of the British give them a first look at the ancient society. By careful study and explication, these historians add daily to an understanding of the ancient past.

Will the efforts of indigenous historians become part of the resources of the western scholar? Probably not. It appears at present that the thinking of the Westerner and the Native are too far removed from each other. Consider one of the most revealing aspects of the Cook story in the question the *Lono* priest asked Captain Clerke and Lieutenant King when the two were negotiating for a cessation of the warfare between the Hawaiians and the British. 'A Singular question was askd by them, & that was when Erono would return, this was demanded afterwards by others, & what he would do to them when he return'd.'[49] When British ships came again to the Islands, beginning in 1786, Hawaiians again asked the questions: 'Was Lono angry with them?' 'Would Lono forgive them and come again to see them?' The questions were reported by the British with amazement and confusion as to their possible meaning. The ability of Hawaiians to connect human life with divinity baffled these early visitors. And what of present-day Hawaiians who can say with calm authority: 'The myth was true. Lono came and he will come again'?[50]

There are elements where it seems there is a coincidence of thought between the two views of history. A hint of this can be seen in the article of Valerio Valeri, 'The Transformation of a Transformation: A Structural Essay on an Aspect of Hawaiian History (1809–1819)'.[51] Valeri notes that a major problem of the great Chief/King was to unify the islands that he had conquered. An important aspect of the process of unification was to turn away from a society addicted to war to one that placed peace as the foremost objective of society. To accomplish this change, Valeri writes that Kamehameha began to emphasise the worship of *Lono* and to diminish the superiority of the worship of *Ku*. He was assisted in this endeavour by the fact that his *niaupiʻo/naha* son, Liholiho, was a master of the worship of the *Lono* temples and one not trained as a warrior.

---

[48] Dennis Foley, Lecture at University of Hawaii, 4 October 2001.

[49] *RDV*, p. 561.

[50] Comment made to author by Hawaiian language scholars, summer 2002.

[51] In *Social Analysis*, 10 (March 1982), pp. 3–41.

According to Valeri, Kamehameha restored the old *Lono* temples and built new ones where his son dominated the rituals. While Kamehameha, according to Valeri, restored Ku temples and built new ones, he kept them secondary to those temples dominated by Liholiho. These ideas coincide with those of Paglinawan. Indeed, each exponent of the period and the problems of the man, Kamehameha, can contribute information to others on aspects of the period. Valeri, however, is writing from the perspective of a specific historical model, while Paglinawan is investigating modes of thought from a Native Hawaiian perspective.

A Hawaiian historian has said, 'I have read some of the discourses on structuralism, especially those reaching a limen of a new paradigm explaining my ancestors to me so that I can understand how I have come to be what I am today. Interesting.'[52]

---

[52] Remark made to the author, spring 2001.

7

Captain Cook's command of knowledge and space: chronicles from Nootka Sound

DANIEL CLAYTON

Introduction

In an elliptical line in the preface to his edition of Cook's journal of his third voyage, J.C. Beaglehole writes: 'Where Cook went, why he said what he did, the accidents of the weather: all this may be taken as matter of historical geography.'[1] Beaglehole was interested in the geographical circumstances in which Cook worked, and had a great feel for how Cook's writing was influenced by his personality and the diverse pressures placed upon him as a naval commander. Yet in important respects, matters of historical geography, at least as they are construed in the recent critical literature on European exploration, are quite incidental to his portrayal of Cook. Beaglehole whittles down the range of ways in which it is possible to think about Cook's voyages geographically to an underlying, and almost unrelenting, spatial project. Cook is represented as 'a great dispeller of [geographical] illusion', and as a judicious and disinterested observer who was a 'genius of the matter of fact' and had 'a perfectly unassuming and primary wish to tell the truth'.[2] In Beaglehole's mind, Cook painstakingly pursued what one of his midshipmen on the third voyage, George Vancouver, subsequently described as the 'ardour of the present age, to discover and delineate the true geography of the earth'.[3] Beaglehole also saw Cook as an increasingly confident and adept journalist, who, by his third voyage (when he was happy to sail without a civilian naturalist), had gained a firm command over the knowledge that his voyages yielded and how it was to be publicly disseminated by the Admiralty. The agendas and chronicles of Cook's supernumeraries, officers and Admiralty editors, which had an important influence on public perceptions of Cook's voyages, are not ignored by Beaglehole so much as placed in a subordinate position to Cook's 'official' voice.

[1] RDV, p. vii.
[2] J.C. Beaglehole, *The Life of Captain James Cook* (London, 1974), pp. 698, 702; idem, *Cook the Writer: 6th George Arnold Wood Memorial Lecture* (Sydney, 1970), p. 20.
[3] W. Kaye Lamb, ed., *The Voyage of George Vancouver, 1791–1795*, 4 vols (London, 1984), I, pp. 275–6.

In these ways and more, Beaglehole referred questions of knowledge and space – of how the Pacific was represented and encountered – back to Cook, and reinforced the late eighteenth-century image of him as 'the most moderate, humane and gentle circumnavigator who ever went upon discoveries', as Fanny Burney famously described him.[4] Overall, Cook emerges from Beaglehole's immense scholarship as a champion of the European Enlightenment, and particularly its ideals of empirical observation and peaceful contact, which were enshrined in Cook's instructions from the Admiralty.

A latter-day generation of scholars has significantly revised this image of Cook, in part by no longer treating him as the primary focus of attention. It has become commonplace to treat exploration as a complex cultural and spatial practice that mobilised a range of material and imaginative resources (equipment, patronage, publicity, scholarship, myths, and so on), and that stretched well beyond the initiatives and texts of individual explorers such as Cook. Scholars from a range of disciplines now talk of cultures and spaces of exploration.[5] They now talk about the significance of Cook's scientists and artists as well as Cook's journals, and suggest that we should not simply treat 'the space' of Enlightenment exploration as an absolute and pre-existing space that awaits discovery and correct representation by the explorer.[6]

It is with these ideas in mind that recent scholarship on Cook pursues the claim that, while he did not pillage or colonise, his voyages should be situated in a wider history of imperial appropriation. Since the late 1950s, a growing body of scholarship has probed the interplay between knowledge, power, profit and dominion that infused Europe's eighteenth-century exploration of the Pacific, and shown that scientific, commercial and political motives for Cook's voyages were deeply intertwined.[7] It now seems clear that the Pacific was a

---

[4] Charlotte Barrett, ed., *Diary and Letters of Madame D'Arblay*, vol. 1: *1778–1781* (London, 1904), p. 318. On late eighteenth- and nineteenth-century images of Cook, see Bernard Smith, 'Cook's posthumous reputation', in Robin Fisher and Hugh Johnston, eds, *Captain James Cook and His Times* (Vancouver and London, 1979), pp. 159–86.

[5] See, for example, Felix Driver, *Geography Militant: Cultures of Exploration and Empire* (Oxford, 2000); Rod Edmond, *Representing the South Pacific: Colonial Discourse from Cook to Gauguin* (Cambridge, 1997); Nicholas Jardine, James Secord and Emma Spary, eds, *Cultures of Natural History* (Cambridge, 1996).

[6] See, for example, David Philip Miller and Peter Hans Reil, eds, *Visions of Empire: Voyages, Botany and the Representation of Nature* (Cambridge, 1996); Bernard Smith, *Imagining the Pacific: In the Wake of the Cook Voyages* (New Haven, 1992); Nicholas Thomas and Diane Losche, eds, *Double Visions: Art Histories and Colonial Histories in the Pacific* (Cambridge, 1999); David N. Livingstone and Charles W.J. Withers, eds, *Geography and Enlightenment* (Chicago, 1999). These assumptions about space are enshrined in Beaglehole's work and can still be found in more recent work on Cook – see, most recently, John Robson, *Captain Cook's World: Maps and the Life and Voyages of James Cook R.N.* (Seattle, 2000).

[7] See Vincent T. Harlow, *The Founding of the Second British Empire*, 2 vols (London, 1953, 1964); Bernard Smith, *European Vision and the South Pacific, 1768–1850: A Study in the History of Art and Ideas* (Oxford, 1960); Glyndwr Williams, *The British Search for the*

crucial testing-ground for the imperial ambitions of European empirical science. The practices of navigation, mapping, surveying, collecting, classification and textual and visual representation that were brought to, and honed in, the Pacific did not merely advance European knowledge. They also worked as tools of empire by encoding cultural difference in Eurocentric terms and by fostering new forms of governmentality over people and nature.[8] Greg Dening, for example, has observed that in 'acting out their scientific, humanistic selves' in the Pacific, European nations also 'jostled to see what the Pacific said to them of their relations of dominance'. The late eighteenth century, he continues, 'was as a time of intensive theatre of the civilised to the native, and of even more intense theatre of the civilised to one another'.[9]

Such critical perspectives have flourished in the context of post-war decolonisation and the postcolonial recognition that, while formal colonial power has largely been dismantled, Eurocentric understandings and colonial stereotypes regarding non-European lands and peoples live on. Cook is still celebrated as a culture-hero in countries such as Australia and New Zealand, and remains a focal point for narratives of patriotic discovery in Britain. But for some formerly colonised peoples, and many Native groups, he stands for a history of colonial violence and dispossession.[10] Indeed, some of Cook's senior officers attributed his death in Hawai'i in 1779 to their captain's violent temper, and this side of Cook was not lost on members of British high society.[11] In other words, how the history of European exploration is to be written has long been and remains a profoundly contested question.

Rod Edmond has recently noted that Cook's voyages continue to fascinate diverse scholars and a scattered 'postcolonial' public because they are 'emblem-

---

Northwest Passage in the Eighteenth Century (London, 1962). More recently, see Patrick Brantlinger, *Fictions of State: Culture and Credit in Britain, 1694–1994* (Ithaca, 1996); John Gascoigne, 'Motives for European exploration of the Pacific in the age of Enlightenment', *Pacific Science*, 54 (2000), pp. 227–43; David Mackay, *In the Wake of Cook: Exploration, Science and Empire, 1780–1801* (London, 1985); Glyndwr Williams, 'The Pacific: exploration and exploitation', in P. J. Marshall, ed., *The Oxford History of the British Empire*, II, *The Eighteenth Century* (Oxford, 1998), pp. 552–75.

[8] See, particularly, John Gascoigne, *Science in the Service of Empire: Joseph Banks, the British State and the Uses of Science in the Age of Revolution* (Cambridge, 1998).

[9] Greg Dening, *Performances* (Chicago, 1996), p. 109.

[10] On Australia, see Deborah Bird Rose, 'Worshipping Captain Cook,' *Social Analysis*, 34 (1993), pp. 43–9. For broader genealogies and wider discussions of this anti-Cook sentiment, see Gananath Obeyesekere, *The Apotheosis of Captain Cook: European Mythmaking in the Pacific* (Princeton, NJ, 1992); Robert Borofsky, 'Cook, Lono, Obeyesekere, and Sahlins', in CA Forum on theory in anthropology, *Current Anthropology*, 38 (1997), pp. 255–65.

[11] Edmund Burke, for example, was acquainted with a number of Cook's officers and noted that one of them, James King, 'never spoke of him [Cook] but with respect and regret. But he lamented the Roughness of his manners and the violence of his temper.' P.J. Marshall and John Woods, eds, *The Correspondence of Edmund Burke*, VII, *January 1792 – August 1794* (Cambridge, 1968), p. 589.

atic of our own period's difficult relation to the Enlightenment'. They continue to raise important questions about that period's belief in the potentially universal 'brotherhood of humankind', and our current postcolonial awareness of the insidious and violent ends to which this Enlightenment worldview was put.[12] Cook's voyages remain meaningful to us, as they did to Cook's contemporaries, precisely because they open up much wider questions about the impossibility of producing a true or authentic knowledge about the other. Among other things, then, scholarship on figures such as Cook has to be mindful of what Edward Said has called 'the power to narrate'.[13] It has to account for how and why some stories about exploration and contact became authoritative, and others were denigrated and ignored.

This chapter brings these issues to bear on Cook's encounter with the Nuu-chah-nulth people of 'Nootka Sound' on 'Vancouver Island' in 1778, during his third voyage.[14] Cook stayed at Nootka Sound for a month, repairing and re-supplying his ships before he advanced north. This was the first encounter of any length between Europeans and Native people in the region, and, as I will explain at the end of the chapter, one that has a special place in the annals of western Canadian history. One of my aims here is to fracture the idea that this encounter confers a single or simple historical meaning. Rather, I try to read this encounter geographically, and as a point of both dialogue and departure between the past and present. I will draw on a range of historical information and some rich but little-known ethnographic material pertaining to initial contact at Nootka Sound in order to decentre established ideas (like Beaglehole's) about Cook's command of knowledge and space. Conceived thus, the chapter explores the relationship between authorship and authority on Cook's voyages, with particular reference to Nootka Sound, and concludes with some observations about the benefits and pitfalls of decentring historical truth into a plethora of partial and situated positions.

The central premise of the chapter is that questions of geography and space should not be construed as independent or inconsequential variables in the

---

[12] Rod Edmond, review of the 1999 re-issue of *The Journals of Captain Cook on his Voyages of Discovery* in *Journal of the Royal Anthropological Institute*, 7 (2001), p. 366.

[13] Edward W. Said, *Culture and Imperialism* (New York, 1993), p. xiii.

[14] I put these two place-names in quotation marks this once in order to register the fact that they are not indigenous names and highlight that processes of naming and mapping were integral to the appropriation of Native land and life by European powers. The Native groups of the western coast of Vancouver Island took Nuu-chah-nulth as their collective name in 1978. Before that Europeans called them 'Nootkans'. Cook initially named the inlet 'King George's Sound', but changed the name at a later date, thinking that 'Nootka' was the indigenous name for the sound. But the Native group he met did not have a single name for the inlet. There are many interpretations of Cook's mistake, starting with that of the Spanish naturalist José Mariano Moziño, who visited the sound in 1792. See his *Noticias de Nutka: An Account of Nootka Sound in 1792*, ed. and trans. Iris H. Wilson Engstrand (Seattle, 1970), p. 67.

contact relations and representational strategies developed and deployed on Cook's voyages. I suggest that there were a number of geographies and spaces inscribed within Cook's travels and encounters, and that it is by delineating their shape that we might start to gain a fuller understanding of the construction of knowledge on Cook's voyages. I will treat Nootka Sound in 1778 as a compound *space of contact* – as a relative space (involving boundaries and divisions), a social space (cross-cut by class and cultural differences), a rhetorical space (involving books and journals), and a cultural space (shaped by competing European and Native worldviews).

Initial contact at Nootka Sound: authorship and representation

Cook entered Nootka Sound on 29 March 1778, and, by evening, his ships, the *Resolution* and *Discovery*, had anchored near the south end of the island in the centre of the Sound (see Plate I). Following is an excerpt from the official account of Cook's third voyage, published in 1784, which was based on Cook's journal of events, reporting his passage into the Sound. By 'official' I mean that this was the account that was sanctioned by the British Admiralty. I also refer to it as 'Douglas's account' because, in the wake of Cook's death, the Admiralty commissioned John Douglas (Canon of Windsor and St Paul's) to edit Cook's journals for publication.

> We no sooner drew near the inlet than we found the coast to be inhabited; and at the place where we were first becalmed, three canoes came off to the ship. In one of these were two men, in another six, and in the third ten. Having come pretty near us, a person in one of them stood up, and made a long harangue, inviting us to land, as we guessed, by his gestures. At the same time he kept strewing handfuls of feathers towards us; and some of his companions threw handfuls of a red dust or powder in the same manner. The person who played the orator, wore the skin of some animal, and held, in each hand, something which rattled as he kept shaking it. After tiring himself with his repeated exhortations, of which we did not understand a word, he was quiet; and then others took it, by turns, to say something. . . . After the tumultuous noise had ceased, they lay at a little distance from the ship, and conversed with each other in a very easy manner; nor did they seem to shew the least surprize or distrust.[15]

For almost two centuries, it was assumed that these were Cook's words. This passage was read as a factual account of first contact at Nootka Sound. It established that Cook and his crew had *been there*, looking and recording.

---

[15] James Cook and James King, *A Voyage to the Pacific Ocean . . . in His Majesty's Ships the Resolution and Discovery . . .*, 3 vols (London, 1784), II, pp. 265–6.

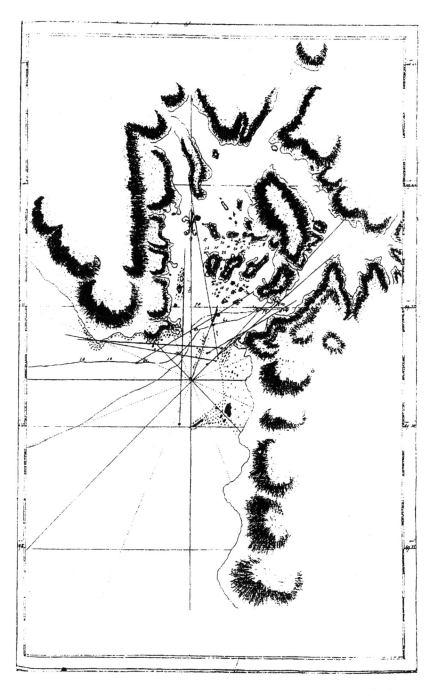

Plate I Thomas Edgar, 'A Plan of King George's Sound' (Nootka Sound), showing the track of Cook's vessels, 29 March 1778. PRO: ADM 55/21, Part 1, fo. 150.

During the eighteenth century, exploration became a resolutely empirical science and European thinkers put a premium on the power of the senses and firsthand observation. As Dorinda Outram and Barbara Stafford have shown, the authority and public appeal of explorers' narratives rested in good measure on the fact that they had seen new lands and people with their own eyes and compiled their observations on the spot. Scientific exploration revolved around what Stafford describes as 'the valorization of the instant' and what Outram sees as the establishment of 'the new' as a category of experience and representation.[16] This passage in the official account undertook to mimic the immediacy of first contact. Cook apparently had no preconceptions about these people, and he recorded what happened in clear, factual prose. Communication at first depended on body language. The inhabitants seemingly showed little surprise at the sight of Cook's ships, and invited Cook to land.

Objectivity, and the supposition that an account was therefore reliable and true, was based on a particular textual stance toward the world. The task of the explorer was to find a transparent mode of literary expression that could duplicate the experience of encountering the new. This stance was tied to notions of disinterestedness and detachment – to the explorer's dedication to observation and commitment not to let the eye wallow in distant memories. The scientific explorer was 'committed to the living of actuality', Stafford observes, yet was meant to work as an 'interloper in a raw world that functions without him'.[17] The passage in the official account contains no value judgements about the Natives' behaviour. Rather, it relates the facts of contact from this position of detachment and implies that the behaviour of the inhabitants was endemic to this particular group of people.

This account of first contact may be objective in the sense that I have sketched the term, but how factual is it? When Beaglehole compared Cook's holographic journal with what was printed in Douglas's account, he discovered that Douglas had altered and embellished Cook's descriptions. Beaglehole's magisterial edition of Cook's journal of his third voyage appeared in 1967, and scholars now generally rely on it rather than the official account, perhaps in the belief that they are reading a truer or more authentic Cook.

This, then, is how first contact at Nootka Sound is recorded in Beaglehole's edition:

> We no sooner drew near the inlet than we found the coast to be inhabited and the people came off to the Ships in Canoes without shewing the least mark of fear

---

[16] Barbara Maria Stafford, *Voyage into Substance: Art, Science, and the Illustrated Travel Account, 1760–1840* (Cambridge, Mass., 1984), p. 28; Dorinda Outram, 'On being Perseus: new knowledge, dislocation, and Enlightenment exploration', in Livingstone and Withers, *Geography and Enlightenment*, pp. 285–7.

[17] Stafford, *Voyage into Substance*, p. 408.

or distrust. We had at one time thirty two Canoes filled with people about us, and a groupe of ten or a dozen remained along side the Resolution most part of the night. They seemed to be a mild inoffensive people, shewed great readiness to part with anything they had and took whatever was offered them in exchange.[18]

This is a shorter statement than Douglas's one, but it is still matter-of-fact and seemingly objective. But is it a disinterested, on-the-spot account? I.S. MacLaren has studied the four basic stages in the evolution of explorers' narratives – from the log book entry, to the journal, to the book manuscript, and finally to these 'official, published accounts'.[19] He shows how, from stage to stage in this sequence, the physical scene of writing becomes more distant, the author relies more on memory, and questions of narrative structure become more central. Cook's journal, MacLaren points out, is a second-stage journal, composed after the fact.

MacLaren's argument can be expanded. Explorers' firsthand observations were tempered by the recollection of other lands and peoples. The particular words and details that gave Cook's and Douglas's accounts of first contact at Nootka Sound their own vitality were drawn from a space of comparison and contrast that had been opened up during the course of Cook's voyages. Each new meeting was made novel by virtue of a singular collection of statements employed to make it differ from others. Here, for example, at Nootka Sound, the Native inhabitants apparently showed little surprise at the arrival of strangers on their shores and threw feathers and dust, whereas in other parts of the Pacific, they appeared hostile and brandished spears.

Historians might read only those parts of Cook's journals that relate to their region of study, but for Cook's eighteenth-century readers, encounters with different peoples made sense as part of a whole.[20] Douglas knew that Cook's journals had a textual momentum and stressed that on his third voyage, especially, Cook had tried to '*relate* as well as to *execute*' his voyage by weaving his observations into a narrative.[21] It is partly for this reason that Douglas's editing of Cook's journal of his third voyage is generally lighter than is his editing of the second voyage, and considerably lighter than John Hawesworth's controversial – and publicly much-discussed – editorial job on the first voyage.[22]

---

[18] *RDV*, p. 295.
[19] I.S. MacLaren, 'Exploration/travel literature and the evolution of the author', *International Journal of Canadian Studies*, 5 (1992), pp. 39–68.
[20] On the consumption and reading of eighteenth-century travel narratives, for which there was a lucrative market, see Charles Batten Jr., *Pleasurable Instruction: Form and Convention in Eighteenth-century Travel Literature* (Berkeley, 1978).
[21] Cook and King, *Voyage to the Pacific Ocean*, I, p. lxxvii (emphasis in original).
[22] For some information on Douglas, see Helen Wallis, 'Publication of Cook's journals: some new sources and assessments', *Pacific Studies*, 1:2 (1978), pp. 163–94.

Cook took on board what Outram sees as one of the Enlightenment's basic epistemological concerns regarding explorers' knowledge: how testimony about the distant and new was to become meaningful and authoritative in metropolitan eyes. This was basic, Outram explains, because Enlightenment philosophers placed great store by probability, the experimental replication of knowledge in the laboratory, and the development of systematic treatises (or what were then often called 'universal histories'). And it was deeply problematical, she continues, because while the metropolitan scientist and scholar depended on the data about the world provided by explorers, explorers' knowledge itself brushed against the grain of probabilism and synthesis precisely because it accentuated novelty and particularity. Outram tries to show how scientific exploration opened up a potentially crippling epistemological chasm between the two spaces of knowledge on which Enlightenment science and philosophy based its cognitive and moral outlook: the field and the study, and their different projects of 'passage and immobility'. 'In the end', she notes, an explorer's knowledge 'could only be accepted on the basis of trust', and a prime way of building trust was through authorship – through a narrative that was based on recognisable and respectable principles of composition.[23]

Nigel Leask has shown that, during the eighteenth century, the most esteemed, if still ultimately awkward, travel narratives were ones like Cook's: narratives that were self-conscious vehicles for the creation of precise knowledge about foreign lands and peoples, and in which curiosity did not lapse into sensationalism.[24] The trustworthy narrative of exploration was one that grappled with similarities and differences, both between non-European peoples and between Europe and the non-European world. Nicholas Thomas observes that Enlightenment explorers were situated within this broad discursive framework in a range of ways, and thinks that it is 'misleading to suggest that there is a divide between the travel narrative and the systematic inquiry or treatise', not least because during the eighteenth century the former underwent 'a good deal of systematization'.[25] Yet he acknowledges that a few works (Forster's *Observations* on Cook's second voyage being one of them) successfully bridged these different modes of enquiry.

Cook was not a savant of science, but he arguably carved himself out a distinctive niche in this general horizon of thought. One of his main narrative tactics was to err towards the elucidation and description of human and material differences between the indigenous peoples he met. Another was to

---

[23] Outram, 'On being Perseus', p. 283.
[24] Nigel Leask, *Curiosity and the Aesthetics of Travel Writing, 1769–1849: 'From an Antique Land'* (Oxford, 2002), pp. 2–12 and *passim*. Also see Dorinda Outram, *The Enlightenment* (Cambridge, 1995), pp. 63–79.
[25] Nicholas Thomas, 'Introduction' to Johann Reinhold Forster, *Observations Made During a Voyage Round the World*, ed. Nicholas Thomas, Harriett Guest and Michael Dettelbach (Honolulu, 1996), p. xv.

judge the similarities and differences between Europeans and Pacific Islanders on the basis of his immediate – visceral and institutional – requirement to protect his ships and crews. And as we will see, yet another was to use the rhetoric of detachment to represent himself as a messenger of British and European civilisation. Cook highlighted differences between indigenous peoples he encountered by pinpointing their specific 'dispositions', and did so, in part, we might surmise, to make his journal more intelligible and trustworthy in the eyes of both a patriotic and science-conscious public. But he also drew comparisons and contrasts between Natives and the British/Europeans that alluded to the corporeal and disciplinary aspects of his command. He wrote at length about Native attitudes to property, trade and theft, and the prostitution of Native women to his sailors, because they weighed heavily on his sense of duty and of the moral distance between the civiliser and the Native.[26] For example, he distinguished the Nootkans from other indigenous groups by emphasising their trading abilities and strong notions of property.[27]

Douglas embellished these narrative tactics (and particularly the first and third of them), both structurally and semantically. He accentuated the Native differences discerned by Cook by dividing the captain's various encounters into chapters that were adorned with lithographs worked up from the sketches and paintings produced by Cook's artist, John Webber.[28] And he filled out the 'manners and customs' sections of Cook's journal, which conventionally follow Cook's chronicles of daily proceedings, in ways that made the 'dispositions' observed by Cook seem more fixed (or given by nature) and less a part of a dynamic and fluid contact situation. Douglas worked with a journal that was less polished than it might have been had Cook lived, and we know that he relied quite heavily in places on the journals of some of Cook's officers (especially that of William Anderson, which, unfortunately, has been lost, and that of James King).

Douglas's editing bears witness to the eighteenth-century propensity to compare and contrast natural and human worlds by projecting European values and models on to other lands and peoples, and ascribing ideas of similarity and difference to particular places, spaces, environments and natures. Thomas notes that Cook's voyages were well equipped to address a set of questions that had long been fundamental to European scholarship and philosophical debate: how a variety of factors (climatic, geographic, demographic, civil and

---

[26] On how this relates to Cook's first voyage, see Alan Bewell, 'Constructed places, constructed peoples: charting the improvement of the female body in the Pacific', *Eighteenth-Century Life*, n.s. 18:3 (1994), pp. 37–54; Bridget Orr, '"Southern passions mix with northern art": miscegenation and the *Endeavour* voyage', *Eighteenth-Century Life*, n.s. 18:3 (1994), pp. 212–21.

[27] See *RDV*, pp. 296–7, 301, 303, 312.

[28] On Webber, see Rudiger Joppien and Bernard Smith, eds, *The Art of Captain Cook's Voyages*, III, *The Voyage of the Resolution and Discovery, 1776–1780* (Melbourne and Oxford, 1987).

historical) created 'material' differences between societies.[29] Douglas entered this broad field of enquiry by trading on the binary of civilisation and savagery that was frequently mobilised to set Europeans apart from 'other' peoples. Cook, he surmised, had sought to spread 'the blessings of civilization' under the guise of trade. And Douglas declared that, 'Comparing themselves with their visitors, they [Pacific Islanders] cannot but be struck with the deepest conviction of their own inferiority, and be impelled, by the strongest motives, to strive to emerge from it.'[30] In this scheme of things, the Nootkans' trading abilities were to be viewed as a sign of such emulation, whereas Native theft was to be taken as confirmation of the steps that the Nootkans still had to take to reach 'civility'.[31]

Yet the relationship – or discursive slippage – between Cook and Douglas does not end here. Cook's textual fabrication of similarity and difference was also connected to the geographical momentum of his voyages. Paul Carter has suggested that Cook tried to capture in writing, and especially in the place-names he bestowed, 'the zigzag map created by his passage' and the physical and imaginative act of exploring.[32] Cook's naming of the eastern Australian coast (with place-names such as 'Botany Bay' and 'Repulse Bay') alludes to his journey itself, Carter suggests; to its dead ends and successes, and to a disagreement between Cook and Banks about how to represent the new. By extension, as Cook approached Nootka Sound and glimpsed what appeared to be an inlet, he bestowed the name 'Hope Bay', signalling his hope at that juncture that he would find a good harbour where he might repair his ships and rest his crews.[33] Cook was not mistaken, of course, but he kept the name because it alluded to his aspirations as he started to close in on the Northwest Passage.

Furthermore, Cook's representations became more intricate as each new encounter proceeded. Cook went back over his journal, adjusting statements and polishing his observations. While his ships were stationary, his journal was still on the move. Toward the end of his journal of events at Nootka Sound, for instance, he tried to reassess the Natives' readiness to trade, and their use of iron. Had such facets of Native life been picked up from Europeans, or were they indigenous? Cook knew that the Spanish had sent explorers to the north Pacific in the mid-1770s, though where, exactly, he did not know. He could not resolve the issue and simply noted that these people 'have been so many years in a manner surrounded by Europeans . . . and who knows how far these

---

[29] Thomas, 'On the varieties of the human species: Forster's comparative ethnology', in Forster, *Observations*, p. xxxci.

[30] Cook and King, *Voyage to the Pacific Ocean*, I, p. lxxvi.

[31] See ibid., II, pp. 270–1. For a fuller discussion of these issues, see Daniel Clayton, *Islands of Truth: The Imperial Fashioning of Vancouver Island* (Vancouver, 2000), pp. 40–9.

[32] Paul Carter, *The Road to Botany Bay: An Essay in Spatial History* (London, 1987), p. 27.

[33] *RDV*, p. 294.

Indian nations may extend their traffick with one another'.[34] Douglas, too, expounded upon the possibility that these people had been contacted before by Europeans, writing that 'They were earnest in their inquiries, by signs, on our arrival, if we meant to settle amongst them; and if we came as friends . . . the inquiry would have been an unnatural one, on a supposition that any ships had been here before; had trafficked . . . and had then departed; for, in that case, they might reasonably expect we would do the same.'[35] In this passage, sixty-five pages on from that which chronicles Cook's arrival at Nootka Sound, Douglas informs us that Cook did understand the Natives' harangues – that they wanted to know why he had visited them. Yet Douglas still suggested that the Natives had only one culturally endemic way of viewing strangers: that they would have reacted to Cook and the Spanish in the same way. Cook, on the other hand, seemed to put parameters around the objectivity of his account of first contact, implying that the inhabitants' initial reaction to his ships was influenced by contact with other strangers.

These complex processes of textual revision and accentuation point to another possible interpretation of the two accounts of initial contact at Nootka Sound that I have been discussing: that Cook, and then Douglas, wrote them as a prospect of things to come; that they served a rhetorical purpose. I will return to this line of enquiry shortly. For now, I want to assess first contact from the margins of Cook's field of vision – in terms of what, retrospectively, we can now say he could not have known and did not discover.

Decentring Cook I: Native testimony

A Spanish vessel anchored near Nootka Sound for two days in August 1774, and in 1789 Native people told an American trader that this Spanish ship had terrified them.[36] Then, in 1792, Native people told a Spanish botanist that they thought this Spanish ship was 'Quautz' (a deity), who was coming 'to punish the misdeeds of the people'.[37] These Native perceptions might usefully be put together with other ethnographic fragments dealing with the arrival of Cook's ships.

In the early twentieth century, Chief George of Nootka Sound related a story about how, one day, the tops of three sticks were seen on the horizon. The sticks were soon identified as a watercraft, and people thought that

---

[34] *RDV*, pp. 321–2.
[35] Cook and King, *Voyage to the Pacific Ocean*, II, pp. 330–1.
[36] Joseph Ingraham to José Estéban Martínez [1789], Mexico City, Archivo General de la Nación, Ramo Historia 65, fos 52–65, in the Freeman Tovell Collection, BCARS Add. MSS. 2826. Also see Martín Fernández Navarette, 'Viajes en las costa al norte de las Californias, 1774–1790', pp. 770–83, Bancroft Library, University of California, P-B 26.
[37] Moziño, *Noticias de Nutka*, p. 66.

Haitetlik, the lightning snake, was propelling it. Others considered it a salmon changed by magic. Still others thought it was the work of Quautz. As the craft got closer, people 'grew very much afraid' and were advised to hide. 'A woman doctor named Hahatsaik, who had power over all kinds of salmon, appeared with a whalebone rattle in each hand; she put on her red cedar bark cape and apron and sang, saying that it must be a salmon turned into a boat.' She called out: 'Hello you, you spring salmon, hello you dog salmon, hello you coho salmon.' A canoe containing another doctor, Wiwai, then went out; then another canoe with Chief Nanaimis and ten strong men went to offer the thing two fine beaver skins. Nanaimis stayed in his canoe but got close enough to the thing to see 'that Cook was not an enchanted salmon, but only a man'. Maquinna, an important Nuu-chah-nulth chief, then went out, saying to Cook, 'I want you to come and stay with me next year.'[38]

Other accounts recorded in the 1970s, and included in a publication that formed part of the Cook bicentennial celebrations, complement this text. In a Native story related by Winifred David, the Native people of the Sound 'didn't know what on earth' was approaching. One of the strange men that appeared had a hooked nose and was thought to be a dog salmon. Another, a hunchback sailor, was in Native eyes a humpback salmon. In another account related by Gillette Chipps, Cook's ship was viewed as a floating island and the Indians danced around it: 'They say Indian doctors go out there singing a song, find out, try to find out what it was. Rattling their rattles.' Cook apparently visited their village, and his blacksmith, Tom, fell asleep in the big house as the Natives danced and entertained the Captain.[39]

In these Native texts, the new and the strange, remembered from the past, have undergone historical translation. The Native people who related these accounts all identified Cook by name. British and American traders came to Nootka Sound in increasing numbers from the mid-1780s onwards, and it is possible that oral histories of these first dealings with non-Natives may have been adapted and improvised so as to incorporate such a famous figure as Cook. Floating islands, a white man and his blacksmith, now signify Cook and his ships. The anthropologists who went to Nootka Sound in the 1970s were probably looking for stories about Cook. We will see shortly that some of the details in these accounts can be found in the white record, and others cannot.

Other Native texts, which I am confident refer to Cook's visit rather than that of some other voyager, do not carry as many of these historical traces, though that is not to say they are necessarily any truer or more authentic than the accounts presented above. When the missionary C.M. Tate was at Nootka

[38] F.W. Howay and E.O.S. Scholefield, *British Columbia: From the Earliest Times to the Present*, 4 vols (Vancouver, 1914), I, pp. 81–3.
[39] Barbara S. Efrat and W.J. Langlois, eds, 'The contact period as recorded by Indian oral tradition', in Efrat and Langlois, eds, *Nutka: Captain Cook and the Spanish Explorers on the Coast, Sound Heritage*, VII (1978), pp. 54–62.

Sound around 1880, he recorded some details that had been passed down by Native elders. 'We were all down at the ocean beach cutting up a large whale', he was told, 'when, looking across the big water, we saw something white that looked like a great seagull.' Some thought it was a large bird from the sky that had come to earth to eat the people. 'This made us all afraid', the account continues, 'and we ran off to the woods to hide'. The old people 'got very much afraid', but the younger ones 'were anxious to know what it was'. The wise men of the tribe said it was a moon from the sky using a sea serpent for its canoe. It was suggested that two of the young men should take a canoe and see what it was. 'If they were swallowed up, then we would know that it was dangerous.' The two men who went out were afraid to go near the moon 'for some time', but eventually decided to make 'a bold dash' towards it. They found men with a great deal of hair on their faces, and were frightened until one of 'the strange men beckoned with his hand for them to go near'. They plucked up the courage to paddle alongside the moon's canoe. 'Very soon', the account states,

> a rope ladder was dropped down, and one of the moon men beckoned for them to come up. They tied their canoe to the rope ladder, and climbed up the side of the moon's canoe, when they were surprised with everything they saw. One of the men, with bright buttons on his coat, spoke to another man, who went down into the very heart of the moon's canoe, and soon came back with two dishes, one of which was full of round flat bones, and the other full of blood [biscuit and molasses]. The man with the bright buttons pointed to the bones and the blood then pointed to his mouth; but the young man did not understand that they wanted them to eat, until one of the moon men took up a piece of the bone, dipped it in the blood, then put it in his mouth . . . at the same time holding out the dishes for them to eat also; but they were afraid to touch the moon's food.

The two Natives soon realised that the moon men wanted the skins they were wearing, and an exchange took place. When the two men returned to shore, people were interested in the beads and strange clothing that they had received but 'felt afraid' when they were told that the people of moon's canoe lived on bones and blood. The next day some of the moon men came ashore and one of them had a 'crooked stick [flintlock gun] which he made speak with a very loud noise'. 'After a while', the story concludes, 'the moon went away, and everybody felt glad.'[40]

The last history I will draw on was told to the ethnographer Philip Drucker in the 1930s. Muchalat Peter related how two people from the community of Tcecis saw an island with people and fire on it that looked like 'a spirit thing', a TcExa. When this news reached the village the chief held a meeting and a group of men and a shaman were sent to find out more. As the ship came into sight again the female shaman began to sing in order to see the spirit in the

---

[40] Tate Family Papers, BCARS Add. MSS. 303, box 1, file 3.

thing. 'I don't think that's a TcExa', she remarked; 'I don't see the spirit of it'. When they got alongside the thing they saw men eating fire who asked about 'pish'. The Natives didn't understand them. When they returned to the village they looked back, expecting the thing to have disappeared, but it had not. The old people of the village thought: 'That's our great-great grandchildren coming from the other side of the ocean.' Many more canoes returned to the thing, and were beckoned to board it. Chief U'kwisktcik was the first to go up, and exchanged cedar bark mats for blankets. When he and others returned, the white men wanted to trade clothes, but the Natives were not interested because they did not know how to wear them. Back at the village, the chief wanted to know if any one had had a bad dream about the ship. When they said they hadn't it was surmised that the ship was not a bad spirit. All the people then went to trade furs. A Native warrior met a man with a gun. He 'went up to the man, placed [the] muzzle of the gun against [his] own breast, because he had on armor . . . that could stop [the gun from] "blowing". The white signed that [the] Ind[ian] would fall dead, took the latter's garment, folded it, placed it at the end of the ship, [and] shot [a] hole in [it]. Then they knew that was another Tc'Exa, for no arrows could pierce his armor.' The people returned to the village and wondered what kind of TcExa this was. A fleet of canoes then came from another village to wed a woman to a TcExa man. As they began their feast, '2 boatloads of whites came ashore and stood looking in the doorway. The white captain gave a hat to the chief of the manuasatxa' (people from another village) but his host 'became jealous and said the gift had been meant [for] them', and so it was surrendered.[41]

I have paraphrased these accounts (some of which are long), but have tried to retain their narrative progression and structure. They were collected for different reasons, and obviously provide a different set of understandings about Cook's arrival.[42] As such, they help us to probe his way of seeing. Like Cook's journal, these accounts are culturally and geographically situated statements about contact. They also point to aspects of this encounter that are obscured in Cook's journal and Douglas's account but shine more brightly in the journals of Cook's officers: a more face-to-face, bodily process of interaction, where

[41] Philip Drucker, 'Nootka Field Notebooks', 2, pp. 19–24. Photocopy from the Smithsonian Institution, National Anthropological Archives, housed in BCARS Add. MSS. 870. Drucker does not state whether this account refers specifically to Cook. His notebook entry is headed: 'First contact with whites'.

[42] With regard to Tate, it should be noted that missionaries' enthusiasm for recording native oral histories of contact was tied to a politics of conversion, and that some of Cook's earliest and most vehement critics were missionaries in Hawai'i. Such stories were deemed to mark the spiritual gulf between (Native) heathenism and (white) civilisation which was to be closed by the missionary. Nevertheless, it appears that this story was proffered by a Native person rather than solicited by Tate. See Tate's reminiscence in J.S. Matthews, ed., *Early Vancouver: Narratives of Pioneers of Vancouver, B.C.*, 2 vols (Vancouver, 1933), II, pp. 130–1.

touch met sight, words failed to translate the meaning of gestures, and human activity on and around the ships could not be easily summarised.

These Native stories relate a mixture of wonder, astonishment, curiosity and fear at the sight of strange objects and people. In the official account, gestures, speeches and songs are registered matter-of-factly, whereas in these Native accounts such actions are invested with spiritual meaning. Chiefs, shamans and wise people were called upon to interpret the appearance of a strange phenomenon. Native people had their own discriminatory categories of knowledge, just as Cook did. There is no space here to provide a detailed (if perhaps still only tentative) interpretation of these Native stories, and my aim is not to use them to prefigure or deconstruct an alternative Native history of contact. Suffice it to say that at Nootka Sound, contact was embedded in a complex Native human geography that involved different groups, villages, families and chiefly prerogatives and rivalries, and the use and control of esoteric knowledge. Native histories are passed down along chiefly and family lines, and in Native stories events happen at the intersection of family routines and geopolitical rivalries, material and spiritual life, and the bonds of kinship and the exploits of individuals. Ethnographers such as Drucker and Michael Harkin have reflected at length on how the social and political 'ethno-logics' of Nuu-chah-nulth societies are encoded in the occurrence, telling and performance of narratives about events that bring the past into the present, and merge human and animal worlds.[43]

Decentring Cook II: Cook's officers

Comments about first contact made by some of Cook's officers tally with these Native accounts. Cook's surgeon, David Samwell, for one, observed that the Indians 'expressed much astonishment at seeing the Ship'.[44] Nor does the serenity of Cook's first encounter exist in Lieutenant James King's journal, which states that:

---

[43] See Philip Drucker, *The Northern and Central Nootkan Tribes* (Washington, DC, 1951), and Michael Harkin, 'Whales, chiefs and giants: an exploration into Nuu-chah-nulth political thought', *Ethnology*, 37 (1998), pp. 317–33. I am fairly certain that these Native accounts relate to Cook rather than to subsequent voyagers. After 1778, Nootka Sound was not visited again by Europeans until August 1785, when the British brig *Sea Otter* arrived to trade furs. Natives of the Sound attacked the vessel and a London newspaper reported that they were 'repulsed with considerable slaughter'. Surely, the Native accounts that I have presented would have related this slaughter if they were chronicling the arrival of this ship; the actions of its captain, James Hanna, are recounted in other Native accounts. See Clayton, *Islands of Truth*, pp. 69–161; James R. Gibson, *Otter Skins, Boston Ships and China Goods: The Maritime Fur Trade of the Northwest Coast, 1785–1841* (Montreal and Kingston, 1992).

[44] *RDV*, pp. 1088–9.

The first men that came would not approach the Ship very near & seemed to eye us with Astonishment, till the second boat came that had two men in it; the figure & actions of one of these were truly frightful; he workd himself into the highest frenzy, uttering something between a howl & a song, holding a rattle in each hand, which at intervals he laid down, taking handfulls of red Ocre & birds feathers & strewing them in the Sea; this was follow'd by a Violent way of talking, seemingly with vast difficulty in uttering the Harshest & rudest words, at the same time pointing to the Shore, yet we did not attribute this incantation to . . . any ill intentions towards us.[45]

As this passage proves, many of the 'facts' of first contact included in the official account come from King's journal, although Douglas toned down King's animated prose.

Cook and his officers recorded some events that are recounted in the Native accounts, though in a different narrative order. In Chief George's story, Maquinna invites Cook to come and stay next year. Cook and some of his officers state that this invitation was extended as the ships were leaving the Sound.[46] Cook did visit two Native villages, in two boats, with some marines (with 'crooked sticks'), and gave out presents. The first village he visited, Yuquot, is that mentioned in the accounts related by Winifred David and C.M. Tate. On the basis of Cook's journal, the second village was Tcesis, as Muchalat Peter's testimony confirms. The 'Surly chief' whom Cook reported meeting there may have been offended because the captain gave a present to a chief from another village and ignored him.[47] Midshipman Edward Riou noted that when Cook visited this second village, on 20 April, he 'found more of our Old acquaintances than at the town to the So:ward', confirming that these people had been trading regularly with Cook's ships.[48] Lieutenant John Williamson reported that some Native people asked him how his musket worked, and that they laughed when he told them the ball would pierce their armour. Williamson folded a Native garment about six times, pinned it to a tree, and fired at it, putting a hole through it and embedding the ball in the tree.[49] The only difference between this account and that given by Drucker's informant is that the event occurred on shore.[50] Finally, within two days of Cook's arrival, the Natives of the Sound had boarded the ships and were

[45] *RDV*, p. 1394.

[46] *RDV*, p. 308; John Rickman, 'Log', n.d., PRO ADM 51/4529[46], fo. 217.

[47] *RDV*, p. 304.

[48] Edward Riou, 'A log of the proceedings of his majesty's ship Discovery', 20 April 1778, PRO ADM 51/4529 [42], fo. 78v.

[49] *RDV*, p. 1350.

[50] Thomas Edgar also recorded this event in his 'Journal', 4 April 1778, BL Add. MS 37,528, fo. 91v, a partial copy of which was deposited in the Provincial Library in Victoria, B.C., but not until after Drucker had interviewed Muchalat Peter. Some 'facts' from the European

trading furs and cedar blankets for metal goods and beads. In short, these European and Native texts relate similar details about this encounter, but from radically different cultural perspectives.

Why were these sentiments of fear and astonishment, picked up by some of Cook's officers, excluded from the official account – especially the observations of King, who helped Douglas to edit Cook's journal? To return to my earlier line of enquiry, I suggest that Cook's and Douglas's accounts served a rhetorical purpose. During this era of scientific exploration, and especially in Cook's case, statements about first contact served as parables of Europe's scientific, civilising mission. Such statements traded on the belief that 'successful intercourse' would be had with the Natives.[51] Their lands were discovered, their cultures were recorded, people were treated fairly, and few got hurt, because contact was executed and related in the pacific blink of a scientific eye.

Statements about first contact mesh past, present and future, and the Native accounts compound the sense that contact had composite – and in some ways incommensurable – meanings, with ship's biscuit and molasses appearing as bones and blood (as signs, perhaps, of cannibalism). When Cook met a new group of people, he assessed the progress of his voyage and shaped its broader message at the site of his discovery. The images of friendship and the prospect of trade that Cook worked into his journal helped to confirm his status as a gentle and humane explorer trading the trappings of European civilisation. And his factual prose confirmed his status as an objective, detached observer who only recorded what he saw.[52] Douglas bolstered Cook's self-estimation as an Enlightenment explorer by giving Cook's account of first contact at Nootka Sound a scientific and almost ceremonial quality – a quality that was central to what Dening means by the theatre of the civiliser to the native. And as Bernard Smith suggests, during his third voyage Cook also used his artist, Webber, to portray images of peace and harmony that functioned as a 'highly selective truth'.[53] Cook narrated contact at Nootka Sound using the collective pronoun 'we' and Douglas followed suit. Cook tried to emphasise that he contacted the inhabitants of this region as a representative of his country, an

record may have been smuggled into Native oral histories over the years. However, it seems unlikely that this event was. Beaglehole was the first scholar that I know of who cited either Williamson's or Edgar's observation.

[51] I borrow this phrase from Tom Dutton: '"Successful intercourse was had with the natives": aspects of European contact methods in the Pacific', in Donald C. Laycock and Werner Winter eds, *A World of Language* (Canberra, 1987), pp. 152–71.

[52] The same idea applies to Cook's cartography. He depicted the northwest coast with a thin line and showed no interior detail; it was a record of what he himself had seen. See the reproduction of Cook's 'Chart of part of the NW Coast of America' in Andrew David, ed., *The Charts and Coastal Views of Captain Cook's Voyages*, III, *The Voyage of the Resolution and Discovery 1776–1780* (London, 1997), p. 114.

[53] Smith, *Imagining the Pacific*, p. 206.

ambassador of European civilisation, and as the official author of what he and others on his ships saw.[54]

Discipline and the spatiality of representation

These ways of visualising and representing Native peoples hinged on a set of disciplinary practices. They hinged on the control that Cook could wield over his own narrative, the discipline he could exercise over his crews, the confidence he could place in his military might over Native people, and how he might keep a lid on other – distracting and dissenting – voices. But in order to maintain these forms of discipline, which, as Daniel Baugh and others have shown, were central to the eighteenth-century development and imperial prestige of the British Navy, Cook had to delegate responsibility.[55] He (and the Admiralty) expected his officers to keep detailed logs, in part so that he might consult them to flesh out his own observations. And he had to base his dealings with Native peoples on a division of labour, and plan for the possibility of attack. He had to allow his crews to see and do things out of the scope of his own vision.

The principles of consultation and exactitude that Cook forged to maintain his status as the chief author of his voyage disrupted the authority of his representations. Cook's officers paid close attention to their captain's actions, but their journals still drift off in different directions. These officers recorded many things that are not in Cook's journal, some of their observations contradict those of their captain, and they traded observations and borrowed passages from each other.[56] And what about the 'ordinary' sailors who made up the bulk of the ships' companies and were left mostly in the dark about official matters: instructions imparted by Cook and the Admiralty about what

---

[54] Captain Charles Clerke of the *Discovery* saw himself in a similar light, and his statement about initial contact is similar to Cook's. See his 'Log and proceedings', 29 March 1778, PRO Adm 55/22, fo. 151.

[55] Daniel Baugh, 'The eighteenth century navy as a national institution, 1690–1815', in J.R. Hill, ed., *The Oxford Illustrated History of the Royal Navy* (Oxford, 1995), pp. 120–45. Also see Christopher Lawrence, 'Disciplining disease: scurvy, the navy, and imperial expansion, 1750–1825', in Miller and Reil, *Visions of Empire*, pp. 80–106. One obvious and important theoretical reference point in this literature is Michel Foucault's *Discipline and Punish: The Birth of the Prison* (Harmondsworth, 1979). But it should be noted that Foucault's hugely influential work on the development of a disciplinary regime of power in Europe hinges, by and large, on an appreciation of built and immobile spaces of control such as prisons, hospitals and asylums. Foucault did not consider the mobile and dynamic disciplinary environment of the ship.

[56] The logs and journals of Cook's officers vary enormously in length and insight. Some logs focus almost entirely on shipboard activities and scarcely mention Native people. Cook's senior officers, and some of his aspiring junior officers, such as Edgar and Burney, were the keenest observers.

to observe, and how to represent what they saw? 'Is it not quite a different path that he travels and can this path ever cross that of the more experienced observer?' wrote one such sailor; 'is it not possible for one traveller to recall what another might forget?'[57]

In fine, Cook's crews found the time and space to do things behind his back, and at Nootka Sound, truth and objectivity became dispersed and decentred. When, for instance, on 4 April 1778, a large number of canoes full of armed men circled Cook's ships, and a Native attack seemed possible, Cook dismissed the event in his journal with a measured, dispassionate prose. He felt sure that his ships had been in no danger. He understood by signs from the Natives that 'it was not us they were arming against', was satisfied that this was a quarrel between rival Native groups, and implied in his journal that he simply sat back and observed these rival groups arguing with one another.[58] But Cook's officers wrote different accounts of this event. Cook evidently did not just sit back. He sent out King and some armed marines in a boat to assess the danger of the situation.[59] Midshipman George Gilbert reported that while Cook did not want to intrude on what seemed to be a Native affair (this being part of his humanitarian mandate), he came very close to firing on some canoes that came alongside the ships.[60] Samwell did not trust the Natives' signs, and judged that 'from every appearance' the Natives meant to attack the ships.[61] In sum, some of Cook's officers were quite frightened and reported their agitation in their journals.

And these officers assessed the meaning of these events in a variety of ways. Many of them focused on Native songs and interpreted them very differently. Nathaniel Portlock, speaking for some of his fellow officers, stated that the Natives' war songs were 'the most warlike and awfull thing they ever heard' and indicative of native savagery, whereas Samwell thought that they showed that these people had a 'brave' and 'resolute' disposition.[62] Lieutenant James Burney, on the other hand, appreciated the harmonies of the Native songs, and suggested that while these people were 'very apt to take offence at the slightest indignity . . . to do them justice . . . any degree of submission imme-diately pacifies them'.[63] Riou noted that Native verbal altercations were passionate, but also emphasised that one protagonist would not interrupt

---

[57] F.W. Howay, ed., *Zimmermann's Captain Cook: An Account of the Third Voyage of Captain Cook Around the World, 1776–1789* (Toronto, 1930), pp. 21–2.

[58] *RDV*, p. 299.

[59] *RDV*, p. 1397.

[60] Christine Holmes, ed., *Captain Cook's Final Voyage: The Journal of Midshipman George Gilbert* (Horsham, 1982), p. 70.

[61] *RDV*, pp. 1092–3.

[62] Nathaniel Portlock, 'Log', 4 April 1778, PRO ADM 51/4531[68], fo. 293v.; *RDV*, p. 1100.

[63] James Burney, 'Journal of a voyage in the Discovery', 4 April 1778, PRO ADM 51/4528[45], fo. 227.

another's speech, and harangues seldom resulted in fighting.[64] Midshipman James Trevenen put this down to their 'fearless independent spirit which apprehended no danger from any other than the person with whom they had particularly quarelled'.[65] William Bayly, Cook's astronomer, added that the orderliness of Native harangues showed that these people were 'free from malice & design'.[66]

These officers had different personalities, backgrounds and literary talents, and such differences are reflected in their journal writing. What they recorded, and the kinds of dealings they had with Native people, also hinged on what they could see from their positions on the ship or shore, and on their rank. Bayly, for example, complained that he saw very little of the Natives' manners and customs because Cook's ships were tucked away in a cove distant from their villages, and Native people came mostly to trade.[67] Cook's emphasis on the Nootkans' trading abilities, then, was conditioned by the location of his ships. King noted that because of 'the narrow confind sphere' of observation at Nootka Sound, it was difficult to distinguish the 'invariable & constant springs' of Native life from fashion and improvisation.[68]

All of this fractures the idea that Cook and his officers captured something original and immediate about the distant and the new in a transparent fashion. Indeed, in 1776 Cook himself confided to an associate in London that he and his officers 'could not be certain of any information they got' on their travels 'except as to objects falling under the observation of sense'.[69] This testimony from Cook's officers, combined with that from Native people, points to important micro-geographical aspects of contact and representation: to the variety and physicality of this encounter. And as I think my discussion shows, Cook's command of knowledge was a spatial problematic. It revolved around his 'zigzag' path across the Pacific, the location of his ships amidst Native peoples, the position of his officers and crew on those ships, and the physical and rhetorical demarcation of similarity and difference between Europeans and Natives.

Conclusion: the chimera of historical truth

Finally, I want to suggest that critical appreciation of Cook's command of knowledge and space is far from a quaint scholarly matter. In historical

---

[64] Riou, 'Log', 4 April 1778, fo. 80v.

[65] James Trevenen, 'Notes regarding the death of Captain Cook', 3. Transcript BCARS A/A40/C77T/A2.

[66] William Bayly, 'Journals and a log kept on Capt. Cook's second and third voyages around the world', 2nd journal, 12 August 1777–30 June 1778, n.d., fo. 105, Alexander Turnbull Library, National Library of New Zealand, Wellington, micro 343.

[67] Bayly, 'Journals and log', n.d., fo. 102.

[68] RDV, p. 1406

[69] James Boswell, The Journals of James Boswell, 1760–1795 (London, 1991), pp. 306–7.

discourses on British Columbia, truth is most precious at its putative point of origin, when Native people 'entered history' by being contacted by literate Europeans. In the 1920s, historians of the region argued that Cook's sojourn at Nootka Sound launched history proper in the region and did so with a specific promise: that Cook was invited to land – and, by implication, to take nominal possession of the coast – by friendly Natives who were eager to trade and please.[70] More recently, historians have argued that the images of trade and tranquillity that pervade Cook's journal capture a basic difference between the pre-colonial and colonial periods of contact: that until colonists arrived in the mid-nineteenth century, contact was mutually beneficial for Natives and Europeans.[71] There is much to debate here about the nature and balance of power in these different periods of contact, not least the fact that the observations Cook and his officers made about the resources of the coast nurtured a turbulent and sometimes violent trade in sea otter pelts. The issue at hand, however, is that when it comes to Cook's place in the annals of British Columbia's history, scholars have generally sidelined issues of representation.[72] I suggest that an awareness of such issues should make us more cautious and self-conscious about the ways in which we pattern the past and connect it to the present.

I have tried to suggest that Cook's encounter at Nootka Sound does not point in any single direction. Comparatively and by all accounts, Cook's sojourn at Nootka Sound was peaceful; but we should be cautious about how or whether we should derive some grander historical motif from this. The images of peace and trade that pervade his journal are, in part, fabricated truths, or situated knowledges. None of the texts I have considered define Cook's stay at Nootka Sound. They each contain partial truths hatched at the intersection of Native and European perceptions of the other in 1778. Such issues are important in British Columbia because Native peoples pursuing land claims in the courts have encountered judges who think that the observations of white explorers are more factual, objective and reliable than Native oral traditions. There are strict legal rules about what counts as admissible evidence in court, of course, but in applying such rules to Native land issues judges have also drawn on and reinforced a long-standing discourse of scientific exploration. Judges, and some historians, have assumed that the texts of explorers are reliable because they conform to a European model of what counts as truth – that these texts are trustworthy because they are firsthand reports. The view expressed here is that while Cook and his officers tried to adhere to this model of truth, they did not, and perhaps could not, conform to it entirely, and partly for geographical reasons.

[70] On this historiography, see Clayton, *Islands of Truth*, pp. 3–5, 50–62.
[71] This idea has been argued most forcefully by Robin Fisher in his *Contact and Conflict: Indian-European Relations in British Columbia, 1774–1890* (Vancouver, 1977).
[72] For a sense of what I mean, see Stephen Haycox, James Barnett and Caedmon Liburd, eds, *Enlightenment and Exploration in the North Pacific, 1741–1805* (Seattle, 1997).

The most controversial judgement concerning Native land claims in British Columbia in recent times is *Delgamuukw et al. v. the Queen*, involving the Gitksan and Wet'suwet'en people. In his 'Reasons for Judgement', Chief Justice Allan McEachern observed that he worked with 'a different view of what is fact and what is belief' than the Native plaintiffs, who, he thought, had 'a romantic view of their history', and one based on hearsay.[73] And he added that while he accepted most of what historians (concerned with 'the facts') put before him, he was generally sceptical of what anthropologists (working in the land of 'hearsay') had to say. Over the last ten years this judgement has been the subject of considerable debate about the public and legal uses of history, and the historical reasoning in it has been challenged by higher Canadian Supreme Court judgements. There is also now a treaty process in place, which seeks, in part, to redress the fact that very few land treaties with Native people were signed in colonial times. However, as Cole Harris has recently argued, the white (ex-colonial and immigrant) culture out of which judgements like McEachern's arise has not become sympathetic to Native causes overnight.[74] Numerous questions remain about how marginalised Native perspectives and ties to land are to be incorporated into mainstream history and a postcolonial land policy, both of which have long been regulated by a white colonising culture.

As this foray into the present suggests, texts of exploration are bound up with cultural relations of power, and we need to think carefully about how we want to read the past in relation to the present. There are, of course, many dangers involved in trying to decentre historical understanding, which, in effect, is where my discussion of Cook leads. If this project is taken too far it can relativise questions of exploitation and historic injustice, especially towards Native people, out of existence. Yet in the British Columbian context, this tactic of decentring is of perhaps greater critical importance than the more pervasive postcolonial critical tendency to routinely connect travel writing and narratives of exploration to a domineering imperial gaze and ineluctable colonial project. Thomas, for example, has suggested that, 'If it is in many ways unavoidable, and even appropriate, that the Cook voyages are seen as an early chapter in the colonization of the Pacific . . . it remains important that this historiography not merely invert that which celebrated Cook's navigational accomplishments', and Enlightenment credentials.[75] Both kinds of narratives, he argues, tend to impoverish understanding of the languages of description and adjudication that shaped European knowledge of the Pacific. Likewise, Leask has argued that European colonial discourse should be viewed

---

[73] Chief Justice Allan McEachern, unreported 'Reasons for Judgement', no. 0843, Smithers Registry, in the Supreme Court of British Columbia, 8 March 1991, p. 49 and *passim*.
[74] Cole Harris, *Making Native Space: Colonialism, Resistance and Reserves in British Columbia* (Vancouver, 2002), especially pp. 293–323.
[75] Thomas, 'Introduction', Forster, *Observations*, p. xxxiii.

in a more contingent and transitive relation to other peoples and places than it is often represented.[76] I suggest that in British Columbia, decentring Cook forms part and parcel of the task of decolonising historical knowledge and returning Native issues to a cultural and political present that does not use the past as a prop and prompt for the dismissal and denigration of Native claims and grievances.

Europeans sometimes struggled to impose their discursive will on the 'Other', and their texts often bear greater witness to that struggle than they do to the expansion of empire through a self-assured process of conceptual and intellectual appropriation. As I have tried to show, contact at Nootka Sound in 1778 was one place where we can see in vivid detail some of the tensions and contradictions embedded in the production of knowledge about the 'Other' in the age and name of Enlightenment. I have said little about the make-up of the Native texts I have used, and it would be presumptuous to say that Cook has a special place in Native historical imaginations. I quote from these texts, but with little deconstructive commentary, mainly in order to unmask how Cook faced up to otherness. If there is a methodological double-standard here, then it is tied to the recognition that these Native stories have long been overshadowed by the work of Cook and his officers, and that a wider force-field of historical representation has long drowned Native voices and dressed them up as myth.

Acknowledgements

I thank Sophie Forgan, Dan O'Sullivan and Nicholas Thomas, who made many useful comments on a draft of this chapter, an earlier and different version of which appeared in Jennifer Brown and Elizabeth Vibert (eds), *Reading Beyond Words: Contexts for Native History* (Peterborough, Ontario, 1996).

---

[76] Leask, *Curiosity and the Aesthetics of Travel Writing*, p. 5.

Part III

Captain Cook and his Contemporaries

Captain Cook and his Contemporaries

8

A comparison of the charts produced during the Pacific voyages of Louis-Antoine de Bougainville and James Cook

JOHN ROBSON

Introduction

European voyages to the Pacific in the eighteenth century did not always carry good quality charts, nor did all the voyagers make an effort to improve matters by drawing new ones. However, by the second half of the century, this attitude was changing and the need to possess good and accurate charts had been realised.[1] Able cartographers now accompanied or led many of the voyages, and instruments for making accurate surveys and drawing correct charts had been developed.

Against this background, two expeditions set off from Europe in the late 1760s to explore the Pacific. The first was French, led by Louis-Antoine de Bougainville; the second was British, led by James Cook. History has remembered them very differently. The name and achievements of Cook are known throughout the world, while the name Bougainville is associated with an island and a colourful tropical flower, Bougainvillea. Few people, though, would be able to explain the reasons for those names, least of all in France where Bougainville is almost forgotten. The cartographic output of the two men and their voyages is one of several reasons for their different standing in history.

At the time the expeditions set out, European knowledge of the Pacific was limited. Scholars such as Charles de Brosses in France and Alexander Dalrymple in Britain had produced volumes that brought together all that was known from earlier voyages. Both expeditions carried a copy of de Brosses' work, which included a copy of Giles Robert de Vaugondy's map of the Pacific, while Cook's *Endeavour* had on board Dalrymple's recent book with its 'Chart of the South Pacifick Ocean'.[2]

---

[1] France established its Dépôt des cartes et plans de la marine in Paris in 1720, beginning a systematic collection of naval charts; Britain did not follow suit until its establishment of the Hydrographic Office in 1795.

[2] Charles de Brosses, *Histoire des Navigations aux Terres Australes* (Paris, 1756); Alexander Dalrymple, *An Account of the Discoveries made in the South Pacifick Ocean* (London, 1767).

137

Objectives of the two voyages

The instructions issued to the two expeditions were quite different and show clearly the contrast in emphasis given to the production of new charts by the two governments. The British voyage of 1768 had two broad objectives: first, to transport a scientific party to Tahiti in the Pacific Ocean to observe the Transit of Venus expected in 1769, and second, to search for the Great Southern Continent. Before Cook sailed on his first voyage in 1768 his instructions stressed:

> You are at all opportunities when the Service upon which you are employed will admit of it, to make such farther Surveys and Plans, and take such Views of the Island, its Harbours and Bays, as you conceive may be useful to Navigation or necessary to give us a more Perfect Idea and description than we have hitherto received of it.[3]

After he had observed the Transit of Venus at Tahiti, Cook followed his secret instructions, which included a note that he was 'to employ yourself diligently . . . surveying and making Charts, and taking Views of such Bays, Harbours and Parts of the Coast as may be useful to Navigation'.[4] Cook would receive similar instructions on both his later voyages. The British Admiralty had realised the need for good charts and had chosen Cook as commander of the *Endeavour* voyage largely because of his proven ability to carry out surveys and prepare charts. The Admiralty also ensured that Cook was assisted by skilled and experienced men by appointing Richard Pickersgill and Robert Molyneux to the *Endeavour*'s crew.

The French had different priorities. Bougainville's voyage originated during the aftermath of the Seven Years War which had finished in 1763, when France, at the Peace of Paris, had ceded territory in Canada, the Caribbean and India to Britain. It now began looking for new territory to colonise and Bougainville himself had been involved in a project concerning the Îles Malouines (Falkland Islands) until Spain objected. As a consolation, Bougainville was offered the opportunity of a round-the-world voyage to look for possible sites for French colonies and opportunities for trade. First, though, he would to have to represent France in the handing over of the Malouines to the Spanish.

The French Ministry of the Marine drew up instructions for Bougainville but without mentioning surveys and charts. During October 1766, the Ministry reworked the instructions several times, and the French historian, Etienne Taillemite, has summed them up as orders to discover new lands and search for propitious locations for future colonies to counter-balance those lost in the Seven Years War; to open up a new route to China to test and develop

---

[3] *EV*, p. cclxxx.
[4] *EV*, p. cclxxxii.

trade with that country to offset the loss of trade with India; and to search for new spice plants for the Île de France (Mauritius). Taillemite adds that 'none of these objectives was attained, but Bougainville was not solely responsible for this failure'.[5] Despite charts not being mentioned in the instructions, a cartographer, Charles Routier de Romainville, was included in the French party, but sailed in the expedition's second ship, the *Etoile*.

The expedition commanders

James Cook and Louis-Antoine de Bougainville were born a year apart, in 1728 and 1729 respectively, and later led expeditions that circumnavigated the world in the late 1760s. There, however, the similarities end, and their backgrounds, their achievements and their places in history have been very different. Cook was born in humble, rural conditions in northeastern England, received a basic schooling and was destined for an ordinary life.[6] In contrast, Bougainville was born into the semi-noble family of a Paris notary which had close connections to the Court.[7] An uncle was a confidant of Madame de Pompadour. Bougainville was a gifted student, versed in the classics, and attended the University of Paris, where he is believed to have studied law. However, he excelled in mathematics and received special tuition from d'Alembert, later one of the authors of the *Encyclopédie*. At the age of 28, Bougainville wrote a treatise on calculus that led to him being elected a member of the Royal Society in Britain. A polymath, Bougainville excelled at most things.

Cook, meanwhile, had become a seaman in the coal trade operating between Newcastle and London along the North Sea coast of England. For eight years he applied himself, learning seamanship and navigational skills in ships working in some of the worst sailing conditions possible. Through his ability, Cook impressed his employers so much that he was promoted and was offered the command of his own ship, when he astounded everyone by enlisting as an able seaman in the Royal Navy in 1755. Over the next dozen years, Cook added to his skills. In 1758 he learned to survey and draw charts and plans

---

[5] Etienne Taillemite, ed., *Bougainville et ses compagnons autour du monde: 1766–1769, journaux de navigation*, 2 vols (Paris, 1977), I, p. 27 (author's translation).

[6] J.C. Beaglehole, *The Life of Captain James Cook* (London, 1974), the definitive source for details of Cook's life.

[7] Details of Bougainville's life are harder to locate as no good biography of him has been published. Jean Etienne Martin-Allanic, *Bougainville, navigateur et les découvertes de son temps*, 2 vols (Paris, 1974), is the most comprehensive work. J.C. Robson has written *A Short Biography of Louis-Antoine de Bougainville* (Hamilton, N.Z., 2001) that appears on the internet (http:pages.quicksilver.net.nz/~boug2.html). However, since the writing of this chapter John Dunmore's edition of *The Pacific Journal of Louis-Antoine de Bougainville 1767–1768* (London, 2002) has been published.

while on Cape Breton Island. Between 1759 and 1762 he honed those skills by charting in the Gulf of St Lawrence during the campaign against Quebec and in Halifax harbour. He accompanied the expedition which retook Newfoundland in late 1762, and when peace came he spent five summers from 1763 to 1767 surveying the intricate coast of Newfoundland. He returned to Britain each fall to draw up his results (Plate II), and his reputation for diligent and accurate charts gradually led to his work becoming known to senior officers at the Admiralty in London. He also added astronomy to his skills and successfully observed a solar eclipse on the south coast of Newfoundland

Plate II James Cook, 'A Sketch of the Island of Newfoundland', 1763, drawn by Cook before he had surveyed the north, west and southwest coasts, which here lack detail

in 1766. Cook sent a record of the eclipse to the Royal Society in London, thus bringing himself to the attention of that body. When, in early 1768, the Admiralty wanted a commander for its expedition to the Pacific to observe the Transit of Venus, Cook was an obvious choice and one acceptable to the Royal Society, co-sponsors of the expedition.

In the meantime, Bougainville had not been idle. In 1756, he travelled to Canada as aide-de-camp to Montcalm, the commander of the French army in its war with Britain in North America. Bougainville remained in Canada until the French surrendered in 1760 (Bougainville, who was fluent in English, even negotiated on behalf of the French with General Amherst, the British commander). Cook and Bougainville were on opposing sides at the Battle of Quebec in 1759, though there is no evidence that they ever met. Bougainville was bitter towards the British when he returned to France as a prisoner of war on parole, and he began formulating plans for France to regain some of its glory by making new settlements overseas. His brother had introduced him to the ideas of Pierre de Maupertuis and the writings of Charles de Brosses, concerning the possibilities of continents in the South Pacific waiting to be discovered and exploited. Bougainville put forward a plan to colonise California and to use the Îles Malouines as a staging post. He received the backing of the Duc de Choiseul, the French Marine Minister, and, from 1763 until 1766, Bougainville was involved in establishing a settlement in the Malouines. His hopes were shattered when France acceded to Spanish demands and agreed to withdraw from the islands. Bougainville had sailed twice to the South Atlantic. The voyages had introduced him to a naval life and he was quickly becoming a sailor with an appetite for exploration.

Cook's personality and background ensured that he always strove to carry out his instructions, and his skills in leadership, seamanship, astronomy and navigation ensured that he was able to do so with a high degree of success. He could not afford to fail, however, for his lack of social standing meant he had nothing to fall back on. His determination, especially on his second voyage, amazed his colleagues and crew and led to his failing health and, ultimately, to his death on the third. During his three voyages he criss-crossed the Pacific, laying to rest the idea of the Great Southern Continent and delineating the map of the Pacific as we know it. 'Cook's chart legacy, and the painstaking method by which he achieved it, placed maritime exploration and surveying on a new footing. Cook built up his coastal outlines from running surveys . . . but his base was now established by astronomical observation.'[8]

As much as Cook would have preferred to continue doing the surveying himself, he realised that he must increasingly delegate the practical work to members of his crews while he carried out the duties of captaining the ships. Fortunately, there were competent men on all three voyages, allowing him

---

[8] Peter Whitfield, *The Charting of the Oceans: Ten Centuries of Maritime Maps* (London, 1996), p. 110.

to do this. Cook further added to the pool of skilled cartographers by instigating a regimen of training for his junior officers and midshipmen in surveying and cartography. To begin with, these young men were employed to copy charts and eventually, as their skills improved, they were given responsibility for preparing original charts. In later voyages, Cook's role changed from hands-on to that of an overseer, safe in the knowledge that his men were more than capable of producing acceptable charts. 'Cook was a seminal figure in British hydrography, and the men he trained, such as George Vancouver and William Bligh, shaped a tradition.'[9]

Louis-Antoine de Bougainville, on the other hand, was a more traditional commander, typical of the time. He was not a career sailor and had little experience of the sea before his Pacific voyage. Bougainville was in overall charge of the expedition, while his two captains, Duclos-Guyot, on the *Boudeuse*, and Chesnard de la Giraudais, on the *Etoile*, were experienced sailors who would carry out the day-to-day running of the ships. Bougainville, no doubt, was prepared to include chart-making in these duties, but charts do not appear to have been a high priority for him. Little or no mention is made in his or his officers' journals of people carrying out surveys or drawing charts. Romainville, his cartographer, sailed on the consort vessel, the *Etoile*, and so was not in regular contact with Bougainville. Nor did Bougainville often display an inquisitive bent. For example, he sailed past Samoa without attempting to investigate the islands, whereas one feels that Cook, in a similar position, would have made every effort to land and to delineate the outline of the land sighted.

The voyages

Bougainville set off on his world voyage in November 1766 but from the beginning fortune was not with him. The precaution of using a second ship, the storeship *Etoile*, was undone immediately when that ship was unready to sail and Bougainville set off in November 1766 with only the *Boudeuse*. It was provisioned for a voyage of two years but it took Bougainville over a year just to reach the Pacific. The handing over of the Malouines took longer than anticipated and then linking up with the *Etoile* forced Bougainville back to Rio de Janeiro. Repairs to the storeship at Montevideo and Buenos Aires further delayed their progress, as did the need to wait for summer months to negotiate the Strait of Magellan. It was December 1767 when they began a slow passage through the Strait, during which some new inlets were charted.

Finally, on 26 January 1768, Bougainville reached the Pacific. Having already wasted so much time, Bougainville was now under some pressure to make a quick crossing as his whole voyage was supposed to last only two years.

[9] Ibid.

He reached Tahiti but was asked by the Tahitians to leave after two weeks. Sailing on, the French passed Samoa, and the islands of Wallis and Futuna, without attempting to stop. They arrived next at Espiritu Santo (Vanuatu), previously visited by Quiros in 1606, but they stayed for only five days. By now supplies were low and Bougainville felt under a greater imperative to reach the comparative safety of Indonesia than to spend time exploring.

In early June, Bougainville neared the northeast coast of Australia but retreated in the face of the outliers of the (still unknown) Great Barrier Reef. He turned north and headed past the Solomon Islands and round the north of New Guinea. In doing so Bougainville passed the island that now carries his name. He made two stops in this region and honoured his two sponsors by naming the anchorages Baye Choiseul (at the western end of the Solomon Island now carrying that name) and Port Praslin (at the southeastern tip of New Ireland). These stops allowed Romainville the opportunity to produce two reasonable small charts of these harbours.

Bougainville brought his ships to safety in Buru, one of the Muluka Islands in Eastern Indonesia, in September 1768. He had put the lives of his crew and the safety of his ships ahead of spending time looking for new lands and producing new charts. It could have been a very different story had the expedition not wasted so much time in the Atlantic. In advance of Cook's first voyage by two years when they began, the French carried Philibert Commerson as naturalist, Pierre-Antoine Véron as astronomer and Charles Routier de Romainville as cartographer, so could have claimed their place in history as the first scientific voyage of exploration. As it was, matters were compounded at the Île de France, where the three men left the expedition.

The *Boudeuse* departed alone from Île de France as the *Etoile* needed repairs, so Bougainville reached France in March 1769 with only one ship. His reception in France was warm if not enthusiastic. He was received at Court and was the attraction in Paris salons for some time. However, the general population was unaware of the voyage and the thinkers and scientists largely ignored both it and its commander. Bougainville set about writing up the narrative of the voyage but it lacked the input of Commerson and Romainville. It was published in 1771, selling sufficiently to go into a second printing, and was also translated into several other languages, including an English edition by Johann Reinhold Forster.[10] Forster travelled as naturalist on Cook's second voyage and took the original French edition with him.

James Cook set sail in HM Bark *Endeavour*, which was a success from the time it left from Plymouth, on 26 August 1768, on the first of his voyages. The largely unknown Cook, who had been promoted to Lieutenant, was soon learning the problems of leadership and diplomacy at Rio de Janeiro,

---

[10] Louis-Antoine de Bougainville, *Voyage autour du monde par la frégate du roi la Boudeuse et la flûte L'Étoile* (Paris, 1771), translated into French by 'John' Reinhold Forster as *Voyage round the world, 1766–1769* (London, 1772).

where he encountered a mistrustful Viceroy of Brazil (the same man had been a problem for Bougainville a year earlier). Sailing on, Cook entered the Pacific in January 1769, reaching Tahiti in time to observe the Transit of Venus, his first objective. He then set out in search of the Great Southern Continent and went on to survey New Zealand and the east coast of Australia. The outlines and positions of Tahiti and the Society Islands, and New Zealand, were determined, while Cook also charted the length of the eastern coast of Australia. Joseph Banks and Daniel Solander, the naturalists on board, collected a host of botanical and zoological specimens, and when the ship arrived home in July 1771 the voyage was hailed for its achievements. The voyage received the praise that so easily could have been Bougainville's. 'Cook's may without exaggeration be called the first scientific voyage of discovery. This "good mathematician, very expert in the business", drew the modern map of the Pacific.'[11]

After the success of that first voyage, Cook went on to make a second voyage from 1772 to 1775, probably the single most impressive of all discovery voyages. He circumnavigated the Southern Ocean as close to Antarctica as possible and made two majestic sweeps of the Pacific, being among the first to visit several island groups. He was certainly the first to chart most of them and he was already well on the way to producing the map of the Pacific we know today. A third voyage followed from 1776 but Cook was killed on Hawai'i in 1779, after adding many more features to the Pacific map. He had become a tired and sick man, and his condition may have contributed to his death. He was also not as inquisitive and determined as he had been on his earlier voyages. Even so, 'his three expeditions not only revealed the geography of the Pacific but also set new standards in the survey and hydrography of unknown coasts'.[12]

Cook's reputation was already made. The journals of his voyages were published and became bestsellers. Later they were translated into many languages. Since then his voyages have been described countless times. Copies of many of his charts have appeared extensively and have become well known in their own right.

The cartographers

Charles Routier de Romainville was the cartographer for the French expedition and had principal responsibility for producing new charts. However, he sailed aboard the *Etoile*, rather than with Bougainville on the *Boudeuse*, and the fact that the two ships were separated from each other during the early part of the voyage further reduced Romainville's output and effectiveness.

Romainville was born in 1742 and had served in the French army during the Seven Years War in Europe, where he had been wounded at the battle

---

[11] John Noble Wilford, *The Mapmakers* (2nd edn, New York, 2000), p. 243.
[12] Ibid., p. 235.

of Johannesberg in 1762. Promoted to Lieutenant in 1764, Romainville came to Bougainville's attention when he joined the second voyage to the Îles Malouines. His army background meant he was more suited to land surveys and had little or no experience of surveying at sea. This rendered him of little use during the crossing of the Pacific, when only short periods were spent ashore. Bougainville made only a few landings and these were often of short duration, which limited Romainville. However, given the opportunity to land and establish proper bases, Romainville produced excellent charts of harbours, as those of Baye Choiseul and Port Praslin testify (Plate III).

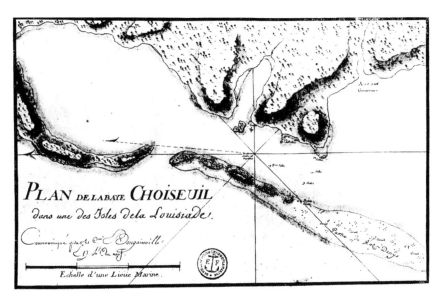

Plate III Charles Routier de Romainville, 'Plan de la Baye Choiseul' (Choiseul Bay, Solomon Islands)

At the Île de France Bougainville agreed to a request from Dumas, the Governor, that Romainville should stay on to assist in building up the defences of the island. This prevented Romainville being involved in the preparation of charts for the printed narrative that Bougainville published in 1771. It also contributed to the dispersal of those charts that had already been prepared.

In 1778, Romainville was sent to establish a French settlement on Mahe Island in the Seychelles. He remained there for two years on islands named after Moreau de Sechelles, the father of Helene de Sechelles, who had been Bougainville's adopted mother. Romainville died in 1818.[13]

---

[13] Taillemite, *Bougainville*, p. 86.

On board the French ships were several other people with varying experience and ability to carry out surveys and prepare charts and maps, though not necessarily with formal training. Nicolas Pierre Duclos-Guyot, Captain of the *Boudeuse,* and his two sons, Pierre and Alexandre, were career sailors from St Malo. Bougainville had met Nicolas when Duclos-Guyot had commanded the *Chezine,* the ship that had carried Bougainville back to Canada in 1759, and, together, the two men had later carried out the French campaign to settle the Îles Malouines in 1763. All three men would have known how to prepare charts, and several survive, including ones by Alexandre of the Malouines and the Strait of Magellan. The son, Pierre, sailed on the *Etoile,* where he formed a close working relationship with Philibert Commerson, the naturalist. Their collaboration produced several small charts of harbours in the Strait of Magellan, some of which survive.

Bougainville himself showed little or no interest in charts or their production. There is no evidence that he ever drew one and his journals and narrative rarely make mention of them. This is somewhat surprising given his mathematical background, the fact that he had been taught by the astronomer Alexis Clairaut, and his extensive travels. He must have been aware of the value of producing and possessing good charts.

Cook, by contrast, was the best marine surveyor and cartographer of his generation, 'the most practiced surveyor on board the *Endeavour,* and he was not the man to leave so essential a task to officers less well equipped than himself'.[14] By the time Cook was chosen for the voyage in 1768, the preparation of new charts was his main *raison d'être* for going to sea, and time and resources would always be given to their production. Cook had managed to assimilate and combine the techniques of land surveying using triangulation, and existing marine techniques, and he took them to a new level. He had learned land surveying originally from Samuel Holland while in Nova Scotia as Master of HMS *Pembroke* in 1758, and he had probably read Murdoch Mackenzie's work on surveying.[15] Employed from 1762 to 1767 to survey the south and west coasts of Newfoundland, Cook improved his skills to the point where he became a most proficient surveyor (Plate IV).

It is also possible to trace a development over the same period in his ability to draw a chart. Two versions of a chart of Carbonnear (the right-hand chart is the later one) show a softening of style, and by the time he was selected for the *Endeavour* voyage his style is much neater and more artistic (Plate V).

Cook often used the technique of a running survey, in which a traverse was made along a coastline, carefully noting the course and distance sailed. As the ship proceeded, sightings were made of features on land from different locations, the use of a compass or quadrant cross-bearings enabling the positions

---

[14] R.A. Skelton's essay, 'The Graphic Records', in *EV,* p. cclxv.

[15] Murdoch Mackenzie, *Orcades or a Geographic and Hydrographic Survey of the Orkney and Lewis Islands* (London, 1750).

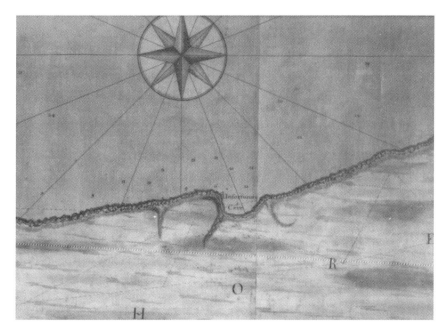

Plate IV James Cook, Unfortunate Cove, Newfoundland, 1764. The dotted lines denote sight lines used to take bearings during a triangulation survey

of land features to be plotted. If time allowed, a landing was made and the exact co-ordinates of one or more features were fixed. As R.A. Skelton has pointed out,

> Hydrographers were at this time rapidly absorbing the techniques of land survey, which equipped Cook in Newfoundland . . . to construct his marine surveys on a network of shore triangulation. . . . The thoroughness and rapidity of his running surveys in the *Endeavour* and *Resolution* testify to his skill in inshore navigation, learnt from his early training in coastal waters.[16]

Time and conditions in the Pacific did not always allow Cook the opportunities to carry out his surveys in the exact manner he had used in Newfoundland and he rarely had the chance to measure a base on land as a basis for an accurate survey. In the Pacific, 'the charts had generally to be drawn by a continuous running survey from the ship, with compass bearings or sextant angles taken on shore features, and a good deal of masthead sketching'.[17] Even so he turned the running survey into a fine art, and his chart of the New Hebrides is a supreme example (see Plate XIII below). Interestingly, this chart did not satisfy

---

[16] R.A. Skelton, 'Captain James Cook as a hydrographer', *Mariner's Mirror*, 40 (1954), pp. 94–5.
[17] Wilford, *The Mapmakers*, p. 243.

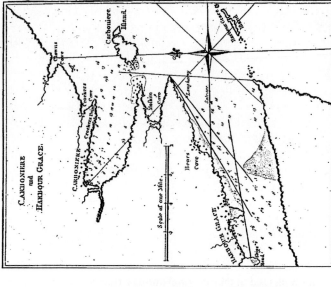

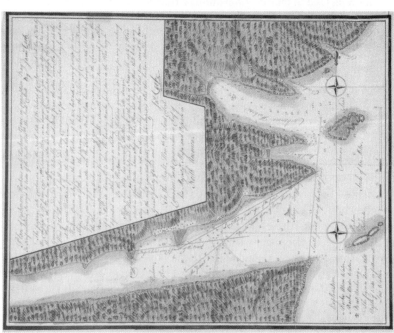

Plate V James Cook, Carbonear, Newfoundland, 1764. Two versions by Cook showing a softening of style in the later chart to the right

the perfectionist Cook, who explained that 'The word Survey, is not to be understood here, in its literal sence. Surveying a place, according to my Idea, is takeing a Geometrical Plan of it, in which every place is to have its true situation, which cannot be done in a work of this kind.'[18]

Cook himself carried out many of the surveys during his first voyage, but gradually he handed over responsibility to members of his crew. On British ships of the time, the responsibility for sailing the ship rested with the Master, a rank Cook had held since his time on the *Pembroke*. Among the Master's duties was the compilation of charts, though not all Masters were equally skilled in this. Cook was fortunate in that the Masters of his ships were all able surveyors, though Cook was a more competent surveyor and cartographer than any of them. Robert Molyneux (*Endeavour*), Joseph Gilbert (*Resolution*, second voyage), Peter Fannin (*Adventure*), William Bligh (*Resolution*, third voyage) and Thomas Edgar (*Discovery*) all contributed charts, and the work of Gilbert and Bligh deserves special mention.

Of the midshipmen, Cook's cousin, Isaac Smith, drew many of the early charts, while Henry Roberts, Master's mate on the *Resolution*, prepared the charts of the third voyage for publication. Several others among those who sailed with Cook, including James Colnett and Nathaniel Portlock, went on to become captains of their own ships and prepared charts in their own right. The most successful of Cook's disciples was George Vancouver, who led a surveying voyage of the Northwest Coast of America from 1791 to 1795, from which the resulting charts can even be said to surpass those of Cook in their meticulous detail. Cook had trained his men well, and he realised that the charts were only part of the task. Wherever possible, coastal views were drawn and notes added describing the navigational problems, details of anchorages, fishing potential, and any other relevant facts about the area. Cook, more than anyone else, entered the Pacific realising the need for good, accurate charts, and he made it his responsibility to chart as much of the Pacific as possible. 'Beginning in 1768, James Cook led three expeditions that remain a model of reconnaissance mapping.'[19]

When the expeditions of Cook and Bougainville entered the Pacific they were both carrying copies of charts prepared by earlier voyagers and drawn by cartographers back in Europe. The reliability, though, of these charts was open to question. They were usually small-scale, very general and often full of supposed but non-existent lands. The exact location of real island groups was vague and one group, the Solomons, visited by Mendaña in 1568, had been 'lost' for two hundred years. The situation was understandable as equipment to fix latitude and longitude had not been available and few sailors, at the time, were given any training in chart making. Equipment for taking more correct measurements, such as sextants and marine chronometers, was only just being

---

[18] *RAV*, p. 509 n. 4.
[19] Wilford, *The Mapmakers*, pp. 168–9.

developed. 'The construction of charts was a neglected discipline in the seamen's education during the 18th century, particularly in the British Navy.'[20] And Cook himself wrote of 'the few [seamen] I have known who are Capable of drawing a Chart or sketch of a Sea Coast'.[21] A similar situation existed in the French navy, whose earlier charts could only act as rough guidelines. The expectations for both expeditions were that they would not only locate new lands but fix their locations more correctly than had been achieved before.

Not all the charts of the period possessed a scale and the charts of Cook and Bougainville usually lacked one. Most possessed a north point, though north was not necessarily at the top of the chart. The British, especially, often drew charts with south at the top. Joseph Gilbert, Master of the *Resolution* on the second voyage, drew a chart of Vanuatu (the New Hebrides) with this orientation. Latitude and longitude were both shown, the British relating longitude to Greenwich, the French to Paris (it would be more than a hundred years before the meridian at Greenwich was set as the international standard). Cook had lunar tables to help him determine longitude and on his second and third voyages also carried copies of John Harrison's marine chronometers, which allowed more precise calculations. Although Bougainville's ships carried *Connaissance des Temps*, the French nautical almanac which allowed navigators to observe the occultations of the moons of Jupiter, the longitudes determined by the French were not as accurate as those of the British.

Both Cook and Bougainville made efforts to use local knowledge in the production of their charts. Tupaia, the Raiatean high priest and navigator, helped Cook on the first voyage as a guide and translator, and he drew a schematic chart that showed the relative locations of islands to Tahiti (Plate VI). He was also able to predict the *Endeavour*'s arrival at Rurutu after the ship left the Society Islands in August 1769. Local nomenclature was used if it could be established, though it was often difficult to determine because of problems with communication and translation. It was not always possible to know whether all features carried local names before European arrival. Cook occasionally recorded names that bear no relation to local language or tradition, Tolaga Bay in New Zealand and Tanna in Vanuatu being examples. In other places, he used local names that have not been in general use since, Te Wai Pounamu for the South Island of New Zealand being an example. The name Tahiti (in different spellings) does appear on the charts of both Cook and Bougainville. However, where local names could not be established, the Europeans bestowed names of their own choosing.

Bougainville's crew prepared and drew charts during their voyage, but the number that survived and that have been published is not large. On his return to France, Bougainville prepared a narrative of his voyage and, when it was

---

[20] Skelton, *Explorers' Maps* (London, 1958), p. 233.
[21] *EV*, p. 413.

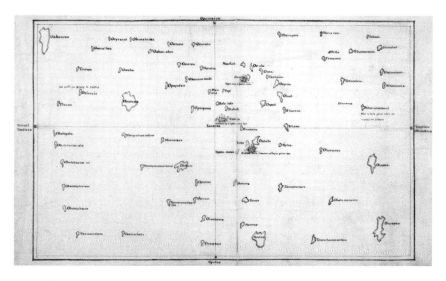

Plate VI James Cook, Pacific Islands, after Tupaia, 1769. A schematic chart drawn by Cook from information supplied by Tupaia

published, it included twenty plates containing maps, which had been redrawn for the work. When Forster's translation into English was published in London in 1772, these maps had been copied but grouped together in a different way. Several charts were combined, while some smaller charts were repositioned as insets in larger ones. Since that time, Bougainville's voyage has been largely ignored, even in France, and the few studies that have been published have included only one or two maps showing the overall course of the ships. Originals of the published and unpublished charts have been dispersed and reside in various archives in France so that it is difficult to determine the total number of charts that were produced. Not until 1977 was a scholarly French edition of the original journals published, and this included several more reproductions of charts drawn on Bougainville's voyage.[22]

The charts were redrawn for inclusion in the published narrative of 1771, not by Romainville, but by another cartographer. They are somewhat bare, reflecting the paucity of new information that Bougainville actually gained. The track of the two ships is shown as they crossed the Pacific, together with outlines of islands and coasts that were sighted. The relative rapidity of Bougainville's crossing, the small number of landfalls made by him, and the lack of time spent ashore, all combined to reduce the amount of cartographic detail that could be incorporated in new charts.

[22] Taillemite, *Bougainville*.

The standard of the charts improves where Bougainville anchored and was able to spend some time ashore. Also, places that had already been visited by Europeans, and for which Bougainville had copies of earlier charts, received better coverage. For these reasons, the Strait of Magellan, especially between Cabo San Isidro and Isla Carlos III, is far better served. Bougainville and several of his officers had visited the Strait in 1765. The *Boudeuse* and *Etoile* were based here for seven weeks and, in this time, officers went off in small boats to survey bays and inlets that were incorporated in new charts.

The charts prepared by James Cook and his crew on his three voyages have been extensively reproduced. Various editions of the narratives of Cook's voyages contained selected charts and, since then, many have been reproduced in various formats. For example, Cook's chart of New Zealand has appeared on calendars, posters, biscuit tins and T-shirts, amongst other formats, ensuring that Cook's charts are recognisable and well known (Plate VII). Cook's charts,

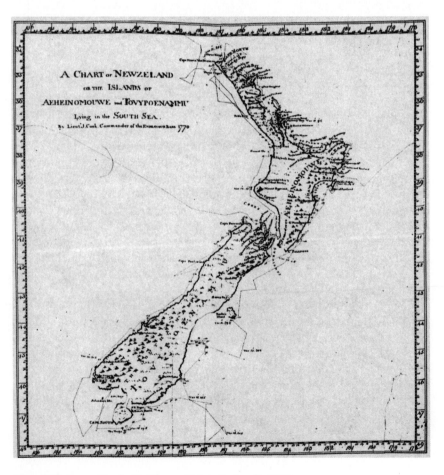

Plate VII James Cook, 'A Chart of New Zealand', 1770

therefore, have always been better served than those of Bougainville. The culmination of this attention came in the late 1980s and 1990s when three volumes were published, devoted to the charts from his Pacific voyages.[23] Cook was scrupulous in his attention to detail and any harbour or anchorage where he stopped would be surveyed. As he stated: 'The world will hardly admit of an excuse for a man leaving a coast unexplored he has once discover'd.'[24] He would always chart them sufficiently well so that he never had to waste effort resurveying locations he had already visited. Matavai Bay on Tahiti and Queen Charlotte Sound in New Zealand, which Cook revisited several times on his second and third voyages, are hardly represented by new charts on the later voyages.

Comparison of the charts

The quantity of charts produced by Bougainville on his single voyage is dwarfed by the production of Cook on his three voyages. This is to be expected given that Cook spent much more time in the Pacific, covered far greater distances and visited far more locations than his French counterpart. In terms of quality, also, Cook's charts are generally superior. For a fair judgement, it is necessary to compare charts of locations visited and charted by both explorers. There are only a few locations that meet these requirements and Tahiti and Vanuatu are the best examples.

Bougainville visited Tahiti in June 1768 and spent two weeks anchored at Hitia'a on the east coast of Tahiti Nui. The French were invited to land and erect a small camp but the Tahitians restricted French movement and prevented them going far beyond the camp. The Tahitians soon asked the French to leave, which meant that French cartographical knowledge was mainly restricted to observations made from the sea as they arrived and departed. The resulting chart shows the route of the ships and the north coasts of Tahiti Iti and Tahiti Nui, with very little extra information. Romainville also produced a freehand sketch chart of the anchorage at Hitia'a. It does not appear that surveying equipment has been used in its compilation, and it is a cross between a chart and a coastal view (Plate VIII). Bougainville was unaware of a visit to the island a few months earlier by the British navigator, Captain Samuel Wallis. Bougainville records the local name Taiti on his chart but calls it and some neighbouring islands the Archipel de Bourbon (Plate IX). He also called Tahiti Nouvelle Cythere, reflecting his classical education.[25]

---

[23] Andrew David, ed., *The Charts and Coastal Views of Captain Cook's Voyages*, 3 vols (London, 1988–97).

[24] Skelton, 'Cook as hydrographer', p. 92.

[25] Cythere or Kythira is an island situated off the south coast of mainland Greece.

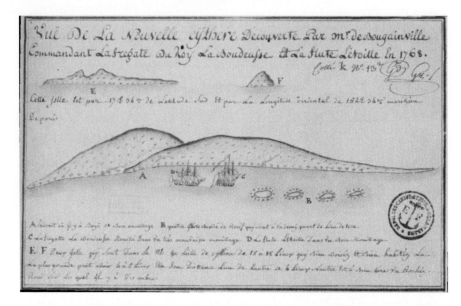

Plate VIII Charles Routier de Romainville, Hitia'a, Tahiti Nui, 1768. A coastal view of Bougainville's anchorage

Cook of course knew of the existence of Tahiti before he sailed, Wallis on his return having reported on his visit to the island, which he called King George the Third's Island. It was identified as a suitable location to observe the Transit of Venus in June 1769 and Cook arrived there in April, without the benefit of detailed charts but knowing of the safe anchorage on the north coast of the island from a sketch by George Pinnock (Plate X). Cook produced many charts of Tahiti, especially on his first visit in 1769, when he spent nearly three months on the island. Cook anchored at Matavai Bay on the north coast of Tahiti Nui and immediately struck up a friendly relationship with the local Tahitians. It would become his favourite place in the Pacific and one he would return to many times. Cook invariably called the island Otaheite and the group of islands the Society Islands. Unlike the French, Cook and his crew were able to travel freely and Cook even made a tour of the perimeter of the island.

As a result, Cook was able to produce detailed and reasonably correct charts of the whole of Tahiti (Plate XI). The overall shape of the island and the positioning of most of its features are excellent so that it is immediately recognisable as Tahiti. The coast and hinterland are portrayed exactly, although the interior of the island is far less well served, owing to the terrain and its covering of dense tropical bush. The mountainous interior is therefore portrayed somewhat stylistically. The surrounding reef is depicted with soundings shown inside the reef. Potential anchorages are marked, while Matavai Bay, where the *Endeavour* anchored, is given a more detailed chart. On his second

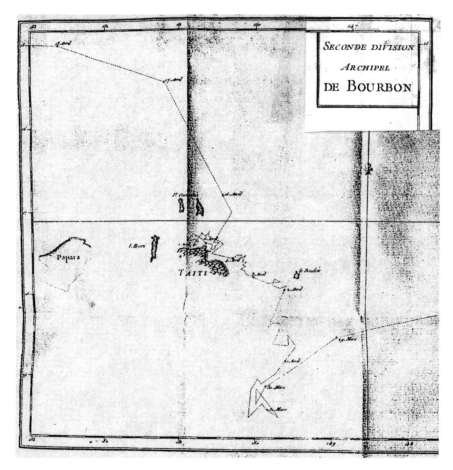

Plate IX 'Archipel de Bourbon' (Tahiti), 1768, published in Bougainville's *Voyage autour du monde* (1771)

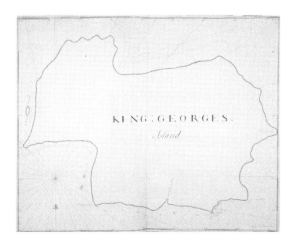

Plate X George Pinnock, King George's Island (Tahiti), 1767. North is at the bottom, Matavai Bay is bottom left

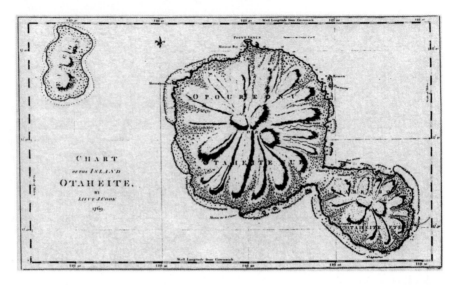

Plate XI James Cook, 'Chart of the Island Otaheite', 1769. North is at the bottom

voyage, a very good chart of Tautira, near the eastern tip of Tahiti Iti, was produced. Future visitors would be safe to use Cook's charts when approaching and anchoring at Tahiti. Cook had had the opportunity to make better charts and had taken it.

Bougainville sailed west from Tahiti, aware that Quiros had discovered land in 1606 which he named Austrialia de Espiritu Santo. Its precise location was uncertain and various charts, including that of Vaugondy, which Bougainville was carrying, tentatively linked it to New Holland. On 22 May 1768, Bougainville reached land, which, after a short visit of five days, he correctly identified as the land previously visited by Quiros. The island group is now known as Vanuatu. The French ships rounded Aurora Island (Maewo) and approached a second island, off which they anchored as they needed fresh water and wood. The French went ashore for a few hours and had the briefest of meetings with the Melanesian inhabitants of the island. Some of the local people had a skin complaint, which caused Bougainville to call the island Île des Lépreux (Leper Island) though its local name was Aoba. Going back on board, Bougainville made to leave but was becalmed for two days. Eventually, on the 26th, he was able to sail through a passage (now known as Bougainville Strait) between two islands and continue his voyage to the west.

During the time the ships were becalmed a small chart was drawn showing all the land fronting onto their location at sea off the west end of Aoba. The chart is recognisable as being of part of Vanuatu, though there are pronounced distortions of some of the islands depicted. The Île de la Pentecoste (Pentecost Island) is especially distorted. No depth soundings or anchorages are given. The chart, therefore, is a basic representation of islands that Bougainville called the Archipel des Grandes Cyclades, once more using a classical allusion to the Aegean (Plate XII).[26]

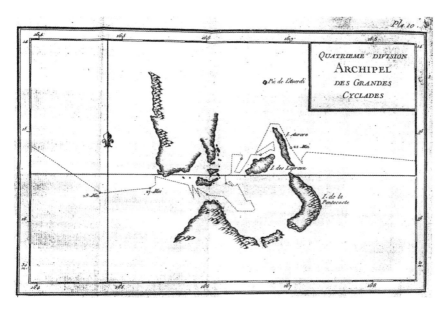

Plate XII 'Archipel des Grandes Cyclades' (Vanuatu), 1768, published in Bougainville's *Voyage autour du monde* (1771)

On his second voyage, James Cook knew about Bougainville's voyage and carried a copy of his chart. In July 1774, Cook happened to approach the same island, Aurora Island (Maewo), from the east as Bougainville had done. Over the next forty-five days he carried out a remarkable piece of marine surveying and put the island group firmly on the map. He made brief landings at Port Sandwich on Malekula, Port Narvin on Erromango and near the Jordan River on Espiritu Santo, but only for an hour or two at each location. A longer stay of fifteen days took place at Port Resolution on Tanna. The other twenty-nine days were spent coasting the 750-kilometre-long archipelago. Using a running survey, Cook produced a chart that shows all the islands in their correct locations, their shapes mostly correct, and with soundings added. It is a magnificent chart and the survey is among the highlights of Cook's career (Plate XIII). Cook obviously felt that he had achieved more than Bougainville, as he wrote:

> They were next visited by M. de Bougainville in 1768, who . . . did no more than discover that it was not a connected land, but composed of islands which he called the great Cyclades; but as we, not only, ascertained the extent and situation of these

[26] The Cyclades or Kyklades is a group of islands between the Greek mainland and Turkey.

islands, but added to them several new ones which were not known before and explored the whole, I think we have obtained a right to name them and shall for the future distinguish them under the name of the *New Hebrides*.[27]

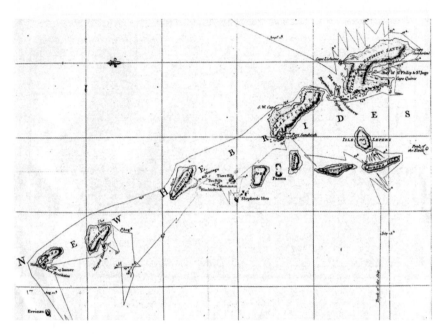

Plate XIII James Cook, New Hebrides (Vanuatu), 1774. North is to the right

Cook's charts are demonstrably superior to Bougainville's for several reasons: no priority was given to charts in the French instructions; Bougainville was not a cartographer; little time, encouragement and training were given on the voyage to surveying and charting; Romainville, the cartographer, sailed on the *Etoile*, separated from Bougainville; delays in the Atlantic led to pressure for a quick crossing of the Pacific; Romainville stayed in Mauritius and so made no contribution to the charts in the published account of the voyage; and Cook, on his second voyage, carried copies of Bougaunville's charts and was able to improve on them.

After the voyages

Bougainville arrived back in France in March 1769 and soon began writing up the narrative of his voyage. However, before the work was published in 1771

---

[27] *RAV*, p. 521.

the Ducs du Choiseul and Praslin both lost power and were dispatched from Paris in disgrace. Bougainville's scheme to settle the Malouines and his round-the-world voyage owed much to the patronage of Choiseul and Praslin and it is probable that Bougainville lost standing and prestige through being involved and identified with them. Certainly the *Voyage autour du monde* when it appeared drew little comment from the Paris establishment of learned societies and the like, even though the book sold sufficiently well to warrant a second edition. The description of Tahiti as an earthly paradise, particularly in Commerson's writings, helped fuel the debate about the 'noble savage'. Ahu-toru, the Tahitian brought back by the expedition, and the first Polynesian to reach Europe, proved of more interest to fashionable Parisians than Bougainville himself. Nor was Bougainville offered the chance to command another expedition. The Pacific voyages of Surville (1769–70) and Marion-Dufresne (1771–3) were private commercial ventures, while Kerguelen's two voyages in search of a southern continent (1771–2, 1773–4) were Indian Ocean affairs. Official France turned its back on the Pacific and was more preoccupied with Europe. The government was nearly bankrupt and the Ministry of Marine changed its priorities completely. It would be fourteen years before Jean-François Galaup de La Pérouse was given command of his prestigious naval expedition to the Pacific which left France in 1785.

La Pérouse's expedition was an effort to combat the prestige that Britain had gained through the voyages of James Cook. Cook had died but men such as Sir Joseph Banks, who had sailed on Cook's first voyage, ensured that the explorer's memory lived on. Gradually Cook's achievements gained near mythical status. Even French explorers placed Cook on a pedestal. Julien Crozet, who visited New Zealand with Marion-Dufresne in 1772, wrote:

> As soon as I obtained information of the voyage of the Englishman, I carefully compared the chart I had prepared of that part of the coast of New Zealand along which we had coasted with that prepared by Captain Cook and his officers. I found it of an exactitude and of a thoroughness of detail which astonished me beyond all powers of expression, and I doubt much whether the charts of our own French coasts are laid down with greater precision. I think therefore that I cannot do better than to lay down our track of New Zealand on the chart prepared by this celebrated navigator.[28]

By the time France acted to restore some pride, Bougainville, although he had continued to pursue a naval career, was too old at 56 to lead the expedition that was to be commanded by La Pérouse. He had fought in the War of American Independence with mixed results, distinguishing himself in one sea battle and being blamed for defeat in another. He survived a duel and

---

[28] Beaglehole, *Life of Cook*, p. 221 n. 2, quoting H. Ling Roth, *Crozet's Voyage to Tasmania . . .* (London, 1891), p. 22.

the guillotine before becoming a favourite of Napoleon, who made him a Comte. Bougainville was also one of the first recipients of the Légion d'honneur. He was one of the few explorers who reached old age and he died in his bed in 1811.

Sadly, this most interesting man has been largely forgotten by history. He deserves to be remembered, if not as the equal of Cook, then as the commander of a notable eighteenth-century expedition. For Bougainville, it is a case of what might have been. If Commerson, Veron and Romainville had returned to France with him and had made botanical, zoological, astronomical and cartographical contributions to the voyage's narrative, they might have been applauded as members of the first scientific voyage of exploration to the Pacific. As it is, they remain only adjuncts to history.

It was James Cook, not Bougainville, who became identified with the Pacific. Henry Roberts's chart after the third voyage showed virtually every island and island group fixed firmly in its correct position with the tracks of Cook's ships weaving amongst them. Like a pinball Cook had bounced from island to island, finding islands where no one else seemed able. His curiosity to search, his drive to search further, and his ability to read conditions and to sense where new islands might be situated placed him apart from other explorers. But his attention to detail was also phenomenal, as the wealth of charts contained in the three volumes of *The Charts and Coastal Views of Captain Cook's Voyages* testifies. Cook's

> chief memorial is the modern conception of the Pacific, derived from his superbly accurate charts, in which every island and every coastline had its latitude and longitude properly fixed for the first time through Cook's care and Harrison's chronometer. After Cook, no navigator could have an excuse for failing to find a Pacific island that Cook had visited or for being wrecked on a coastline appearing from nowhere.[29]

In conclusion, Bougainville left the map of the Pacific much as he had found it. His voyage may be regarded as one of the last made by a gentleman-amateur explorer. Cook, on the other hand, drew the map of the Pacific as we know it today and his voyage was the first made to the Pacific by a professional hydrographer. Cook had more than fulfilled the expectations of Lord Colvill, Commodore of the squadron in Canadian waters on which Cook served who, a few years earlier, had written: 'Mr Cook late Master of the Northumberland acquaints me that he has laid before their Lordships all his Draughts and Observations . . . I beg leave to inform their Lordships, that from my Experience of Mr Cook's Genius and Capacity, I think him well qualified for the Work he has performed, and for greater Undertakings of the same kind.'[30]

---

[29] Simon Berthon and Andrew Robinson, *The Shape of the World* (London, 1991), p. 131.
[30] Beaglehole, *Life of Cook*, p. 59.

9

Successors and rivals to Cook: the French and the Spaniards

ROBIN INGLIS

The discovery of the Pacific not only determined its entry into the conscious-ness of Europe, but also confirmed that its destiny was to reflect the shifting balance of power in the struggle for continental hegemony. At the same time, the ebb and flow of European interest in the vast and seemingly empty 'great south sea' reflected the navigational uncertainties and huge distances involved in approaching and sailing through it, as well as the existence of colonial settle-ments and trading opportunities in more easily accessible regions – North America, the Caribbean, Africa, and even India. Historians can speak in terms of James Cook's 'opening of the Pacific' as late as the eighteenth century only because of its essential remoteness from the centre of the action, which always remained Europe itself.

Early activity in the Pacific in the sixteenth century reflected the domination of Spain and her American empire.[1] In the seventeenth century, independent Holland emerged as a sea power, and the renewed rivalry of England and France became more evident. Then, in the eighteenth century wealth and imperial ambition, advances in shipbuilding and navigation, and the age of the Enlight-enment made Europe ever more ready to explore and exploit overseas lands. Anglo–French rivalry reached new heights, and Spain under Carlos III wit-nessed a renaissance in her political and cultural life, and a determination to preserve her imperial legacy.

Spain's early confrontation with Portugal was defused by a papal division of the world, and her assumption of sovereignty in the Pacific led to a series of voyages to its western reaches. Here she concentrated on the occupation of the Philippines and, following their conquest in 1564–5, on the establish-ment of a trade route between Acapulco and Manila, which until 1815 was the world's most sustained maritime enterprise. Once Spanish power had estab-lished itself in the Philippines, the cycle of exploration shifted south of the Equator. Its focus was one of the great geographical assumptions of the time – the existence of *Terra Australis* – but Spain had to be content with discoveries

---

[1] An accessible survey is Carlos Martínez Shaw, *Spanish Pacific: From Magellan to Malaspina* (Madrid, 1988).

in the Marquesas and Melanesia. Coincident with these southern initiatives were voyages of exploration and commerce along the American littoral, north and south of Lima and Acapulco respectively, where Spanish ships fought an ongoing battle with pirates and interlopers. The northern voyages towards California, however, had two specific purposes – the finding of safe harbours for use by the Manila galleons as they approached New Spain, and the search for the second great assumption of the age, that there was a navigable passage between the Pacific and the Atlantic, the northern mystery which was causing British adventurers to thrust their ships into the icy waters west of Greenland.

Spain's early domination in Pacific waters, and the concept of a 'Spanish Lake' that she was able to sustain during a period of over two hundred years, had less, however, to do with papal directives than with the existence of two practical advantages.[2] First, only Spain had settlements on both sides of the ocean, and settlements were crucial to support extended voyages. As long as other powers could not find convincing reasons to establish their own settlements, they were at a clear disadvantage. They were limited to individual, if profitable, strikes against coastal towns or the pursuit of treasure ships, and even these were easier and safer in the Atlantic where there was less expense and no need to negotiate Cape Horn. Even more substantial exploratory efforts such as those of Le Maire and Schouten (1615), Abel Tasman (1643), William Dampier (1698), and Jacob Roggeveen (1721) only provided the exceptions that proved the rule, and they did not lead to any substantial change in the situation. The second reason was that the current and wind systems reduced the ability of navigators to sail outside the routes first taken and areas first visited early in the sixteenth century. The westerlies and South Pacific drift forced ships north where they picked up the trades and equatorial currents to sail west in the wake of Magellan. In the North Pacific the trades and currents made the westbound galleon run relatively easy but made a return voyage eastbound impossible except in high latitudes with the help of Kuro Siwo; but even here the winds and weather made it a risky business.

To explore further in the Pacific, or to extend commercial enterprise throughout it, required new outlooks, new technologies and more compelling reasons to undertake the continuous expense and ongoing risk.[3] When Spain's position was finally challenged in the middle of the eighteenth century this is exactly what happened, and it led to the predictable response of any power whose position of ascendancy and control was more apparent than real: initially Spain was only able to counter the challenge with diplomatic bluster. For example, during the years of peace that followed the War of Austrian Succession

[2] O.H.K. Spate, *The Pacific since Magellan*, 3 vols (Canberra, 1979–88), is an exhaustive study. In the subtitle to vol. I Spate uses the phrase 'The Spanish Lake' to reflect early Spanish domination.
[3] Alan Frost, *The Voyage of the Endeavour: Captain Cook and the Discovery of the Pacific* (Sydney, 1998), p. xxvii.

and George Anson's remarkable voyage across the Pacific in the 1740s, many in British government and maritime circles became convinced of the need to move on the Pacific to establish new avenues of commerce, and above all to discover and lay claim to *Terra Australis*. A key element was the occupation of the Falkland Islands as a staging post. When Spanish foreign minister José de Carvajal heard of this he protested that 'the islands had long been since first discovered and inhabited by the Spaniards' and he dismissed as nonsense suggestions of exploration in the South Pacific for the advancement of knowledge without intent to settle. He scoffed at the idea that Spain could allow the British to plant themselves at the mouth of the Strait of Magellan. The British agreed to 'lay the scheme aside', but not without insisting that this was temporary and that 'his Majesty cannot in any respect give in to the reasoning of the Spanish ministers as his Right to send ships for the discovery of unknown and unsettled parts of the world, must indubitably be allowed by everybody'. The British Ambassador in Madrid wrote,

> if after all our intentions these people should be stubborn and testy, I should be the first to advise a contrary behaviour, and if they would vex us We have matters and ways to vex them in Our turn without infringing our Treaties and one of my first steps should be the setting out of discoveries in the South Seas.[4]

This was the first clear warning to Spain of a coming British policy of freedom of the seas: to roam, touch and trade at will away from places already settled. The policy was later most obviously tested in Britain's favour in the Nootka Sound Crisis of 1789–90. The time was not yet right for the Pacific, however, because of a continuing preoccupation with the Northwest Passage, but it would arrive with the end of the Seven Years War in 1763, when Britain, in a period of four years – 1764 to 1768 – sent out the voyages of John Byron, Samuel Wallis and James Cook.

* * *

Like Britain, France approached the 'Spanish Lake' as a disadvantaged outsider.[5] Spain continued to control the track around Cape Horn from her settlements in the Americas, and the northern route in the east from the Philippines. France watched with growing concern the Dutch establishment of a foothold in the central route in the East and the growing British power

---

[4] Quotations in ibid., pp. 5–6. See also Frost, 'Shaking off the Spanish yoke: British schemes to revolutionise America, 1739–1807', in Margarette Lincoln, ed., *Science and Exploration in the Pacific* (Woodbridge, 1998), pp. 19–37.

[5] This section of the chapter has benefited from John Dunmore's 'Anglo-French rivalry in the Pacific, 1700–1800', paper presented to the Vancouver Conference on Exploration and Discovery, Simon Fraser University, 1992. See also Dunmore, *Visions and Realities: France in the Pacific, 1695–1995* (Waikanae, 1997), chs 2–4.

in the Indian Ocean. The capture of Mauritius in 1715 and its establishment as Île de France gave the French a vital naval base but it was still too far away for more than sporadic forays. More obvious success resulted from growing Spanish–French co-operation against English and Dutch power at the end of the seventeenth century, and an ultimate alliance in the War of Spanish Succession. From 1695 to the end of the war in 1713, numerous French ships traded openly in the Americas and indeed across the ocean. However, again, without settlements there was no continuity for future growth, but the French came to appreciate the immense value of the Falkland Islands as a base for Pacific operations.

On the eve of the outbreak of the Seven Years War in 1756, when Anglo–French imperial rivalry began to reach its peak in what was the first global conflict of the modern age, Charles de Brosses wrote a maritime history of the Pacific, *Histoire des Navigations aux Terres Australes*, in which he outlined France's urgent need to promote exploration and the establishment of settlements and naval bases to balance Spanish power and thwart British expansion. The war, in which France suffered major losses in North America, the Caribbean and India, only proved how desperate the French predicament had become. The Pacific was still open, 'but it was evident to many prominent Frenchmen that it was likely to fall into British hands before the century was out'.[6] De Brosses' work was translated into English and his communications with Alexander Dalrymple also helped to determine and orient British exploration. Just as the end of the war in 1763 served to launch British voyages to explore and exploit the Pacific, so also the French made a move. Louis-Antoine Bougainville developed, and set out to implement, a strategy to establish a naval base in the Falkland Islands using displaced French Canadians, and a trading post on a Pacific island in the direction of Asia. Spanish pressure obliged Bougainville to terminate his Falklands adventure, but in following Wallis to Tahiti he laid claim to a French presence that was ultimately to endure. In his journals and on his return to France he expressed deep anxiety about British activities in the Pacific. When word reached Paris of the intentions of Cook's first voyage and then reports of its activities, there was quick official endorsement of, and hopes invested in, the expeditions of Jean François de Surville and Joseph de Kerguelen, who in 1769 and 1771 respectively embarked from India and Île de France.[7]

Surville's voyage grew out of French setbacks in India, and was encouraged by vague reports of a major English discovery – in reality Wallis's visit to Tahiti. Arriving off New Zealand at the same time as Cook (at one stage they were only a few miles apart), Surville then sailed northeast in search of the mysterious new land. After failing to find it he reached Peru where he was

---

[6] Dunmore, 'Anglo-French rivalry', p. 5.

[7] See John Dunmore, *French Explorers in the Pacific*, I, *The Eighteenth Century* (Oxford, 1965), pp. 144–65 (Surville), pp. 196–249 (Kerguelen).

detained by Spanish authorities for over three years. Next, the ambitious voyage of Kerguelen set out to search for the southern continent and to lay claim to an element of French control in the high latitudes. When he discovered what is today Kerguelen Island and hastened back to France to announce the great discovery of 'a fifth part of the world' that could become French, a second voyage was hastily arranged to verify the existence of the land and to forestall any English designs on it once the news got out. Indeed at this point rumour and speculation were important in determining the direction of rival voyages, Cook's second voyage having as a principal objective 'the land said to be discovered by the French'. There was of course no *Terra Australis* able to provide grain crops, precious stones and metals, and once Kerguelen's fiction was exposed he returned home in disgrace to a court martial.

The embarrassing and costly failures of Surville and especially Kerguelen forced the French into a self-enforced hiatus while Cook continued his exploration work with a third voyage that only served to marginalise them further and to cause anxiety to their geostrategists. But for all the concern among his ministers, Louis XVI, a student of geography who was fascinated by the new discoveries that were an integral part of the Enlightenment, was persuaded that Cook's achievements were part of the larger story of mankind and an understanding of his world. Although France and Britain were at war he gave the royal order that, if encountered, Cook was to be left alone by ships of the French navy so that he could complete his work.[8]

The war in question was that of the American Revolution in which France intervened successfully. The navy performed honourably after a period of restructuring under the capable Duc de Choiseul. After the disastrous Seven Years War he had used peace to build new ships and to create an effective, well-trained officer corps; the French fleet at least proved itself enough to neutralise Britain's assumed advantage. One of the officers who had distinguished himself, particularly in engaging a British convoy off Louisbourg and in a raid on forts in Hudson Bay, was Jean François Galaup de La Pérouse. In the glow of success, he was chosen to lead an expedition to restore a French presence in the Pacific. As the American war wound down, so information about Cook's third voyage emerged, ultimately in the 1784 publication of his journal. French interest in the potential of the fur trade of the North Pacific was particularly strong since France was still smarting from the loss of Canada twenty years earlier. Discussions between Claret de Fleurieu, Minister of Ports and Arsenals, and Navy Minister Marechal de Castries soon determined that an initiative to increase the national commerce was too important to leave to private traders, and that a commercial reconnaissance should be carried out by the French navy. The royal geographer, Jean-Nicolas Buache de la Neuville, and Louis XVI himself became involved, and during the winter of 1784–5 a proposed commercial enterprise expanded into a full-blown voyage of Pacific

---

[8] Archives National, Paris, Fonds B4, 313.

exploration. Cook's achievements loomed large and in the end the planners formulated an itinerary to rival his exploits, and to win for France some of the glory that the great navigator had brought to England. In its vision to explore all four corners of the ocean, and to contribute to science through exploration, the development of accurate charts and the amassing of natural history and ethnographic collections, along with reports and drawings on people and places designed to complete Cook's work, the voyage of La Pérouse must be considered equal to Cook's great third voyage.[9] In six months of feverish preparation two solid, heavy storeships were refitted as the *Boussole* and *Astrolabe*, and the best officers of the post-war period were recruited along with a full complement of scientists, artists, astronomers and a military engineer. The latter, Paul Monneron, was dispatched to London to investigate Cook's success and to purchase instruments, and during this time he received from Sir Joseph Banks two inclination compasses which had been in the Pacific with Cook. La Pérouse later received these 'with a religious feeling of respect towards the memory of that great man'.[10]

The King's final instructions ran to over two hundred pages in the account of the voyage that was finally published in 1797.[11] In the plan La Pérouse was enjoined 'particularly to endeavour to reconnoitre those parts which have not been examined by Captain Cook, and of which the . . . Russian and Spanish navigators have given no idea'. Political and commercial matters included the study of the production of the different islands and the manner and customs of the natives, their religion, government and mode of making war. Geographical and scientific concerns were to recognise that 'the object of greatest importance to the safety of navigators is to fix with precision the latitudes and longitudes of the places visited' and the need for 'exact charts of coasts and islands'. La Pérouse was also to oversee a full programme of scientific research. The conduct expected of him in his dealings with native peoples underlined that one of the hallmarks of the voyage was its genuine spirit of generosity and a desire to assist the peoples encountered. Seeds and implements were distributed at a number of places – at Easter Island, in California, and at places on the Asian mainland. The King's 'special instructions' stressed the need to encourage friendship, and to act with gentleness and humanity, and there is no reason to doubt the King's sincerity when he ordered that he would 'consider it as one of the happiest events of the expedition if it should end without costing the life of a single man'. Health issues were mentioned in the context of Cook's experiences, with its reliance on the procurement of

---

[9] For the genesis of the voyage of La Pérouse see Catherine Gaziello, *L'Expédition de Lapérouse 1785–1788: réplique française aux voyages de Cook* (Paris, 1984); also the Introduction in John Dunmore, ed., *The Journal of Jean-François de Galaup de la Pérouse, 1785–1788* (London, 1994), I, pp. xvii–ccxl.

[10] Ibid., I, p. 9.

[11] Ibid., I, pp. cx–cl.

wholesome food at every stopover and strict attention to the cleanliness of both ships and men. Finally, the enlightened dynamic of the whole endeavour was underlined by the drawing up of extensive *mémoires* from the *Académie des Sciences* and the *Société de Medicin*.

The departure of the *Boussole* and *Astrolabe* from Brest in August 1785 was witnessed by a huge crowd including the young René de Chateaubriand, the future romantic novelist and politician who later wrote: 'my uncle pointed out La Pérouse in a crowd, the new Cook, whose fate is a mystery of the tempests'.[12] The original route was around Cape Horn to Tahiti and Australia, but it seems likely that the priority was always the Northwest Coast, and after stopping at Concepción, Easter Island and Maui, La Pérouse reached modern-day Alaska in June 1786. If the aim was to complete the work of Cook the results were disappointing, After a boat accident that drowned twenty-one men and caused an extended stay in Port des Français, time and fog did not permit more than a cursory run down the coast to Monterey. The coastal perspective in front of him and his discussions with the British fur-trader and explorer Samuel Hearne four years earlier in Hudson Bay meant that La Pérouse harboured few illusions about the existence of a navigable passage across America, but he did improve slightly on existing Spanish and British charts, and Paris became as knowledgeable about the coast as London and Madrid. But there were still great gaps, particularly around latitudes 55° and 56°N. Nevertheless an act of possession and the dubious purchase of an island were achieved at Port des Français, strategically positioned between what La Pérouse understood to be the northern limits of Spanish activity and the Russian presence in the Aleutians. He also traded for furs and wrote a detailed *mémoire* about the prospect of establishing a factory manned by up to eighty people.[13]

In terms of expanding the knowledge developed by Cook's voyages, La Pérouse's work on the Tartary Coast was his single most important accomplishment. After stopovers in Macao and Manila, the ships set sail for the north, through the East China Sea and Sea of Japan into a region of the world previously unexplored by European navigators. Past Taiwan and into the Strait of Korea, La Pérouse was in waters and along coasts known only from the sketchy maps of missionaries, and for the first time a European ship had the chance to undertake a proper survey; but currents, contrary winds and fog made it a difficult task. Swinging east, La Pérouse came within sight of the coast of Japan, but this was not his focus; rather he moved on to visit a coast rumoured by the occasional Russian travellers to be uninhabitable. In his journal he noted: 'we were all anxious to examine this land . . . the only part of the globe

---

[12] Quoted in Alan Barrès, 'Lapérouse, marin et voyageur au siècle des lumières', *Revue du Tarn*, 17 (1985), p. 35.
[13] See Robin Inglis, 'Lapérouse 1786: a French naval visit to Alaska', in Stephen Haycox, James Barnett and Caedmon Liburd, eds, *Enlightenment and Exploration in the North Pacific, 1741–1805* (Seattle, 1997), pp. 49–64.

Plate XIV La Pérouse at Langle Bay, Sakhalin, 1787. In this engraving of a sketch by Duché de Vancy a portly La Pérouse looks on while one of the expedition's surgeon naturalists, Simon-Pierre Lavaux, questions a local elder to learn words for the dictionary he was compiling

that had escaped the indefatigable activity of Captain Cook, and we are indebted, perhaps, to the sad event that ended his life of being the first to land there'.[14] Voltaire had once dismissed the Tartars as 'rough stupid and brutal' but La Pérouse, during four meetings, found them friendly and accommodating. At one, Duché de Vancy drew the famous sketch showing the *Astrolabe*'s surgeon questioning elders in order to compile a dictionary of their language (Plate XIV).[15] The natives discussed their trading relationships and informed the Frenchmen that Sakhalin was an island, a fact later confirmed by their own observations. At another there were five days of intense charting and the botanist Collignon rushed about planting seeds. Although the damp, foggy weather was debilitating, when the *Boussole* and *Astrolabe* sailed through what is still named La Pérouse Strait between Sakhalin and Hokkaido, eight weeks of slow and dangerous navigation had provided a unique survey.

The port of St Peter and St Paul (Petropavlosk) on the Kamchatka peninsula was the farthest outpost of the Russian Empire, and La Pérouse stayed there for three weeks before sending his Russian interpreter home across Siberia with the expedition's reports and charts. The scientists visited a nearby volcano,

[14] Dunmore, *Journal of La Pérouse*, II, p. 276.
[15] Archives of the Société Historique de la Marine, Vincennes, Paris, Fonds 352, No. 19; *Atlas du Voyage de La Pérouse* (Paris, 1797), Plate 50.

replaced the plaque on the tomb of Captain Charles Clerke (Cook's successor as commander on the third voyage), and were fêted with a grand ball during which mail arrived from Paris ordering La Pérouse to abandon his planned visit to Guam, Tahiti, the Solomon Islands and New Zealand in favour of checking rumours that the British were about to settle at Botany Bay. After a long monotonous voyage south, even fresh fruit and water could in no way compensate for a second disaster, the massacre of eleven men and the wounding of twenty more during a landing to gather water at Tutuila in the Samoan Islands. It was a sad and dispirited group that limped into Botany Bay on the heels of Arthur Phillip's First Fleet, which was in the process of moving up the coast to Port Jackson. La Pérouse was in no position to do more than send another package of documents to France including a report on the British plans to establish a settlement, which could only have increased the sense of frustration and unease in Paris. But relations were cordial. 'All Europeans are compatriots at such a distance from home' he wrote,[16] and this is confirmed by the journal of Philip Gidley King. He had dinner with the Frenchmen in their shore settlement and later visited the French ships to be given a tour of the expedition's activities, both achieved and proposed; drawings, navigational observations, charts and collections were displayed. For La Pérouse, meeting with the British officer meant that Cook was never far from his thoughts, and he again expressed a generous attitude toward his predecessor. King noted that 'M. de Lapérouse informed us that at every place where he touched at or had been near, he found all the astronomical and nautical works of Captain Cook to be very exact and true and concluded by saying "Enfin, Monsieur Cook a tant fait qu'il ne m'a rien laissé à faire, que d'admirer ses oeuvres."'[17]

The tragedy of Vanikoro in the Santa Cruz Islands, where both ships were lost in a cyclone in March 1788, has clearly diminished the legacy of the sad and tragic La Pérouse expedition, and we are all the poorer for the loss. When one considers the wealth of material that came home with Alejandro Malaspina in 1794, we can only imagine the extent of material that never found its way into the official reports and dossiers that fortunately were sent home, and the results of the scientific investigations that went down with the ships. One of the more interesting aspects of La Pérouse's expedition was the commander's attitude towards the native peoples he encountered.[18] Certainly the generosity of his actions, as set out in his instructions, was increasingly at odds with his personal feelings. The idea of the noble savage had become well entrenched in French intellectual thought, and the reports of Philip Commerson, Bougainville's botanist, had only confirmed the impression that

---

[16] Dunmore, *Journal of La Pérouse*, II, p. 446.
[17] 'Journal of Philip Gidley King, 1786–90', Mitchell Library, Sydney, CY Reel 13, c.115, pp. 142–3.
[18] See J.F. McKenna, 'The noble savage in the voyage of La Pérouse', *Kentucky Foreign Language Quarterly*, 12 (1965), pp. 45–62.

man had been depraved by his development from the natural state into the false environment of an artificial and complex society, and that it was indeed possible to find happy, noble man close to nature. But La Pérouse had no time for the philosophers who assumed that native peoples in distant lands were intrinsically better than Europeans. The idea was nonsense as the death of Cook had shown. La Pérouse, like other European explorers and traders, was initially merely frustrated by the persistent thievery of the natives who had little concept of private property and regarded as fair game the belongings of strangers who took their wood and water. During the voyage his attitude hardened; at Easter Island he showed his displeasure at people who had responded to the French willingness to leave animals, implements and seeds with a desire to rob us of 'everything they could carry away'. Leaving in the middle of the night, he suggested optimistically that 'when they no longer saw us they would consider our speedy departure to our just discontent at their actions, and that this reflection would render them better people'.[19] At Port des Français, in the despair brought on by the loss of his men, he railed against academic philosophers with a bitter denunciation of their sentimental speculations:

> They write their books by their firesides while I have been voyaging for thirty years. I have witnessed the knavery and injustice of people whom they depict as good because they are so near to the state of nature; but nature is sublime only in the larger view, in detail it is less so. It is impossible to go into the woods where the hand of civilized man has not stretched to meet with the man of nature, because he is savage, deceitful and malicious.[20]

In Samoa he had thought the islanders were

> the happiest beings on earth, they spend their days in idleness surrounded by their wives and have no other care than to adorn themselves, to tame birds, and like the first man to pick fruit growing above their heads without any effort on their part. We saw no weapons, but their bodies were covered with scars which was evidence that they were often warring and quarreling, and their features indicated a ferocity one did not see in the women's appearance . . . man in an almost savage state and living in anarchy is a more malevolent being that the wolves and tigers of the forests . . . .[21]

He lamented the misguided thinking of his botantist Lammanon, who, the night before he was cut down on the beach, praised the local natives as 'better men than us'. Nevertheless, a comment in his journal suggests that he was not insensitive to the enlightened concept of the essential equality of men and

[19] Dunmore, *Journal of La Pérouse*, I, pp. 68–9.
[20] Ibid., I, p. 133.
[21] Ibid., II, p. 394.

the potentially harmful results of European exploration. Although he considered the French arrival in Maui to be the first in modern times he refused to take possession, scorning the idea of claiming it in the name of a faraway king, and instead gave further evidence of his sceptical and practical mind:

> The European practice is too utterly ridiculous, and philosophers must reflect with some sadness that, because one has muskets and cannons, one looks upon sixty thousand inhabitants as nothing, ignoring their rights over a land where for centuries their ancestors have been buried, which they have watered with their sweat. . . . Modern navigators have no other purpose when they describe the customs of newly discovered people than to complete the story of mankind. Their navigation must round off our knowledge of the globe, and the enlightenment which they try to spread has no other aim than to increase the happiness of the islanders they meet as they add to their means of subsistence . . . .[22]

If this is a naïve sentiment it is no less a noble one and a worthy epitaph to a courageous navigator who comes as close as anyone to Cook as a representative of an age when raw imperialism was tempered by enlightened thinking and the quest for knowledge.

It is perhaps not usual to relate the voyage of Bruny d'Entrecasteaux, sent to search for La Pérouse, in the context of Cook's voyages, but the expedition of the aptly named *Recherche* and *Espérence* was a significant undertaking, which included scientists and made a full programme of scientific and hydrographic research an important secondary objective. While it failed in its principal, daunting task and finally disintegrated after the death of its commander amid recriminations between royalists and republicans, the expedition circumnavigated Australia almost twice in the years 1792 and 1793. The collapse of the voyage overshadowed some real achievements, particularly the detailed examination of Tasmania, the southwest central coast of Australia, New Caledonia and the Solomon Islands, resulting in a wealth of charts, accounts of native life and natural history observations. But France's response to Cook had fallen short. As revolution gripped the nation and the long period of the Napoleonic adventure engulfed Europe, the Pacific remained beyond her sphere of interest for more than twenty years except for the well prepared and enlightened voyage of Nicolas Baudin, which again concentrated on the seas around Australia. Although the French were to establish a significant presence in the South Sea in Tahiti and New Caledonia (both first discovered by the British) and in the New Hebrides, the larger prizes of Australia and New Zealand fell firmly into British hands.

* * *

---

[22] Ibid., I, p. 88.

The historian of the Pacific Ocean, Oskar Spate, has maintained that Spain was never able to resolve the dilemma of whether it was a continental European and Mediterranean power or an American and Atlantic one. Her rulers not only tried to be both at once, but also attempted to extend and maintain their influence over the Pacific as well.[23] In the eighteenth century this latter ambition could not be sustained for the simple reason that the resources available could never match the size of the problem. Nevertheless, the British and French did not act in some kind of Spanish vacuum, and in the 1760s Spain began a new round of exploration aimed at the defence of her American empire and the safeguarding of her interests in the Philippines and the wider Pacific. During the reign of Carlos III there was a renaissance in the nation's intellectual and cultural life that brought it into the mainstream of the Enlightenment; and a series of able, reformist ministers began to pay long-overdue attention to the empire. Spain, like France and Britain, fully realised the importance of maintaining superiority at sea, and for the best part of the century was fully committed to the development of a modern navy. Her ships, armament, instrumentation and officer training, driven by such reformers as Jorge Juan and Francisco Gautier, surpassed in many respects those of her principal rivals.[24] Voyages to the Americas and the Pacific became a symbol of Spain's eighteenth-century recovery and were powered by an effective duality: a political agenda involving military, strategic and commercial concerns, and a sincere desire to use and contribute to scientific progress and the expansion of knowledge.

Between 1767 and 1795, eight major Spanish expeditions were engaged in a systematic survey of the Atlantic and Pacific coasts in the region of the Strait of Magellan, signalling its importance as a gateway to the South Sea that merited fuller understanding and control. In the same period no less than seven hydrographic expeditions were sent to the Philippines, while Viceroy Manuel de Amat organised four expeditions in the southern latitudes from Peru, which followed the voyages of Wallis and Cook. The only lasting result of these latter initiatives, however, was the seizure of Easter Island and its incorporation into the Hispanic world. The Spanish crown also sponsored a number of specifically scientific endeavours following the establishment in Madrid of a Botanical Garden, Academy of Medicine and astronomical observatory. Inspired by the work of Linnaeus and Buffon, the French *philosophes* and the publication of the *Encyclopédie*, Spanish naturalists were keen to apply the new methods of identification and classification to the flora and fauna and minerals of both North and South America. Principal among these expeditions were the Ruiz/Pavón travels in Peru and Chile, Mutis in New Granada, Cueller in the Philippines, and Sessé and Moziño in New Spain.[25]

---

[23] O.H.K. Spate, 'The Spanish Lake', in Shaw, *Spanish Pacific*, p. 42.

[24] See John Harbron, *Trafalgar and the Spanish Navy* (Annapolis, 1988), pp. 11–52.

[25] The scope of these major endeavours can best be appreciated in Iris H.W. Engstrand, *Spanish Scientists in the New World* (Seattle, 1981).

In the world of the Spanish Pacific in 1760s, a particular area of concern was the Northwest Coast of America. Reports were reaching Madrid from St Petersburg about Russian designs in the region, and these coincided with continuing speculation about whether or not the legendary Northwest Passage existed. Two voyages in 1774 and 1775 respectively introduced the world to a surprisingly vibrant Native culture, but found no Russians. When information emerged about Cook's forthcoming third voyage, however, the alarm was raised and the reaction immediate. From his time as *Visitador* to New Spain, José de Gálvez had dreamed of extending the empire into the western half of North America. Control of the coast was vital, and if the British had found the passage the real threat to New Spain and its galleons would have been obvious. Now, as Minister of the Indies he instructed the Viceroy Bucareli 'to be vigilant and cause [Cook] to fail in every way possible without using force but by taking measures to restrict assistance and supplies'.[26] When Bucareli doubted the existence of the passage, suggested that there were no supplies to spare anyway, and expressed his opinion that it was absurd to think of Cook creating settlements which Britain could not possibly support, Gálvez replied that Cook was to be detained, imprisoned and tried in accordance with the Laws of the Indies. 'I expect you to comply',[27] he wrote tersely. After the success of Bodega y Quadra's voyage in 1775 another voyage had been planned. When news of Cook's intentions became clear this expedition was ordered to find and arrest him. Even if this might have been possible for ships sailing from San Blas, which it clearly was not, the voyage only got under way in 1779, long after Cook had left the coast.[28]

The distraction of the American War included the transfer of officers from the San Blas naval station on the Pacific coast of Mexico to Havana, and Spain did not refocus on her previous concerns about Pacific North America until La Pérouse appeared. When Spain acted, it was less a direct response to what Cook had done or where he had been than a reaction to the French response to Cook's achievements. La Pérouse put into the Chilean port of Concepción in February 1786, and following his visit the local military commander, Ambrosio Higgins, sent a long memorandum to Gálvez expressing grave concern about the Russian, British and now French threats to the Northwest Coast. During La Pérouse's visit, a Spanish official who read French was shown a chart that seemed to indicate Russian trading posts on the coast as far south as Nootka. While this was a misreading of a chart which had been prepared

---

[26] Royal Order of 23 March 1776, quoted in Bucareli's letter to Gálvez of 26 June 1776; No. 2296 in *La Administratión de D. Antonio María de Bucareli y Ursúa* (Publications of the Archivo General de la Nación, Mexico, XXIX, 1936).
[27] Royal Order quoted in No. 2702 (see note 26 above) from Bucareli to Gálvez, 27 January 1777.
[28] See Christon Archer, 'The Spanish reactions to Cook's third voyage', in Robin Fisher and Hugh Johnston, eds, *Captain Cook and His Times* (Vancouver, 1979), pp. 99–119.

for the voyage and which detailed Spanish and British activities, Higgins wrote forcefully of the dangers inherent in the perceived challenges and urged Gálvez to occupy Hawaii and Cook Inlet in Alaska.[29] This did not happen, but it was enough to touch off another round of Spanish voyages in the North Pacific with the expeditions of Lopez de Haro and Esteban Martínez to the Aleutians in 1788, the decision to occupy Nootka in 1789, and the voyage of Salvador Fidalgo to Prince William Sound in 1790.

It was not unexpected that the Spain of Carlos III, with its growing concern about the challenges to its sovereignty in the Pacific, and its enthusiasm for the scientific study of its vast dominions, should seek to respond to the La Pérouse voyage with one that should stand alongside Cook's voyages of the 1760s and 1770s. What became the Malaspina expedition was designed to complement and complete the significant hydrographic and scientific surveys, already under way or planned, with a round-the-world expedition led by a group of the finest officers in the navy accompanied by the best scientific corps that the nation could provide. Highly educated and well-connected, the 34-year-old Alejandro Malaspina evoked the spirit of Cook and La Pérouse when in September 1788 he and his colleague José Bustamante submitted their plan for the voyage to the Navy Minister Antonio Valdés.[30] Malaspina had already completed a circumnavigation in the naval vessel *Astrea* which had been chartered by the Royal Philippine Company in an effort to investigate better trading relationships between Spain, the Americas and the Far East. On this voyage he became conscious of the need to reform the empire, particularly in relation to trade, and more appreciative of the work of Cook, Bougainville and La Pérouse. Indeed he was disappointed to have missed the latter (by a month) when he arrived in the Philippines and, when he visited Ambrosio Higgins in Concepción in February 1787 there is little reason to doubt that he was inspired by the latter's enthusiasm, expressed repeatedly in correspondence and reports to Madrid, for a similar voyage to match the benefits that the British and French expeditions had secured. There seems to be a direct link between the Higgins memorandum of 1786 and Malaspina's plan presented in 1788.

Although certainly inspired by his predecessors, Malaspina was clear that it was not possible to equate his proposed expedition with the voyages of the 1760s and 1770s. He understood that the essential scope and nature of the Pacific had been clearly established; that its peoples, their origins, customs and products had been examined; and that there had been significant progress in shipbuilding and navigation, and particularly in the whole approach to the

---

[29] *Nota* from Ambrosio Higgins to the Marques de Sonora (Gálvez), Concepción, 20 July 1786, in Archivo Histórico Nacional, Madrid, Estado 4289; see also Robin Inglis, 'The effect of Lapérouse on Spanish thinking about the Northwest Coast', in Inglis, *Spain and the North Pacific Coast: Essays in Recognition of the Bicentennial of the Malaspina Expedition, 1791–1792* (Vancouver, 1992).

[30] 'Plan de Viage', Museo Naval, Madrid, MS 316.

health of crews. For him it was important to complement the work already done, to confirm the work of his predecessors, and to contribute to the expansion of knowledge. Most important was to meet some crucial needs of the Spanish state: to investigate further the immense range of the King's possessions, to create and publish up-to-date hydrographic charts, and to look at ways of increasing the security, defence and commercial potential of the empire, recommending reforms as necessary.[31] For this the expedition was backed by royal orders to officials in the Americas and the Philippines to lend all assistance possible, and Malaspina was even permitted to remove, if necessary, original documents from government offices and archives. The results of the voyage in this regard are staggering: in the Museo Naval, Madrid alone there are some four thousand documents including reports and letters, diaries, scientific papers, statistical records, drawings and charts. When one considers that the Malaspina scholar Dolores Higueras has listed eight other major respositories, one can only agree with her assessment that, considering the geographic sweep of the voyage, this volume of documentation amounts to 'one of the fullest bodies of knowledge available as an insight into the century of the Enlightenment' (Plate XV).[32]

The specially-built *Descubierta* and *Atrevida* left Cadiz at the end of July 1789. Because of the calibre of officers and scientists assembled, it followed that the collections amassed and the documentation produced were of the very highest quality. A full nineteen months were spent reaching Acapulco, from where Malaspina expected to do some important new exploration work in the Hawaiian Islands. But a revival of the story of Ferrer Maldonado's fictitious voyage through the passage from the Atlantic to the Pacific at the end of the sixteenth century, through a memoir presented by Buache de la Neuville (the same who had played a key role in drawing up La Pérouse's instructions) to the Académie des Sciences in Paris on 13 November 1790, led to a swift order to Malaspina to make a detour to the Northwest Coast of America. Here in the summer of 1791 he visited Yakutat Bay in southern Alaska; he found no passage but he was more successful further south in bolstering Spanish control at Nootka, where an important military settlement was already well established. The work of his officers Dionisio Alcalá Galiano and Cayetano Valdés, whom he detached from the main party for more exploration in 1792, went on to prove the insularity of Vancouver Island and complemented the surveying achievements of George Vancouver.[33]

---

[31] See Malaspina's 'Introducción' to his journal in Andrew David, Felipe Fernández-Armesto, Carlos Novi and Glyndwr Williams, eds, *The Malaspina Expedition 1789–1794: Journal of the Voyage by Alejandro Malaspina*, I (London, 2001), pp. lxxix–xcvi.
[32] See Dolores Higueras, 'The Malaspina expedition (1789–1794): a venture of the Spanish Enlightenment', in Shaw, *Spanish Pacific*, pp. 158–62.
[33] The Northwest Coast visit is covered in Donald C. Cutter, *Malaspina and Galiano: Spanish Voyages to the Northwest Coast, 1791 and 1792* (Vancouver, 1991).

Plate XV A sketch by Juan Ravenet (outside the tent) showing Alejandro Malaspina and his colleague José Bustamante observing the pendulum as part of a gravity experiment at Port Egmont, Falkland Islands, 1794

The strictly Pacific phase of the voyage began after the return to Acapulco. Rather unenterprisingly, Malaspina followed the track of the Manila galleons, visiting Guam and reaching Cavite, the port of Manila, in March 1792. Bustamante visited Macao, and it was eight months, after waiting out the typhoon season, before the expedition sailed south. The Spaniards visited Dusky Sound on the South Island of New Zealand before arriving in March 1793 in Port Jackson to undertake a little polite espionage. They were warmly received, relations were cordial and they were impressed by the progress of the colony. But Malaspina's secret report underlined the real threat such a British outpost could pose to the Spanish position in the southern latitudes, all the way to the Americas. He saw in it a haven for the promotion of smuggling and piracy, and a base from which to control the whale fishery. His visionary response, however, was not to attempt, in the words of an official in Chile, 'to root out once and for all these interlopers',[34] a hopelessly futile tactic by this time, but to suggest regular communication and freer trade.[35]

[34] José Miguel Urezberoeta to Ambrosio Benavides, Concepción, 24 March 1786, in Archivo Histórico Nacional, Madrid, Estado 4289.
[35] For a translation and discussion of Malaspina's report see Robert J. King, *The Secret History of the Convict Colony: Alexandro Malaspina's Report on the British Settlement of New South Wales* (Sydney, 1990).

Malaspina performed the act of possession only twice during the whole expedition: at Puerto de Desengaño in Alaska, and at Vavao in the Friendly Islands of Tonga, where he was keen to confirm the discoveries of Francisco Mourelle in 1781. Two activities were necessary for this latter – first a full scientific examination of the Vavao archipelago, and secondly a public ceremony of possession. The latter was an elaborate affair, as religious as it was political. However disingenuous we might view his position today, the commander took pains to record that it was performed with the consent of the natives, whose chief Vuna was present and who apparently encouraged his people to recite the phrase 'Long live the King!'[36] Interestingly enough for a representative of a nation that condemned such acts as meaningless without settlement, James Cook had on several occasions carried out acts of possession, not only without any immediate prospect of settlement, but also in breach of his instructions which required him to secure 'the consent of the natives' for such annexations.[37]

By now Malaspina had decided not to return to Spain via the Indian Ocean and Cape of Good Hope. He was becoming weary and disillusioned, and even harboured fears of a mutiny.[38] But after crossing east to Peru he subsequently rounded the Horn and returned home to a triumphant welcome in September 1794. The Spain he found, however, was very different from the one he had left five years previously. The world of Carlos III had vanished with his death and the succession of his dull and incompetent son; the enlightened world of liberal despotism was long gone in the turmoil unleashed in Europe by the French Revolution and by the various reactions and counter-reactions that followed. Although Malaspina was well received, promoted and encouraged to start preparing for publication a multi-volume account of the expedition, along with all the requisite drawings, charts and scientific reports, his views were often scathing in their criticism of Spanish colonial policy and attitudes, and radical in their proposals for a lessening of centralised political control and the introduction of freer trade. Despite these opinions, he might have been able to complete the task had he not openly challenged Prime Minister Manuel Godoy with strident personal criticism and plans for a ministerial coup. Malaspina was arrested and condemned to prison for ten years. With him went any hope of publication of a grand account of the expedition, and it was close to one hundred years before Pedro Novo y Colson produced an edited version in 1885, and promptly reburied it in a folio of 681 pages, 573 of them double-columned with no index. It meant that Malaspina's expedition, despite its worthy results, became the least known of all the great Pacific voyages, rarely,

---

[36] See Mercedes Palau, Blanca Saiz and Aránzazu Zabala, eds, *Viaje científico y politico: Diario de Viaje de Alejandro Malaspina* (Madrid, 1984), p. 462.

[37] See p. 244 below.

[38] See John Kendrick, *Alejandro Malaspina: Portrait of a Visionary* (Montreal and Kingston, 1999), pp. 86–94.

and then often inaccurately, mentioned in most historical accounts of the ocean.

Alexander Humbolt suggested that Alejandro Malaspina was better remembered for his misfortunes than for his discoveries. The voyage was a prodigious effort and magnificent in its scope, but as he himself wrote, 'Ours was not a voyage of discovery', and he understood that it came too late to add very much to the history of exploration.[39] He really seems to have believed that Spain could best be served if, as he wrote to Sir Joseph Banks, he and his colleagues were 'to add to the efforts of other nations towards progress in the fields of physics and natural history as well as geography and navigation'.[40] Given that it was the early 1790s, Malaspina was certainly naïve about Spanish rights to exclusive sovereignty over the Pacific Ocean, which had clearly disappeared in practice and were close to complete rejection at the diplomatic level. The failure to undertake a thorough investigation of the Hawaiian Islands, which might have been followed by an aggressive programme of settlement – as the British were undertaking in New South Wales – lost them for Spain.[41] Likewise, he never followed up his original intention to visit the Lui Chiu or Ryuku Islands, northeast of Taiwan, which would have provided the first accurate and extensive survey of that region.

It is remarkable, given the predilection of European nation states to engage in frequent warfare on land or at sea as a natural consequence of their evolving relationships and competing interests, that their rivalries in the Pacific were rarely expressed in belligerent terms – at least against each other – as the great south sea became more open and accessible. The Natives of course were much less fortunate, but the eighteenth-century voyagers were for the most part sensitive imperialists who tried with what little understanding they had during their various encounters, to treat the peoples they met as fellow human beings, inferior only in their progress in the ascent of man. The enlightened impulse of scientific investigation in its broadest sense meant that, rivals though they were, they were also successors and predecessors engaged in a larger human drama.

---

[39] Malaspina, 'Introducción', in David et al., Malaspina Expedition, p. lxxxvii.

[40] Malaspina to Joseph Banks, 20 January 1789, translation (from the French) in The Spanish at Port Jackson (Sydney, 1967), p. 34.

[41] See Donald C. Cutter, 'Malaspina and the Shrinking Spanish Lake', in Lincoln, Science and Exploration in the Pacific, pp. 77–8.

10

Russian responses to the voyages of Captain Cook

SIMON WERRETT

In 1790, the radical Russian social critic Alexander Radishchev published his *Journey from St. Petersburg to Moscow*. Amidst a harsh critique of political absolutism and serfdom which would earn him exile in Siberia, Radishchev attacked Russia's navy for its indifference towards voyages of discovery. The navy, he said, was an institution of apathy and petty careerism, where officers might advance themselves without ever leaving a harbour. Radishchev contrasted this dismal state to the inspirational voyages of Captain James Cook: 'O Cook! Why did you pass your life in travail and privations? If you had boarded [Russian] ships you would have begun your voyage in delightful ease, and in delightful ease you would have ended it.'[1]

Commentators on Russian reactions to the voyages of Cook, in particular Terence Armstrong in his appraisal of 'Cook's reputation in Russia', have identified a more enthusiastic response to Cook than Radishchev's comments would suggest.[2] Armstrong identified a steady growth in Cook's reputation in Russia following the conclusion of the third voyage and interactions between Cook and the Russians in the Aleutians and Kamchatka in 1778–9. Despite an initial caution at foreign incursions into what was perceived as Russian territory, the Russian government soon began its own voyages of exploration to the region, beginning with those led by Cook's former crew member Joseph Billings in 1785–93. Armstrong notes that in a series of subsequent Russian circumnavigatory voyages in the early decades of the nineteenth century, many were commanded by Russians trained in the British navy, whose British

---

[1] Alexander N. Radishchev, *A Journey from St. Petersburg to Moscow*, trans. Leo Wiener, ed. R.P. Thaler (Cambridge, Mass., 1958), p. 74.

[2] Terence Armstrong, 'Cook's reputation in Russia', in Robin Fisher and Hugh Johnston, eds, *Captain Cook and His Times* (Vancouver, 1979), pp. 121–8; James R. Gibson, 'A notable absence: the lateness and lameness of Russian discovery and exploration in the North Pacific, 1639–1803', in Robin Fisher and Hugh Johnston, eds, *From Maps to Metaphors: The Pacific World of George Vancouver* (Vancouver, 1993), pp. 85–103. Much of the literature on Cook and Russia focuses on his visit to the North Pacific on the third voyage. See James R. Gibson, 'The significance of Cook's third voyage to Russian tenure in the North Pacific', *Pacific Studies*, I (1978), pp. 119–46, and note 7 below.

experience helped foster an enthusiasm for Cook. Examining these voyages, by captains such as Adam von Krusenstern, Otto von Kotzebue and Thaddeus von Bellingshausen, Armstrong was surprised by the extravagance of Russian praise for Cook, noting, 'A stage was even reached at which no wrong could be imputed to Cook.'[3] He also remarks, 'the oddity here is that the hero is not Russian'.[4]

In this chapter, two issues relating to Cook's reputation in Russia raised by accounts such as Armstrong's are addressed. First, it is proposed that the growth of Cook's reputation in Russia was more uneven than has been suggested. The first part of the chapter examines the decade following Cook's final voyage, and argues that enthusiasm for Cook and voyages of discovery was restricted to scholarly circles, failing to penetrate to the court and government. Glyndwr Williams has shown how uneven British Admiralty interests were in promoting voyages of discovery, including Cook's, during the eighteenth century, and a similar case may be made for the Russian government.[5] Exploring the context leading up to Billings's expedition to the North Pacific shows how government interest in the fur trade, rather than interest in Captain Cook or a desire for discoveries, motivated the expedition. Other Russian expeditions of the 1770s and 1780s similarly rested on strictly commercial and imperial concerns. It is also suggested that when the Russians did send ships to the North Pacific, they followed the precedent of earlier Russian voyages rather than those of Cook, despite their employment of Billings. While Russia's scholarly community responded enthusiastically to Cook, it was not self-evident that the British navigator should be admired or emulated in a land which had its own traditions of voyaging and exploration.

Undoubtedly the delay in positive responses to Cook in Russia was partly a result of the time needed for knowledge of Cook's voyages and activities to spread among the Russians, and undoubtedly much of the enthusiasm which did eventually appear owed its origin to Russians training in the British navy. However, as Armstrong points out, this enthusiasm quickly became adulation. This is the second issue examined in this chapter. The transition from enthusiasm to adulation may be understood by taking into account the nature of late eighteenth-century Russian culture and its intense fascination with the foreign. Recent anthropological studies of enlightened exploration have stressed the theatricality of eighteenth-century voyages of exploration. The historical anthropology of Greg Dening in particular has explored the cultural performances of officers, crews, strangers and natives in their efforts to display

---

[3] Armstrong, 'Cook's reputation', pp. 127–8.

[4] Ibid., p. 125.

[5] Glyndwr Williams, 'To make discoveries of countries hitherto unknown: the Admiralty and Pacific exploration in the eighteenth century', in Alan Frost and Jane Samson, eds, *Pacific Empires: Essays in Honour of Glyndwr Williams* (Melbourne, 1999), pp. 13–31.

national and cultural agendas and 'make history' during voyages.[6] In this chapter, another dimension of theatricality in voyages of discovery is presented. The Russian semiotician Yuri Lotman has proposed that the lives of eighteenth-century Russians were peculiarly 'theatrical' as they were obliged by the state to imitate the lifestyles and habits of western Europeans, following the westernising reforms of Peter I (r. 1689–1725) earlier in the century. By the 1790s such theatrical imitation had become deeply embedded in Russian culture, and its forms and nuances help make sense of the circumnavigators' attitudes. At the same time, many of the circumnavigators came from a distinctive group within Russian society, the Baltic German nobility. This group had its own particular agendas and position within the Russian service, and examining these interests also helps to explain Russia's peculiar veneration of Captain Cook.

The Russian tradition in exploration

In October 1778, the *Resolution* and *Discovery* arrived at Unalaska, where Captain Cook met a community of Russians who had settled there to pursue the lucrative trade in sea otter furs.[7] Cook seems to have had a good opinion of these fur traders, and he entrusted the leading Russian, Gerasim Izmailov, with charts and reports for the British Admiralty to be sent back to London by way of St Petersburg. In his journal, Cook described the Russians with the same ethnographic eye he used to describe the many other communities he had visited during his voyages. But he also noted something which Radishchev would later pick up. The Russian government, Cook wrote, had made no effort to explore the North American coast, and what had been learnt of it was for the most part due to the efforts of independent Russian fur traders. 'What has been done . . . has been by traders', he wrote in his journal.[8]

---

[6] Greg Dening, 'The theatricality of history making and the paradoxes of acting', *Cultural Anthropology*, viii (1993), pp. 73–95; Dening, *Mr. Bligh's Bad Language* (Cambridge, 1992); Dening, *The Death of William Gooch: A History's Anthropology* (Melbourne, 1995); Dening, *Performances* (Chicago, 1996).

[7] On the expedition in Russia see *RDV*, pp. 448–58 (Cook's journal), pp. 645–83 (Clerke's journal), pp. 700–7 (Edgar's journal), pp. 1140–1, 1240–60, 1272–82 (Samwell's journal); Russian documentation of events may be found in J.C. Beaglehole, *Cook and the Russians. An Addendum to the Hakluyt Society's Edition of the Voyage of the 'Resolution' and 'Discovery', 1776–1780* (London, 1973); Ia.M. Svet, 'Novyie danniie o prebyvanii na Kamchatke tret'ei ekspeditsii Dzh. Kuka (1779 g.)', in K.V. Malakhovskii, ed., *Novoe v izuchenii Avstralii i Okeanii*, (Moscow, 1972), pp. 219–27; Y.M. Svet, S.G. Fedorova, 'Captain Cook and the Russians', *Pacific Studies*, II (1978), pp. 1–19; see also anon., 'The English in Kamchatka in 1779', *Geographical Journal*, LXXXIV (1934), pp. 417–19.

[8] *RDV*, p. 450 (11 October 1778).

This comment was not without truth. Voyages of exploration had once been one of the most prestigious signs of Russia's new status as a member of the 'civilised' European nations. Under the leadership of the Danish seaman Vitus Bering, Russian expeditions had set out from St Petersburg to Kamchatka and the North Pacific in 1725–30 and again in 1734–43, bringing great imperial and scientific gains to the Russian court.[9] But after Bering's death in 1741 and the premature conclusion of the second expedition in 1743, Russian interest in the North Pacific dwindled. Nevertheless, in subsequent decades a variety of independent Russian and Cossack adventurers pushed east towards the Aleutian Islands in pursuit of the fur trade. Building up families and communities with the indigenous peoples of Siberia, these traders became known as *Sibiriaki*, Russian-Siberians, and together with other traders they formed the community which Cook met in Unalaksa.[10] Early in the reign of Catherine II, naval expeditions under the command of Captains V. Ia. Chichagov and Petr Kuz'mich Krenitsyn had been sent from St Petersburg to try to gain government control over these traders, but the missions proved abortive.[11] Traders retained their independence and, as Cook said, most of the recent Russian exploration in northern America was the result of these people's search for trade.[12]

While the *Sibiriaki* were exploring the coasts of the North Pacific in search of furs, the response to Cook's voyages in the capital, St Petersburg, was mixed. St Petersburg's scholars did take an interest in Cook. Shortly before his death, Captain Charles Clerke gave a large collection of Polynesian artefacts and engravings from Cook's third voyage, described as 'an assortment of curiosities' by Lieutenant James King, as a gift to First-Major Magnus von Behm, the

---

[9] Frank A. Golder, ed., *Bering's Voyages* (New York, 1922–5); Raymond H. Fisher, *Bering's Voyages: Whither and Why* (Seattle, 1977); Evgenii G. Kushnarev, *Bering's Search for the Strait: The First Kamchatka Expedition, 1725–1730*, trans. and ed. E.A.P. Crownhart-Vaughan (Portland, Oreg., 1990); O.W. Frost, ed., *Bering and Chirikov. The American Voyages and Their Impact* (Anchorage, 1992).

[10] J.R. Gibson, *Feeding the Russian Fur Trade: Provisionment of the Okhotsk Seaboard and the Kamchatka Peninsula, 1639–1856* (Madison, 1969). See also V.N. Berkh, *Khronologicheskaia istoriia otkrytiia Aleutskikh ostrovov, ili podvigi rossiiskogo kupechestva* (St Petersburg, 1823).

[11] Glyn Barratt, *Russia in Pacific Waters, 1725–1825* (Vancouver and London, 1981), pp. 42–73; A.P. Sokolov, 'Ekspeditsiia k Aleutskim ostrovam kapitanov Krenitsyna i Levashova 1764–1769 gg.', *Zapiski Gidrograficheskogo departamenta Morskogo ministerstva*, x (1852), pp. 70–103.

[12] Cook took with him a copy of a book by the professor of rhetoric at the St Petersburg Academy of Sciences, Jakob Stählin, *An account of the new northern archipelago lately discovered by the Russians in the seas of Kamtschatka and Anadir* (London, 1774), which described and provided a chart of the discoveries of islands in the North Pacific by fur traders under Lieutenant Sind. Cook was disparaging of Stählin's work, since it described Alaska as an island separated from America by a channel of water and contained many other errors, 'a Map that the most illiterate of his illiterate Sea-faring men would have been ashamed to put his name to'. *RDV*, p. 456 (19 October 1778).

governor of Kamchatka. These reached St Petersburg in 1780, and were deposited in the Kunstkammer of the Imperial Academy of Sciences.[13] Members of the Academy also took note of Cook's health measures on board ship, and a short account of them was published in 1778.[14] In April 1779, the Imperial Academy of Sciences' chief naturalist, the German Peter Simon Pallas, wrote to naturalist Thomas Pennant in England, 'Everyone here is very desirous to learn the issue of Capt. Cook's expedition.'[15] When Clerke's reports of Cook's demise reached St Petersburg, Pallas quickly dispatched news of 'the sad account of Cap[tn] Cook's misfortune' in letters to Joseph Banks and Thomas Pennant in London and to the philosopher and publisher A.F. Büsching in Berlin. Pallas would subsequently play an important role in organising the Billings expedition.[16]

However, aside from this scientific interest, a relative indifference to voyages of exploration reigned at the Russian court during the 1770s. When reports of Cook's third voyage reached Empress Catherine, she is said only to have ordered that copies of Cook's charts be drawn up for the Russian navy.[17] Sir James Harris, a British diplomat in St Petersburg, trying to secure news about Cook's death, lamented, 'Besides the Empress herself . . . there are to be found very few persons here who have directed their investigations to this interesting object.'[18] Some government ministers expressed indignation that the British

---

[13] Journal of Lieut. King, 22 May 1779, quoted in Beaglehole, *Cook and the Russians*, p. 1; L.G. Rozina, 'The James Cook Collection in the Museum of Anthropology and Ethnography, Leningrad', in A.L. Kaeppler, ed., *Cook Voyage Artifacts in Leningrad, Berne, and Florence Museums* (Honolulu, 1978), pp. 3–17; L.A. Ivanova, 'Kukovskaia kollektsiia Petrovskoi Kunstkammery: mif i real'nost'. Gavaiskie per'evye nakidki', *Etnograficheskoe obozrenie*, IV (1999), pp. 65–6; L.A. Ivanova, 'Graviury po risunkam Uil'iama Khodzhesa v Kukovskoi kollektsii Petrovskoi Kunstkammery', *Etnograficheskoe obozrenie*, I (2000), pp. 140–52. The artefacts, numbering thirty-eight and mostly from Hawaii and Tahiti, Tonga, and the northwest American coast were exhibited in the St Petersburg Kunstkammer in 2002.

[14] (Author and title unknown) *Mesiatsoslov na 1779 god*, St Petersburg, 1778, pp. 21–83.

[15] Peter Simon Pallas to Thomas Pennant, 4/15 April 1779, quoted in Folkwart Wendland, *Peter Simon Pallas (1741–1811)*, *Materialen einer Biographie*, 2 vols (Berlin and New York, 1992), I, p. 634.

[16] Peter Simon Pallas to Joseph Banks, 10/21 December 1779 (BL Add. MS 8094. fols 242v. and 245), reproduced in Wendland, *Peter Simon Pallas*, I, p. 636. See also ibid., I, pp. 184, 190, 518, 632–8 for Pallas's further correspondence with Banks, Pennant and Büsching; *RDV*, p. 1555. In March 1781, Pallas presented to the Academy seeds collected on Cook's third voyage sent with instructions from Banks in England, Wendland, *Peter Simon Pallas*, I, p. 207.

[17] Sir James Harris reported to Lord Sandwich from St Petersburg on 7/18 January 1780, 'The Empress feels the great utility which must result from such a voyage, & is anxious to promote its success – she expressed a very earnest desire of having Copys of such Charts as may tend to ascertain more precisely the extent & position of those remote and unexplored Parts of her Empire'. *RDV*, pp. 1553–4.

[18] Sir James Harris to Lord Sandwich, St Petersburg, 7/18 January 1780. Ibid., pp. 1553–4.

had succeeded in entering Russian territories without their knowledge. How-ever, nothing was done about it and there was no organised response to Cook for another six years.

If there was an interest in voyaging at the Russian court in the 1770s, it prevailed not among the Russians but among foreigners. Catherine's reign was famous for its pretensions to Enlightenment, and the Empress's generous patronage was well known among the elites of polite society around Europe. It is important to recognise that Russia itself had long been perceived as an exotic and distant land by Europeans, and like other distant lands it was surrounded by stories and rumours of rich bounties and opportunities for the traveller. This was mostly thanks to a long tradition of popular travel accounts of westerners visiting Russia.[19] After Peter the Great opened up Russia to the west at the beginning of the century, such accounts enticed an increasing number of English, French, Italians and Germans to set out on the long voyage to Russia during Catherine's reign. Among the most celebrated were the philosopher Denis Diderot, the sculptor Etienne Falconet, and the enterprising brothers Samuel and Jeremy Bentham.[20] Another was the Cambridge-educated historian and clergyman, William Coxe, whose exploits would be of signifi-cance to the Russian response to Cook.

Coxe travelled to Russia as tutor to the son of an English nobleman in 1778. With the assistance of Pallas at the Academy of Sciences, he entered St Petersburg's Free Economic Society and made extensive studies of Russian commerce and culture.[21] In 1780, Coxe published in London a book entitled *Account of the Russian Discoveries between Asia and America*.[22] The book indicates that while Russians were relatively indifferent to Cook's voyages, British audiences were certainly interested in Russian exploration. Coxe's account explored the fur traders' exploits, in an effort to inspire his readers to further voyages of discovery. He wrote so that his audience might compare the feats of the Russians with those of Cook. His intentions are made clear

---

[19] Francesca Wilson, *Muscovy: Russia Through Foreign Eyes, 1553–1900* (New York, 1970); A.G. Cross, ed., *Russia Under Western Eyes, 1517–1825* (London, 1971); Lloyd E. Berry and Robert O. Crummey, *Rude & Barbarous Kingdom: Russia in the Accounts of Sixteenth-century English Voyagers* (Madison, 1968).

[20] I. Bischoff, 'Etienne Maurice Falconet: sculptor of the statue of Peter the Great', *Russian Review*, XXIV (1965), pp. 369–86; I.R. Christie, 'Samuel Bentham and the Western Colony at Krichev, 1784–1787', *Slavonic and East European Review*, XLVIII (1970), pp. 232–47; Isabel de Madariaga, 'Catherine and the Philosophes' in A.G. Cross, *Russia and the West in the Eighteenth Century*, (Newtonville, Mass., 1983), pp. 30–52; A.G. Cross, *By the Banks of the Neva: Chapters from the Lives and Careers of the British in Eighteenth-century Russia* (Cambridge, 1997).

[21] On Coxe, see 'Coxe, William', *Dictionary of National Biography*, IV (New York, 1908), pp. 1346–7.

[22] William Coxe, *Account of the Russian Discoveries between Asia and America* (London, 1780).

in a supplement to the *Account*, published seven years later, entitled *A Comparative View of the Russian Discoveries, with those made by Captain Cook and Captain Clerke*. Here Coxe told his British readers that Captain Cook was rightly being hailed in Britain as the greatest navigator of all time. But it would be wise for the British to consider Russia's feats in Pacific exploration. He wrote,

> It reflects the highest honour on the British name that . . . our great navigator extended his discoveries much further in one expedition . . . than the Russians accomplished in a long series of years . . . yet we ought not to withold that portion of praise due to the Russians, for having first navigated those seas, and made those discoveries which the English have confirmed.[23]

There followed detailed accounts of Russian voyages published in the *Account*, mostly chronicling the travels of the Russian fur traders. These Coxe carefully compared to the voyages of Cook in order to determine precisely which regions remained unexplored. Thus Russian traders' travels were made to feed the British appetite for exploration.[24]

In 1784 Coxe's *Account* was translated into French and given to Catherine the Great, who read the work with enthusiasm. Soon everyone at court was reading it. But Russians did not read with the same enthusiasm for discovery as their British counterparts. Rather, 'the amazing extent of dominion acknowledging the sovereignty of Russia . . . became now the fashionable topic of conversation at Court'.[25] Evidently gaps in scientific knowledge were far less interesting than realities of dominion. Catherine's chief concern was that Russia's territories in the North Pacific had fallen into the hands of independent traders rather than those of the central government. With the encouragement of Coxe, Catherine ordered new voyages to the Pacific to take control of the trade.[26] Crucially, Cook was still of little significance in this at court. Coxe had revived Russian interests in their distant imperial domains, but Russians did not share his concerns for extending Cook's voyages of discovery. Nevertheless, when the voyage set out, it was captained by a former crew member of Cook's

---

[23] William Coxe, *A Comparative View of the Russian Discoveries, with those made by Captain Cook and Captain Clerke*, supplement to the third edition of Coxe's *Account of the Russian Discoveries between Asia and America* (London, 1787), pp. 430–1.

[24] In his *Comparative View*, Coxe suggested 'considerable information' could be ascertained from the fur traders' explorations, and noted that even Cook had used the charts supplied by Ismailov. Coxe deflected anglocentric assumptions, 'it must not be thought surprising, that a collection of voyages, performed by ignorant traders merely for the sake of obtaining furs and not with a view of discovery, should be defective in determining the position and number of so many islands. We ought rather to wonder that the descriptions . . . are tolerably accurate.' Coxe, *Comparative View*, pp. 447–8.

[25] Martin Sauer, *An Account of a Geographical and Astronomical Expedition to the Northern Parts of Russia . . . by Commodore Joseph Billings in the Years 1785, &c. to 1794* (London, 1802), p. viii.

[26] Ibid., p. viii.

third voyage, able seaman and 'astronomer's assistant' to William Bayly, Joseph Billings.[27] The academician Pallas proposed Billings to the government as leader of the expedition, no doubt reflecting the naturalist's enthusiasm for Cook.[28] But for the Russian government Billings's connection with Cook was less valuable than his recent experience of the Pacific and the fur traders. The government appointed a Russian, Gavriil Andreevich Sarychev, to accompany Billings as second-in-command.[29] As for Billings's own intentions, he came to Russia in search of patronage, 'with the intention of putting a finishing hand to Cap[n] Cook's & Clark's discoveries in the Eastern Ocean'.[30] Like other Englishmen travelling to Russia, Billings came after his hopes for advancement were dashed at home.[31]

In the event, Billings's expedition did prove to be a voyage of discovery. It provided an opportunity for the Academy of Sciences to advance its interests in exploration (Billings's ship was named *Pallas*), and Billings's instructions, prepared by the Admiralty, the Academy of Sciences, and the Commerce Colleges, included demands for geographical, ethnographic, astronomical and commercial observations. The Russian Admiralty formally described the expedition as a survey of the coastline of Siberia and the islands between Asia and America, though its central, secret, objective remained surveillance and control of the fur traders. Another Englishman, Martin Sauer, was chosen as the expedition's secretary and 'journalist'. Sauer was certainly inspired by Cook's voyages. He dedicated his account of the Billings expedition, published in England in 1802, to Sir Joseph Banks, and made numerous references to Cook's voyages in the text.[32] Meeting Russians who had encountered Cook's ships at Kamchatka, for example, Sauer noted,

---

[27] On Billings, see A.I. Alekseev, 'Joseph Billings', *Geographical Journal*, CXXXII (1966), pp. 233–8; Cross, *Banks of the Neva*, pp. 216–18.

[28] Peter Simon Pallas to Sir Joseph Banks, 2/13 June 1785 (BL Add. MS 8096. fol. 148v), reproduced in Wendland, *Peter Simon Pallas*, I, p. 649. Pallas also notes in the letter, 'The Copy of Cook's Voyage for the Priest at Patorinka is just arrived at time to be sent by an Officer, who was in Captain Cook's expedition & knows the Priest personally. It is Mr. Billings . . .', indicating that accounts of Cook's voyages in English were circulating in Russia.

[29] For Billings's orders, see Sauer, *Account of a Geographical . . . Expedition*, appendix v, pp. 29–54; Barratt, *Russia in Pacific Waters*, pp. 77–8. Sarychev published an account of the voyage in Russian in 1802, translated into English as *Account of a Voyage to the North-East of Siberia, the Frozen Sea and the North-East Sea* (London, 1806).

[30] Peter Simon Pallas to Joseph Banks, 2/13 June 1785 (BL Add. MS 8096. fol. 148v), reproduced in Wendland, *Peter Simon Pallas*, I, p. 649.

[31] Billings's plans for a voyage sponsored by the British navy were turned down, Cross, *Banks of the Neva*, p. 216; On British navy men who travelled to Russia, see R.C. Anderson, 'British and American Officers in the Russian Navy', *Mariner's Mirror*, XXIII (1947), pp. 17–27; Philip H. Clendenning, 'Admiral Sir Charles Knowles and Russia, 1771–1774', *Mariner's Mirror*, LXI (1975), pp. 39–49; A.G. Cross, 'Samuel Greig, Catherine the Great's Scottish Admiral', *Mariner's Mirror*, LX (1974), pp. 251–65.

[32] Sauer, *Account of a Geographical . . . Expedition*. In the 'Preface', p. 13, Sauer indicates

Nothing in nature could be more pleasant than the glow of friendship which animated their countenances . . . when they mentioned the names of King, Bligh, Webber, and others; names that will be handed down to posterity by tradition in a Kamchatka Song to their memory, with a chorus to the tune of God Save the King.[33]

Sauer and Billings both saw themselves as following in Cook's footsteps, but the expedition as a whole owed as much to the model of earlier Russian voyages by Bering and Krenitsyn as to those of Cook. Thus Bering's grandson, Lieutenant Christian Bering, shared the command with Billings and Sarychev, and the expedition followed the same route that Bering, and after him Krenitsyn, had taken, setting out for Kamchatka overland, before sailing out into the Pacific on ships built in Eastern Siberia. References to Bering and Krenitsyn featured prominently in Billings's instructions and even in Sauer's subsequent account. Bering also appears to have been uppermost in the minds of Billings's Russian crew. Sauer records how they refused to land at Bering's Island because 'the misfortunes of Captain Bering in 1741 were so strong in the minds of all the sailors'.[34]

So in the 1780s, interest and enthusiasm for Cook's voyages of discovery remained largely restricted to Russia's scholarly community, while the court and government concerned themselves with more immediate, pragmatic issues surrounding the fur trade. Certainly the Russian government had a respect for the British navy and hired Cook's crew members. Following Billings, in 1787 the government agreed to sponsor a second expedition under James Trevenen, the heavily-tattooed 16-year-old midshipman of Cook's third voyage.[35] Yet Trevenen, like Billings, came to Russia of his own accord in search of patronage. He was not sought out by a Russian government inspired by Cook, though his experience under Cook, like that of Billings, would be considered a practical advantage.[36] In fact, the Russian government remained deeply suspicious of

the lack of Russian interest in Cook, 'the extraordinary discoveries of the ever-memorable circumnavigator Cook inspired all Europe with an enthusiastic desire of being acquainted with the parts of the globe still remaining unknown. Russia . . . being engaged in different pursuits, did not consider the distant and barren regions belonging to her own Empire as of sufficient importance to justify the expense and trouble of exploring them.'

[33] Ibid., p. 146.

[34] Ibid., p. 207.

[35] C. Lloyd and R.C. Anderson, eds, *A Memoir of James Trevenen, 1760–1790* (London, 1959); *RDV*, p. 1466; Cross, *Banks of the Neva*, pp. 210–16.

[36] When another of Cook's former crew members, John Ledyard, sought patronage from Catherine for a scientific expedition to America via Siberia in 1786, the Empress flatly refused, calling the plan 'chimerical'. See Eufrosina Dvoichenko-Markov, 'John Ledyard and the Russians', *Russian Review*, XI (1952), pp. 211–22; Stephen D. Watrous, ed., *John Ledyard's Journey through Russia and Siberia 1787–1788; The Journal and Selected Letters* (Madison, 1966).

foreign nations' exploration at this time. A further expedition, under Captain G.I. Mulovskii, was planned to take 'two vessels armed like those employed by Captain Cook' to annex territorial possessions claimed by foreign explorers on the American coastline above 55°N.[37] As it turned out, both this and Trevenen's plans came to nothing. As in the 1760s, the Russian government easily turned its attention away from voyaging, this time to wage war on Turkey over new Russian territories in the Crimea. Another lull in Russian interests in exploration ensued.

The rise and fall of Captain Cook's reputation

It was three years later, in 1790, that Radishchev wrote his lament for the state of Russian exploration. In contrast to his apathetic government, Radishchev celebrated Cook, and his comments are indicative of a new, more positive attitude to Cook which was to prevail in the Russian navy for several decades.

First, Cook became much more visible in Russian literature. Throughout the 1790s numerous translated accounts of Cook's voyages appeared, including the first biography of Cook by Andrew Kippis, and accounts of the second and third voyages translated by the naval officer Longin' Ivanovich Golenishchev-Kutuzov, later head of the Admiralty and a promoter of Russian voyages of exploration.[38] The 1790s also witnessed a new era of Russian voyages of discovery undertaken not by hired foreigners but by Russian officers of the nobility, who set out on circumnavigations which followed closely the voyages of Cook in their aims, routes and methods. There were some thirty-six of these between 1803 and 1849.[39] Between 1803 and 1806, the nobles Adam Johann von Krusenstern and Yuri Lisianskii led the first Russian expedition

---

[37] Decree of 22 December 1786, quoted in Barratt, *Russia in Pacific Waters* p. 92. Georg Forster, who had accompanied his father Johann Reinhold Forster as a naturalist on Cook's second voyage, was invited to join this expedition, but he declined. See ibid., p. 93. On the plans for Mulovskii, see L. Golenishchev-Kutuzov, *Predpriiatie imperatritsy Yekateriny II dlia puteshestviia vokrug sveta v 1786 g.* (St Petersburg, 1840); A.P. Sokolov, 'Prigotovlenie krugosvetnoi ekspeditsii 1787 goda pod nachal'stvom Mulovskogo', *Zapiski Gidrograficheskogo departamenta Morskogo ministerstva vi* (1848), pp. 142–91.

[38] For a complete list of translated accounts of Cook's voyages, see Armstrong, 'Cook's Reputation', p. 128. Accounts of Cook's second and third voyages first appeared in Russian translation in 1780 and 1786 respectively. An account of the first voyage appeared in 1798. On Golenishchev-Kutuzov, see 'Kutuzov' (Golenishchev'-Kutuzov'), Longin'-Ivanovich', *Russkii biograficheskii slovar'*, ed. A.A. Polvstov *et al.*, 28 vols (St Petersburg, 1896–1991); *Knappe-Kiukhel'beker'* (St Petersburg, 1903), pp. 627–8.

[39] A.E. Sokol, 'Russian expansion and exploration in the Pacific', *American Slavic and East European Review*, XI (1952), p. 97.

to explore the full extent of the Pacific Ocean and circumnavigate the globe. On board Krusenstern's ship *Nadezhda* were two other nobles who would command their own voyages of exploration a few years later. Otto von Kotzebue made two round-the-world voyages between 1815 and 1826, and Thaddeus von Bellingshausen commanded a trip to the Antarctic in search of a southern continent between 1819 and 1821.[40] These figures all maintained a view of Cook which contrasted with the relative indifference of the preceding decades. As Armstrong noted, they practically worshipped Cook, and most took Cook as the standard by which to calibrate their own careers.

The causes of this increased attention to Cook and the initiation of new voyages of discovery modelled on Cook's own are varied. The new interest in Cook was partly a delayed result of Russian naval officers who had trained in Britain.[41] Russians held a respect for the British navy throughout the eighteenth century and co-operated with it in many ways. This co-operation had diminished with British resentment of Russia's policy of armed neutrality in the 1780s, but in 1793, when the situation improved, fourteen Russian officers were sent to train on British ships. These included Krusenstern and Lisianskii, who when they returned to Russia fostered the first of the Russian circumnavigations which owed a great deal to Cook and British navy practice. Adopted practices included new degrees of scientific observation and accurate navigation, and the use of British instruments and even British ships.[42] The Russians also introduced dietary and disciplinary practices then current in the British navy. Then, such methods were spread through the Russian navy

[40] For accounts of Russian voyages in this period, see Barratt, *Russia in Pacific Waters*; Sokol, 'Russian Expansion and Exploration in the Pacific'; N. Novikov, *Russian Voyages round the World* (London, 1945); A.I. Andreev, *Russian Discoveries in the Pacific and in North America in the Eighteenth and Nineteenth Centuries*, trans. Carl Ginsburg (Ann Arbor, Mich. 1952); V.A. Yesakov, A.F. Plakhotnik and A.I. Alekseev, *Russkie okeanicheskie i morskie issledovaniia v XIX – nachale XX v.* (Moscow, 1964); R.V. Makarova, *Russians on the Pacific, 1743–1799*, trans. R.A. Pierce and A.S. Donelly (Kingston, Ontario, 1975); N.A. Ivashintsev, *Russian Round-the-World Voyages, 1803–1849: With a Summary of Later Voyages to 1867*, trans. Glyn Barratt (Kingston, Ontario, 1980).

[41] On Anglo–Russian naval co-operation, see A.G. Cross, *'By the Banks of the Thames': Russians in Eighteenth-Century Britain* (Newtonville, Mass., 1980), pp. 165–72; M.S. Anderson, 'Great Britain and the growth of the Russian Navy in the 18th century', *Mariner's Mirror*, XLII (1956), pp. 132–46.

[42] Krusenstern used two ships built in London, the 450-ton *Leander* and 370-ton *Thames*, re-named *Nadezhda* and *Neva*, Barratt, *Russia in Pacific Waters*, p. 114; Kotzebue's *Rurik* carried a life-boat built in London, Otto von Kotzebue, *A Voyage of Discovery into the South Seas and Beering's Straits*, trans. H.E. Lloyd, 3 vols (London, 1821), I, p. 99. Many of the circumnavigators used British instruments. Kotzebue, for example, used sextants, compasses, marine barometers, thermometers and hygrometers by Edward Troughton, a chronometer by Paul Phillip Barraud, and a mountain barometer and camera lucida by Thomas Jones, an apprentice of Jesse Ramsden, A.J. von Krusenstern, 'Introduction' to Kotzebue, *Voyage of Discovery into the South Seas*, I, p. 16.

as Kotzebue and Bellingshausen 'followed . . . the track of Vice-Admiral Krusenstern, who . . . set an example for such voyages'.[43]

All this was accompanied by a healthy respect for Cook, whose expertise could provide a model for the Russians' own commands. Thus the Russian explorer Vasilii Mikhailovich Golovnin, whose ship *Diana* began a two-year circumnavigation in 1807, met James Trevenen during a period of training in the British navy. Golovnin was inspired to learn English and read Cook in the original.[44] However, the officers' respect for Cook was more than just healthy. Cook became a figure who took on heroic proportions, and the noble officers paid a special deference to him. Cook was held as 'the immortal navigator'. As Krusenstern noted, 'that which was impossible to Cook could hardly be possible for another'.[45]

The way Russian officers approached Cook at this time was not simply a result of their training in the British navy. An examination of the cultural identity of the noble officers, their local backgrounds, expectations and values, sheds further light on their attitudes to Cook. In other words, to understand the Russian response to Cook, it is necessary to understand the Russians who were responding. The Russian nobility were a distinctive group with an unusual position in the cultural geography of Europe, and considering that position helps to explain the new adulation of Captain Cook. In fact, two groups of noble explorers are discernible in the decades after Cook's voyages. Many of the officers, such as Golovnin, Lisianskii, and Bellingshausen's second commander Mikhail Lazarev came from Russian stock, but, as their names suggest, Krusenstern, Kotzebue, and Bellingshausen himself, were Baltic German nobles, raised among the ancient German nobility who ruled over the region of present-day Estonia, Lithuania and Latvia. To understand the attitudes of Russia's explorers, then, the cultural identities of both groups need to be considered.

---

[43] L.I. Golenishchev-Kutuzov, 'Preliminary memoir' to Thaddeus Bellingshausen, *The Voyage of Captain Bellingshausen to the Antarctic Seas, 1819–1821*, ed. Frank Debenham, 2 vols (London, 1945), I, p. 2.

[44] Barratt, *Russia in Pacific Waters*, p. 159. On Golovnin, see R.I. Fraerman and P.D. Zaikin, *Zhizn' i neobyknovennye prikliucheniia kapitana-leitenanta Golovnina, puteshestvennika i morekhodsta*, 2 vols (Moscow, 1946–8); Iu. Davydov, Golovnin (Moscow, 1968); E.L. Wiswell, 'Introduction' to V.M. Golovnin, *Around the World on the Kamchatka, 1817–1819*, trans. E.L. Wiswell (Honolulu, 1979), pp. xix–xxxix.

[45] A.J. von Krusenstern, introduction to Kotzebue, *Voyage of Discovery into the South Seas*, I, p. 3. That the Russians deified Captain Cook aligns them with other nations who thought Cook a god – the British, and, more controversially, the Hawaiians. See the comments on mythologising Cook in Dening, *Performances*, pp. 139–40, 160; Marshall Sahlins, 'Captain James Cook; or, The Dying God', in Sahlins, *Islands of History* (Chicago, 1985), pp. 104–35. Marshall Sahlins, *How 'Natives' Think: About Captain Cook, For Example* (Chicago and London, 1995), pp. 99–100, deals with Hawaiian responses to Cook recorded on Kotzebue's voyage.

According to Yuri Lotman, the Russian nobility of the eighteenth century was, like Russia itself, caught midway in the Enlightenment. Neither members of a nation like England or France secure in its sense of being the highest point of civilisation, nor members of the so-called barbarian or savage peoples, Russian nobles were easterners who were always in the process of becoming western. From the reign of Peter the Great, when the old Muscovite nobility had been forced to shave their beards and lose their kaftans in favour of Dutch and German dress, the Russian noble had internalised a set of values whereby the imitation of foreigners was deemed crucial to social and political success at court: 'To conduct oneself correctly was to behave like a foreigner, that is to act in an artificial way according to the norms of an alien life-style.'[46] French manners and language famously became *de rigeur* among the nobility during the eighteenth century, but any number of national cultural identities could become fashionable, from the practical Dutch and German during Peter's reign to the more commercial British who became the model during the reign of Catherine the Great.

So when Russians travelled to Britain to learn naval skills, they studied more than just skills. The Russians' desire to imitate foreigners meant that the whole British form of life was there to be explored and adopted. Peter the Great, fashioning himself as a model for the nobility, had dressed in the clothes of a common shipwright to work in the shipyards of England and Holland during his Grand Embassy to Europe in 1697–8.[47] Back in Russia, Peter held 'naval assemblies', shipboard parties where nobles were encouraged to handle the ships and learn the form of life of the skilled naval officer.[48]

A similar situation was discernible in the case of the Baltic Germans. The Baltic Germans' relationship to Russia was close.[49] This conservative nobility provided many of the highest courtiers and military officers in the Russian service for much of the eighteenth and early nineteenth century. Proud of their nobility and cautious of any career, such as trade, which entailed deference to the 'lower orders' of native Balts, Baltic German families made an imperative of entering the Russian civil and military service at a young age. Here, they would only serve the Emperor, and, indeed, soon gained a reputation as the

---

[46] Ju. M. Lotman, 'The poetics of everyday behaviour in Russian eighteenth-century culture', in Ju. M. Lotman and B.A. Uspenskij, *The Semiotics of Russian Culture*, ed. Ann Shukman (Ann Arbor, Mich. 1984), p. 233. See also Ju.M. Lotman, 'The theater and theatricality as components of early nineteenth-century culture', in ibid., pp. 141–61.

[47] A.G. Cross, *Peter the Great Through British Eyes: Perceptions and Representations of the Tsar since 1698* (Cambridge, 2000), pp. 8, 14.

[48] Lindsey Hughes, *Russia in the Age of Peter the Great* (New Haven and London, 1998), p. 265.

[49] For a detailed analysis of the Baltic German nobility and their relationship to Russia, see Heide W. Whelan, *Adapting to Modernity. Family, Caste, and Capitalism Among the Baltic German Nobility* (Köln, 1999).

'most loyal subjects of the Russian Czar'.[50] Equally, Baltic Germans disdained their neighbour Prussia, where 'her order, her equality, her national education'[51] threatened noble privilege. Many Baltic Germans knew Russian poorly, but this was also true among the Russian nobility, and both groups preferred the courtly French language for most of the eighteenth century.

The Baltic Germans did not aspire to 'western' European culture in quite the same way as the Russians, though most spent their careers in St Petersburg and, in the case of the explorers, trained there from an early age.[52] However, their noble heritage did intersect with Russian cultural identity in at least one crucial area. With their service ethic and disdain of the 'lower' orders, Baltic German noble families took up technical and scientific-oriented careers within the Russian service. It is remarkable how many Baltic Germans became prominent in the sciences in early nineteenth-century Russia, many training or working first in the Estonian University of Dorpat before moving to St Petersburg.[53] These included the physicist Heinrich Lenz, geologist Alexander von Keyserling, zoologist Alexander von Middendorff, and the well-known embryologist Karl Ernst von Baer. Kotzebue's physician and botanist was another Baltic German and Dorpat professor, Johann Friedrich Gustav von Eschscholtz. For these men, scientific interests necessarily combined with an interest in western Europe, where technological and scientific developments far outstripped those of their native land, which like Russia was founded on an archaic agricultural economy. Many travelled to the German states, France and Britain to develop their scientific careers. This Baltic German interest in the sciences may also have drawn noble officers such as Krusenstern, Kotzebue and Bellingshausen to voyages of discovery, and to Captain Cook.[54] All these

---

[50] J.G. Kohl, *Russia, St. Petersburg, Moscow, Kharkoff, Riga, Odessa, the German Provinces on the Baltic, the Steppes, the Crimea, and the Interior of the Empire* (London, 1842), p. 395. Kohl provides a detailed account of the relations between Baltic German and Russian nobility, ibid., pp. 394–6.

[51] Ibid., p. 396.

[52] Krusenstern, Kotzebue, and Bellingshausen trained in the St Petersburg Naval Cadet Corps during the 1780s–1790s. *Russkii biograficheskii slovar'*, ed. A.A. Polvstov *et al.*; *Aleksinskii-Bestuzhev'-Riumin'*, pp. 682–3 ('Bellingsgauzen, Faddei Faddeivich'); *Knappe-Kiukhel'beker'*, pp. 356–8 ('Kotsebu, Otto Evstaf'evich'); Charlotte Bernhardi, *Memoir of the Celebrated Admiral Adam John de Krusenstern, the First Russian Circumnavigator* (London, 1867).

[53] On Baltic Germans and the sciences, see Whelan, *Adapting to Modernity*, p. 158. Dorpat (now Tartu) University was opened in 1798 by Emperor Paul I as a gesture to the Baltic German nobility who had previously sent their sons to German universities, see Alexander Vucinich, *Science in Russian Culture. A History to 1860* (Stanford, 1963), p. 190; E.V. Petukhov, *Imperatorskii Iur'evskii, byvshii Derptskii, universitet za sto let ego sushchestvovaniia (1802–1902)* (Iurev, 1902).

[54] Similarly, Baltic German savants embraced opportunities of voyaging. The Dorpat-trained physicist Heinrich Lenz accompanied Kotzebue to the Pacific where he made extensive oceanographic studies. Von Baer and Middendorff conducted their own land

men exhibited skill and enthusiasm for the scientific aspects of their voyages, and Krusenstern noted, 'the bounds of human knowledge are more effectually extended by [voyages of discovery] than by other enterprises which have science for their object. When it is considered what the sciences have gained by the voyages of Cook and his successors, my assertion will not be thought exaggerated.'[55] As will be seen, British navigation, instrumentation, shipbuilding and science, much of it advanced under Cook, drew Baltic German officers to western Europe in the same way as it did their Russian counterparts. Exploration constituted an arena where the Russians and Baltic Germans shared in a desire to imitate aspects of the western form of life.

This peculiar situation sheds light on the new Cook-inspired Russian voyages of exploration. First there were the routes. Where Billings had followed Bering and Krenitsyn across land to Kamchatka, Krusenstern and his successors all took a route more suited to their western-looking noble identity – all travelled first to Europe, principally England, before embarking south. In other words, the noble officers first went west to view states they considered superior to their own before going south to view states they regarded as lesser. When Bellingshausen arrived in Portsmouth, for example, 'all the officers with their telescopes . . . began to examine the ships . . . anchored there, commenting on their beauty and good qualities'.[56] Bellingshausen then took his officers to visit the sights of London before leaving for the African coast. He also bought instruments from Troughton and Dolland, and visited Sir Joseph Banks in search of a naturalist for the voyage.[57]

Many of the Russian navigators joined enthusiasm with imitation. Once they set out from Europe, the noble officers followed more than just the aims and practical techniques of the British navy – they actually followed Cook. All made a point of stopping in places Cook had visited, even making sure to be on the exact spot where some historic event in Cook's world had taken place. Lisianskii visited 'the village of Tavaroa, to see the memorable spot where Europe had been deprived of her most celebrated navigator. . . . We landed at the very rock on which this truly great man lost his life.'[58] Lisianskii also ordered his crew to read accounts of the voyages of Anson and Cook, as a 'source of amusement . . . of a most rational kind'.[59] Kotzebue noted that his trip to Matavai Bay, Tahiti, was on account of 'the celebrity bestowed upon it by

---

expeditions to Lapland and Siberia respectively. See Vucinich, *Science in Russian Culture*, pp. 301–5.

[55] Krusenstern, 'Introduction' to Kotzebue, *Voyage of Discovery into the South Seas*, I, p. 28.

[56] Bellingshausen, *Voyage . . . to the Antarctic Seas*, I, p. 37.

[57] Ibid., I, pp. 39–40.

[58] Urey Lisiansky, *A Voyage Around the World in the Years 1803, 4, 5, & 6; performed, by Order of His Imperial Majesty Alexander the First, Emperor of Russia, in the Ship Neva* (London, 1814), p. 109 (15 June 1804).

[59] Ibid., p. 21 (30 October 1803).

Cook'.[60] He then set up an observatory at Cape Venus on 'precisely the same spot where Cook's Observatory had formerly been erected'.[61] Golovnin 'visited the rock where Cook had been put to death . . . and saw the gap made by the cannonball from English ships that fired at the inhabitants after this misfortune'.[62] Bellingshausen's journey provides the best case, since he more or less retraced Cook's second voyage to the Antarctic, deviating only to explore regions uncharted by the Captain himself. Bellingshausen copied numerous of Cook's habits. He named new discoveries after his first lieutenants as Cook had done, though he regarded Cook's own place-names as sacrosanct. At the Sandwich or Hawaiian Islands he noted 'the names given by [Cook] must remain unchanged that the memory of this daring explorer may be handed to posterity'.[63] He, and the other nobles with him, also took Cook's measurements and positions as standards against which to set their own. Bellingshausen's journals, for example, are full of comments such as 'We . . . accepted the latitude . . . as fixed by Captain Cook as true, correcting our own reading.'[64] Cook literally set the standard for the noble explorers' actions.

According to Lotman, the imitation of foreigners in Russia gave the nobility a distinctively theatrical sensibility, a consciousness of their own and others' need to be constantly acting a role. However, throughout the eighteenth century, there was no sense in which the theatre itself provided a model for nobles' behaviour. This changed at the end of the century, when, as Lotman puts it, 'the theater invaded life'.[65] Embracing a European-wide neo-classicism, the nobility now looked to ancient Greece and Rome as models for conduct, behaviour and style. Nobles began to see their lives as taking on elements of the heroic, and they imagined themselves participants in some great historical drama. This is important for understanding their relationship to Cook because from the early nineteenth century, contemporary figures began to take the place of classical figures as heroes for dramatic imitation. Cook was perhaps

---

[60] Otto von Kotzebue, *A New Voyage Round the World in the Years 1823, 24, 25, and 26*, 2 vols (London, 1830), I, p. 145.

[61] Ibid., I, p. 176.

[62] Golovnin, *Around the World on the Kamchatka*, p. 178.

[63] Bellingshausen, *Voyage . . . to the Antarctic Seas*, I, p. 107. Bellingshausen noted of one of these islands, 'I called it Cook island in honour of the great explorer who had been the first to see this shore.' Later the island was re-named 'Bellingshausen'. On Bellingshausen's voyage, see Hugh Robert Mill, 'Bellingshausen's Antarctic Voyage', *Geographical Review*, XXI (1903), pp. 150–9; Robert Cushman Murphy, 'Captain Bellingshausen's voyage 1819–21', *Geographical Review*, XXXVII (1947) pp. 303–6; Glynn Barratt, *Bellingshausen. A Visit to New Zealand, 1820* (Palmerston North, New Zealand, 1979).

[64] Bellingshausen, *Voyage . . . to the Antarctic Seas*, I, p. 102; Similarly, Kotzebue wrote 'My calculation of the longitude of the Pallisers, agreed with that of Cook, within three minutes. Between our latitude and Cook's there was no difference; I therefore had no reason to complain of my time-keepers.' Kotzebue, *Voyage of Discovery into the South Seas*, I, p. 155.

[65] Lotman, 'Theater and theatricality', p. 145.

one of them, further explaining the Russians' particular hero-worship of the explorer.

Lotman proposes that this is particularly evident in the realm of warfare. The nobility in Russia of the Napoleonic era understood war as a romantic tragedy, the battlefield a place where they might find their place in history.[66] If the Russian Empress's bed had once offered a means for advancement at court, it was now replaced by the battlefield, a space where social distinctions dissolved, and where there was every opportunity for heroic initiative and enterprise. Thus the poet Denis Davydov wrote of the military life, 'This calling, filled with poetry, demands a romantic imagination, a passion for adventure; it is not satisfied with dry, prosaic bravery. It's a stanza by Byron!' Byron himself became a modern hero for the swashbuckling noble to imitate, evident in the case of Alexander Pushkin, as did other romanticised poets such as Goethe, Schiller, and Shakespeare.[67] Even Napoleon provided a hero worthy of emulation, evident in the character of Prince Andrei Bolkonsky in Tolstoy's novel of this era, *War and Peace*.

The noble explorers' adoration of Captain Cook in Russia appears to have followed this trend. For officers such as Krusenstern, Kotzebue, and especially Bellingshausen, Cook was a kind of Napoleon, and the voyage of exploration a kind of battlefield, another fluid space of adventure where the officer might overcome great odds to achieve his place in history next to the 'immortal Cook', as Krusenstern called him. Unlike Billings, all the explorers made sure to leave published accounts of their journeys for posterity, and those of Krusenstern, Kotzebue and Bellingshausen at least were prefaced with romantic prose locating their journeys within the broader historical context of global exploration. Krusenstern compared Kotzebue's search for the Northwest Passage with Cook's demolition of the idea of a southern continent, quoting Shakespeare's epitaph to glorify Cook's achievement.[68] Cook's Russian translator Golenishchev-Kutuzov romanticised Bellingshausen as an intrepid figure pitted against a wild and hostile nature, whose travails – exactly those which Radishchev had lamented were absent in Russian exploration – earned

---

[66] Ibid., pp. 153–6.

[67] Faddei Bulgarin, writing in 1837, said Pushkin 'posed as a Byron and died like a hare', quoted in V.V. Veresaev, *Pushkin v zhizny*, 2 vols (Moscow, 1936), II, p. 464; See also Iuri M. Lotman, *Aleksandr Sergeevich Pushkin: biografiia pisatelia: posobie dlia uchashchikhsia* (Leningrad, 1981).

[68] 'Before Cook, [the southern continent] sunk to the bottom of the ocean, and, like the baseless fabric of a vision, left not a rack behind!', Krusenstern, 'Introduction' to Kotzebue, *Voyage of Discovery into the South Seas*, I, p. 2. Kotzebue's voyage carried other poetic resonances. Kotzebue's father, August Friedrich, was a poet and playwright, though no Romantic, while the naturalist on Kotzebue's voyage, Adelbert von Chamisso de Boncourt, was a poet of some renown. See Sokol, 'Russian expansion and exploration', p. 100; Heinrich Döring, *August von Kotzebues Leben* (Weimar, 1830); Robert Fischer, *Adelbert von Chamisso: Weltbürger, Naturforscher und Dichter* (Berlin, 1990).

him a place in the 'annals of Russian navigation'.[69] Cook was thus taken up not only as a standard but also as the precursor and model for an increasingly historicised and romantic culture of heroic exploration.

Conclusion

In Tom Stoppard's play, *The Coast of Utopia*, the Russian nineteenth-century literary critic Vissarion Belinsky is heard to complain of his native land, 'What we have', in Russia, 'isn't ours, it's like a party where everyone has to come dressed up as someone else – Byron, Voltaire, Goethe, Schiller, Shakespeare and the rest.'[70] James Cook might be added to Belinsky's list. Stoppard draws attention to a widespread sense among the mid-nineteenth-century Russian nobility that the previous generation had been consumed with the imitation of foreigners to gain a sense of themselves. It was this generation who, besides following Shakespeare and Byron, also set out on the first Russian circum-navigations of the globe, voyages of exploration which were closely modelled on the voyages of James Cook. A quotation from a play is appropriate here because the response to Cook in Russia was itself fundamentally theatrical. Noble officers responded to Cook within a world where the fashionable imitation of foreigners, particularly the British, was flourishing. Certainly, nobles' training in the British navy helped establish Cook's reputation in Russia, but the theatricality of noble cultural identity did as much to shape the response to Cook.

The high point of Russia's romantic infatuation with Cook and exploration came early in the reign of Emperor Alexander I (1801–25). By the close of his reign, with a rising mysticism and reaction setting in at court, voyaging lost its former place in the elite imagination. When Bellingshausen returned from his trip to the Antarctic his ship was met with relative indifference in St Petersburg, and only through the efforts of Golenishchev-Kutuzov was his travel account published.[71] Nevertheless, the impact of the voyages inspired by Captain Cook was profound. Not least, the arrival of new knowledge of diverse ethnic groups and their material culture brought to Russia by the explorers helped contribute to the rise of extensive discussion on the place of Russia in the world and the character of the Russian nation, that is, to the famous debates between 'Westernisers' and 'Slavophiles' of the mid-century. The intensity of the Slavophile reaction of the 1830s and 1840s, with its stress on local Russian traditions and beliefs, is testament to the degree to which

---

[69] Golenishchev-Kutuzov, 'Preliminary memoir' to Bellingshausen, *Voyage . . . to the Antarctic Seas*, I, p. 3.
[70] Tom Stoppard, *The Coast of Utopia: Voyage* (London, 2002), p. 39.
[71] Golenishchev-Kutuzov, 'Preliminary memoir' to Bellingshausen, *Voyage . . . to the Antarctic Seas*, I, pp. 1–3.

the previous generation of the elite had given themselves over to heroic foreign ideals. Conversely, the language of westernisers determined to modernise Russia was infused with imagery of sea voyages to unknown shores. Reformers such as Belinsky and Alexander Herzen found meaning in the accounts of voyagers such as the Baltic German noble and Petersburg academician Karl Ernst von Baer, who, returning from a voyage to Novaia Zemlia (New Land) in 1830, proclaimed, 'Novaia Zemlia is a real land of freedom, where each man may act and live as he wishes. It is the only land where there is no police force or other ruling force besides hospitality . . . in Novaia Zemlia each man who arrives is greeted as an honest man.'[72]

By the 1830s, as Russians were taking their voyages of discovery and exploration into new directions and giving them new meanings, Cook's reputation among the nobility began to decline. Indeed, it was never clear that Cook established a firm place in the Russian imagination as he had done in Britain and elsewhere.[73] Russians today, asked the value of Cook to Russia, are as likely to mention John Cook, a British physician working in eighteenth-century Russia, as they are the Captain. For a few decades at the turn of the nineteenth century, Cook's voyages had enjoyed an outstanding reputation and a profound influence on Russian navigation. Yet it was only a combination of socialisation of Russian and Baltic German nobles within the British navy, and a short-lived fashion among them for worshipping the contemporary heroic, which made Cook into an idol. That moment was enough to secure a place for Cook in Russian history, but it was perhaps only as temporary as Cook's own brief stay in Russian waters.

[72] Karl Ernst von Baer, quoted in James H. Billington, *The Icon and the Axe: An Interpretive History of Russian Culture* (New York, 1970), p. 309. For imagery of sea-voyages in Russian nineteenth-century thought, see ibid., pp. 361–70.

[73] On Cook's ambiguous reputation in Soviet Russia, see Armstrong, 'Cook's reputation', pp. 125–8.

Part IV

The Legacy of Captain Cook

Part IV

The Legacy of Captain Cook

11

Redeeming memory: the martyrdoms of Captain James Cook and Reverend John Williams

SUJIT SIVASUNDARAM

Almost half a century had passed after Cook's death, when the Revd William Ellis of the London Missionary Society sat in a house in Oahu with several local chiefs, a folio edition of Cook's *Voyages* spread before him. While poring over the image of the navigator's demise together with the chiefs, Ellis observed: 'They were greatly affected with the print which represented [Cook's] death . . . I perceived Karaimoku more than once wipe the tears from his eyes, while conversing about this melancholy event.'[1] Substituting the name of a British evangelical for that of Karaimoku would change nothing in this narrative. The intended message is that times have changed: the Hawaiians have converted and adopted the civilised manners of the British. Their absorbed interest in Cook's *Voyages* supplies evidence of how they can read and write; and Ellis proudly parades the fact that even their emotions have been tamed. The chiefs are now willing to cry on account of Cook's death without celebrating it. Ellis's emphasis on how his charges had achieved the mastery of their selves was again evident when he wrote: 'More than once, when conversing with us on the length of time the missionaries had been in the Society Islands, they have said, "Why did you not come here sooner? Was it because we killed Captain Cook?"'[2] The Hawaiian memory of Cook was then a truly British and evangelical one. It encompassed civilised remorse, controlled grief and literary safe-keeping.

Although this chapter is not about Captain Cook, it uses the explorer as a departure point for a study of memory and replication.[3] My aim is to characterise the early nineteenth-century Pacific, by discussing how evangelicals modified the memory of Cook, and re-embodied their remembrance of the navigator, in the lives of others who they hoped would become martyrs for

---

[1] William Ellis, *A Narrative of a Tour through Hawaii or Owhyhee* (London, 1826), p. 102.
[2] Ibid.
[3] In doing this I follow broadly in the wake of Chris Healy's excellent book, *From the Ruins of Colonialism: History as Social Memory* (Cambridge, 1997).

their cause. Evangelical theology and rhetoric are quite distant from the way we remember Cook. Yet the passage of memory into history is helpful in stimulating a closer reflection on our memories than would be possible if I were to select a thread of commemoration which we share with this period. The evangelical focus, in what follows, is also appropriate given the dramatic impact that missionaries had on the Pacific. By the middle of the century, the transformation of the Pacific islands was presented by the missionary world as its chief accomplishment.[4] The region had been chosen by the Directors of the London Missionary Society as the first location to which missionaries should be sent, after evangelicals had been captivated by reading Cook's *Voyages*.

A study of how evangelicals used accounts of Cook to characterise their expansionist ideologies reveals how history may be used in colonialism. Evangelicals prided themselves on reconciling myth with biblical tradition and differentiating error from fact. Their narrations of Cook were consciously set against local traditions of the arrival of Europeans in the Pacific, which were said to be vague and superstitious. While making these claims about their ability to interpret the past, missionaries transported printing presses to the Pacific and reported how local people responded with awe and confusion to the possibilities presented by reading and writing.[5] Words and histories were closely linked therefore with articulations of difference. Should we then reflect on the status of our histories of Cook? Missionary practice suggests that it is far too easy to privilege the production of rational words and empirical accounts in coming to terms with the celebrated navigator.

Analysing how an individual's life is retold and re-inscribed in the lives of others can also be the means of studying changing notions of self.[6] By showing how evangelicals moulded the memory of Cook, erasing the negative connotations of his alleged deification, what it means to be religious becomes identifiable.[7] In the climate of the early empire, difficulty and pain were to be cherished as signifiers of divine instrumentality; an acknowledgement of the relation between humans and the Deity was crucial in defining self. When

---

[4] *Westminster Review*, 1856, p. 25. For more on the South Pacific mission see Niel Gunson, *Messengers of Grace: Evangelical Missionaries in the South Seas, 1797–1860* (Melbourne, 1978); Sujit Sivasundaram, 'Nature speaks theology: colonialism, cultivation, conversion and the Pacific, 1795–1850' (University of Cambridge, Ph.D. thesis, 2001).

[5] For more on the placement of literature in the Pacific mission see Vanessa Smith, *Literary Culture and the Pacific: Nineteenth-century Textual Encounters* (Cambridge, 1998); also Rod Edmond, *Representing the South Pacific: Colonial Discourse from Cook to Gauguin* (Cambridge, 1997).

[6] For more on the definition of the self see Jonathan Lamb, *Preserving the Self in the South Seas* (Chicago, 2001).

[7] Recent work on missionary history includes Susan Thorne, *Congregational Missions and the Making of an Imperial Culture in Nineteenth-Century England* (Stanford, 1999), and Brian Stanley, *The Bible and the Flag: Protestant Missions and British Imperialism in the Nineteenth and Twentieth Centuries* (Leicester, 1990).

the Revd John Williams, the most celebrated Pacific missionary, voyaged through the Pacific discovering new islands, he wrote of the loss of his children, the plots on his life, his near drowning and how he constructed a ship from scratch while stranded on Rarotonga. When he was killed and allegedly eaten on the shores of Eromanga in 1839, he ended his life of willing suffering in fitting fashion. He earned himself the title of martyr and exemplified the religious hero: an individual who underwent trials in order to allow the Deity to work. Williams was readily compared with Cook. Instead of a strangely impassioned moment of deification, the missionary was said to have taken the pain of martyrdom while in full control of his passions and in communion with God.[8]

Just as Cook's *Voyages* was important in creating the navigator's name, Williams also published what became a best-seller, under the title *A Narrative of Missionary Enterprises* (1837). In its pages Williams made a case for being an explorer on a par with Cook. He wrote of Rarotonga:

> This splendid island escaped the untiring researches of Captain Cook, and was discovered by myself, in 1823. It is a mass of mountains, which are high, and present a remarkably romantic appearance. It is situated in lat. 21° 20′ S., 160° W. long. It has several good boat harbours, is about thirty miles in circumference, and is surrounded by a reef. The population is about 6,000 or 7,000.[9]

As Williams translated islands into numbers, he authenticated his own claim to be a discoverer and he filled Cook's chart. The created order was designed to have humans at its head. To live in unison with nature – as the islanders had done – was to oppose that divine plan.[10] The heroic coloniser was the pious individual who rose against the land and put it in its place, firmly in the bounds of human control. In that process he never came under its sway, like Cook had done, in confusing the Creator and the created, and blurring the boundaries between what needed to be worshipped and what needed to submit to duty. Williams became a better Cook for a religiously awakened public.

---

[8] There is a vast literature on how to die well in this period. See Pat Jalland, *Death in the Victorian Family* (Oxford, 1999), Doreen Rosman, *Evangelicals and Culture* (London, 1984), Nigel Llewellyn, *The Art of Death: Visual Culture in the English Death Ritual, c.1500–1800* (London, 1991), John McManners, *Death and the Enlightenment: Changing Attitudes to Death Among Christians and Unbelievers in Eighteenth-century France* (Oxford, 1981).

[9] John Williams, *A Narrative of Missionary Enterprises in the South Sea Islands; with Remarks upon the Natural History of the Islands, Origin, Languages, Traditions, and Usages of the Inhabitants* (London, 1837), p. 18.

[10] For more on the operation of natural theology see Boyd Hilton, *Age of Atonement: The Influence of Evangelicalism on Social and Economic Thought, 1785–1865* (Oxford, 1988), and Richard Drayton, *Nature's Government: Science, Imperial Britain and the 'Improvement' of the World* (New Haven, 2000). For the placement of natural theology in the missionary project see Sujit Sivasundaram, 'Natural history spiritualized: civilizing islanders, cultivating breadfruit and collecting souls', *History of Science*, 32 (2001), pp. 417–43.

Although evangelicals engaged in what Gananath Obeyesekere has identified as myth-making, these myths were certainly not 'inflexible' with 'almost no internal debate'.[11] Missionaries dealt creatively with Cook's death, denouncing him as an idolater at the same time as they hoped to emulate his voyages. I do not mean to go into a full analysis of the over-heated anthropological debate between Obeyesekere and Marshall Sahlins.[12] Yet this chapter will demonstrate, in passing, that Obeyesekere's claim for the Hawaiians works with as much force for the evangelicals. The missionaries were also able to combine myth with reasoning. If this is the case both Sahlins and Obeyesekere should reflect more on their use of the dichotomous pairing of European and non-European. Forms of reasoning need to be historically particularised and located on a spectrum without being categorised under the competing terms of 'them' and 'us'. The evangelicals' relation to the site of Cook's death and the landscape of Williams's demise is reminiscent of Pacific islanders' natural historical traditions. The shared features of these approaches to the environment are forgotten in accounts that suppose that reasoning is diametrically opposed on either side of the encounter.

I will begin by studying nineteenth-century retellings of Cook, before widening my gaze in order to take in this dialectic between the celebrated missionary and the commemorated navigator.

Religious narrations

When the King and Queen of Hawai'i died in England in July 1824, after being taken ill with pulmonary inflammation caused by their introduction to a cooler climate, their bodies were taken back to the Pacific in HMS *Blonde*.[13] According to the missionaries, the ceremony that accompanied the return of these remains was put on at least in part because of the islanders' claim that an act of terrible revenge had been inflicted on their monarchs. The Revd George Young wrote, 'The death of their King and Queen in London, was regarded by many of them as a judgement of God, inflicted on the islands for the murder of the great Captain.'[14] Captain Byron's voyage aboard the *Blonde*

---

[11] Gananath Obeyesekere, *The Apotheosis of Captain Cook* (Princeton, 1992), p. 168.

[12] For the reply see: Marshall Sahlins, *How 'Natives' Think: About Captain Cook, For Example* (Chicago, 1995); also Michael Bravo, 'The anti-anthropology of highlanders and islanders', *Studies in History and Philosophy of Science*, 29A (1998), pp. 369–89.

[13] George Byron, *Voyage of H.M.S. Blonde to the Sandwich Islands in the Years 1824–1825* (London, 1826). According to the American missionary Sheldon Dibble the monarch decided to visit London from a state of restlessness; see his *History and General Views of the Sandwich Islands' Mission* (New York, 1839), p. 87.

[14] George Young, *The Life and Voyages of Captain James Cook, Drawn up from his Journals and other Authentic Documents; and Comprising much Original Information* (London, 1836), p. 462.

therefore had the specific aim of recasting the memory of the Cook tragedy in the islands. The bodies of the monarchs were deposited in lead coffins, enclosed in wood, covered with crimson velvet, and richly ornamented, with inscriptions in Hawaiian and English.[15]

At this time Cook's reputation amongst evangelicals had two threads to it. On the one hand, the Revd Thomas Haweis, founder of the South Pacific mission, had cherished the pages of Cook's *Voyages*. An early historian of the mission observed:

> These pictures of lovely scenes, of stirring adventure, of human degradation and need . . . powerfully touched the imagination of Dr Haweis. A mission to these dusky islanders, so gentle, so favoured by nature, so likely to be so easily influenced for good, as he pictured them in his mind, had become the cherished purpose of his heart.[16]

In fact Cook's discovery of the islands was said to have set the stage in a divinely ordained plan for mission work. In an address composed to encourage exertions towards missionary work, the Revd George Burder wrote,

> Captain Cook and others have traversed the globe, almost from pole to pole, and have presented us, as it were, a new world. . . . May we not reasonably hope that a well-planned and well-conducted mission . . . will be attended with the blessing of God and issue in the conversion of many souls?[17]

But at the same time as Cook's travels were thought to have been the first step in God's master plan for the unfolding of the Pacific islands, evangelicals derided Cook for losing control of himself and acting irreligiously at his death. The missionary, the Revd Hiram Bingham, wrote that Cook's death was a divine judgement for the sin of allowing the Hawaiians to adore him: 'we can hardly avoid the conclusion, that for the direct encouragement of idolatry, and especially for his audacity in allowing himself like the proud and magisterial Herod to be idolized, he was left to infatuation and died by the visitation of God'.[18] Bingham went on to suggest that Cook had violated the proper relation between humans and the Deity. The missionary noted that it was vain and rebellious for 'a worm to presume to receive religious homage and sacrifices'.[19]

---

[15] James Jackson Jarves, *History of the Hawaiian or Sandwich Islands, Embracing their Antiquities, Mythology, Legends, Discovery by Europeans in the Sixteenth-Century, Rediscovery by Cook* . . . (London, 1843), p. 233.

[16] Richard Lovett, *The History of the London Missionary Society 1795–1895* (London, 1899), I, p. 117.

[17] Ibid., p. 20.

[18] Hiram Bingham, *A Residence of Twenty-one Years in the Sandwich Islands or the Civil, Religious, and Political History of those Islands* (London, 1848), p. 35.

[19] Ibid.

The Revd George Young added, 'in this instance, our illustrious countryman suffered his curiosity to overcome his sense of duty'.[20] This was thought to be unusual for the celebrated voyager, who had condemned the human sacrifice of Tahiti, and whose journal contained many references to Providence.[21] Cook seemed to have fallen prey to a momentary but consequential temptation.

Religious biographers were insistent that Cook's folly could not be compromised; the navigator was said to have consented to being adored with the full knowledge of what was happening. James Jackson Jarves who first arrived in Hawai'i in 1837 as a sympathiser of missions, and who edited the weekly paper, *The Polynesian*, wrote that Cook had observed how the inhabitants of the island worshipped him and allowed this to continue. Poking fun at local traditions, Jarves noted, 'the punctilious deference paid Cook when he first landed was both painful and ludicrous . . . as soon as he walked passed [past], all unveiled themselves, rose and followed him'. In all there were said to be 'ten thousand half-clad men, women and children' chasing or following Cook 'on all-fours'.[22] These actions could not be misinterpreted and so Jarves wrote: 'The natives say that Cook performed his part in this heathen farce, without the slightest opposition.'[23] In the meantime, Young criticised those who argued that Cook's curiosity was sufficient excuse for his folly, by pointing to the fact that he allowed himself to be worshipped twice.[24] Cook's intention to be worshipped, and the implication that full blame for his actions should rest on his own shoulders, were a shared feature of religious narrations of his demise.

These criticisms need to be contextualised in a wider account of evangelical views of British contact in the Pacific. Navigators and travellers were often accused of neglecting to introduce local people to the benefits of religion, while encouraging alcoholism, and spreading venereal disease.[25] The American missionary the Revd Sheldon Dibble observed, 'Captain Cook might have directed the rude and ignorant natives to the great Jehovah, instead of receiving divine homage himself. If he had done so, it would have been less painful to contemplate his death.'[26] In a document written to the directors of Bible and missionary institutions, this opinion came to fever pitch with the criticism of sailors whose 'vicious practices cannot fail to subvert and banish every virtuous feeling; – whose example only teaches them to sin as with a cart-rope and who are like a swarm of destructive locusts that eat up every green thing

---

[20] Young, *Life and Voyages*, p. 421.

[21] Ibid., pp. 421–3.

[22] Jarves, *History of the Hawaiian Sandwich Islands*, p. 102.

[23] Ibid., p. 103.

[24] Young, *Life and Voyages*, p. 421.

[25] For more on the representation of mariners in this period see Jane Samson, *Imperial Benevolence: Making British Authority in the Pacific Islands* (Honolulu, 1998).

[26] Dibble, *History and General Views*, p. 28.

wherever they come'.[27] The self-presentation of missionaries as benevolent and selfless was forged in opposition to the image of godless mariners who sought their own gain. Where missionaries brought the benefits of British rule through pain and suffering, worldly mariners were said to destroy everything in their path.

This rhetoric explains why religious commentators on Cook's last days were quick to combine the navigator's irreligiosity with his supposed selfishness. Ephraim Eveleth, an American evangelical, wrote for instance of how Cook had insisted on a *heiau*, or sacred enclosure, being desecrated to supply the needs of his crew, just prior to his death. As payment for a piece of wood from this site, where the bones of kings and chiefs were deposited, Cook offered two iron hatchets.[28] Exasperated at the Hawaiians' denial of this request, Cook ordered his men to break down the fence of the *heiau* and to take it to the boats. Cook's lack of benevolence was amply proved for Eveleth by the unequal nature of this exchange. Jarves also wrote of the selfishness of Cook's crew:

> [the] most cogent reason operating to create a revulsion of feeling, was the enormous taxes with which the whole island was burthened to maintain them. Their offerings to senseless gods were comparatively few; but hourly and daily were they required for Cook and his followers. . . . The magnitude of the gifts from the savage, and the meanness of those from the white men, must excite the surprise of anyone who peruses the narrative of this voyage.[29]

In these and other ways, Cook and his contingent were demoted to the lowly rank of other travellers, characterised by greed and worldliness.

While accusing Cook of acting irreligiously and selfishly, and wanting to distance themselves from his mistakes, evangelicals wished to follow in the navigator's path. One solution to this paradox was to set about redeeming and remoulding the memory of the death. The Revd William Ellis, for instance, wrote that it will be 'gratifying for the Christian reader to know' that a missionary station has been formed in the village near where Cook was killed; and close to where the navigator was murdered 'a school has been opened, and a house erected for Christian worship'.[30] The physical features of the site also came under the natural theological gaze of the evangelicals. The cave where Cook's remains were deposited for a while was described thus:

---

[27] R. Ferguson, *Affecting Intelligence from the South Sea Islands. A Letter Addressed to the Directors and Friends of Bible and Missionary Institutions in Great Britain and America* (London, 1839), p. 3.

[28] Ephraim Eveleth, *History of the Sandwich Islands, with an Account of the American Mission Established there in 1820* (Philadelphia, 1831), p. 13.

[29] Jarves, *History of the Hawaiian Sandwich Islands*, pp. 108–9.

[30] William Ellis, *Polynesian Researches During a Residence of Nearly Six Years in the South Sea Islands* (London, 1839), IV, p. 138.

The cave itself is of volcanic formation, and appears to have been one of those subterranean tunnels so numerous on the island, by which the volcanoes in the interior sometimes discharge their contents upon the shore. It is five feet high, and the entrance about eight or ten feet wide. The roof and sides within are of obsidian or hard vitreous lava; and along the floor, it is evident that in some remote period a stream of the same kind of lava has also flowed.[31]

Evangelicals attempted to redeem Cook's mistake not just by rearranging the landmarks of the bay; they brought the site of the death securely within the boundaries of geography and science.

There was also a persistent desire to track down those who were associated with the events surrounding Cook's demise, to suggest that their behaviour had been altered under the redeeming influences of evangelicalism. Ellis wrote that there were a number of persons at Kaavaroa, and other places in the island, 'who either were present themselves at the unhappy dispute . . . or who, from their connexion with those who were on the spot, are well acquainted with the particulars'.[32] Dibble noted that, 'the heart, liver, &c. of Captain Cook were stolen and eaten by some hungry children, who mistook them in the night for the inwards of a dog'. Emphasising the contact that these men had since had with missionaries, he added that they were now 'aged . . . and reside within a few miles of the station of Lahaina'.[33] Captain Nathaniel Portlock, one of Cook's crew who later commanded a voyage through the Pacific that lasted from 1785 to 1788, first set this tradition in motion in publishing the account of his conversation with a man named Ta-boo-a-raa-nee.[34] This man turned out to be the brother of the chief who was killed by Cook's men, and whose death sparked the uproar just prior to Cook's death. He apparently told Portlock that 'the present king Co-ma-aa-ma-a and other chiefs were very much afraid of coming on board; dreading our resenting the fate our countrymen'.[35] This encounter provides an insight into an earlier attempt to track the perpetrators of Cook's death, which was shrouded in fear and regret, and which predates conversion.

Attempts to change the people and landscape of Hawai'i and to assert the superiority of Christianity are evident outside the missionary corpus. After depositing the remains of the King and Queen, Captain Byron steered for Kealakekua Bay. He noted upon meeting the chiefs of the district, 'Theft is punished, murder almost unknown, and infants enjoy all the benefits of parental love.'[36] Yet even in the context of all of these changes there was still more

---

[31] Ibid., pp. 130–1.
[32] Ibid., p. 131.
[33] Dibble, *History and General Views*, p. 31.
[34] Nathaniel Portlock, *A Voyage Round the World, but more Particularly to the North-west Coast of America performed in 1785, 1786, 1787 and 1788* (London, 1789), p. 309.
[35] Ibid.
[36] Byron, *Voyage of H.M.S. Blonde*, p. 198.

converting that had to be done. Byron visited the spot where it was believed that Cook's body had been burnt and took away many pieces of the dark lava that lay at the spot. According to Ellis, few visitors left Hawai'i without making a pilgrimage to the spot where Cook died. Such tours customarily included the collection of lava, the commentary of a Hawaiian guide, and the study of two coconut trees that were perforated by balls shot from the boats on the occasion of Cook's death.[37] Yet Byron was not content with these gestures of commemoration. He went to the royal *morai*, where the son of the high-priest of Cook's time was still in charge of relics. He described it as 'filled with rude wooden images of all shapes and dimensions, whose grotesque forms and horrible countenances present a most extraordinary spectacle'.[38] Viewing the artefacts of this district where Cook had been deified, Byron hastily collected some to display in Britain.

The regret of the high-priest's son at the desecration of a holy place is noted and yet paraded as a sign of powerlessness. The structures of a culture that allowed a navigator to perish were dismantled and transplanted with Christianity. By the collection of artefacts, Byron asserted the passage of time, and put Cook's folly firmly into history. At the spot where the body was burnt, he erected a cross of oak to the memory of the man. 'Sacred to the memory of Capt. James Cook, R.N. who discovered these Islands in the year of our Lord, 1778. This humble monument is erected, by his countrymen, in the year of our Lord, 1825.'[39] A new artefact and a new memory: the signification of a landscape and a people changed and Christianised.

The memory of Cook's death therefore stimulated a range of positions amongst evangelicals and religious travellers. His last actions were said to violate the proper ordering of creation: he had allowed himself to be worshipped, and had acted in a way that was unfitting for a British navigator. He had also displayed a selfishness that was common to all worldly explorers who sought their own gain before the conversion of the Pacific islanders. Yet evangelicals were forced to portray themselves as following in Cook's path, since the missionary enterprise rose out of the seeds of Cook's voyages. This ambiguity was resolved by their reorganisation of the site of Cook's death and the civilisation of the people associated with the events of the navigator's last days. As places and people were redeemed it became possible to atone for the past and to move beyond Cook's folly.

[37] Ellis, *Polynesian Researches*, IV, pp. 137–8; also p. 144.
[38] Byron, *Voyage of H.M.S. Blonde*, p. 200.
[39] Ibid., p. 202.

Debunking myth

A brief consideration of secular accounts of Cook is useful in placing these religious narrations in perspective. For example, a cheap biography of Cook published in 1831, and aimed at the lower and middling classes, played down the events of Cook's alleged deification. Cook's mistake could have no place here, given the pamphlet's aim to instil in its readers, the 'important truth, that industry, prudence, honesty, and perseverance, are ever sure of being rewarded, even in this world'.[40] The Hawaiians' actions were said to suggest their high respect and opinion and the name 'Orono' was parenthesised, 'a title of high honour given to Captain Cook'.[41] A host of other sources also drew on this rhetoric of improvement, by stressing Cook's successes and showing how they could be emulated by those dedicated to hard work. One author hoped, for instance, that Cook would soon be revered in the Pacific, with 'the rational respect and affection due by an enlightened people to him who was the harbinger of their civilisation'.[42] Typifying self-help literature, these accounts went to great lengths in suggesting that anyone could become like Cook: 'In whatever soil genius or merit is sown, it will burst forth, according to its strength, with as much splendour as the sun from behind a cloud: if difficulties obstruct its progress, the more furious it will burn, till it is properly cultivated, and advantageously employed.'[43]

Yet common to both evangelical and improving accounts of Cook's death was the use of the navigator's memory as a commodity. All of these writers reshaped Cook's life in order to suit their own ideology. Ironically, the use of Cook as cultural currency was characterised in these very works as a feature of the mentality of Pacific peoples. Young wrote, for instance, that when the mutineers of the *Bounty* wanted a stock of cattle in Tahiti, they 'made the demand in the name of Captain Cook; a name which operated on the natives like a charm, and made them furnish in more than three days, more than was required'.[44] Pacific peoples were thought to be in the grip of memory and incapable of rational history. This was why Dibble noted:

> The *early history* of the Hawaiian nation is involved in uncertainty. It could not be otherwise, with the history of a people entirely ignorant of the art of writing.

[40] Anon., *The Life of Captain James Cook the Celebrated Circumnavigator, compiled from the most Authentic Sources* (Dublin, 1831), Preface.
[41] Ibid., p. 148.
[42] Anon., *An Historical Account of the Circumnavigation of the Globe and of the Progress of Discovery in the Pacific Ocean, from the Voyages of the Magellan to the Death of Cook* (Edinburgh, 1837), p. 490.
[43] Anon., *The Voyages of Captain James Cook, Round the World with an Account of his Unfortunate Death at Owhyhee* (London, 1823), Preface.
[44] Young, *Life and Voyages*, p. 460.

Traditions, indeed, are abundant; but traditions are a mass of rubbish, from which it is always difficult to extricate truth. Very little can be ascertained with certainty, beyond the memory of the present generation, and the records of Europeans who first visited the islands.[45]

Cook's arrival in Hawai'i was also said to provide evidence for the tyranny of memory and myth. Missionaries recounted how, in mistaking the navigator for the god *Lono*, islanders had come to a superstitious view of the past. They believed that a chief who 'slew his wife in a fit of passion' became 'gloomy and sullen' and left the island in his canoe; and that this chief was actually a god who would return.[46]

Some religious commentators attempted to reconcile detailed descriptions of the islanders' traditions of the past with established narratives of history. Jarves wrote, for instance, how local people believed that in the reign of Kahoukapu, 'a *kahuna* (priest) arrived at Kohala. . . . He was a white man, and brought with him a large and a small idol.' Jarves then interjected with clinical precision: 'Kahoukapu reigned eighteen generations of kings previous to Kamehameha I. . . . If such were the case, it would bring the arrival of Paao [the priest] to somewhere between the years 1530 and 1630, a period brilliant in the annals of Spanish maritime discovery in the Pacific.'[47] By these means superstition was aligned with truth. Yet scripture was the prime arbiter of truth for evangelicals and provided a source of the firmest certainties. Therefore, Hawaiian accounts of their past needed to be compared with the Bible. Bingham wrote that the islanders were part of the lost tribe of Israel, who in their travels over a wide field like Polynesia, 'have lost every vestige and tradition of their literature, and of their language, and of the names of their patriarchs, kings, prophets and heroes'.[48]

Despite priding themselves on coming to a rational and scriptural view of the past, evangelicals traded and moulded memory. They used Cook as a commodity for their own purposes, even as the Tahitians were supposedly beguiled by his name. While oral traditions were represented as inferior to written texts, words themselves came to have mystical power. When printing presses were transported to the region, the evangelists were jubilant in reporting on the awe of Pacific peoples. In Hawai'i, Dibble drew attention to how the monarch Kamehameha confused words with what they referred to:

The people were amazed at the art of expressing thoughts on paper. They started back from it with dread, as though it were a sort of enchantment or sorcery. A certain captain said to Kamehameha, 'I can put Kamehameha on a slate'; and proceeded

[45] Dibble, *History and General Views*, p. 14.

[46] For one example of the use of this story see Eveleth, *History of the Sandwich Islands*, p. 11.

[47] Jarves, *History of the Hawaiian Sandwich Islands*, p. 90.

[48] Bingham, *A Residence of Twenty-one Years*, p. 27.

to write the word Kamehameha. The chief scornfully replied, 'That is not me – not Kamehameha.' . . . They even imagined that letters could speak.[49]

These tales may be explained in part by the missionaries' dedication to the Word.

If words and histories were crucial to the orchestration of colonialism in the Pacific, it is unsurprising that retellings of Cook's life and death could be so ideologically charged. Evangelical narrations of Cook's irreligiosity and selfishness are part of a wider proclivity amongst Europeans to use Cook's name as a commodity. While biographers and historians mythologised the man and made myriad different heroes of him, they rebuked Pacific islanders for being mythical. European accounts of Cook were lauded instead as the triumphs of the press and the Word.

Being selfless

Even as evangelicals attempted to redeem Cook's memory by reshaping the physical appearance of Hawai'i and converting the inhabitants of the bay where the navigator had been slain, they urged others to emulate the great man by living a life like his and then dying for the cross instead of worldly passion. The Society's Directors decided to warn the missionaries about the power of temptation: 'there may be suspecting kings, superstitious priests, a blind and perhaps a ferocious people; [you] may be in perils often, and perhaps in deaths; [you] may expect all that hell and earth can devise or execute; . . . [you] should chiefly dread [your] own heart'.[50] To follow in Cook's wake was to ensure that the self was mastered and that temptations from within as well as without were resisted. In order to exemplify how the navigator's life could be re-embodied in the lives of those that followed him, I will focus on the story of one missionary, who was explicitly compared with Cook. The manner in which this missionary was equated with Cook can also be the lens through which we understand how the definition of the self changed in this period.

John Williams set out for the Pacific in 1817 and became by his death in 1839 the foremost missionary in the region. Despite writing many hundred lines, there is one sentence that religious writers and biographers immediately applied to his life: 'For my own part I cannot content myself within the narrow limits of a single reef.'[51] This statement captured the essence of the man: a

---

[49] Dibble, *History and General Views*, pp. 81–2.

[50] 'Considerations recommended to the missionaries', in *Evangelical Magazine*, 1796, p. 334.

[51] This became the title of a biography of Williams. See J. Gutch, *Beyond the Reefs: The Life of John Williams* (London, 1974). For more on John Williams see also: Niel Gunson, 'John Williams and his ship: the bourgeois aspirations of a missionary family', in D.P. Crook, ed., *Questioning the Past: A Selection of Papers in History and Government* (St Lucia, 1972),

striving to travel and to plot new points on the map of the Pacific. This restless spirit was useful in comparing him with Cook. Yet even as Williams voyaged through the sea, his thoughts were supposedly occupied with a very different journey. As an evangelical, he believed that the earthly life did not provide him with his home, it set a course of spiritual development that prepared his soul for heaven. This was why writers were keen to stress Williams's ordinariness. By emphasising the missionary's origins in the mechanic class, religious commentators suggested that he had become an instrument of divine agency. After his death, the Revd John Campbell described Williams with these words: 'Few men, skilled in the physiognomical attributes of nations, would have pronounced him an Englishman.' Yet having 'been once seen, he was ever after easily recognised; and you could instantly point him out, at a distance, among ten thousand men'. These symptoms of distinction were also combined with a judgement which 'although sound was neither strong, comprehensive nor exact. Its moral movements closely resembled those of his bulky frame; they were heavy and lagging – wanting in rapidity, dexterity, and decision.'[52] To support the claim that Williams had been an instrument of God, evangelicals had to form a view of the man that allowed greatness to be found in weakness.

A similar set of tropes characterises the reception of Williams's book, *A Narrative of Missionary Enterprises* (1837). The *Congregational Magazine*'s reviewer noted: 'To our minds there is a life, and charm in these artless, unvarnished narratives and descriptions fresh from nature and from truth'.[53] In apologising for the defects of his prose, Williams commented that they arose from being 'devoted either to active labour, or to the study of uncultivated dialects, the idiom, abruptness, and construction of which are more familiar to him than the words and phrases – the grace and force of his native tongue'.[54] Difficulties and hard work were essential to the life of a godly evangelist and these characteristics were paraded as signifiers of faith. Williams himself observed in his book: 'I have felt disappointed when reading the writings of Missionaries at not finding a fuller account of the difficulties they have had to contend with.'[55] That his life had been preserved through difficult times became the means of suggesting that God had worked through him. Yet this strategy might have been taken too far. According to the *Monthly Review*, Williams's career

pp. 73–95; Gavan Daws, *A Dream of Islands: Voyages of Self-Discovery in the South Seas: John Williams, Herman Melville, Walter Murray Gibson, Robert Louis Stevenson, Paul Gauguin* (New York, 1980); Sujit Sivasundaram, 'John Williams', in Timothy Larsen, ed., *Biographical Dictionary of Evangelicals* (Leicester, 2003), pp. 737–39.

[52] John Campbell, *The Martyr of Erromanga or the Philosophy of Missions Illustrated from the Labours, Death, and Character of the Late Rev. John Williams* (London, 1842), pp. 196–7.

[53] Review of 'A Narrative of Missionary Enterprises' in *Congregational Magazine*, I (1837), p. 440.

[54] Williams, *A Narrative*, Preface pp. x–ix.

[55] Ibid., p. 117.

has been one that constantly led him to mark the dealings of Providence towards him with more than ordinary closeness and wonder; but it is not less true, that he who orally describes his hair breadth escapes and marvellous experiences – much more he who commits his emotions to a book, where their ardour and intensity of gratitude cannot be witnessed excepting through the medium of literary truth and skill, should be wary lest he spoil the effect of the whole by a neglect of proportions and occasions – by wasting the whole vocabulary of his ecstasies on comparatively unimpressive passages of every-day life.[56]

Despite this criticism, Williams's book was extraordinarily successful in forming the stereotype of the ideal missionary and godly traveller. Williams's faith was apparently evident not just in his rise to fame from lowly origins, but in his awareness of weaknesses and his triumphant celebration of difficulty. The *Congregational Magazine* praised Williams saying: 'the author of this work is entitled to a high place. He is a man of large views, great courage, strong sense, and eminently practical talents, and all his qualifications are dedicated to his work with most simple-minded thorough consecration.'[57] The *Monthly Review* compared him with other missionaries and concluded: 'none have been more eminent and successful than Mr. John Williams'.[58] Campbell noted that 'Williams' "Missionary Enterprises", alone, is of more real value than all the writings of a Clarke, a Butler, a Paley, a Chalmers, a Leland and a Lardner united.'[59] Letters were received from gentlemen of standing who wished to meet Williams and to contribute to the costs of the mission.[60] The sales of the work rocketed. His book sold 7,500 copies from April 1837 to September 1838; when a new edition came out it sold a further 6,000 copies. Subsequently a 'People's Edition' was stereotyped and published unabridged for the sake of the poorer readers at two shillings and six pence, and this version sold 24,000 copies.[61] It was in this climate of acclaim that Williams could be heralded as a new Cook; a better Cook for a religious public. Evangelicals claimed that they had found a mariner who at last sought glory for God, who retained his own sense of identity and the need for a proper relation between himself and the Deity.

---

[56] Review of 'A Narrative of Missionary Enterprises' in *Monthly Review*, II (1837), p. 408.

[57] Review of 'A Narrative' in *Congregational Magazine* (1837), p. 440.

[58] Review of 'A Narrative' in *Monthly Review*, II (1837), p. 407.

[59] Campbell, *Martyr of Erromanga*, Preface, p. ii.

[60] Williams was proud of these letters and used them to support the claim that he had been successful. See John Campbell, ed., *The Missionary Farewell: Valedictory Services of the Rev. John Williams Previous to his Departure for the South Seas with his Parting Dedicatory Address to the British Churches and the Friends of Missions* (London 1838), p. 84.

[61] Review of 'Memoirs of the Life of the Rev. John Williams' in *Eclectic Review* (1843), p. 182.

Replicating Captain Cook's death

Three years after his book was published, Williams was killed and allegedly eaten when he landed on the shores of the island of Eromanga, and it was this event that formed the nub of the comparison between Cook and the missionary. Campbell wrote of the missionary's death: 'for popular effect, for the reputation of Mr. Williams, and for the purposes of history, he died in a proper manner, at the proper place, and the proper time'.[62] In Campbell's thinking, Cook's death also came at the climax of his career.[63] This is why he could write:

> What Cook was in his own department, that Williams was in his; the career of the seaman shone resplendent with maritime, the career of the missionary with moral, glory . . . the one represented England's power and science, the other her piety and humanity; both had earned the confidence of their countrymen, and the admiration of mankind; – both were killed with the club of the savage.[64]

This analogy between Cook's death and Williams's demise had come into such currency that a children's Sunday School book on Williams, published much later in the early twentieth century, could begin with Cook's landing at Eromanga and end with Williams's death at the same location. Despite seeming to compare the two navigators, these images draw attention to Williams's selfless character. In the first image Cook is shown standing over the Eromangans, with weapon in hand (Plate XVI). Williams's landing, however, emphasises his willing death; he does not even resist the attack (Plate XVII). Here it is the assailant who stands above, swinging a club. While Cook has not left the boat, Williams's companions are shown far in the background. The missionary's death is therefore emphatically determined and detached and unlike that of Cook. That this work started with Cook's arrival and ended with Williams's death had a powerful rhetorical thrust: Williams completed what Cook began and he did it far more sacrificially.

Accounts of Williams's death suggested, not only that he died willingly, but that his demise was pre-ordained. Captain Morgan, who was with Williams, wrote that the missionary was adamant to land at Eromanga despite his own hesitation.[65] Mr Cunningham, the Vice-Consul of Sydney, who was with him at the moment of attack wrote:

> I instantly perceived that it was run or die. I shouted to Mr. Williams to run . . . Mr. Williams did not run at the instant I called out to him, till we heard a shell

---

[62] Campbell, *Martyr of Erromanga*, p. 228.
[63] Ibid., p. 226.
[64] Ibid., p. 227.
[65] Ebenezer Prout, *Memoirs of the Rev. John Williams* (London, 1843), p. 578.

Plate XVI Captain Cook landing at Eromanga, from Basil Mathews, *John Williams, The Ship Builder* (Oxford, 1915)

Plate XVII The martyrdom of the Revd John Williams, from Basil Mathews, *John Williams, The Ship Builder* (Oxford, 1915)

blow; it was an instant, but too much to lose. I again called to Mr. W. to run, and sprang forward for the boat. . . . Mr. Williams instead of making for the boat, ran directly down the beach into the water, and a savage after him.[66]

These actions were irrational, both for a thinking man and for the normal frame of mind that Williams possessed. This type of evidence was essential in the evangelical claim that the missionary had been led to his death in a predetermined way. The spirit that resided within him had destined that he would die and guided him to that very death. The last, incomplete entry from Williams's diary was also used to celebrate this thesis of premonition. Two days before his death Williams wrote: 'This is a memorable day, a day which will be transmitted to posterity, and the record of the events which have this day transpired, will exist after those who have taken an active part in them have retired into the shades of oblivion, and the results of this day will be – '[67] Campbell said: 'Did not our departed friend, like the prophets of old, write words which he saw not the full import?'[68] The fact that Williams did not sleep on the night before they reached Eromanga also attracted attention.[69] Williams was said, therefore, not only to have known that he was about to die; his excitement demonstrated his close communion with the Deity, and stood in contrast to how Cook lost his religiosity at the moment of his demise.

In coming to all of these conclusions evangelicals paid particular attention to the manner in which Williams mastered his body at death. It was presumed that he would have prayed like Jesus did: 'Father forgive them, for they know not what they are doing.'[70] The saintliness of Williams became so well accepted, that the image of him dying while pointing to heaven became an accepted trope of evangelical thinking. Images from Sunday School books of the early twentieth century may be used to show the longevity of this tradition (Plate XVIII). Here Williams is focused on the world to come, pointing upwards and looking beyond to the heavens. This is quite unlike the manner of Cook's death. Williams's death therefore highlights the character of the evangelical martyr: an individual in control of his body to the extent that he could give it up, like Christ had at the cross. Although Campbell equated Cook and Williams, it is clear that he believed that Williams was infinitely superior to Cook. He wrote: 'John Williams will be venerated as one of the most illustrious Fathers of the New Era, – as one of the royal line of Stephen and Antipas, and other martyrs of our God'.[71] And this was why

[66] Ibid., p. 580.

[67] Ibid., p. 569.

[68] Campbell, *Martyr of Erromanga*, p. 229.

[69] See Basil Mathews, *Yarns of South Sea Pioneers for the use of workers among boys and girls* (London, 1914), p. 32.

[70] See *Evangelical Magazine* (1840), p. 298 and (1843), p. 117.

[71] Campbell, *Martyr of Erromanga*, p. 243.

**The Savages overtook him and struck him down
with their Clubs.**

Plate XVIII The martyrdom of the Revd John Williams, from Albert Lee, *John Williams* (London, 1921)

progress was at the core of evangelical re-inscriptions of Cook. Williams did what Cook had done much better.

John Williams and nature

In 1841 an engraving made from wood-blocks, entitled *The Massacre of the Lamented Missionary Rev. John Williams and Mr. Harris*, appeared in London and came into wide circulation (Plate XIX). The print depicts Williams falling into the water with his left arm held up to shield his head. He is depicted looking 'with eyes turned up to heaven for that support which he well knew and felt would not fail him even in that dreadful moment'.[72] Over him, 'ready to repeat the blow, stand two of the natives with their clubs upraised, while another by their side, is ready to pierce the heart of the unhappy missionary with his spear'. In all, about a hundred Eromangan men are shown rushing towards the ocean in 'wild commotion, every countenance expressive of the most diabolical malice and rage, armed with spears and massive and murderous clubs, made of the hard wood of the island, slings, and bows and arrows, they all seem intent on the work of death'.[73] The description accompanying the print urged viewers to meditate on the islanders' countenances in order to come to some idea of their sinfulness.

This engraving was produced by George Baxter, who had by this time established a reputation and won a patent for colour printing.[74] The death scene was modelled on a watercolour by J. Leary, who had been on the boat, to which Williams attempted to return before he died (Plate XX). In his engravings George Baxter apparently 'drew from nature'.[75] His first colour print was of butterflies. Robert Mudie's books, *The Feathered Tribes of the British Islands* (London, 1834) and *Man: His Physical Structure and Adaptations* (London, 1838), were illustrated by him.[76] This attention to natural detail is also evident in Baxter's portrayal of the death of Williams. The original watercolour by Leary survives, and is annotated by Baxter with such phrases as 'hilly', 'deep valley', 'the mountain not so steep', 'bushes and men running through', 'these men should be in deeper water' and 'natives – <u>dark</u> complexion' and, most revealingly, 'Williams should be more heavenly'.

[72] 'The last two days of Rev. John Williams and Mr. Harris' from a description accompanying the print at the School of Oriental and African Studies, University of London, p. 7. To help in interpreting the claim that Williams looked heavenly see Elaine Scarry, *The Body in Pain: The Making and Unmaking of the World* (Oxford, 1987).

[73] 'The last two days of Rev. John Williams and Mr. Harris', p. 7.

[74] For George Baxter, see Asa Briggs, *Victorian Things* (London, 1988), pp. 173–8.

[75] C.T. Courtney Lewis, *George Baxter, His Life and Work* (London, 1972), p. 68.

[76] For more on this see C.T. Courtney, *George Baxter, the Picture Painter* (London, 1924). For the *Evangelical Magazine*'s review of Mudie's *The Sea* see *Evangelical Magazine* (1836), p. 21.

Plate XIX The martyrdom of the Revd John Williams by George Baxter, 1841, from *The Massacre of the Lamented Missionary Rev. John Williams and Mr. Harris* (London, 1843)

Plate XX The martyrdom of the Revd John Williams: watercolour print by John Leary

These changes were necessary to make the image consonant with evangelical views of nature and death. Because evangelicals interpreted the mountains, the seas and the rocks anthropomorphically, the appearance of these objects at the moment of death could add meaning to the image. For example, Leary's watercolour had four well-defined peaks quite close to the shore; but Baxter's print had just one mountain which faded into the background. On the last day, Scripture held that 'every valley shall be filled in, every mountain and hill made low. The crooked roads shall become straight, the rough ways smooth. And all mankind will see God's salvation.'[77] For Baxter the fading of the peak on the shore of Eromanga could symbolise the passing of earthly splendour. Here Williams would be killed, while in heaven he would be crowned a martyr. In an article on mountains in the *Evangelical Magazine*, a writer noted that 'Time is every hour committing gradual, but constant depredations on those surprising monuments of almighty power . . . how should it teach us to set our affections on the things which are above!'[78]

Two years after Baxter's print appeared, the *Evangelical Magazine* carried a plate depicting Dillon's Bay, Erromanga, where Williams had been slain (Plate XXI). The page following the engraving carried a description of the landscape, which presented the argument that nature was to blame for Williams's demise. It was 'possible, indeed that the wild barrenness of its rocks and hills have helped, with other more potent causes, to nurture in their bosom those habits which seem to defy, at present, the approach of the Gospel's genial influence'. The spot where Williams was slain was said to have 'a bold and very rugged coast' while the bay was said to show 'stern uncultivatedness'.[79] Leary's watercolour, with its four majestic peaks, did not present a sufficiently fallen view of the environment surrounding Williams's demise. Baxter's changes to the original image must thus be related to evangelical theologies of the mountains. The *Missionary Magazine* for 1842 noted: 'those mountain peaks are the obelisks on which, in the blood of their martyrdom, are inscribed the memorials of devoted zeal, and the glory of the gospel'.[80]

But this connection between the environment and Williams's demise could also be turned on its head, by the suggestion that the Eromangans had revolted against nature in killing Williams, as opposed to conforming to its ruggedness. In an early twentieth-century missionary history of Eromanga, it was observed: 'The contrast between the beauty of the Island of Erromanga and the degradation of its inhabitants is as light and dark.'[81]

---

[77] Luke 3: 5–6, King James version of the Holy Bible.

[78] *Evangelical Magazine* (1806), p. 457. For more on the connection between mountains and the sacred see M.H. Nicolson, *Mountain Gloom and Mt. Glory: The Development of the Aesthetics of the Infinite* (New York, 1959).

[79] *Evangelical Magazine* (1843), p. 414.

[80] *Missionary Magazine and Chronicle* (1841), pp. 89–90.

[81] A.K. Langridge, *Won by Blood. The Story of Erromanga the Martyr Isle* (London, 1922), p. 21.

Plate XXI The coast of Eromanga, from *Evangelical Magazine* (1843)

Just as Baxter changed the appearance of the mountains from Leary's original, he also made the water appear deeper and more turbulent. This modification might also be related to evangelical theologies of nature. The fury of the ocean could, for example, be linked to the spiritual condition of the Erromangans. A poet wrote of the natural features of the island where Williams had fallen:

> But long the powers of darkness had held dominion there;
>   And rites of horrid cruelty polluted all the air;
> And the cliffs that frown above them, and the waves that round them roll,
>   Spoke of wrath, and not of mercy, to the terror-stricken soul.[82]

---

[82] *Evangelical Magazine* (1844), p. 405. For the connection between the sea and the sacred see Cynthia Behrman, *Victorian Myths of the Sea* (Athens, OH, 1977).

References to the relationship between the sea and death were widespread in the early nineteenth century. The sea was at the centre of a popular funeral hymn: 'Abide with me'.[83] Symbolism usually represented the dying as passing over a great sea to the eternal shore beyond. In an early book titled *Contemplations on the Ocean*, Richard Pearsall wrote that 'The wicked are like yon troubled sea, vexations to themselves and one another; they many times blaspheme God. . . . Peace is a stranger to their breasts, for the way of Peace they have not known.'[84] Therefore the connection between Baxter's furious sea and the Erromangan temperament was a real one.

The sea for the evangelical was also an important reminder of the attributes of God. The infinity of the oceans was said to be indicative of the infinity of God's love. The *Evangelical Magazine* carried a sermon preached by the late John Williams. This included the anecdote of a South Sea islander who remarked that 'the love of Christ is like the ocean. In all ages men have been taking from its waters, yet the ocean remains as full as ever; in like manner, men in all ages have been drinking of the stream of Christ's love yet there remains a fullness that can never be diminished.'[85] Evangelicals who were shocked by the death of Williams may have been comforted by reflecting on how the mysterious workings of the ocean were like the unsearchable ways of God. At his death, it was said that Williams had remained in firm control of himself, remaining at the head of creation and willing to submit to the Creator.

Trading in tragedy

Just as much as Williams emulated Cook and recast the navigator's death in an evangelical mould, there were many who followed in Williams's wake who wished to replicate the missionary's life-story. Dozens of books came off the evangelical press that served to commemorate the martyr-traveller. These ranged from philosophical treatises to boys' adventure books. John Campbell's *Maritime Discovery and Christian Missions, considered in their mutual relations* appeared in 1840 and celebrated Williams's life and his achievements in navigation and shipbuilding. Campbell published again under the title: *The Martyr of Erromanga or the Philosophy of Missions illustrated from the labours, death, and character of the late Rev. John Williams*. This appeared in 1842 and went through two further editions. He also reissued the farewell proceedings for John Williams together with an account of his death and 6,000 copies of

---

[83] *Abide with Me* by H.F. Lyte (1793–1847). For a good analysis of this hymn see J.R. Watson, *The Victorian Hymn* (Durham, 1981).

[84] Richard Pearsall, *Contemplations on the Ocean, the Harvest, Sickness and the Last Judgement* (London, 1802), p. 58.

[85] *Evangelical Magazine* (1843), p. 168.

this were published. Within the decade pamphlets celebrating Williams's life also appeared.

For the period up to 1954 I have been able to trace no fewer than ten books published on Williams.[86] Many of these were children's book and carried statements such as: 'Children like to imitate and they like to experiment. Here is an opportunity for both.'[87] Another claimed: 'Its aim is to reach boys of the Scout type, at the age when the new emotions of space-hunger, hero-worship and sex instinct are bringing them into a new world, and the age at which the majority of those who take any decisive line at all come to their decision.'[88] For the evangelical and the Christian, mechanical ingenuity was a manly trait. Male children were expected to be interested in building ships and were provided with the necessary cut-outs. They were also asked to contribute to the cost of a line of ships that were designed to send missionaries to the South Pacific: these were named the John Williams ships. By the launch of *John Williams VI*, the money was said to come from children all over the empire. This, the last ship in the line, was named by Princess Margaret

The desire to raise a generation of missionaries of the calibre of John Williams was not restricted to Britain. The island of Eromanga and others of the region also came to serve as lasting monuments to Williams's memory. Churches were built on several islands in memory of Williams. Monuments were erected very soon after the event in Rarotonga. It was crucial that those who had caused Williams's martyrdom were converted. Particular attention was paid by later missionaries to the family of Williams's murderer. When the Gordons arrived in Erromanga in 1857 they wrote: 'Kowiowi – the murderer of Williams – was killed fighting three months before our arrival. We visited his widow, a dear little woman, living in their war cave. Kowiowi had two sons;

---

[86] Anon., *John Williams, the Missionary* (London, 1849); James Joseph Ellis, *John Williams, the Martyr Missionary of Polynesia* (London, 1890); Arthur John Hallam Montefiore, *Heroes who have Won Their Crown: David Livingstone and John Williams* (London, 1909); Basil Mathews, *John Williams, The Ship Builder* (Oxford, 1915); Albert Lee, *John Williams* (London, 1921); Ernest H. Hayes, *Wilamu mariner-missionary, the story of John Williams* (London, 1922); Norman James Davidson, *John Williams of the South Seas* (London, 1925); William Cecil Northcott, *John Williams Sails on* (London, 1939); Robert and Beryl Collens, *John Williams. A Sunday School Celebration* (London, 1949); Phyllis Matthewman, *John Williams, a Biography for Children* (London, 1954). On the John Williams ships see anon., *The Missionary Ship 'John Williams'* (London, 1844); anon., *The Return to England of the Missionary Ship 'John Williams' Containing an Account of her Voyages During Three Years as Related by Capt. Morgan, and Messrs. Barff, Buzacott and Mills* (London, 1847); Basil Mathews, *The Ships of Peace* (London, 1919); Mary Entwistle, ed., *Islands Everywhere, Stories for 7–9 Year-olds* (London, 1944); anon., *Our John Williams, 1844–1944* (London, 1944); J. Reason, ed., *The Ship Book, 1844–1944, Stories, Games, Poems, Models etc.* (London, 1944); Cecil Northcott, *South Sea Sailor. The Story of John Williams and his Ships* (London, 1965).
[87] Winifred Warr, *Practical Books No 6. South Seas, A Handbook for Leaders* (London, 1947), p. 37.
[88] Mathews, *Yarns of South Sea Pioneers*, p. 2.

the younger son joined our Mission, the other son used to come sulkily about, but remained a heathen in our day.'[89] In time, this 'other son' also embraced the gospel and took part in the laying of a stone for the centennial memorial of the death of Williams. The family of the murderer was therefore redeemed and this brings to mind the quest to redeem the Hawaiians after Cook's demise.

The Missionary Society did not have to wait long to see their desire of emulation fulfilled. The Gordons, who arrived as missionaries to Eromanga in 1857, were martyred, as was their successor, George Gordon's brother. The image of the first Gordon's death demonstrates many conventions used in depicting the death of Williams (Plate XXII). The Eromangan is barely clothed, in contrast to the fully clothed George Gordon, and there is a drama of light and darkness between the skin colours of the two. Gordon reaches his hands to the heavens, as Williams did before him.

Conclusions: colonising history

In the first chapter of the Revd Hiram Bingham's book, which condemned Cook for allowing others to worship him, there are some striking instructions about how evangelicals should use history. According to Bingham, in place of authentic history Pacific islanders produce accounts that are merely 'obscure oral traditions, national or party songs, rude narratives of the successions of kings, wars, victories, exploits of gods, heroes, priests, sorcerers, the giants of iniquity and antiquity, embracing conjecture, romance, and the general absurdities of Polytheism'.[90] In contrast to these histories, Bingham sets out in his book to read the records 'carefully written by men thoroughly acquainted with the people, and friendly to the truth'. At his aid are the pen and the press, science and Christianity, and all of these will lead to 'a just view of facts and motives' and enable him to 'do justice to all classes concerned, and to decide what ought to be done in like circumstances'.[91] This brand of evangelical history is then a didactic one; a set of doctrines that can be used to live life in the present. Bingham explains his ability to write history as arising from his mastery of nature. In contrast to his rational mind, he says that the islanders who have no true history are 'children of nature'.[92]

I have explored how this ideology of history was put into practice in religious accounts of Cook's death. Although Cook was said to have contradicted the proper relation between humans and the Deity and to have acted selfishly at his death, missionaries had to draw on his life in order to place themselves within the tradition of Pacific exploration. To deal with their ambiguous

---

[89] Langridge, *Won by Blood*, p. 17.
[90] Bingham, *A Residence of Twenty-one Years*, p. 17.
[91] Ibid., p. 20.
[92] Ibid., p. 23.

Plate XXII The martyrdom of George N. Gordon, from A.K. Langridge, *Won by Blood The Story of Erromanga the Martyr Isle* (London, 1922)

relationship with Cook, evangelicals modified their memory of the navigator's death by reshaping the geography and religion of the bay where Cook was killed. They called on missionaries to follow in Cook's path, and to die for the cross instead of passion. When the Revd John Williams was slain by Eromangans, his death apparently bettered the manner of the navigator's demise. Williams had died while in control of himself and with a selfless willingness to suffer.

Williams's death supported the evangelicals' providential colonialism and presented the ideal type for the missionary. Evangelicals therefore used Cook as a resource to celebrate their own success in Williams's career, and changed their account of the past. To what extent then did empire depend on shifting interpretations of past moments of expansion? The number of commentaries on Cook's death, and the lengths that evangelicals went to to redeem his mistake, may at first appear surprising. This body of material suggests instead that we often underestimate the importance of typologies in the early nineteenth century. More work is required on the relationship between the commemoration of specific figures and the articulation of ideologies of colonialism. That there was an industrial output of works on Cook also points to the importance of histories in the definition of the empire.

Evangelicals supported their colonial activity by gesturing towards history; their approach to the past was a supremely optimistic one that chartered divinely ordained progress. Although the Hawaiians were alleged to be mythic, the missionaries hoped to train them in language by exporting printing presses, and to place them within the biblical heritage of Zion. Evangelicals believed that the whole of history worked towards the millennium when the world would be converted. They held to the possibility of winding time backwards in order to redeem the mistakes of their nation. Their obsession with progress was such that the written word was privileged above oral accounts; Christianity was said to be superior to Hawaiian myth; and Williams could be a better Cook. These observations provide the platform to reflect on the relationship between accounts of historical progress and colonial activity. Do we continue to favour supposedly rational and empirical accounts of Cook over all others? It is easy to assume that we can know more about Cook than before and that we need to dispense of myths in order to get to that truth. Such assumptions about history may indeed reveal more about ourselves than the past, just as much as this chapter suggests more about evangelicals than Cook.

Also at the centre of evangelical history was a series of dichotomies. The most obvious is that between saved and damned, and yet I have drawn attention to that between Creator and created. Williams's death was interpreted in line with the mountains and seas where he had died, because the evangelical hero was thought to read the land. This was possible only for those who respected the proper distinction between the categories of made and maker. Cook had violated those categories at the moment of his death when he allegedly received homage as a god, and the Pacific islanders were said to pay no respect to these categories by worshipping nature. The relationship between history and nature may quite easily be characterised as Hawaiian; yet evangelical attitudes towards the site of Cook's death and the site of Williams's martyrdom suggest that we need to look beyond the appearance of rational history. Evangelical naturalism seems surprisingly close to Hawaiian worship of nature. Evangelicals used rationality and empiricism with rhetorical force in the identification of their historical tradition, while valuing nature as symbol and Cook as commodity and seeming oblivious to this contradiction.

The events that followed Cook's death are curiously similar to those that followed Williams's demise. There were attempts to convert the alleged perpetrators, and the landmarks of the bay were changed as monuments and mission stations were erected. A vast literature flowed from the religious press commenting on these two navigators and the actions that led to their deaths.

Commemoration therefore combines an injunction to change the present with a retelling of the past. While this may be a peculiarly religious dimension of memory, it is important to consider whether any commemoration, particularly when it is focused on an individual, can lend itself to religious sensibilities. Religious typologies assess character against the life of Jesus: thus Williams's death was ultimately compared with the crucifixion, as was Gordon's demise. The missionaries' deaths could fall into line with a whole list of martyrdoms that went back to the early church; no individual death could be considered in isolation from these chains of representation. Cook's death was sinful because it did not fit into this hierarchy with ease.

This account of Cook may seem particularly local: it emphasises a theology of progress and a theology of nature. Yet the challenge in engaging with this story is to create both a helpful sense of distance and an active sense of presence. Distance comes easily as evangelicalism seems unimportant to the memory of Cook today. Yet distance must not sanction exclusion. How do we mould the stories of great explorers and how do we come to terms with past acts of colonialism? The evangelicals in this account were willing to send men to die to put memory right. We would probably discredit Bingham's view of history as one that has little merit. Yet is has been my aim to stimulate reflection on the way history may be used in colonialism and how we colonise history.

12

'As befits our age, there are no more heroes':[1] reassessing Captain Cook

GLYNDWR WILLIAMS

For long, exploration history remained one of the last literary arenas in which heroic, almost superhuman, figures could be seen performing. It was conceived in essentially personal terms, with its sagas of fearless leaders setting off across uncharted seas or trackless wildernesses. Most histories of exploration were written as a series of biographical capsules, and the names of individual explorers served as stepping-stones to mark the progress of knowledge of the wider world. Some of the most celebrated explorers have biographies by the dozen – Columbus, Lewis and Clark, Livingstone, Shackleton. And in the Pacific there was, of course, Captain James Cook.

When the news of Cook's third and final voyage reached London in January 1780, the response of the Earl of Sandwich, First Lord of the Admiralty, ignored the geographical discoveries of the voyage, but went straight to the heart of the matter. As he wrote to Joseph Banks, 'what is uppermost in our minds must allways come out first, poor captain Cooke is no more'.[2] Cook's death on a distant shore in February 1779 was recognised in the Europe of the time as an event at once momentous and shocking, and the next few years saw a series of attempts to assess the explorer and his achievements. 'Dead men make better myths than live ones', Charles Batten has written,[3] and Cook's reputation after his death 'was submitted quite consciously and deliberately to a heroizing process' through which he entered 'those exalted realms of the imagination where only saints, heroes and martyrs dwell'.[4] The tone was set by his shipboard companions, who mourned his loss – by able seaman Heinrich Zimmermann, for example, who wrote at Kealakekua Bay that 'Everyone

[1] K.R. Howe, *Where the Waves Fall: A New South Sea Islands History from First Settlement to Colonial Rule* (Sydney, 1984), p. 83.
[2] Sandwich to Banks, 10 January 1780. *RDV*, p. 1552.
[3] Charles L. Batten, 'Literary responses to the eighteenth-century voyages', in Derek Howse, ed., *Background to Discovery: Pacific Exploration from Dampier to Cook* (Berkeley and Los Angeles, 1990), p. 136.
[4] Bernard Smith, 'Cook's posthumous reputation', in Robin Fisher and Hugh Johnston, eds, *Captain James Cook and His Times* (Vancouver and London, 1979), pp. 159, 161.

in the ships was stricken dumb, crushed, and felt as though he had lost his father.'[5]

Mention of Zimmermann is a reminder that Cook's voyages had a European dimension in more than one sense. Solander and Spöring on the first voyage, the Forsters and Sparrman on the second – all sailed as supernumeraries with Cook. And after his death European writers produced numerous eulogies of Cook, praising him as a standard-bearer of the Enlightenment in the years before the French Revolution changed everything. Even before the end of Anglo–French hostilities in the American War of Independence, a French representative engaged in the repatriation of prisoners of war asked the Admiralty in 1782 for details of Cook's life since French academicians wished to honour him.[6] A few years later Pierre Lemontey's prize-winning 'Eloge de Jacques Cook' (one of twenty competing essays in the competition) portrayed him as 'representing the best in a European civilization in the process of renouncing its murderous, barbaric practices when confronted with the native inhabitants of regions'.[7] A universal theme was praise for Cook for introducing to the peoples of the Pacific the useful arts of Europe – from new plants and strains of cattle to the latest technology and commercial skills. These were the arts and practices of peace, and John Webber's engraving of 'The Apotheosis of Captain Cook' as he is drawn up to heaven in clouds of glory has him clutching, not a sword, but a sextant. It was the visual representation of one of the earliest literary responses to Cook's death, Anna Seward's 'Elegy on Captain Cook', in which he appears as a 'mild hero', whose goddess is 'Benevolence'. Most of the paintings of the death of Cook show him in unthreatening pose. The best-known, again by Webber, has him with his back turned to his attackers, apparently waving the boats away in a self-sacrificial gesture. Cook's humane approach was contrasted with the brutality of the sixteenth-century conquistadors, and, in Cook's own day, with the horrors of slavery and the slave trade. In her poem 'The Black Slave Trade' (1788) Hannah More made the comparison:

Had these posess'd, O Cook! Thy gentle mind
Thy love of arts, thy love of humankind;
Had these pursued thy mild and liberal plan
Discoverers had not been a curse to man.[8]

---

[5] F.W. Howay, ed., *Zimmerman's Captain Cook: An Account of the Third Voyage of Captain Cook Around the World, 1776–1779* (Toronto, 1930), p. 102.

[6] PRO ADM FP/25, 4 June 1782. I am grateful to Miss Patricia Crimmin for this reference.

[7] See William Scott, 'Cook, France and the savages', in Paul Dukes, ed., *Frontiers of European Culture* (Lampeter, 1996), p. 171.

[8] For the responses of Anna Seward and Hannah More see Rod Edmond, *Representing the South Pacific: Colonial Discourse from Cook to Gauguin* (Cambridge, 1997), pp. 26–7.

At a different level, seafaring men respected Cook for his skills as an explorer and surveyor. To his command of a grand sweep of exploration on an oceanic or continental scale was allied an unrelenting feel for accuracy. One of the most knowledgeable and perhaps surprising tributes came from George Forster, who had accompanied his father Johann Reinhold Forster on Cook's second voyage, and who had witnessed the shipboard discord between the two men and the differences between them after their return. In 1787 the younger Forster wrote 'Cook der Entdecker', a ten-thousand-word introduction to his translation into German of the official account of Cook's third voyage. Forster's piece was at one level a summary of the achievements of Cook's three Pacific voyages, at another an awed recollection of the dominant personality of the navigator. Even as a landsman Forster noticed that when Cook came on deck he would often see slackness in a rope or line which the officer on watch had overlooked. When the officers were reckoning distance by eye it was invariably Cook's estimate that was correct. His handling of his officers and men, his attention to health on his ships, and his sense of when discipline must be rigidly enforced and when it might be relaxed, were all admired by Forster. Above all, he was impressed by Cook's 'iron perseverance' which enabled him to achieve more than all his predecessors put together, so that 'he remains, as a mariner and discoverer, unattainable, unique, the pride of his century'.[9] Long after Cook died, navigators were using his surveys – his own men of course, but also those who never sailed with him, never knew him. His men dominated the British voyages to the Pacific in the last two decades of the century. As the statesman William Wyndham remarked on hearing of Bligh's incredible open-boat voyage after the *Bounty* mutiny, 'But what officers you are! You men of Captain Cook; you rise upon us in every trial.'[10] It is doubtful whether the First Fleet would have been sent fourteen thousand miles to Botany Bay in 1788 on the report of a single brief visit to the spot eighteen years earlier, had it not been Cook who had made the visit. And on the fleet's arrival at Botany Bay there was a perceptible sense of shock that the area was not as Cook and Banks had reported.[11]

Uneasiness about Cook centred on two rather different issues. First was the foreboding about the effect of the European voyages on the peoples of the Pacific. As the younger Forster had famously asked in his account of Cook's second voyage, would it not have been 'better for the discoverers and the discovered, that the South Seas had still remained unknown to Europe and

[9] See Michael E. Hoare, '"Cook the Discoverer": an essay by Georg Forster, 1787', *Records of the Australian Academy of Science*, I (1969), pp. 7–16; I have also benefited from access to 'Cook the Discoverer', a translation of Forster's essay by P.E. Klarwill in the Alexander Turnbull Library, Wellington, New Zealand.

[10] Quoted in *EV*, p. cxxii.

[11] See Glyndwr Williams, 'The First Fleet and after, expectation and reality', in Tony Delamothe and Carl Bridge, eds, *Interpreting Australia: British Perceptions of Australia since 1770* (London, 1988), pp. 27–8.

its restless inhabitants'?'[12] Horace Walpole had already written in similar terms when he said of Tahiti that 'not even that little speck could escape European restlessness'.[13] It was an apprehension that Cook himself shared. In a journal entry on his second voyage he lamented that

> we debauch their Morals already too prone to vice and we interduce among them wants and diseases which they never knew before and which serves only to disturb that happy tranquillity they and their fore Fathers had injoy'd. If any one denies the truth of this assertion let him tell me what the Natives of the whole extent of America have gained by the commerce they have had with Europeans.[14]

In France the Abbé Raynal and Denis Diderot in their influential *Histoire philosophique et politique des deux Indes* were expressing opinions that a later age would call anti-colonial, while James Dunbar wrote in 1780 that discovery voyages 'have never yet been happy for any of the tribes of mankind visited by us . . . that natives of that happy island [Tahiti], so cruelly abused, will have cause to lament for ages, that any European vessel ever touched their shores'.[15]

The second issue concerned the events leading up to Cook's death, and the uncomfortable realisation that on Hawai'i Cook seemed to have been treated as a god, and had perhaps even encouraged such reverence. There was a particular irony about this, for Cook has come down to us essentially as a secular figure. As Bernard Smith has written, 'Cook did not depend much on God; he kept his powder dry, mentioned Providence rarely, and performed the Sunday naval service intermittently.'[16] One of the most illuminating examples of this concern comes from William Cowper, whose first poem on Cook, 'Charity', published in 1782, was a hymn of praise to the explorer and his humanity.

> While Cook is loved for savage lives he saved,
> See Cortes odious for a world enslaved.

The poet's reading of the official account of the voyage published in 1784 produced a change of tone as he recoiled in horror from the realisation that Cook had been 'content to be worshipped', and had incurred 'the guilt of sacrilege'.[17] This was perhaps reading more into the official account than is

---

[12] George Forster, *A Voyage Round the World* ed. Nicholas Thomas and Oliver Berghof (2 vols, Honolulu, 2000), I, p. 200.
[13] W.S. Lewis, ed., *The Yale Edition of Horace Walpole's Correspondence*, II (New Haven, 1937), p. 225.
[14] *RAV*, p. 175.
[15] James Dunbar, *Essays on the History of Mankind* (London, 1780), pp. 356–7.
[16] Smith, 'Posthumous reputation', p. 168.
[17] For both Cowper references see Edmond, *Representing the South Pacific*, pp. 27–8.

there; but in other ways the work, published on George III's birthday in 1784, was a major step in the heroising process. The task of putting Cook's journal into a shape suitable for publication was entrusted to Dr John Douglas, the editor of Cook's second voyage journal. Within a month of the return of the ships in the autumn of 1780 he had Cook's journals in his possession, though there is a mystifying and unfortunate gap in them. The last entry we have is for 16 January 1779; for the crucial four weeks of his stay in Hawai'i from his landing until his death we have not a word from Cook's own pen. For those weeks Douglas relied on James King, first lieutenant on the *Resolution*. So it was King who in the description of Cook's last moments produced an interpretation of the confused scene on the beach in which Cook, 'the last time he was seen distinctly, was standing at the water's edge, calling out to the boats to cease firing . . . it is not improbable that his humanity, on this occasion, proved fatal to him'.[18]

The final result of the collaboration between the dead explorer, Douglas, King, and other members of the expedition was a publication which dwarfed previous voyage narratives: three volumes, 1,617 pages, an accompanying atlas and eighty-seven plates. Until J.C. Beaglehole's edition of the journals of the voyage in 1967 it remained the standard account, the deep quarry from which generations of scholars took the materials for their work on the third voyage. The question therefore of how much of the final product was Cook and how much Douglas is an important one. Recent scholarship has discerned in Douglas's revisions more evidence of the elevation of Cook to hero status after his death. The syntax of Cook's journal was altered to stress the role of the first-person narrator, the commander.[19] He is forever ordering, directing, mastering. Douglas's Cook is heroic and just, stern but compassionate. As he surveys, charts, and takes possession, he is the representative of the monarch, the flagbearer of an imperialism that few questioned. His voyages marked the beginning, not the end, of British enterprise in the Pacific, and Douglas pointed the way forward when he wrote that although Cook's surveys were now available to all nations, 'Great Britain herself, whose commerce is boundless, must take the lead in reaping the full advantage of her own discoveries'.[20]

Standing alongside these mighty volumes as a memorial to Cook was the first biography of the explorer, Andrew Kippis's *Life of Captain James Cook* (1788). It is a mark of the hero that he stands alone, and Kippis, a professional biographer, gave little attention to the role of other officers on the voyage, in the same way that those at home who differed from Cook's views and Cook's priorities were given short shrift. All in all, as Rod Edmond has put it, if we

---

[18] James Cook and James King, *A Voyage to the Pacific Ocean . . . In His Majesty's Ships the Resolution and Discovery*, 3 vols (London, 1784), III, pp. 45–6.
[19] See I.S. MacLaren, 'Exploration/travel literature and the evolution of the author', *International Journal of Canadian Studies*, 5 (1992), pp. 39–68.
[20] Cook and King, *Voyage to the Pacific Ocean*, I, preface.

look at images of Cook in the years after his death, 'enlightenment idealism, entrepreneurial individualism and Christian values overlapped'.[21] Such a combination slots easily into Bernard Smith's insistence that Cook was 'a new kind of hero for a new time', with virtues 'neglected by the old military and naval heroes'.[22] But it is an interpretation that has its limitations. The 'new time' was not so new that it was not able within twenty years of Cook's death to produce a rather old-fashioned type of hero, whose fame was to eclipse Cook's. Members of the same service, Horatio Nelson and James Cook had little in common except the respect of their superiors and the affection of their crews. In terms of temperament, personal morality and professional achievement, the two seamen represented very different strains of national endeavour. During the long years of war with France, while in the Pacific navigators, traders and missionaries followed in Cook's wake, at home his light dimmed before the flamboyance of Nelson's battle honours. And when war finished in 1815, the focus of British naval exploration moved to the Arctic. It might be going too far to call the rather woebegone figure of Sir John Franklin a hero, though he may have some claims to a self-inflicted martyrdom; but of public fascination with his voyages, and those of his fellow explorers in polar regions, there can be no doubt.[23] In the second half of the century Africa took central stage, and in particular the missionary-explorer David Livingstone. In a sense Cook and his contemporaries had been almost too effective as explorers, for in a few decades they had revealed the main features of the Pacific. By the early nineteenth century there were no more mysteries left; to the reading public exploitation would never be as fascinating as first 'discovery', and other regions held more allure. In the Arctic men were pitted against nature in its most forbidding form, with scarcely another human being to complicate the situation. In tropical Africa, Livingstone and his contemporaries appeared as saviours of peoples subjected to the horrors of the Arab slave trade.

After Kippis, only one biography of Cook was of much significance until the twentieth century, that of the Revd George Young of Whitby, a learned parson-antiquary whose *Life and Voyages of Captain Cook*, published in 1836, contained some valuable fragments of Cook's local and family history. Otherwise, there were the occasional short biographies, mostly of what Oskar Spate has called the 'Men who made the Empire' type. The centenary of Cook's death in 1879 seems to have passed without much notice in Britain, whereas in France the Société de Géographie held a special meeting in Paris on 14 February 1879 to commemorate the event.[24] Of more interest was the local reaction to Cook in the Pacific lands he had visited and charted, and especially the

---

[21] Edmond, *Representing the South Pacific*, p. 40.
[22] Smith, 'Posthumous reputation', p. 168.
[23] See Robert G. David, *The Arctic in the British Imagination 1818–1914* (Manchester, 2000).
[24] See Oskar Spate, *The Pacific since Magellan*, III, *Paradise Found and Lost* (Canberra, 1988), p. 148.

widening divide between his reputation in nineteenth-century Hawai'i and nineteenth-century Australia. In Hawai'i the main investigator into Cook's impact was the American missionary Sheldon Dibble, who in the 1830s published a volume of Hawaiian oral tradition about the visit and the circumstances of Cook's death. Dibble had his own agenda, one adamantly opposed to the British presence in Hawai'i, and he put forward a view of Cook as an idolater, a libertine, a bringer of venereal disease, a destroyer, which paved the way for a generation of Hawaiian historians.[25]

In Australia there was no such censure, but Cook's emergence as a founding father was long delayed. A plaque set up in 1822 at his supposed landing place at Botany Bay was one of the few early attempts to commemorate Cook's charting of the east coast in 1770. Later in the century imperially-minded politicians hit on Cook as a more sympathetic founder of white Australia than the uncharismatic figure of Arthur Phillip and his convict fleet. In 1868, 28 April was declared a public holiday since it was the 'anniversary of the landing of Captain Cook and of the first hoisting of the British flag in Australia'.[26] In the heyday of imperialism Cook found a place, in Australia and elsewhere, as a hero of empire. The celebrations to mark the Commonwealth of Australia in 1901 included an 'event' at Botany Bay. There some feeble Aborigines were scattered by musket fire, while an actor playing Solander declaimed, 'So the dark tribes of earth in terror flee'.[27] It was the beginning of a Cook cult in the antipodes. There were to be Cook monuments, Cook playing fields, Cook fountains, Cook hotels and restaurants, Cook stamps, a James Cook University, and even a small cottage transported at great expense from Yorkshire to Australia where in its new location in Melbourne's botanical gardens it was long and wrongly described as Cook's birthplace. There was something odd about this devotion to a British hero at a time when Australia was moving away in terms of material and sentimental ties from Britain. As the Australian journalist Jillian Robertson wrote in 1981, 'Cook's role as a super-hero is a completely false one. Very many Australians still believe that Cook discovered Australia, that in a very real sense he was Australia's founder.'[28]

This was the less excusable since the same period saw an explosion of Cook scholarship. The inter-war period had produced bibliographic research on Cook's voyages, and also the beginning of J.C. Beaglehole's interest in Cook. After writing his *Exploration of the Pacific* in 1934 the New Zealand scholar decided that it was time for a new life of Cook, based on the original journals, and that as a preliminary he would publish those journals in comprehensive,

---

[25] See John F.G. Stokes, *Origin of the Condemnation of Captain Cook in Hawaii* (39th Report of the Hawaiian Historical Society, 1930), pp. 68–104.

[26] See Jillian Robertson, *The Captain Cook Myth* (Sydney, 1981), pp. 110–15.

[27] See 'The Landing of Captain James Cook' [1901] in BL 11781 a. 50.

[28] Robertson, *Captain Cook Myth*, p. 1.

critical editions. It was to be his life's work. After the Second World War one by one the mighty volumes appeared, in 1955, 1961 and 1967, 3,359 pages in all, heavily annotated, to be followed by the long-awaited biography, published in 1974, three years after Beaglehole had died. For the first time, scholars had to hand what Cook had actually written, while Beaglehole's biography – another 760 pages – so massive, so authoritative, was surely the last word on Cook. In fact it marked the beginning of a new stage in Cook scholarship, one that is still evolving.

At the same time that Beaglehole was working on the Cook journals, another distinguished scholar was looking at the same geographical area from a rather different perspective. In 1960 Bernard Smith published his *European Vision and the South Pacific*, a book which had a great impact on several different scholarly areas. Science and art were Smith's preoccupations. In the early chapters Banks and the Forsters, Hodges and Webber, dominate. Smith's order of priorities was shown when he wrote that it was 'widely held by naturalists and writers that Cook's scientists, *aided by his seamen*, would gradually complete the picture of the universe'.[29] Whereas with Beaglehole one feels that in the end the 'supernumeraries' were always subordinate, and sometimes irritating nuisances, in Smith's pages they appear as part of a genuine collaborative enterprise.

One of the first popular attempts to build on the developing Cook scholarship was Alan Moorehead's *The Fatal Impact: An Account of the Invasion of the South Pacific*. In his Author's Note, Moorehead explained, 'I have concentrated upon one aspect of Cook's voyages, namely that fateful moment when a social capsule is broken into, when primitive creatures, beasts as well as men, are confronted for the first time with civilization.' Tahiti is the focal point of almost half the book, and in apocalyptic terms Moorehead wrote about the effect of explorers and their followers on 'the slow, natural rhythm of life on the island as it had been lived till then'.[30] It was, although Moorehead did not much acknowledge the fact, an elaboration of a thesis about the Pacific voyages that had been present from the beginning. Moorehead's book was first published in 1966, only a few years before the modern obsession with centennials, bicentennials and all the rest fastened on Cook's voyages. There were to be conferences and published proceedings, popular events and ceremonies, and finally that great accolade which placed Cook alongside Columbus and Drake, the building of a replica of his first Pacific command, HM Bark *Endeavour*. Anniversaries of this sort have their own momentum and rationale: commercial, patriotic, educational. It is difficult for them to be anything but celebratory, although 1992, Columbus year, began to change all that.

---

[29] Bernard Smith, *European Vision and the South Pacific*, 2nd edn (New Haven and London, 1985), p. 51 (my italics).
[30] Alan Moorehead, *The Fatal Impact: An Account of the Invasion of the South Pacific 1767–1840* (Harmondsworth, 1968), pp. 14, 19.

In terms of scholarship, the various bicentennials of Cook's voyages were marked by an impressive output of new work, though I think it is fair to say that until the bicentennial of the third voyage most publications supplemented rather than challenged Beaglehole's work. The change came in the 1978 conference held at Simon Fraser University, Vancouver, to commemorate the 200th anniversary of Cook's arrival on the Northwest Coast of America. As the editors of the conference volume, *Captain Cook and His Times*, wrote, 'the name that came into discussion almost as frequently as Cook was Beaglehole'.[31] The impact of the voyages was seen to be more far-reaching than ever, but the emphasis on the first-person singular that had survived from Douglas to Beaglehole faded in favour of an interpretation that gave weight to the collective achievement of Cook and his companions. So there were papers on Banks, Dalrymple and the Forsters, while James Watt's critical summation of the antiscorbutic methods followed by Cook as being 'a blunderbuss approach' lent support to the view that Cook's achievement in keeping his crews healthy had perhaps been overstated. Even Cook's competence as an explorer was called into question, with my own paper which claimed that his approach to the Northwest Coast in 1778 was based on information that a more critical mind would have recognised as spurious. Little wonder that the editors found it necessary to display immediately after the title-page Bernard Smith's statement at the conference that 'It has not been part of my intention to discredit the achievements of Cook. My intention has been to suggest that it is timely that they be placed in a new perspective.' Perhaps *Captain Cook and Our Times* would have been a more appropriate title. And a reminder of another viewpoint came with the refusal of the Nu-Chal-Nuth Tribal Council to allow a boatload of Cook enthusiasts from the conference to land at Nootka Sound, Cook's watering place on the Northwest Coast.

As the 1970s gave way to the 1980s the old anti-colonialism gave way to postcolonialism, Edward Said held sway for one hemisphere, and a new generation of scholars came forward to look afresh at indigenous societies before and during the arrival of the Europeans. The work of scholars such as Francis Jennings, followed by Ronald Wright and Thomas Berger, set a trend which reached a climax in the 1992 controversies over the Columbus celebrations.[32] In the South Pacific similar controversies arose, as commemorations loomed. Attempts in Australia in 1988 to celebrate the arrival of the First Fleet met resistance from Aboriginal groups, who saw nothing to celebrate in the beginning of a process which had led to the degradation and disappearance of many of their people. Demonstrations were accompanied by the refusal of Aboriginal

---

[31] Fisher and Johnston, *Captain Cook and His Times*, p. 1.

[32] See Francis Jennings, *The Invasion of America, Colonialism and the Cant of Conquest* (New York, 1976); Ronald Wright, *Stolen Continents: The New World through Indian Eyes since 1492* (New York, 1992); Thomas Berger, *A Long and Terrible Shadow: White Values, Native Rights in the Americas 1492–1992* (Vancouver, 1991).

scholars to participate in conferences and books that were associated with the Bicentennial.[33] A reissue of Bernard Smith's collection of essays, *Imagining the Pacific in the Wake of the Cook Voyages*, was greeted by one reviewer with the dismissive comment, 'It is time for people whose business it is to write history, to present real accounts of Europe's sanguinary exploits in the previously peaceful waters of the Pacific.'[34] In New Zealand the 150th anniversary in 1990 of the Treaty of Waitangi was marked by demonstrations by Maori groups. Interestingly, while the visit to New Zealand shores of the *Endeavour* replica six years later also resulted in protests, these were accompanied by appeals for a new understanding. At a service at Anaura Bay in January 1996 Anne Salmond tried to strike a balance:

> Cook had been portrayed as the great white hero bringing Western civilization to a benighted land. Then it became fashionable to denounce him as the harbinger of white colonisation, with the *Endeavour* a sign of the ills and harms that would follow in her wake. In my view both versions are one-eyed caricatures making propaganda out of past events. . . . In both Ananaura and Uawa (Tolaga Bay) the meetings between the *Endeavour*'s people and the locals were peaceful and untroubled. Both sides might have learned something from the shootings in Tauanga (Poverty Bay) two weeks earlier . . . in his private writings Cook, more than any other explorer, displayed great liking and respect for Maoris.[35]

At the national level there have been attempts to respect sensitivities. There has been some restoration of Maori place-names, and when in 1997 stamps were issued in New Zealand to commemorate six navigators important in the country's early history, a careful balance was struck: two Polynesian names, two French, one Dutch, and one British (Cook, of course).

In academic circles the 1990s were marked by the controversy over the death of Cook. What might have been thought, two hundred years after the event, to be a matter of only antiquarian interest became a hotly contested issue. Beaglehole in his edition of the records of Cook's third voyage had given some

---

[33] An example of this came with the publication of the multi-volume set, *Australians: A Historical Library*, issued to commemorate the Bicentennial. The first volume, published in 1987, *Australians to 1788*, covered the history of Aboriginal Australia. In their Introduction the editors explained the absence of Aboriginal scholars from the contributors. 'We have sought Aboriginal involvement and taken as much Aboriginal advice as we could get in planning and shaping the book. Some potential Aboriginal contributors declined invitations to write because they considered that any bicentennial enterprise was necessarily a celebration of their people's dispossession, extermination and degradation. Some Aboriginal people believe that non-Aborigines should not try to study Aboriginal societies. This view we respect but do not share.' D.J. Mulvaney and J. Peter White, eds, *Australians to 1788* (Broadway, NSW, 1987), p. xvi.

[34] Jeanette Hoorn in *The Age*, 10 October 1992, published two days before Columbus Day, 1992.

[35] *New Zealand Herald*, 19 January 1996. I am grateful to David Mackay for this reference.

attention to the thesis that the Hawaiians regarded Cook as a god, but thought it impossible to reach any definite conclusion. Nor did he add much to this in his biography although in the meantime Gavan Daws had produced, at least in skeletal form, an interpretation of Cook in Hawai'i, not simply as a god, but, crucially, as a flawed god.[36] In other ways, though, Beaglehole's edition, with long extracts from other journals as well as Cook's, revealed a commander who at times seemed near the end of his tether, distracted and infuriated by many of the setbacks of the voyage, and above all by the incessant stealing among the islands. 'He flogged, in ascending dozens, he put in irons, he cropped ears, he slashed with a knife the arms of men he regarded as desperate offenders.'[37] And it was not only Pacific islanders who suffered. On his first voyage Cook flogged 20 per cent of his crew; on his second 26 per cent; on his third 37 per cent. As Greg Dening has pointed out, Captain Bligh, that sadist of popular literature and film, flogged far fewer of his crew on the *Bounty*.[38] In his journal Cook indulged in verbal violence – a harmless way of letting off steam perhaps – but worrying in the general context of the voyage. So, on 7 December 1778, he wrote, and then half-deleted, an entry about his 'mutinous, turbulent crew'. 'In future', he seems to have told them, 'they might not expect the least indulgence from him'.[39] Just over two months later Cook was dead. Beaglehole's thesis is clear: Cook started the voyage a tired man, and the further strains of the voyage blunted his reactions, until on 14 February 1779, with his 'patience tried beyond its limit', he acted with far less than his usual judgement of situations. At the fatal moment, Beaglehole wrote, 'the strained cord snapped'.[40]

There the matter rested until the arrival on the scene of the Chicago anthropologist Marshall Sahlins, who published a series of essays on the death of Cook which argued that the sequence of events at Hawai'i in the winter of 1778–9, which culminated in Cook's death, could only be understood in the context of the acceptance by the Hawaiians of Cook as the incarnation of the god *Lono*.[41] In an ingenious argument based on the shipboard records and on later Hawaiian sources, Sahlins showed how Cook arrived at the right season for *Lono*, the 'makahiki', bearing the god's insignia, and landing at the preordained spot, Kealakekua Bay, 'the path of the gods'. A week after sailing he unwittingly made the portentous error of returning to Hawai'i in a damaged ship, out of season, out of character. Sahlins's interpretation incorporated the view from the shore rather than from the ship. As such it had a wide appeal,

---

[36] Gavan Daws, *Shoal of Time: A History of the Hawaiian Islands* (Toronto, 1968).

[37] *RDV*, p. cvi.

[38] Greg Dening, *Mr Bligh's Bad Language: Passion, Power and Theatre on the Bounty* (Cambridge, 1992), p. 63.

[39] *RDV*, p. 479 n. 4.

[40] *RDV*, pp. cliv, clvi.

[41] See, for example, his 'Captain James Cook; or, The Dying God', in Marshall Sahlins, *Islands of History* (Chicago, 1985), pp. 104–35.

though it did not go entirely unchallenged. Oskar Spate, the Grand Old Man of Pacific historiography, asked whether Sahlins had perhaps fallen into 'an unwarranted cultural determinism'.[42] But such queries were overshadowed by the fierce assault on Sahlins by another anthropologist, the Sri Lankan Gananath Obeyesekere, who in his book, *The Apotheosis of Captain Cook*, condemned the idealisation of Cook the humane explorer, the representative of the Enlightenment, as an exercise in imperialist mythology, and suggested that 'the myth of Cook as the god Lono is fundamentally based on the Western idea of the redoubtable European who is a god to savage peoples'.[43] In Rod Edmond's words, Obeyesekere blew a postcolonial whistle on Sahlins,[44] who responded with an angry book, *How 'Natives' Think: About Captain Cook, For Example*, which in turn drew a fifty-page 'Afterword on De-Sahlinization' from Obeyesekere in the revised edition of his book published in 1997. The debate has now widened far beyond the ill-tempered wrestling match between Sahlins and Obeyesekere, but over and above the details of their quarrel a more general paradox can be glimpsed. The historical records for the matter of Cook's death are at once plentiful and unsatisfactory. They range from the journal entries and other records of dozens of Cook's men, written in a state of bemused uncertainty once they leave the familiar structure of shipboard life for the vagaries of the shore, to the Hawaiian records which by the very nature of their later recollecting and recording are also flawed. One can only wonder at the certainty with which Sahlins and Obeyesekere pick through this material to come up with interpretations of Cook's death which share virtually no common ground. At one level it is a disturbing sight for historians who sometimes take it for granted that anthropology and its practitioners will come to their aid in situations not susceptible to the conventional process of historical investigation.

Away from the specific episode of Cook's death the third voyage has attracted increasing scholarly interest. One aspect must suffice here. The voyage produced the fullest descriptions and illustrations to date of the Pacific peoples, and this has fuelled the debate on the methods and results of the discovery voyages. Scholars who see the lavish official accounts of Cook's voyages as part of a humanising myth which concealed their rough reality can point to the way in which John Webber's set-piece paintings and drawings mostly depict friendly encounters. Receptions, entertainments, ceremonies, loom large – rather than the clashes which became a depressingly familiar feature of the voyage. This selectivity raises large questions about the value-laden nature of visual representation, and the extent to which the recording of native peoples

---

[42] Spate, *Paradise Found and Lost*, p. 145.

[43] Gananath Obeyesekere, *The Apotheosis of Captain Cook: European Mythmaking in the Pacific*, 2nd edn (Princeton, NJ, 1997), p. 177.

[44] Rod Edmond, 'Chronicle of a death foretold? Captain Cook and the anthropologists', *Wasafiri*, 23 (1996), p. 26.

was a form of cultural appropriation; but to see Cook's artists merely as facilitators of imperialist dominance would be crude and misleading. One of the constraints imposed on ethnographic drawing was that its subjects could not, like some natural history specimen, be pinned to a board. Their co-operation and trust had to be obtained, and the nature of the cultural contact between the artist and them was different from the fleeting trading or sexual encounters with most crew members. Yet if the artist represented the soft edge of the contact process, behind him lurked the threat of force, of marines, muskets, and great guns. So Webber's celebrated painting of Poedua, daughter of the chief of Raiatea, was probably done during the tense five days that father and daughter were held hostage by Cook.

Much of this will be familiar to those who study the contact process in other parts of the world. What may be unique to the Pacific is the status of 'the beach'. In one sense this was a well-defined physical entity, a boundary separating land and water; in another it was a more ambivalent area, a zone of confrontation and conflict, but also a space where intercourse, commercial and sexual, took place. It was a stage in Greg Dening's theatre of empire, where explorers 'shouted to the natives, in that loud and slow way that we use to communicate with those that do not share our language, the meaning of flags and cannons and property and trade, and lessons of civilised behaviour'.[45] Robin Fisher is among those historians who have deplored the way in which accounts of the contact experience continue to be written 'in terms of the clash of opposites . . . of two completely different cultures meeting at an absolute line of contact, failing to communicate, and often resorting to violence'.[46] Kerry Howe in turn has pointed to the patronising implications of the Fatal Impact thesis, with its depiction of the Pacific peoples as helpless victims, and he argues in favour of acculturation and adaptation rather than catastrophe and extinction.[47] In her several books as well as in her essay in this volume, Anne Salmond has set her face against traditional exploration narratives with their ancient lineage of intrepid discoverers setting off into the unknown. In the accounts of the Europeans' arrival in New Zealand, she writes, 'Europeans are in charge of the drama, the explorers are the heroes, while Maori people either sit as passive spectators or act anonymously behind cloaks and tattooed masks.' As she notes elsewhere, 'the search is for an intellectual middle ground, a place at the interface between European explorers and local communities'.[48]

[45] Greg Dening, *Performances* (Melbourne, 1996), p. 109.

[46] Robin Fisher, 'George Vancouver and the Native peoples of the Northwest Coast', in Stephen Haycox, James K. Barnett, Caedmon A. Liburd, eds, *Enlightenment and Exploration in the North Pacific 1741–1805* (Seattle and London, 1997), p. 198.

[47] Howe, *Where the Waves Fall*, pp. 348–52.

[48] Anne Salmond, *Two Worlds: First Meetings Between Maori and Europeans 1642–1772* (Auckland, 1991); 'Kidnapped: Tuki and Huru's involuntary visit to Norfolk Island in 1793', in Robin Fisher and Hugh Johnston, eds, *From Maps to Metaphors: The Pacific World of George Vancouver* (Vancouver, 1993), p. 193.

Much of today's scholarship attempts to follow such guidelines, but a continuing problem is the extent to which such reinterpretations percolate through to popular writing and presentation. When the replica of the *Endeavour* reached Whitby on its first visit in 1997, it was greeted by huge crowds. There were flags and bunting, receptions and speeches, guided tours of the ship, and, in the giftshop on the quayside, *Endeavour* sweaters, mugs, postcards and videos – everything except a decent book on Cook's voyages. Just as the vessel was, of necessity, a sanitised version of the original – modern safety equipment, flush toilets and the rest – so the depiction of Cook had been cleaned up for mass consumption. In the town the most readily available book on Cook was the paperback edition of Richard Hough's biography, based on Beaglehole, but ignoring almost all post-Beaglehole scholarship. Dalrymple's work, we read, was 'bogus', Forster was a 'shady bore', and there was no reference to the work of Bernard Smith, Marshall Sahlins and the others.[49]

There are signs that things are changing. Anne Salmond and Nicholas Thomas have recently published books on Cook's voyages that can claim to be the most important since Beaglehole's biography of thirty years ago.[50] The opening in 2002 of a new gallery, 'Oceans of Discovery', at the National Maritime Museum, Greenwich, was accompanied by a book of essays on Cook that encapsulated much recent scholarship.[51] In the late summer of 2002 the BBC put out multi-episode programmes on Cook's voyages, on radio and on television. The latter series, 'The Ship', was accompanied by a lavishly-illustrated book aimed at a wide readership. The book's opening sentences show an awareness of today's scholarship. Captain Cook

> has been lauded as a founding father of modern Australia and New Zealand and celebrated as an icon of discovery and exploration. . . . In recent years, however, Cook has become a more ambivalent figure . . . a symbol of the colonialism, dispossession and oppression that sometimes followed in the wake of his explorations.

This duality – respect for Cook as a seaman, but misgivings about the implications of his voyages – runs through the book. Sailing on the *Endeavour* during the shooting of the television series were – unhistorically – three Maori and three Aborigines. One of the latter, Bruce Gibson, head of the Injinoo Land Trust at Cape York, derided the oft-stated view that the replica was 'a means of learning that provides a bridge to understanding between cultures'. 'The *Endeavour*', he said, 'is a proud symbol for white Australia, but for most

---

[49] Richard Hough, *Captain James Cook* (London, 1994), pp. 303, 322.
[50] Anne Salmond, *The Trial of the Cannibal Dog: Captain Cook in the South Seas* (London, 2003); Nicholas Thomas, *Discoveries: The Voyages of Captain Cook* (London, 2003).
[51] Nigel Rigby and Pieter van der Merwe, *Captain Cook in the Pacific* (Greenwich, 2002).

Aborigines it is an insulting thing – a painful reminder of our tragic history as well as our present, languishing condition as a people in modern Australia.'[52] Aboriginal histories across much of Australia continue to identify 'Captain Cook' as the emblematic invader, the despoiler of their lands and culture over wide expanses of space and time.[53]

* * *

Reassessments of Cook tend to follow two tracks. First, there is a personal reassessment of the explorer, and here today's Cook is not quite Beaglehole's. He is set more firmly in a context of collaboration and mutual help both on shipboard and in England, while there has been a sharpening of Beaglehole's worry about Cook's behaviour on the third voyage. That said, there is not, I think, any significant diminution of regard for Cook's technical achievement as an explorer – he remains, as Sandwich put it after his second voyage, 'The first navigator in Europe'. What is altogether more open to debate is Cook's role as a force in Europe's entry into the Pacific. How far should an explorer following official instructions be held responsible for the long-term consequences of his actions? I conclude by pointing to one moment on the *Endeavour* voyage, the ceremony at Possession Island in August 1770 in which Cook claimed the east coast of Australia for the British crown. Here Cook was both dutifully following his instructions and exceeding them. His sailing orders in 1768 had given him general and (by now) standard instructions that he was 'with the Consent of the Natives to take possession of Convenient Situations in the Country in the Name of the King of Great Britain; or, if you find the Country uninhabited, take Possession . . . as first discoverers and possessors'.[54] Cook's decision in early 1770 to head towards, and survey, that unknown coast, was his own, as was his subsequent decision to take possession without 'the Consent of the Natives' of a region parts of which were clearly peopled, although the inhabitants seemed to be few in number and without recognisable political organisation. The personal nature of his double decision needs stressing because it would be as wrong to regard Cook as an unwitting agent of British imperialism as to fall into the trap of 'judging him according to how we judge what happened afterwards'.[55] He was more sensitive than most

[52] Simon Baker, *The Ship: Retracing Cook's Endeavour Voyage* (London, 2002), pp. 6, 12, 139–40.
[53] The term 'emblematic invader' is Deborah Bird Rose's in 'Hard Times: an Australian study', in Klaus Neumann, Nicholas Thomas and Hilary Ericksen, eds, *Quicksands: Foundational Histories in Australia and Aotearoa New Zealand*; see also Chris Healy, 'Captain Cook: Between Black and White', and Paddy Fordham Wainburranga, 'Too many Captain Cooks', in Sylvia Kleinert and Margo Neale, eds, *The Oxford Companion to Aboriginal Art and Culture* (Melbourne, 2000), pp. 92–5, 96.
[54] *EV*, p. cclxxxiii.
[55] Thomas, *Discoveries*, p. xxxiii.

to the likely repercussions of the European arrival in the Pacific, but his command of successive voyages indicated both his professional commitment, and his patriotic belief that if a European nation should dominate the waters and lands of the Pacific then it must be Britain. He was, after all, a man of his age.

13

Retracing the Captain: 'Extreme History', hard tack and scurvy

ANDREW LAMBERT

In September 2001 I was in hospital on Thursday Island in the Torres Straits. For me the horror of 11 September unfolded in the middle of the night, as I stood in a corridor, watching television. That I was so far from home was, in no small part, due to our enduring fascination with Cook.

Three months earlier I had been sitting in the Courtyard at Somerset House, discussing a BBC project to retrace part of Cook's first Pacific voyage. The idea of picking a volunteer crew, and some contemporary 'experts' to man the replica HMS *Endeavour*, and then sailing from Cairns to Djakarta, was fascinating. As we discussed the social fabric of the eighteenth-century Royal Navy, and the demands of shipboard life, I was already looking forward to watching the series! Then I was asked to join the crew, as historian and foremast hand. I accepted without hesitation, subject only to clearance from my college department (since the trip would overrun the start of term), and my family. Both were agreeable, although my 11-year old daughter was horrified to discover that there would be no place for a 'cabin-person', and was hardly placated by the information that this was a legal stipulation, rather than a personal slight.

The next two months were filled with exams, conferences, and a number of writing tasks that had to be completed before I could set off. As the time drew near I began to have second thoughts: was it really such a good idea? By early August the administration of the trip was in full swing, dates were set, and I had been asked to speak at this conference; it was too late, I was going. But what was I going to be doing? The concept of 'Extreme History' began to appear in conversation; we were going to learn by suffering. We would push our interest in the past to the limits, and see what we found. We would be confronted with hard food, hard work, the removal of twenty-first-century luxuries, and necessities, drug free, out of contact, and deprived of our personal space.

Most of the crew were volunteers, selected for the project after rigorous tests. Some were experienced sailors, from yachting or naval backgrounds, others were adventurous spirits, and at least one was a mountaineer. They would be joined by an American party. I had hoped to go to the team-building day, but a ruptured Achilles put paid to any travel that week, and curtailed my running until after the trip.

The historians, ethnographers and anthropologists would be integrated with the crew, learning alongside the volunteers, developing our understanding of the original voyage and the interface with the new experience as we went along. Being part of a team would offer further potential to develop our understanding. All told there were six 'historians' (Vanessa Agnew, Mereta Kawharu, Jonathan Lamb, Iain McCalman, Alex Cook and me), two navigators, an astronomer, a botanist and a botanical illustrator. The combination of disparate approaches and the long voyage would, I hoped, provide rich opportunities for discussion of the many worlds of Captain Cook, and the many approaches the modern world takes to him. This could be a rewarding voyage of discovery.

On the other hand I had little preparation for my new life as a foremast hand on a working square-rigger. I had not sailed in anything larger than a dinghy for twenty years, and was not entirely sure I wanted to work that far above the deck. Re-reading my favourite book on the subject, Melville's *White Jacket*, brought little comfort, while friends who had already tried the *Endeavour* experience were anxious that I should be under no illusions. It was never entirely clear how the two roles of historian and seaman were to be combined, a problem that would be exacerbated by the introduction of a third player, 'The Ship'.

The main party left London on 20 August, and flew economy class to Sydney, via Bangkok, and then, after a delay, on to Cairns. We checked into a backpacker's hostel on the edge of town, joining the American party and some of the BBC crew. This was an opportunity to recover, and begin to build the crew over a few beers. The historians soon coalesced, and four of us used our last day ashore to drive up to Cooktown, about 300 kilometres, much of it over unmade roads, through a rainforest. After a swim at Cape Tribulation we reached the Endeavour River in the late afternoon. For tired and thirsty travellers Cooktown proved idyllic; we found a phone and on local advice headed for the chip shop, 'Gutted and Gilled'. This sat alongside the pier, roughly where the *Endeavour* had been beached, and served up a barramundi, Morton Bay bugs and chips fit for any gourmet. We sat on the pier, watching the sun go down through a pall of smoke from a bush fire, and reflected that the trip could not get any better than this. It was the beginning of a collective love affair with the shore that would afflict the historians. The questions we wanted to ask were about the interface between the voyagers and the shore, the islands, rivers, hills and forests that so concerned Cook and Banks. Despite three days ashore I was still exhausted; the hostel had been a half-way house, preparing us for life on board ship, not a place to rest.

The next morning we got up early, washed our kit, and packed for sea. We drove to an Aboriginal village, and then walked down to an isolated beach on tribal lands. Here, for the first time, we caught sight of the *Endeavour*, and she was an awfully long way out to sea. We were divided up into three watches. I was very fortunate, joining mainmast watch, which proved to be the best led, best manned, and steadiest. Then we rowed out some three miles to our new home. This was my first lesson. In the eighteenth century everything took a very long time. By the time we were on board, kitted up with hammock, safety belt, reflective vest, clothes and a sea chest, it was dark, and we had to shift anchor. This went surprisingly well, the permanent crew being expert at getting the best out of novices.

The second lesson came with dinner. The mess tables were small, and crowded, the mess deck, with a vast wood-burning stove at work, was hot, and the food was, well, eighteenth-century. I knew we were going to be on a 'historical' diet, but nothing could have prepared us for what was served up. The 'adviser' on this issue had chosen not to join the cruise, probably for her own safety. We were going to live on salt beef, salt pork, salt fish, ship's biscuit, a few vegetables, sauerkraut, the odd cheese day, with gruel and tea or chocolate for breakfast. I had not eaten red meat in twenty-five years, and knew it would be very unwise to start now. Instead I focused on the side orders while my colleagues did their best with the beef. The first lot was still too hard and salt, but our cook, Caroline, quickly mastered the art. Although there were many non-meat eaters among the permanent crew and volunteers, no concessions were made for such foibles. Within days hunger and improved technique intersected; after that there was little left over. Dinner was whatever we had not eaten at lunch. The biscuits had been baked at Townsville gaol, and the prisoners obviously had something against us. While highly nutritious and easy to store, they were rock hard, breaking several teeth, and impervious to all fluids. The best technique was to shatter them, and deal with the fragments. I still have one, round and flat, three inches across and almost an inch thick. I would come to love the biscuit, and always had a few stowed away for emergencies. Most days we had a piece of fruit, and there was always Cook's stand-by. I ate a lot of sauerkraut, and, just in case this diet failed, scurvy was kept at bay with vitamin pills. Later we began to catch some fish, and baked tuna is among the finest meals I have ever tasted. The only drink available all day would be water, straight from a wooden barrel. The unusual taste was tolerable, but it was difficult to get enough, not least because of the salt rations.

More problematic than the menu on offer were the items we did not have. For legal reasons, and our own safety, there would be no alcohol. This was bearable. We were also informed that the eighteenth century had no coffee; this would prove to be my first trial. For two days I was in agony, my head splitting and my spirits depressed by the torment of a drug denied. Gradually the pain subsided, and the occasional breakfast mug of tea helped. Never again will I laugh at people struggling with dependencies.

The *Endeavour* is a small ship, and once all fifty-six crew were on board it was crowded. How Cook's men managed for so long with more than ninety is hard to imagine. The main impact was that only a handful had their own space – the officers, the doctor, navigators, botanist and artist. The historians were too numerous, and too much part of the crew, for any special treatment, so we were pitched up with our watches on the mess deck. We would have no personal space, nowhere to call our own, and precious few moments alone. This might not have been a problem in the more crowded eighteenth century, but we were a group of self-absorbed twenty-first-century creatures, used to a very different regime. We quickly became more tolerant, forgiving and considerate. Inter-personal friction was inevitable, although most found figures outside their immediate social group onto whom they could focus their discontents. We could blame the BBC for our suffering, the permanent crew for our regime, and yet others, unknown to most, for the diet.

The first night in a hammock was interesting. Tying it was OK, although mine was slung in the 'marines'. With only three foot six headroom it required working bent double, but after a long day, or night, it was invariably welcome, and once tightly encased in my canvas trough sleep came quickly. Eighteenth-century facilities for personal hygiene were basic, but we all made a huge effort. The standard drill was to move topside before breakfast and after dinner, with towel and washing kit, haul up sea-buckets of ocean, shower down, wash and rinse. Coconut oil soap was surprisingly effective. Such communal ablutions were adequate for most, but the female crew did ask for, and were granted, an opportunity for single-sex bathing. With the upper deck otherwise cleared they had a morale-building half hour to themselves, and despite a certain amount of wry comment it proved a success.

Keeping a dry towel proved impossible, there was nowhere to hang one in the air, while stuffing it in the sea chest produced unpleasant results. Within a few days most gave up washing their hair, just rinsing it through. This was fine, although perhaps I didn't have enough to notice. Many stopped shaving their chins, although a few hard cases were still shaving their heads three weeks later!

The heads were an altogether more complex issue. For legal reasons we were obliged to use the twentieth-century facilities on the lower deck while inside the Barrier Reef. These required the user to pump out the system, having opened a 'grey valve' to let in sea water. Failure to close the same 'grey valve' on departure was a heinous crime, punishable by an endless belittling harangue. The threat that we would be forced to resort to the seats of ease at the bow, reinforced by the sudden appearance of newly-made shoots, was only a device, and we were soon toilet trained.

As there was only room for a week's supply of clothes we had to wash them, which provided another insight into the dynamics of the ship, the voyage and the television project. For Cook, and indeed any captain, the well-being of the crew was of the utmost importance. He took great pains to ensure they had adequate warm clothing. On wash day sailing ships were festooned with washing, and it was left out until dry. We were given a limited space, and limited hanging time. When mizzen watch were ordered to down their lines there was much grumbling; their clothes were still damp. The Captain had no time for such concerns, he did not want his ship to 'look like a Chinese junk', while the first officer accused us of thinking we were sailing on daddy's yacht. He did not see the incongruity of such a statement while pursuing the neatness of 'The Ship' over our comfort. The incident also made good television, with one of the historians taking the lead.

Each morning after breakfast the entire crew set to communal cleaning, working in watches. The mess deck furniture was shifted, the deck swept and washed down. This was demanding, the deck was stiflingly hot and ventilation hard to come by. Then the heads and cabins were cleaned out. The upper deck was washed down before breakfast, providing an opportunity to sample the ship's only 'power shower'.

Adjusting to life on board was one thing, becoming a sailor was quite another. Small as she is the *Endeavour* is a very vertical environment. When we came on board I looked up at those towering masts, wide spread yards and endless miles of rigging, and wondered how I would deal with the next stage. It came on the second day, the other two watches had already been up and furled sail before our turn came. I looked at my watch, and quickly worked out that one man was going to have a big problem with the task; to my relief it was not me. As soon as the first hands grasped the ratlines I joined, and steadily climbed up to the futtock shrouds. I was not going to be first, or last. *Endeavour* has no lubber's hole, so we all had to clip on our safety lines, climb out hanging off the shrouds and reach up and over the rim of the top to locate the 'Mars bar'. Once this had been grasped it was simply a case of hauling and climbing over, grabbing the shrouds, stepping into the top and unclipping the line. Sounds simple, and after a few goes it was. The first time, one of our watch just could not make that last push. He came up the following day, and, although never a confident top man, worked aloft thereafter. That he persevered, and we encouraged him, made us all feel good. Once in the top there was work to be done. We clipped on to the yard line, stepped out on to the footrope, and worked our way out to furl the sail. It is a strange experience to be bent double a hundred feet off the deck, trying to stow stiff and heavy canvas in a neat parcel, and then tie a proper gasket.

This is where the camaraderie of the watch really comes into play. It is a team task, and only finished when the last gasket is tied. Everyone looks out for everyone else, and the expression 'to lend a hand' gets back to its origins. When you are trying to stow that awkward piece of canvas the hand is much appreciated! The combination of anxiety, exhilaration, satisfaction and spectacle made going aloft the basic building block of the watch, and the key to a close-knit community. If we felt like this after a week, how much closer were Cook's men after three months, or three years?

As we came to terms with the rig it was obvious that some were happier aloft than others. For myself I was comfortable on the yards and topsail yards, but found the topgallant yards a trial. The footropes had been rigged for small boys, and it was impossible to work effectively without a good balance point. I decided to try again, once I had more experience. By contrast the bowsprit and spritsails were a pure joy. The view ahead and the near proximity of the water made this a special place. Furling sail as we came in to anchor off Lizard Island one evening will always be etched on my memory. We lay out there for an hour, while another watch was working on the foredeck, watching the sun set, and the phosphorescent bow wave.

Other tasks on the ship involved strength and teamwork, but little skill. It was 'waisters'' work, fit for marines. We all had our station when wearing and tacking, and joined in the other heavy hauling as required. Taking watch, astern and on the bowsprit, steering or working the wheel all helped to occupy a watch.

Having settled into the routine of the ship, and built our teams, it was time for the historians to develop their professional interests, both as a group, and for the benefit of the BBC. This is where the divergent agendas of the BBC, 'The Ship' and the scholars came to the fore. The permanent crew of 'The Ship' were used to drilling paying volunteers into competent seamen as quickly as possible, using the routines of shipboard life to reinforce the priority given to handling the ship under sail. The prospect of a long voyage with the same company was not unattractive; they also wanted to get some low-level, but labour-intensive maintenance done, including scraping the masts and other decorative work.

Anything that interfered with the handling of the ship was undesirable.

The BBC team had a more complex approach. From the end result it is clear that the big idea was to combine a number of disparate elements within the one series. While we would retrace Cook's voyage, the volunteer crew were also a major subject. How would they cope with the demands of this eighteenth-century world? The 'fly on the wall' documentary method favoured by producer Chris Terrill was always going to generate images and stories that were incidental to the Cook story. There were also more obviously 'set-up' debates to be had about the meaning of Cook for native peoples and 'Europeans', be they white Australians, British or Americans. These proved to be very useful, and the voyage had a positive impact in the reconciling of stories and beliefs. Having two Australian Aborigines, three Maori, including one of the historians, and two 'white Australian' historians generated a wide range of opinions, and proved a highlight of the expedition, for everyone. It made the interaction with the shore especially rich. We could not remain detached observers, we had to engage with the opinions and ideas of fellow crew, and our hosts on shore.

Then there was the second strand of story telling, using actors and reconstructions in some of the same locations. This was done after the voyage; opinion on the utility of these scenes is mixed. Perhaps they lingered too long shooting a kangaroo, but Cook and Banks were our constant companions, and they had to come along on the programme in a more corporeal form. Their traces were everywhere, notably in the remains of a camp recently found on the banks of the Endeavour River.

Part of the problem lay in the division with those 'experts' who were reconstructing aspects of the original voyage, astronomy, botany and navigation. They were given cabins, excused most watch activity and allowed to run their own agendas. By contrast the historians were wholly integrated with the volunteer crew. Once we had settled into a routine the watches were kept busy, and this left little or no time for reflection, especially the priceless opportunities to work together on aspects of both voyages, sharing ideas and insights. On the fourth day we called the BBC team to join us in our cramped work space, the after end of the mess deck, and pointed out that they would get little value from our presence if we could not have more time. It was simply not possible to be a useful scholar and put in eight hours of watch keeping, answer not infrequent calls to wear ship, and carry out the rest of the shipboard routine. Regular duties, sleep and food were eating up all the hours of the day. We secured opportunities to avoid some non-watch tasks, and to spend a little more time on the work at hand. However, this created further problems. I was not happy leaving my watch working hard so I could go and 'read'. I took to spending the evenings, when the mess deck area was inaccessible, working in the ward room alongside the navigators and the botanists. Here again the opportunities for exchange and reflection were invaluable, and helped us to make the most of what we could see, where we landed, and the passages we took. We all had our own interests, but the interaction was far more important. The extent to which Cook exploited the knowledge of his experts to 'read' the ocean, and develop his concept of the area, only became clear as we talked over the evidence. Seemingly insignificant items – drift wood, pumice, birds and peoples – were all employed to answer the big questions, which on our leg of the trip centred on the presence of a sea passage between New Guinea and Northern New Holland. Although Cook believed there was one, he was not going to rush in.

We needed more time, and a bit more space. This became obvious when we went ashore. While we think of Cook as the great navigator, his major work was interacting with the shore, charting, making accessible the new land, and preparing the way for others. Similarly the impact of his work came not on the oceans, but on the peoples of the new worlds he charted.

We stopped at Endeavour Reef, to locate the damage Cook caused when the *Endeavour* struck, and to salute the saving of the ship, before heading north to Cooktown where the *Endeavour* had beached. Those of us who had been there before were salivating at the prospect of a run ashore; the fish, and the other local delicacies, were very appealing. We secured ourselves a place in the boat, which had a long beat into harbour as we were anchored in a safe spot for sailing, rather than motoring in (the engines being restricted to emergencies). This used up half the day, especially as the botanists went in first. Even so, once we had blitzed the Cook's Landing Kiosk, which had its best day in years, we discussed the impact of Cook with local elders, and climbed one of the hills Cook had climbed, which allowed us to view 'The Ship' as a mere toy, shimmering on a brilliant blue ocean. While much time was wasted on setting up film shots it was a very enjoyable day. Chris Terrill resolutely refused to eat anything, he really did want to learn by suffering. The rest of us gave way to temptation, although I was surprisingly unenthusiastic. This was wise, for there were many more weeks of shipboard food to come.

The discussion onshore revealed how Cook's work is now being used as the basis of Aboriginal land rights claims, his limits as an explorer and recorder of the land, and the limits of his age. The land rights issue was fascinating. In a pioneering ethnographic endeavour Banks had taken down the local language, and this has been used to demonstrate continuity of occupation by the local people. By contrast Cook was more interested in sea-going craft and maritime issues. One of the major reasons for his dismissive view of the Aboriginal people was their lack of sophisticated watercraft, and he contrasted them with the 'maritime' people of Tahiti. Reading over Banks's and Cook's journals on a mountain climb to look for a safe passage revealed a clear case of borrowing, and led to a long discussion. Was Banks recording Cook's sentiments in his own language, only for Cook to borrow this more polished version for his own journal? The tribal elders helped us to see the contact in a new light, showing the importance of a third party, the Malay bêche-de-mer fisherman, who had already raided this coast. It was this experience that had prompted Aboriginal warning fires, and initial caution.

This was the most rewarding day of the trip. My journal entry is the longest, and even allowing for the euphoria produced by a sudden and extensive intake of caffeine, the excitement is palpable. After this the historians were convinced that they had found the key to their work, and it lay in a more shore-oriented voyage. After all, Cook spent a long time at the Endeavour River. We wanted more, and communicated our views to Chris, while preparing to land on Lizard Island. This landing was less rewarding. The island is now a high-price resort, and the climb up the hill Cook and Banks had used to spot the gap in the reef was only good exercise, although we did beachcomb some of the same debris that Cook had used to settle the question of priority. The ship did not come for us when expected, so we spent a pleasant morning on the beach, swimming and contemplating. This time there was no food to be had. We rejoined ship that afternoon, and for the first time I saw her under full sail, a complete ship, close up. This is another image that will endure.

That afternoon we sailed through Cook's passage, and left the Reef for the Coral Sea. On both sides a seemingly endless run of white water, while we ran through a gap hardly half a mile wide. Passing from the pale green-blue reef shallows to the deep blue sea, from calm to swell and light air to stiff breeze, was striking, and the upper works were crowded with idlers as we shot through. Sadly one of the volunteers was taken ill, with a blood clot, and we put about for a boat to take him to Lizard Island. He had picked up the problem on the flight out, the same one I had been on.

The next day we headed back into the Reef, and did a little more work on the charts, addressing the knowledge of this area before Cook. I also caught a tuna, and used what credit I had with the BBC to secure a few minutes on the satellite phone, timed to catch my daughter as she left home for her first day at a new school. The next day we anchored off Adolphus Island in the Torres Straits, and went ashore for a barbecue, a beer and general release of tension. It was wonderful, but the only historical issue was which son of George III the island was named after. That evening I reflected on the voyage. I was now comfortable working aloft, our watch having furled the fore course that morning. We also set the foretopsail the next morning to take the ship down to Cape York and the Pajinka tribal area, where most of us went ashore, ate and drank, phoned home and enjoyed another calm day. Three of the crew left, including two historians; it was not a good omen. Moving to Possession Island the next day we overran the anchorage to avoid fouling the propeller, which meant that those of us going ashore to the spot where Cook officially claimed the east coast for King George had a long, wet boat trip. We climbed another hill, joined the astronomer and navigators in some thoughts on the issues, and struggled back.

That night we were meant to set out across the Timor Sea for Djakarta, but the wind shifted. The next day was declared a Sunday, as we had not had one that week, and we were left in our hammocks. It was also the end of my trip. I had spent the night coughing, and sleeping fitfully, and when the time came I could not get up. I rolled down to the doctor's area, and within minutes pneumonia had been diagnosed. I was having trouble breathing, and severely dehydrated. After blacking out and being put on oxygen I was given a big shot of antibiotics, a saline drip and the best possible treatment. The Captain and the doctor quickly decided that I had to go; we were close to the last hospital for two thousand miles. By the time the helicopter arrived I had recovered enough to regret my departure. Overcome with 'nostalgia' I felt that I had let everyone down; in order of concern, my watch, the rest of the crew, the programme makers and 'The Ship'. After four weeks the loyalties and concerns of the modern day had been replaced by those of our own small world. The date was Monday 10 September. 11 September would bring a more communal sense of loss and isolation to my shipmates, but I was quite alone, thousands of miles from home. Hot showers, clean clothes and release from shipboard routine helped me recover quickly. I spent three days in hospital on Thursday Island, where I drafted part of this chapter, and flew home in the aftermath of 11 September. Subsequent diagnosis suggested the original infection dated back to the flight out – the twenty-first century had caught up with me.

* * *

I will always regret failing to make it to Bali, where the trip ended. After a hard week of adjustment it was all coming together, and there was much more to be done. However, it is best to look on the bright side. The opportunity to experience life at sea under 'eighteenth-century' conditions was priceless. We tried 'Extreme History', but not all of us could cope.

I learnt more in four weeks about the working and crewing of a wooden sailing ship than I could have picked up in a lifetime of shore-bound study. Three things stand out: comradeship, skill and self-discovery. Getting up on to the foretopsail yard to furl sail for the first time, a hundred feet above the deck, bent double over a spar, standing on a rope and hauling up a heavy sail with the rest of my watch required concentration, teamwork, dexterity and a steady nerve, not the obvious qualifications for a historian.

In the eighteenth century time was relatively unimportant, and labour-saving was unnecessary. Everything about the ship took far longer than we would imagine, minutes not seconds, hours not minutes, and days rather than hours. This made it essential for Cook, and all great sea officers, be they navigator, mariner or warrior, to be thinking hours ahead, to read the weather, currents and land features, much as a good driver reads the road far ahead. That Cook suffered so few accidents and close calls on this voyage is a mark of his greatness.

My reflections on Cook were profoundly affected by the experience of this trip. The first was his obsession with accuracy, his persistence and anxiety to fill in the gaps, gaps in human understanding of the globe. Secondly his methodical approach, his reluctance to make leaps of faith, instead patiently building the evidence required to answer major questions that were highlighted in the available literature. This was his compensation for the terrible work of sustained coastal navigation inside the Barrier Reef. This calls for the utmost nerve. Yet he knew that his place was on the coast, where he could chart; safe out at sea there was nothing to record. His attitude to longitude reflected his astronomical work, which predisposed him to Maskelyne's lunar distance method. Although imperfect this provided him with a base line for the astonishing running coastal surveys of this voyage. His greatness as a leader, mariner and navigator shines through, unalloyed by the wider questions of his impact on the region. Here he is made to carry the blame for the actions of those who came after, largely because he was transformed into a nationalist icon by white Australians and New Zealanders, for quite other purposes. His original heroic status was a product of the age, one in which Britain needed a new kind of hero.

To retrace Cook's voyages we needed more time ashore, and on the coast, making contact, but this imperative ran counter to the 'experience' element of the programme, and ultimately had to be subordinated. I would have valued more time to reflect and discuss, in essence an evening to deal with the events of one day, and prepare for the next.

I also learnt a great deal about myself. Being ordered about, controlled, directed and confronted with inedible food was a challenge, but once mastered it was not too difficult. Would I go again? Well, maybe if . . .

Index